AF412139

VOGUE DIALOGUES

DEUTSCH

Edited by Condé Nast Germany

PRESTEL   Munich · Berlin · London · New York

CONTENTS

FOREWORD

VOGUE Dialogues are a hallmark of *Deutsche VOGUE*, the German edition of VOGUE magazine, in which two people come together in a relaxed atmosphere and talk. And the topics? They just evolve and are chosen at will. VOGUE Dialogues are not interviews, not a rapid question-and-answer staccato, but conversations between equal partners. Both are stars. And each is curious about the other.

Singers and authors, actors and artists, fashion designers and ballet stars enjoy themselves at VOGUE's pleasure. All of them are well known and admired worldwide and most of them feel at home in more than one country. For this book, the editors have selected the best of the inspired conversations which have taken place since 1991.

VOGUE Dialogues usually last for hours, often leading into dinner or, once the champagne starts flowing, going on into the early hours of the morning. Isabella Rossellini and Sheila Metzner added an additional day at the pool, and Richard Gere stayed at the painter Balthus' house for several days.

This book is a real pleasure to readers, who are able to take part in intellectual ping-pong. Whether Jeanne Moreau philosophizes with Wim Wenders on packing luggage, or Isabelle Huppert and Peter Handke consult each other on their individual reasons for always being too late — we are witness to many intimate revelations: Alexander McQueen succumbs to his obsession for chocolate on Fridays (and only Fridays), and George Tabori still regrets, after decades, having insulted Greta Garbo over her film *Ninotchka*. These living legends reveal how they discovered their talents and surprise us with anecdotes from the beginning of their careers. In these dialogues, the experiences of their lives are distilled into *bon mots*: "Life is like a wave. The important thing is being a good surfer," says Isabella Rossellini. "The greatest distress in a relationship is the result of false expectations," is the recognition of the great architect Frank O. Gehry. And Björk reveals her motto: "In life, you yourself have to make sure that miracles happen."

Of course, in these dialogues VOGUE also shows itself as a style guide, when Manolo Blahnik and John Galliano talk about the principles of chic, Claudia Cardinale and Giorgio Armani agree that a well-groomed appearance is an expression of brotherly love, or when Gianfranco Ferré and André Leon Talley discuss how one can make a good impression at the beach without having a good figure.

A photographer acted as a visual chronicler on every date. The pictures capture intimate moments of friendship, cheerful moments, and show stars in unaccustomed roles. Photographic artists such as Arthur Elgort, Karl Lagerfeld, Bryan Adams, Tyen and Elfie Semotan have all contributed to making these VOGUE dialogues an institution, in which major personalities find time to participate. The photographs at the front section of this book make it a visual delight.

When asked by the VOGUE editors, some say that they would like to see an old friend once again. Stella McCartney and Dinos and Jake Chapman wanted to continue the small talk which had started at a party and asked VOGUE to organize a rendez-vous. Some of them took the opportunity of making contact with a long-admired star. VOGUE was, for example, able to fulfill Christian Lacroix' great desire of meeting Germany's famous choreographer Pina Bausch. Others had already worked together but never found the time for a lengthy, personal chat.

They usually agreed spontaneously and gladly. As a rule, however, months went by before the rendezvous could take place—one had gone into seclusion to write his newest book, a film had to be completed, a collection presented on the catwalk; for another, his summer vacation with his family is sacred, or a promotional tour had to be completed. It can take quite a while until a mutually feasible date can be found. Bernardo Bertolucci, who wanted Edgar Reitz as his partner, holds the record—he had to keep putting him and VOGUE off for three years before the conversation could finally take place in Rome. In spite of everything, a conversation has appeared in every edition of Deutsche VOGUE since 1991. It can happen that a couple meets in a city which is foreign to both of them: Marlene Dietrich's daughter, Maria Riva, happened to be in Paris and her conversation partner, Rosa von Praunheim, flew in from Berlin, where Armin Mueller-Stahl, returning from the Kiel Bay, had also arranged to meet Susan Sontag.

Once a date had been set—often with the help of agents and assistants—we witnessed an often underestimated aspect of all great artists: their discipline and reliability. Even if one had just landed from an overseas flight, he or she appeared at the appointed place on time. But what Pedro Almodóvar was forced to do to his partner, Geraldine Chaplin, rarely happened: he became so nervous about the premiere of his most recent film *Hable con ella* that he fell ill. Happily, Geraldine was on holiday nearby and extended her stay.

VOGUE Dialogues are uniquely candid impressions of encounters which will never again take place in this form.

VOGUE would like to thank those who took part in these dialogues, who along with the photographers and journalists have all renounced their fees for the benefit of UNICEF.

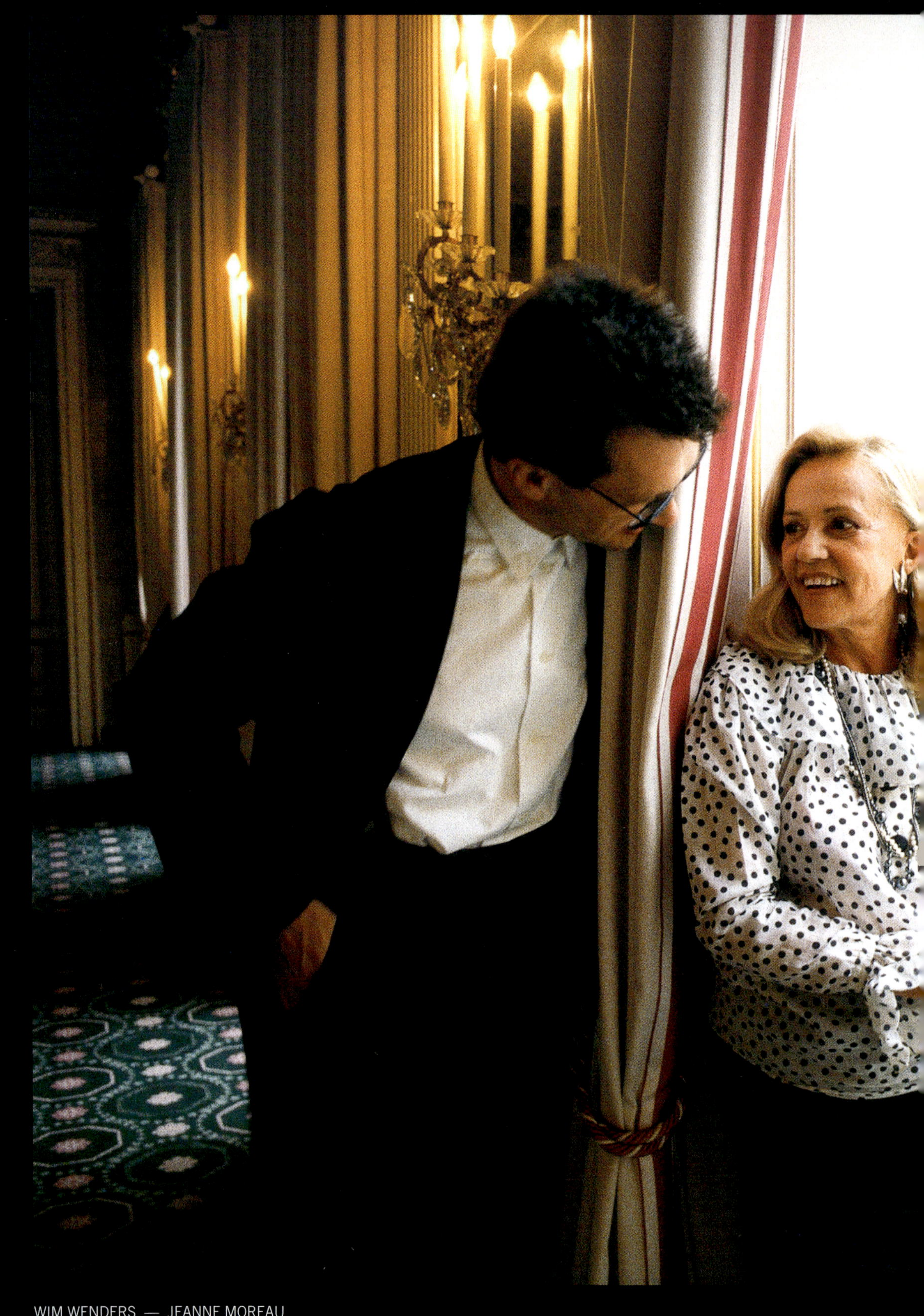

WIM WENDERS — JEANNE MOREAU

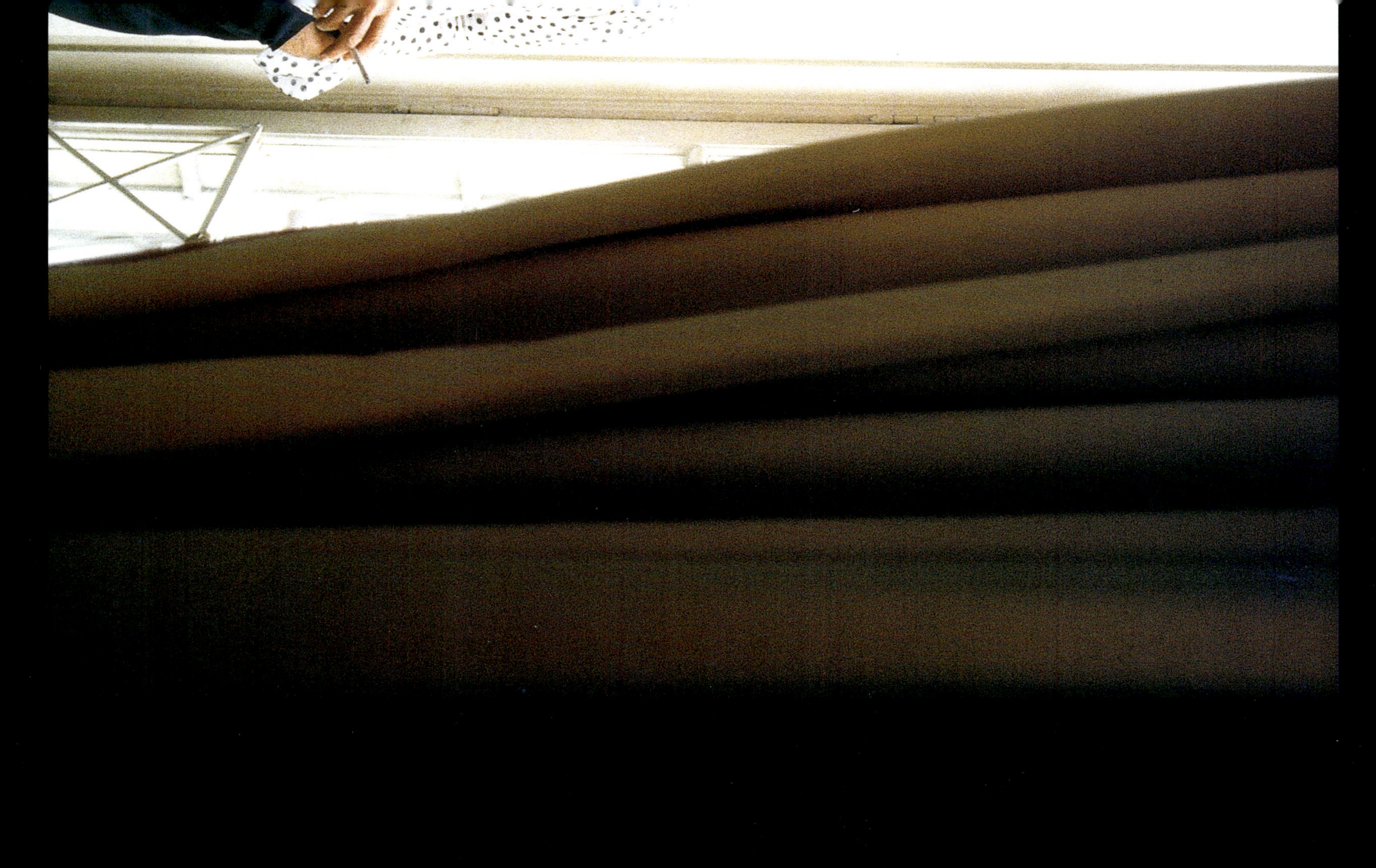
PHOTO: JIM RAKETE

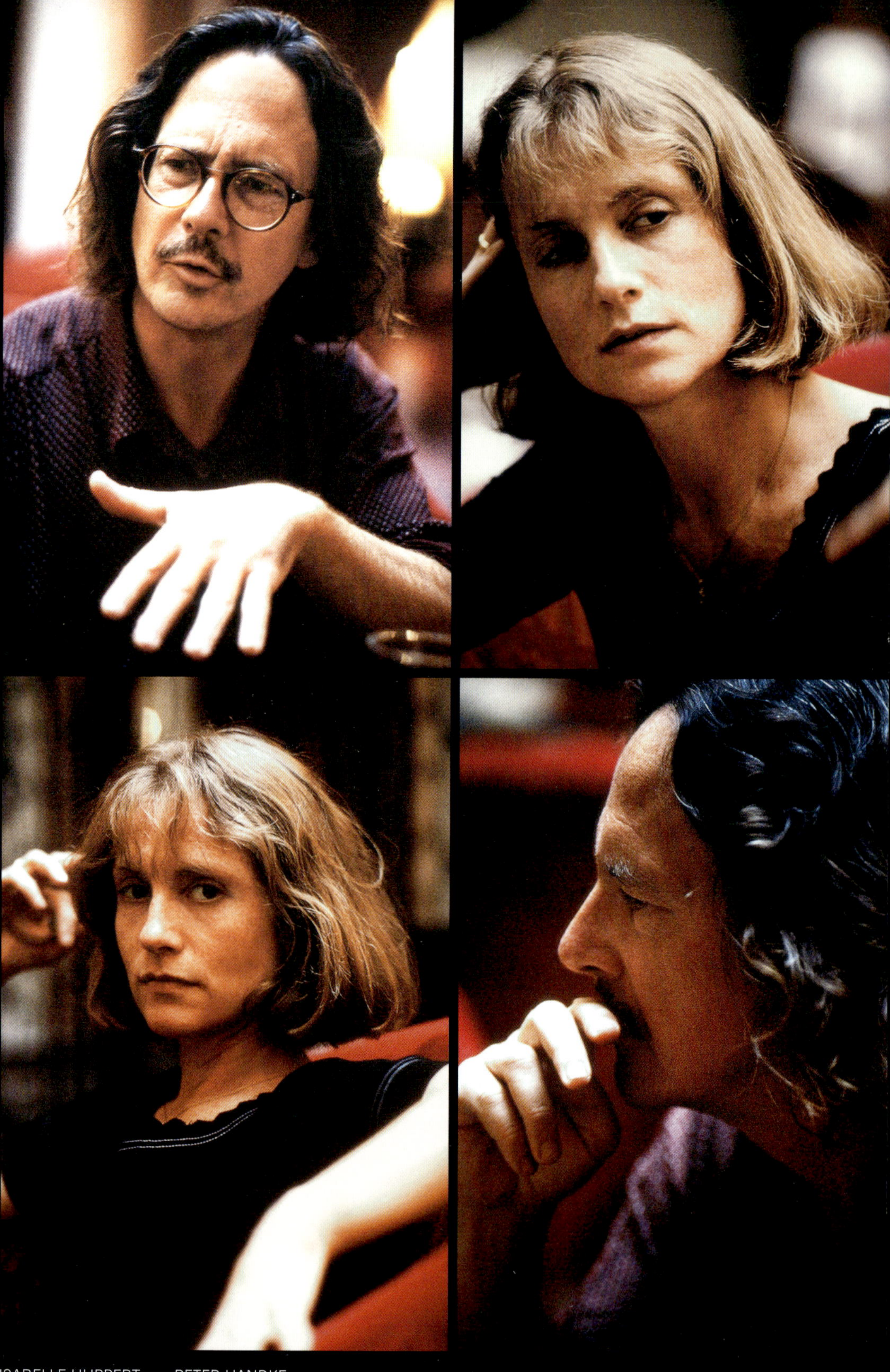

ISABELLE HUPPERT — PETER HANDKE

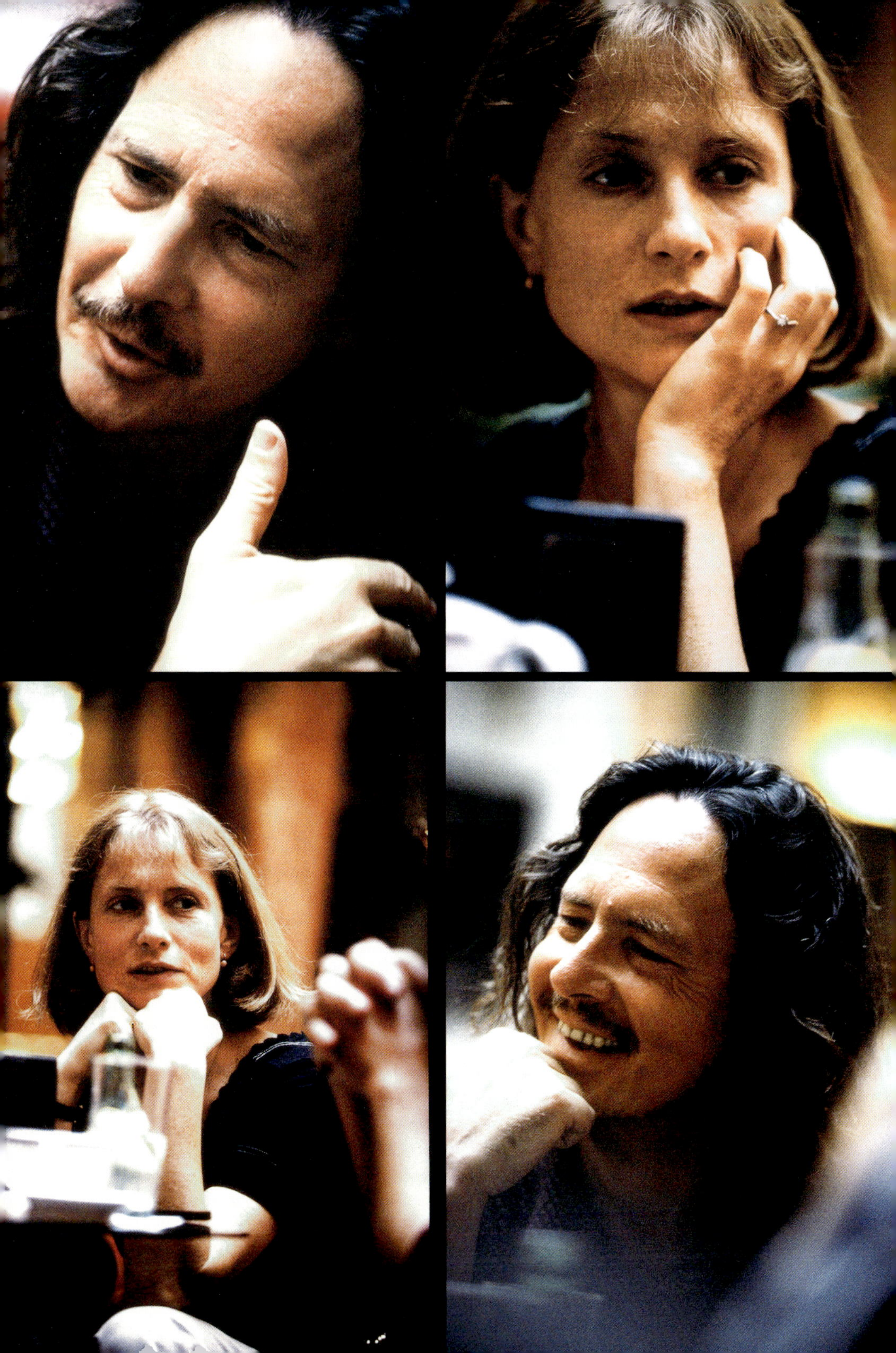

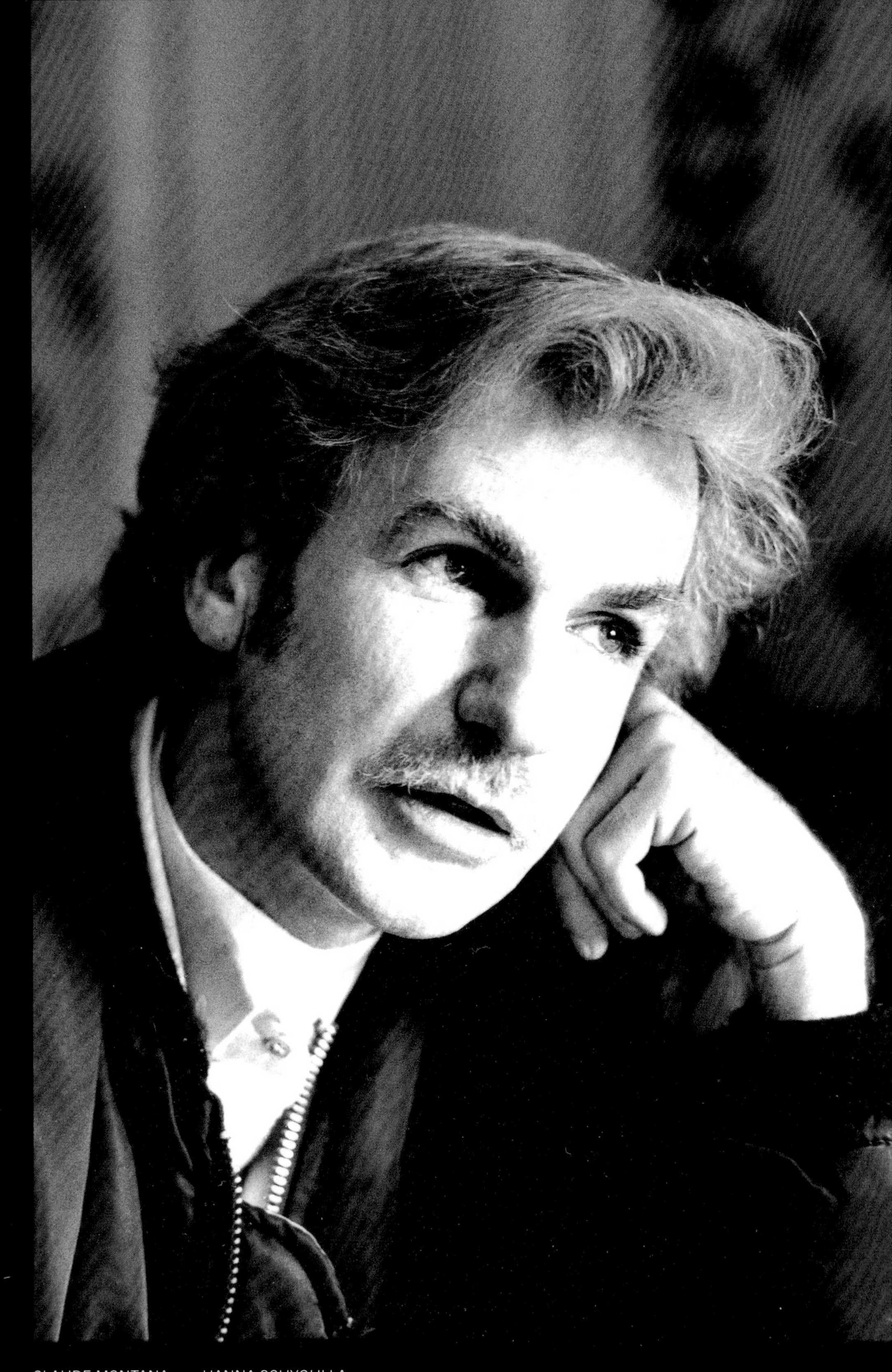

CLAUDE MONTANA — HANNA SCHYGULLA

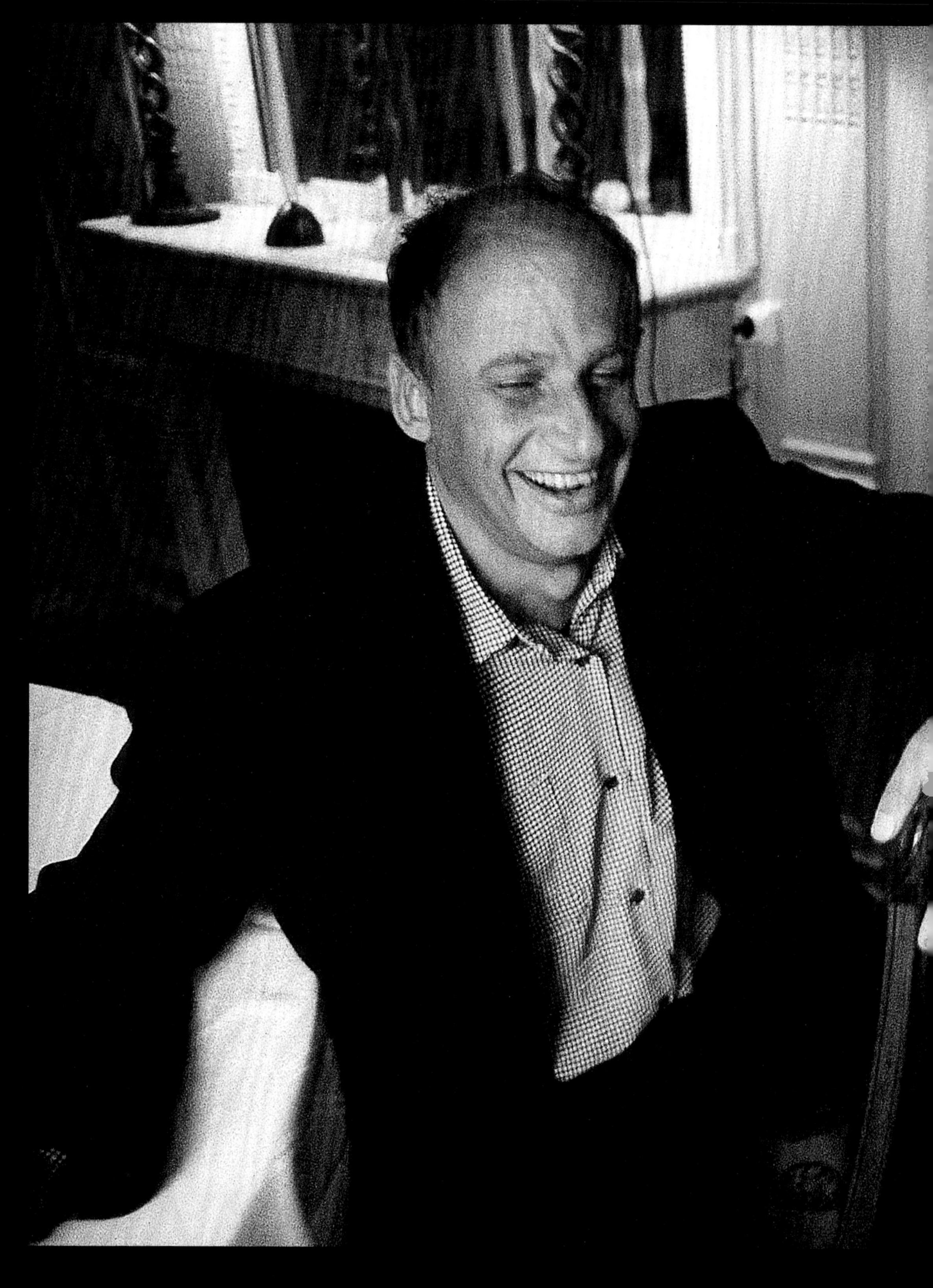

LUC BONDY — MICHEL PICCOLI

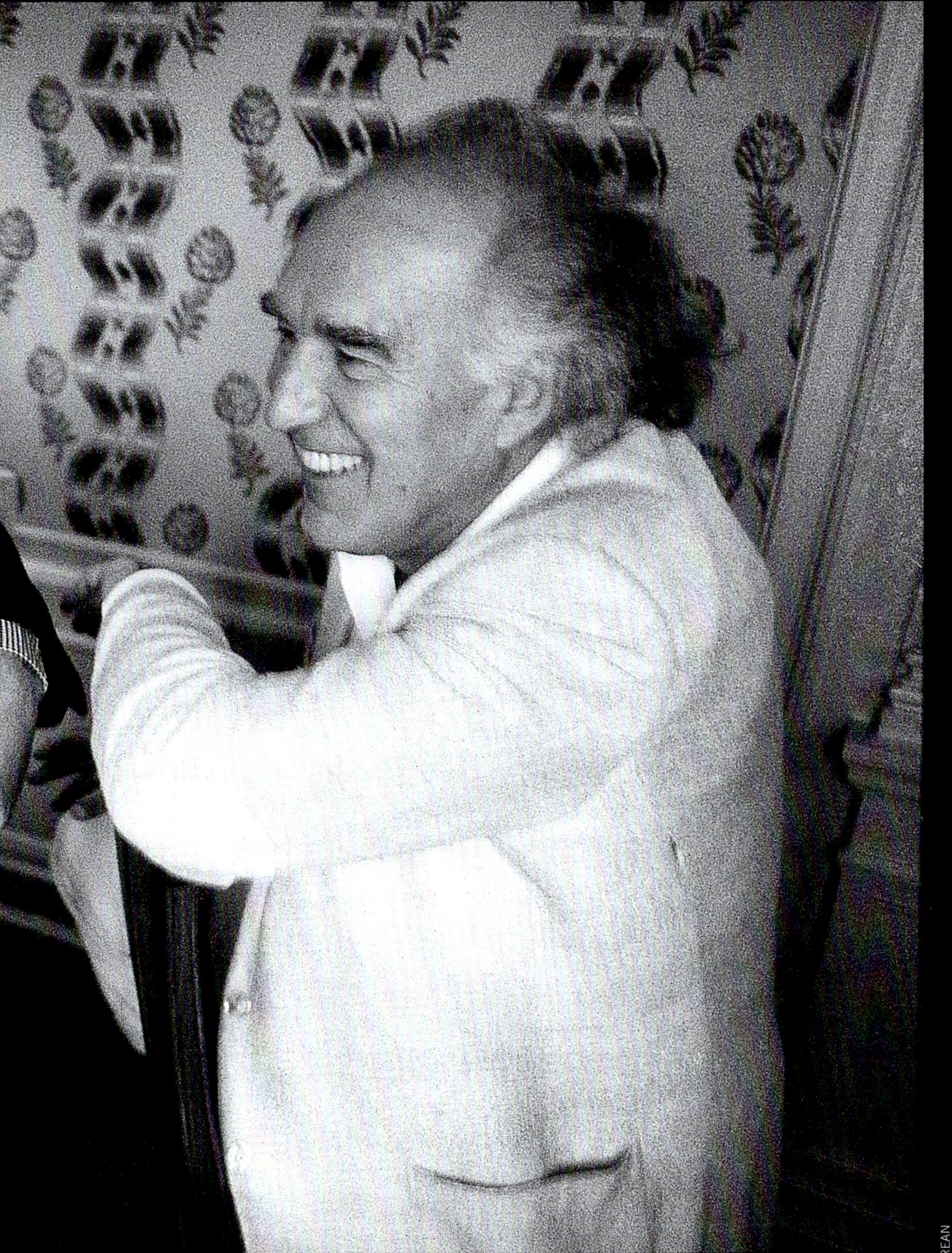
EAN

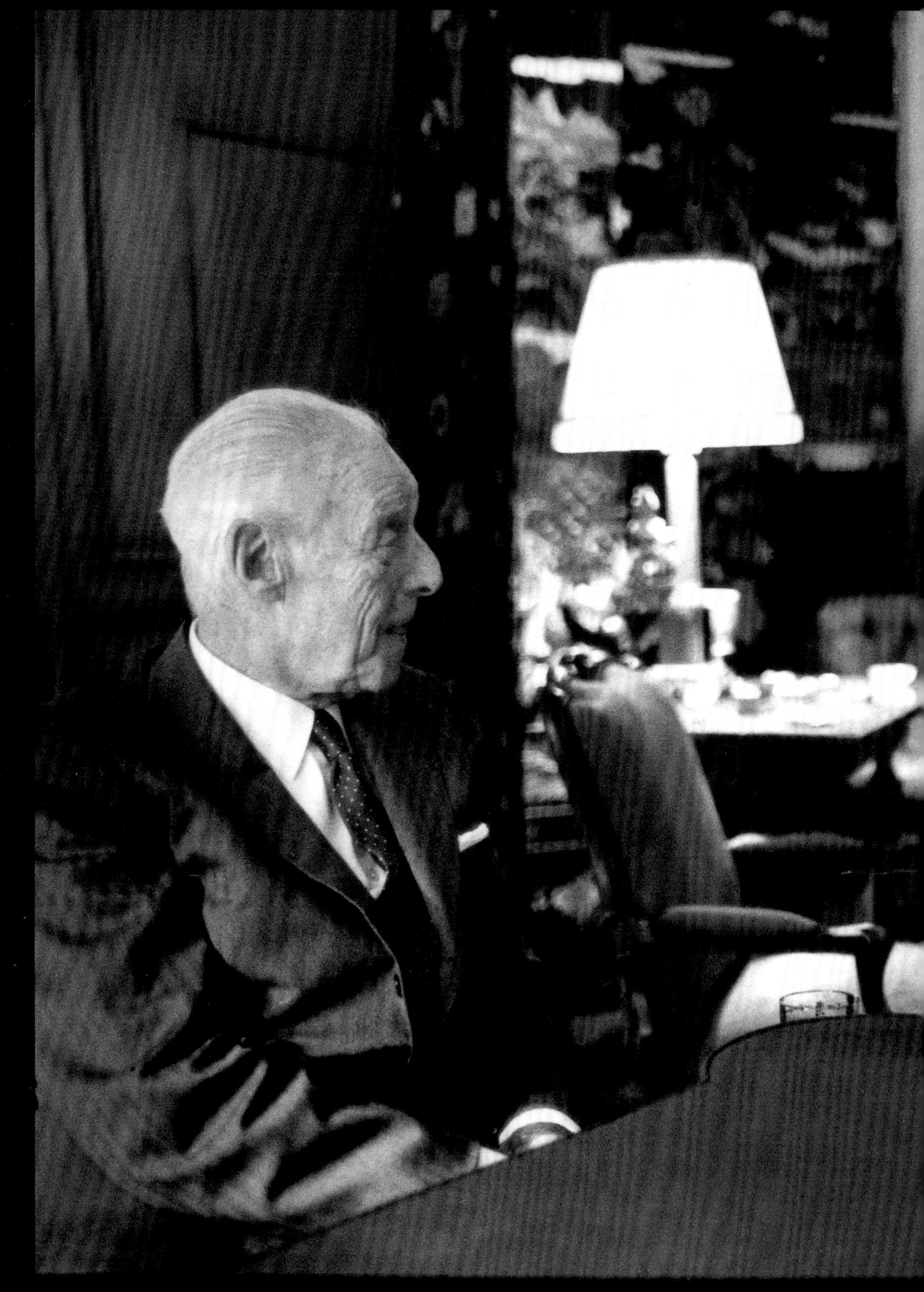

BARON GUY DE ROTHSCHILD — RUDOLF NUREYEV

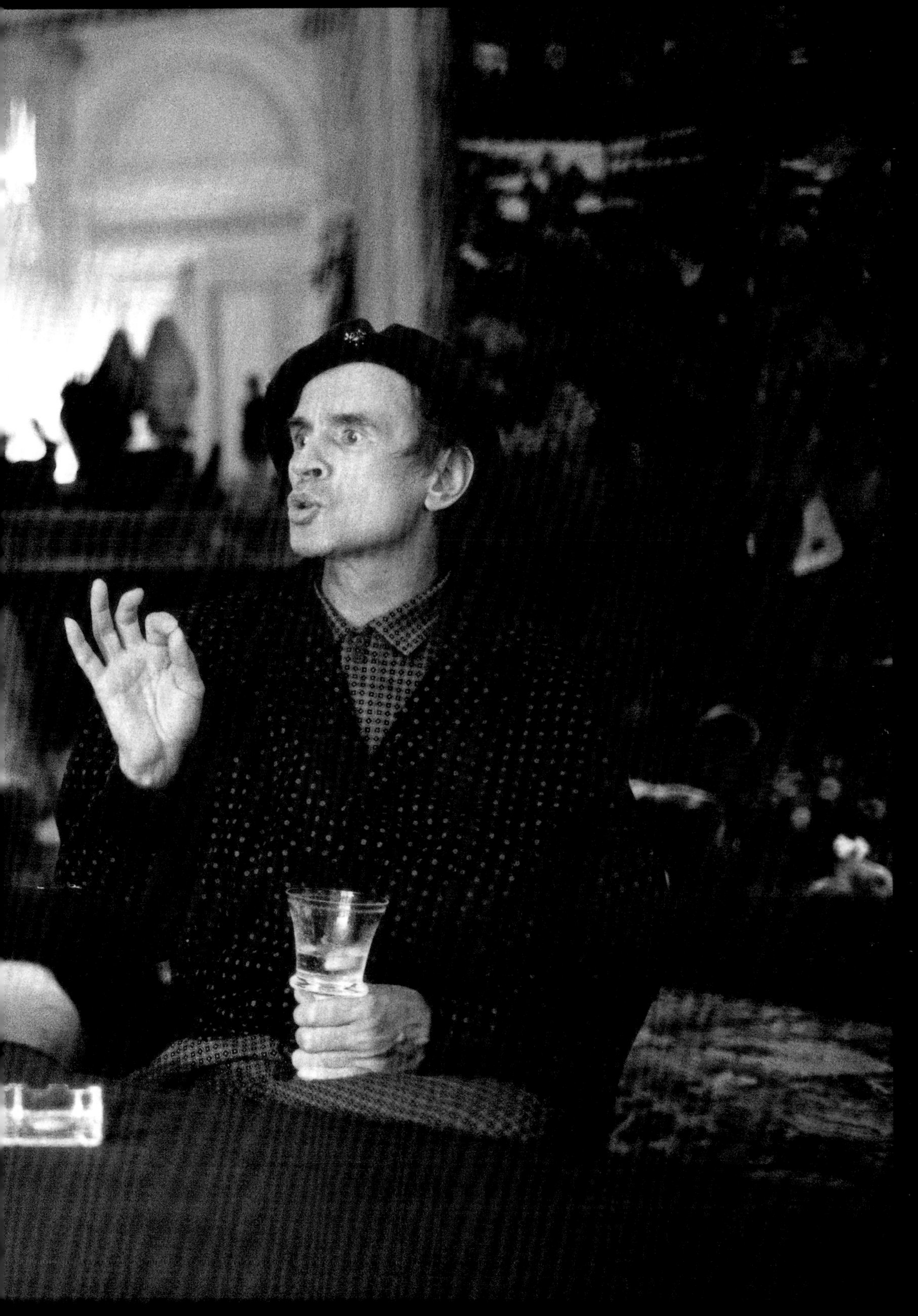

GABRIELE HENKEL — KARL LAGERFELD

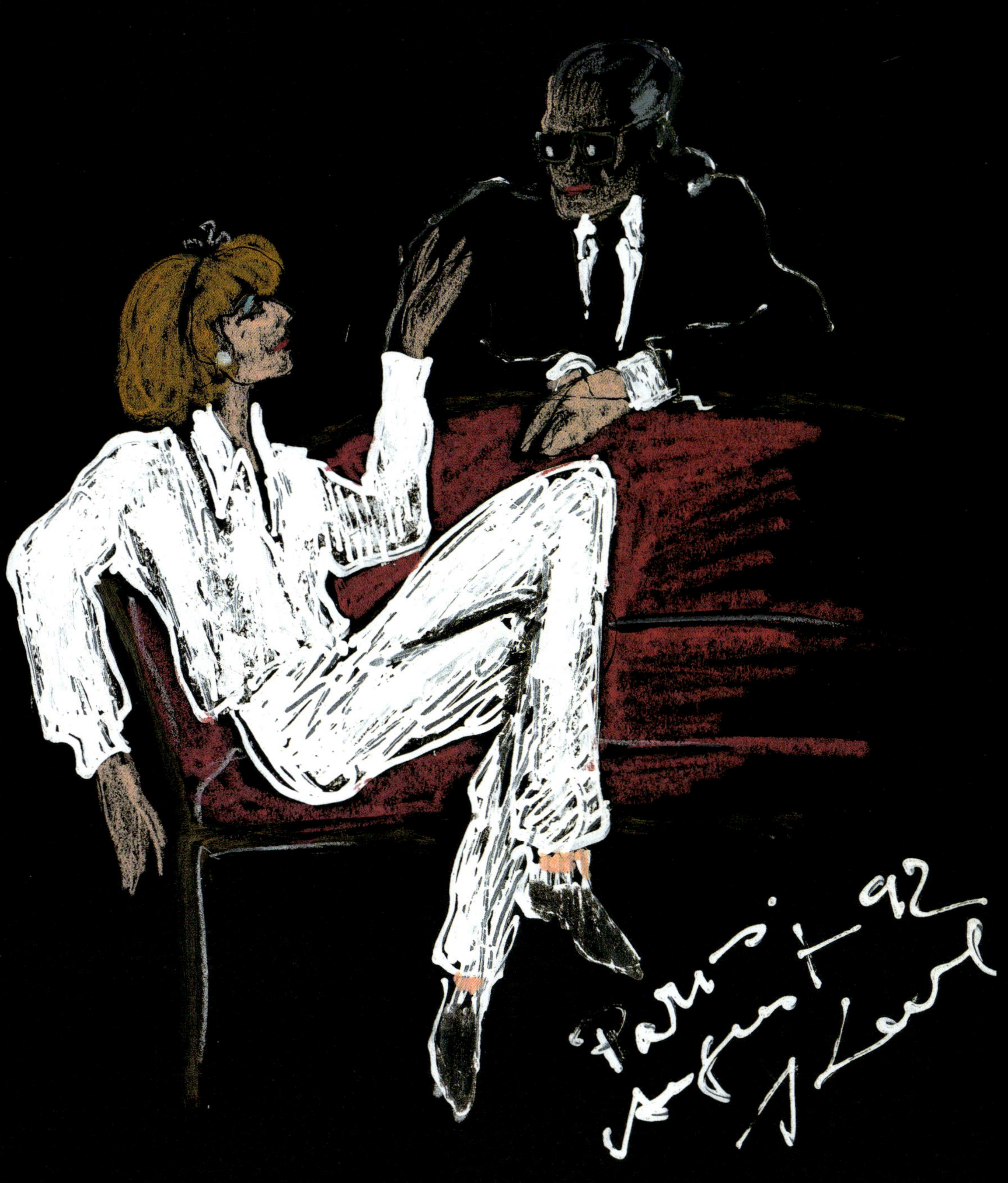

Paris 92

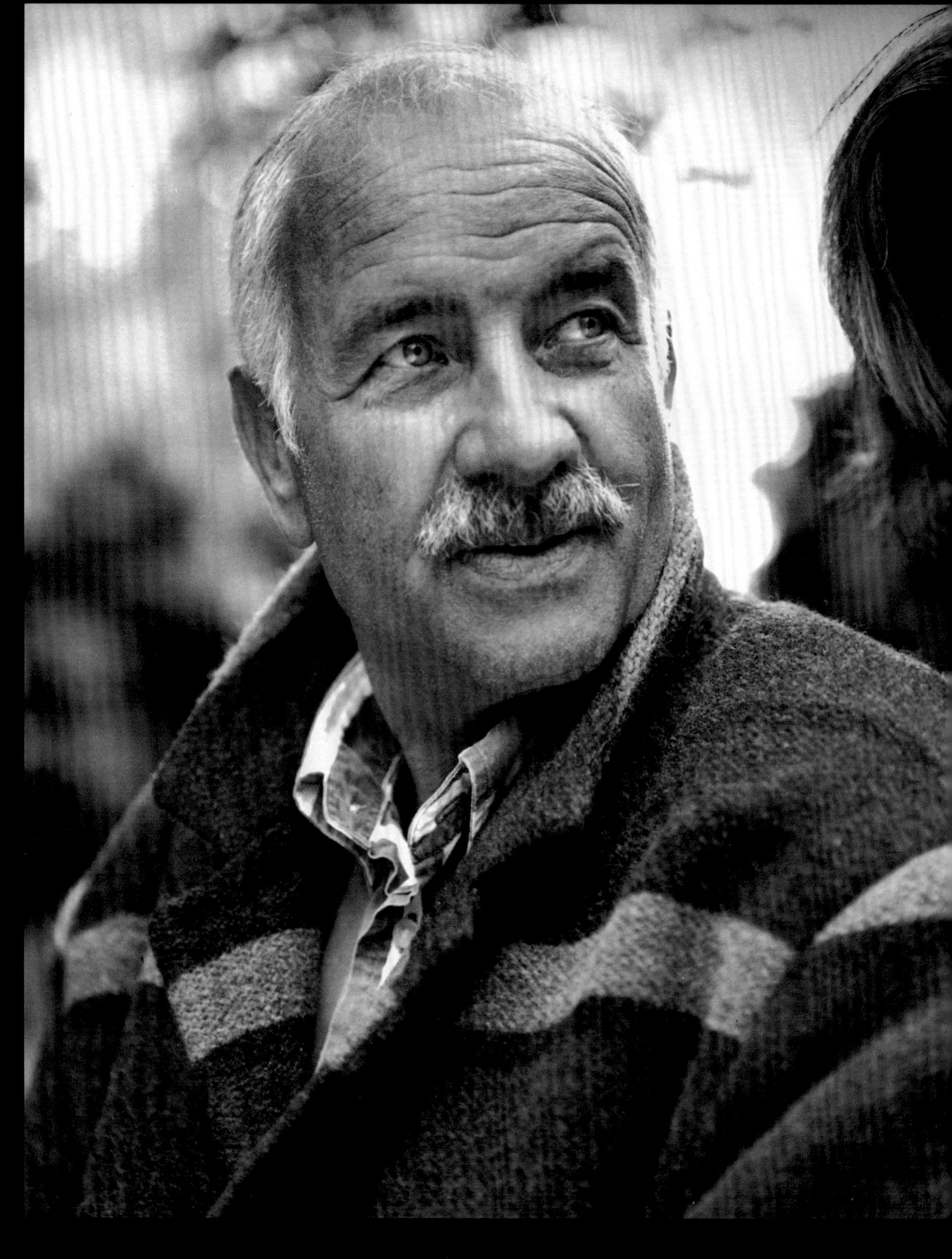

ARMIN MUELLER-STAHL — SUSAN SONTAG

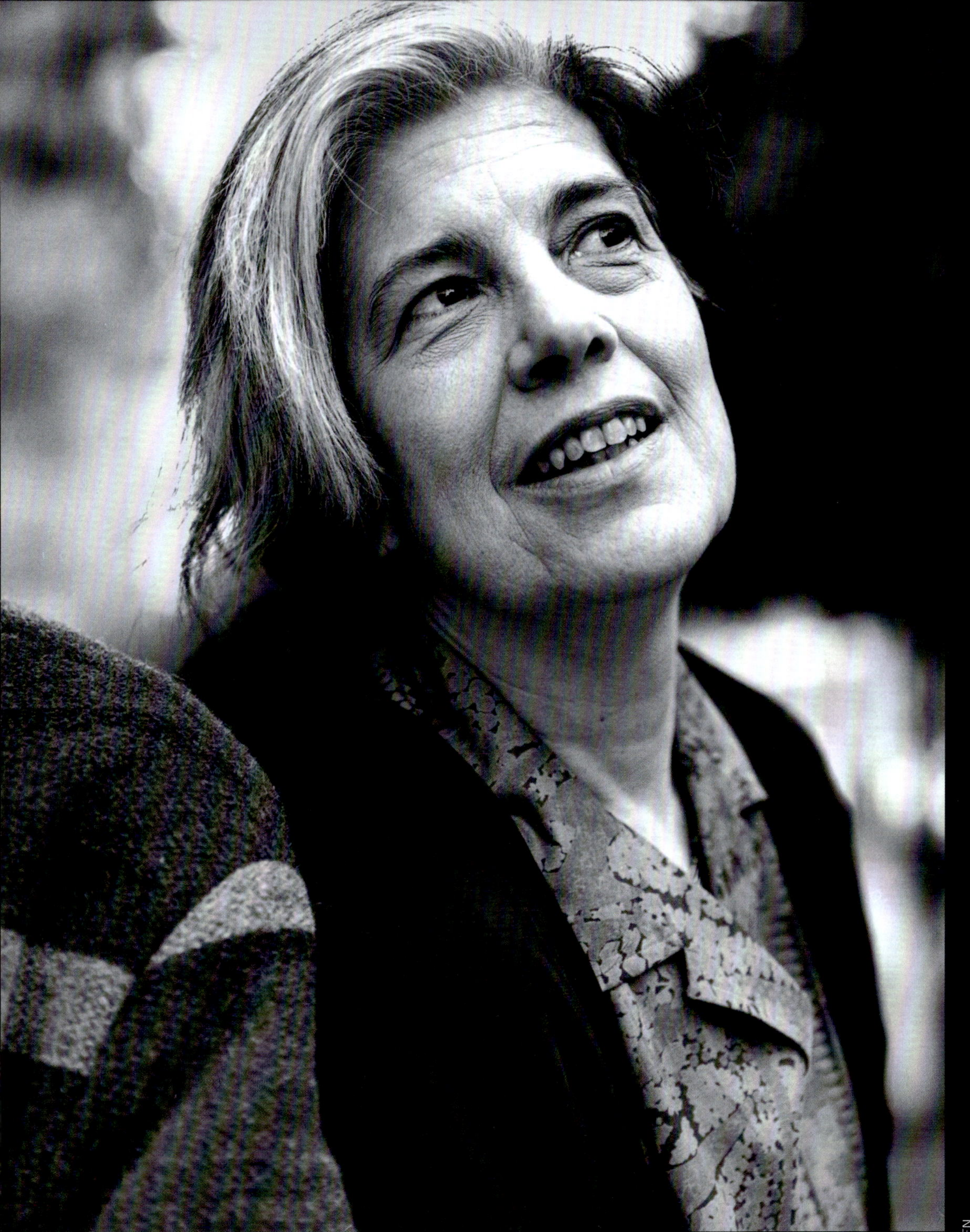

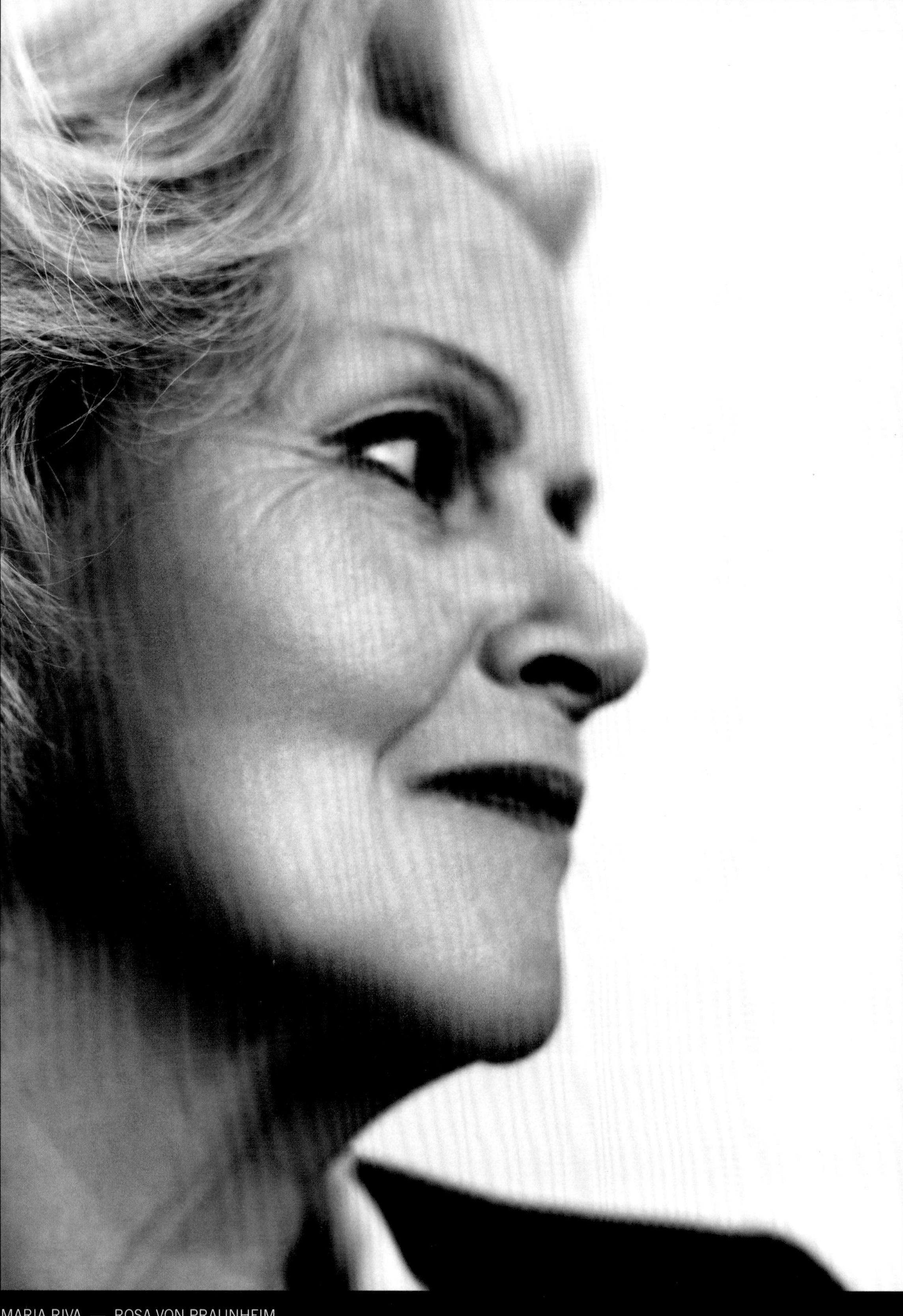

MARIA RIVA — ROSA VON PRAUNHEIM

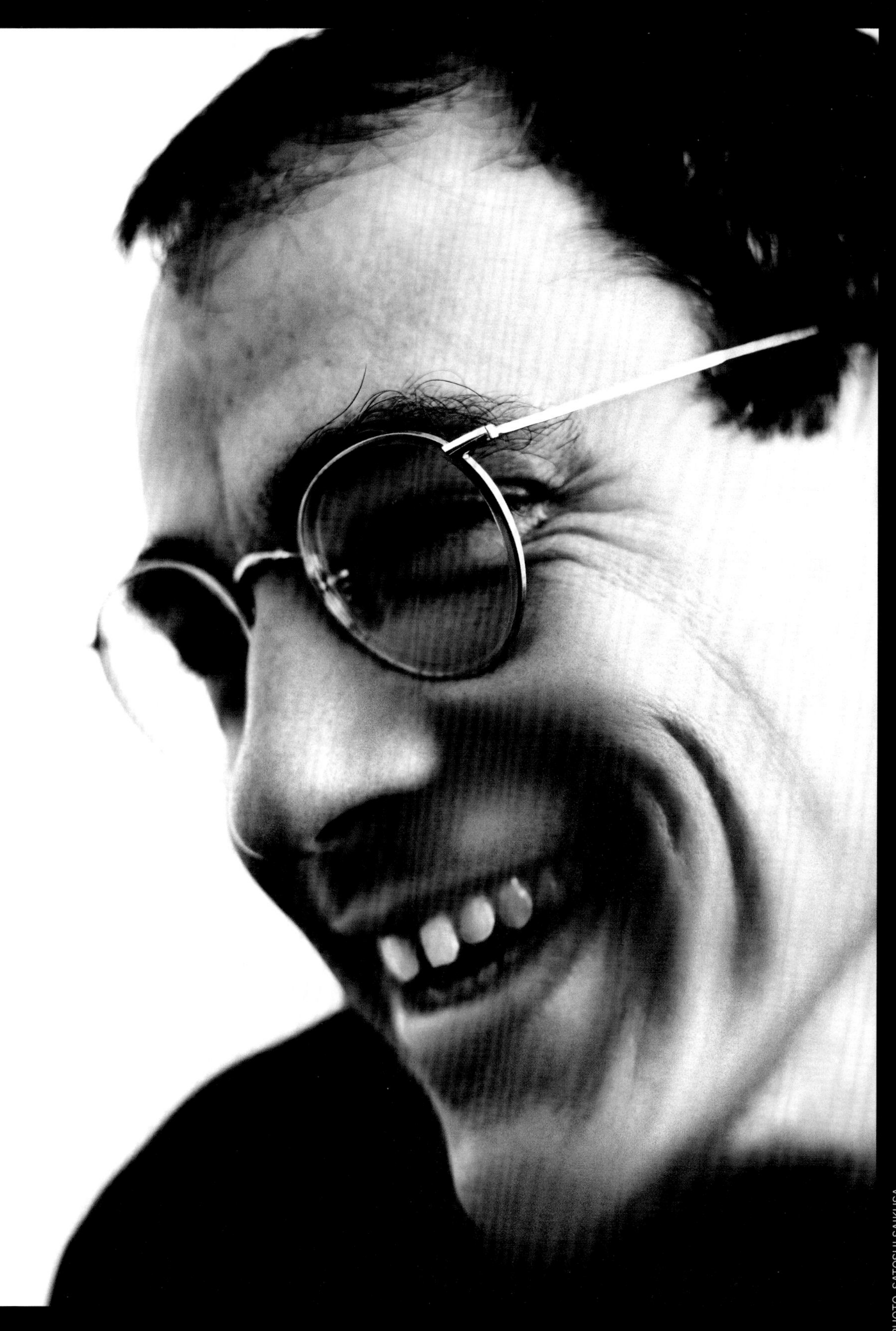

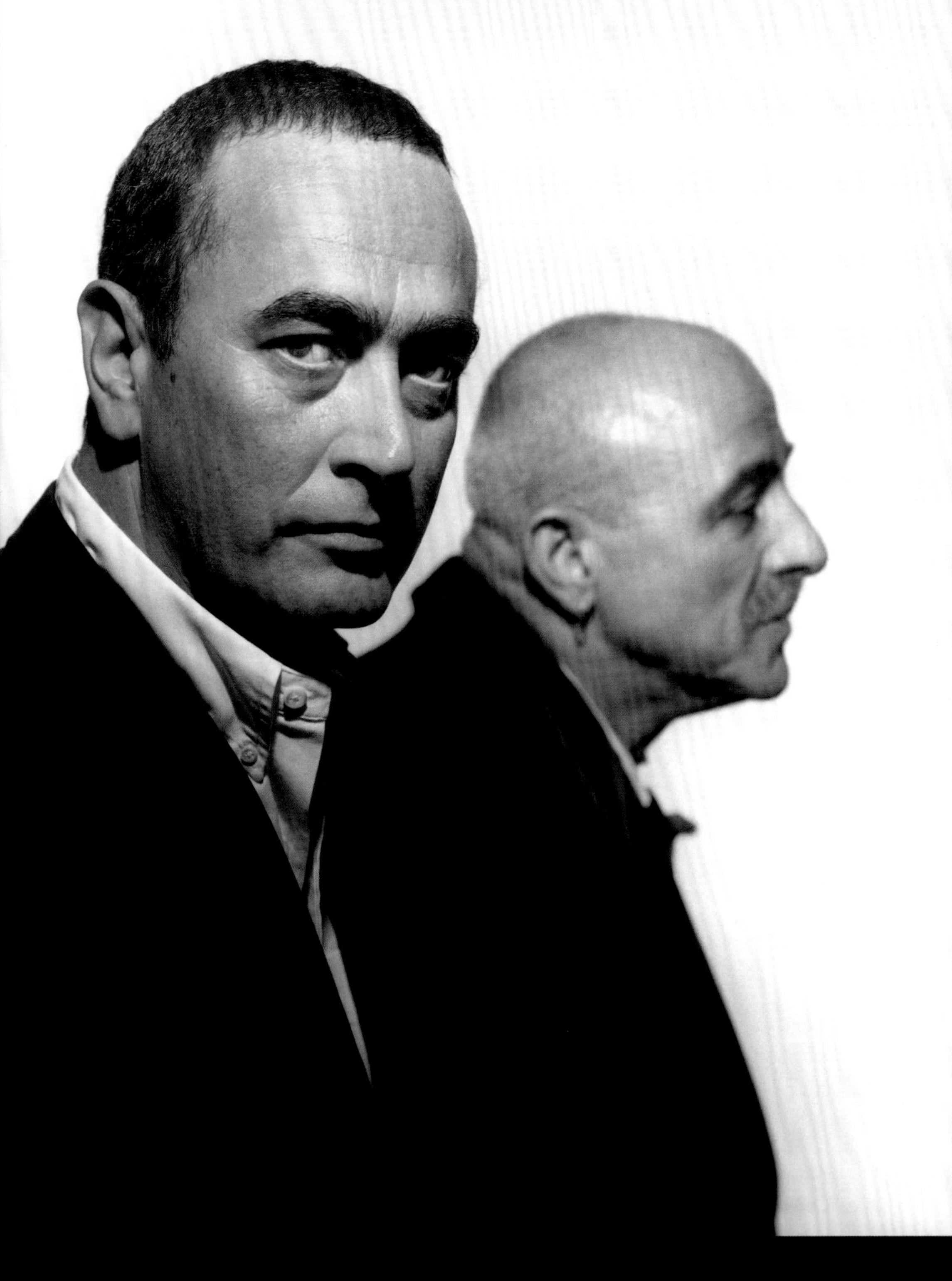

BERND EICHINGER — MARKUS LÜPERTZ

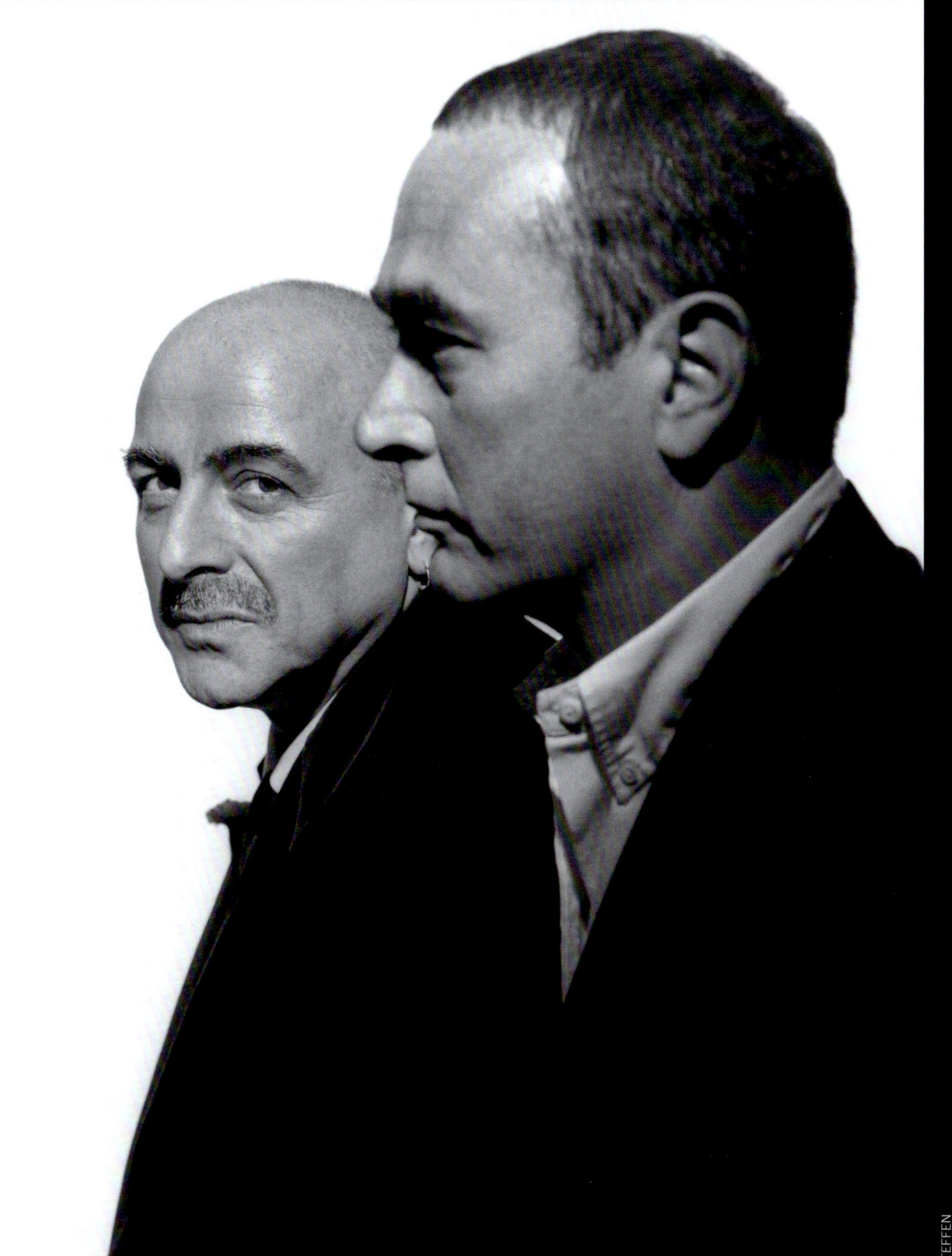

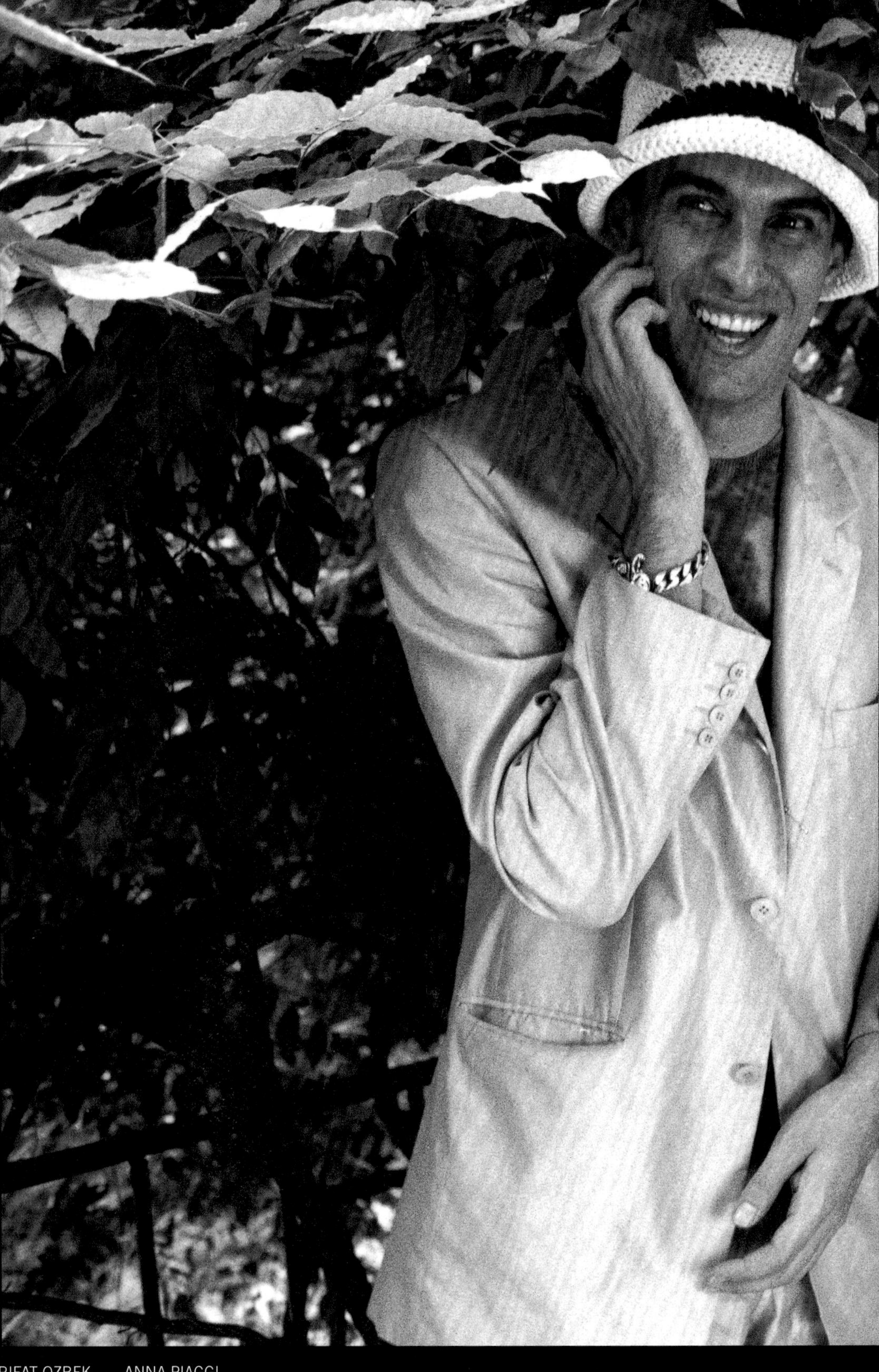

RIFAT OZBEK — ANNA PIAGGI

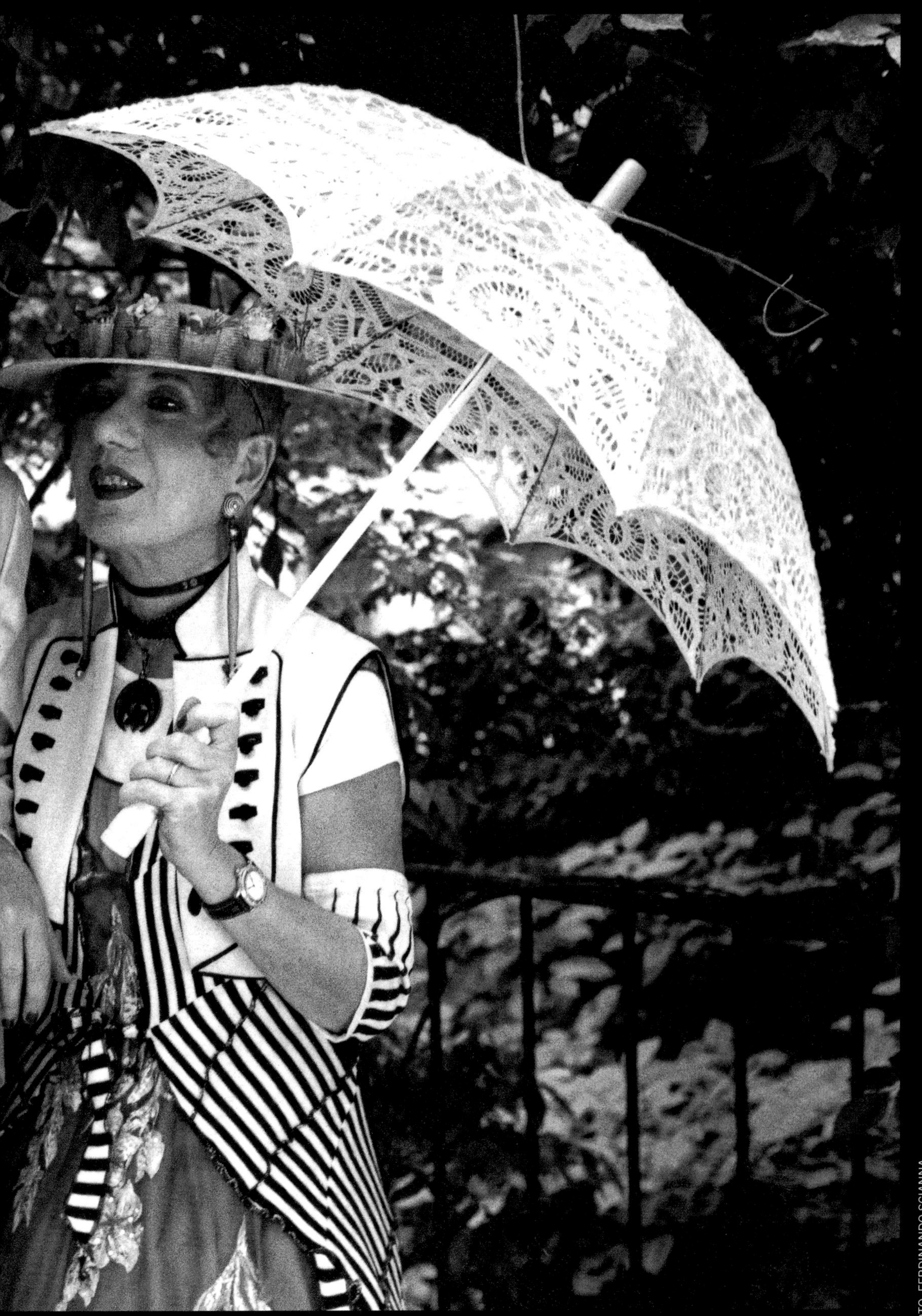

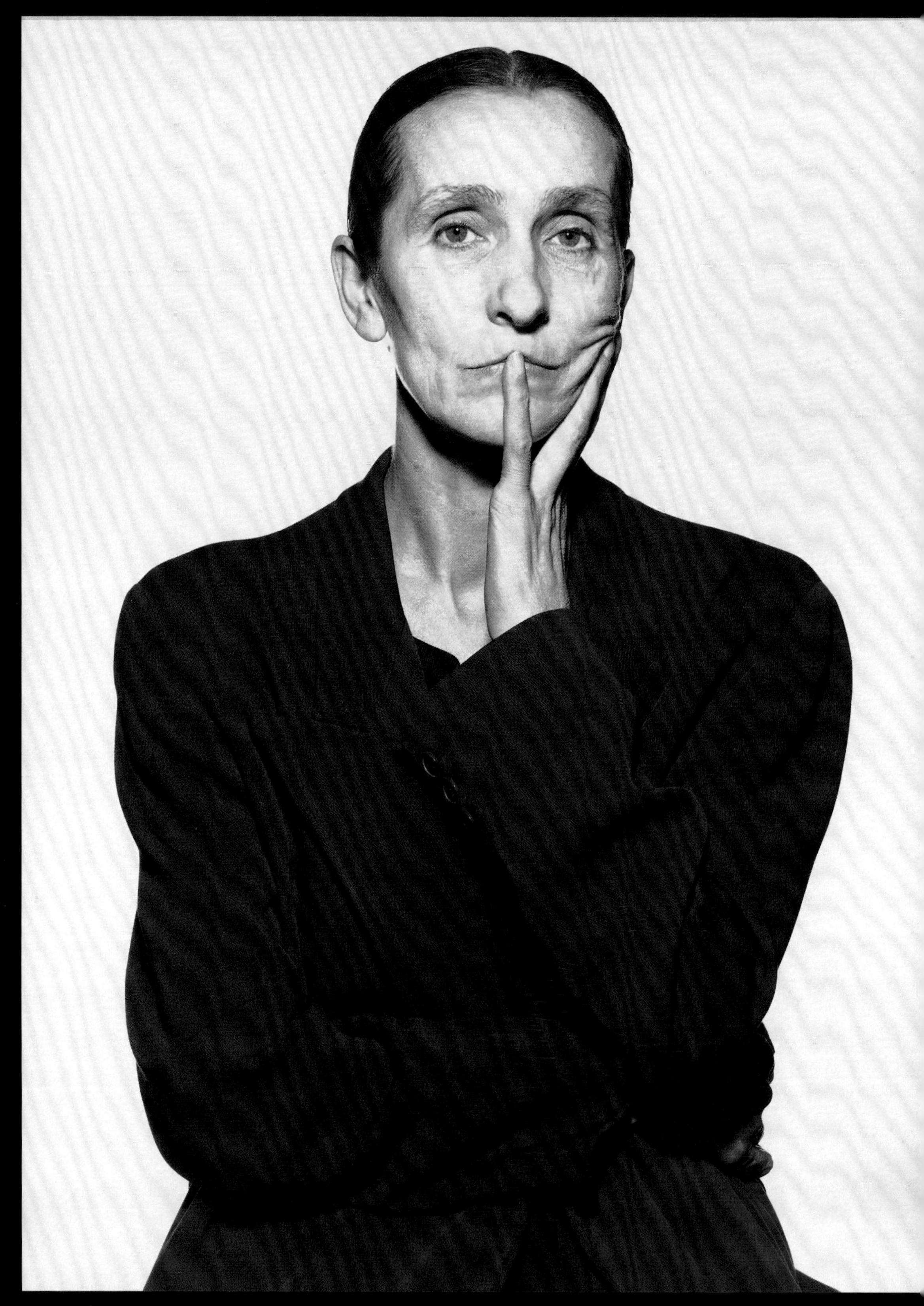

PINA BAUSCH — CHRISTIAN LACROIX

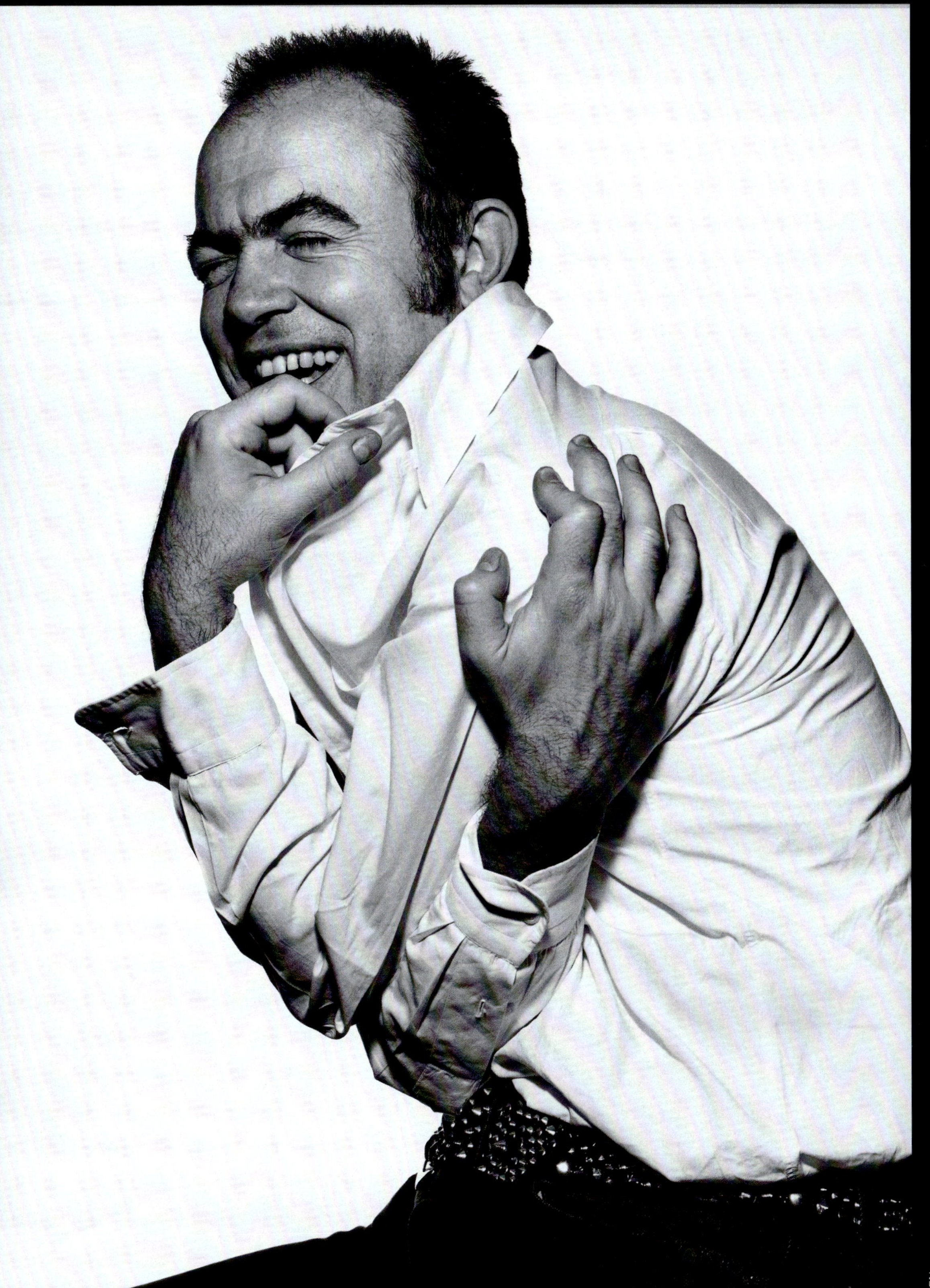

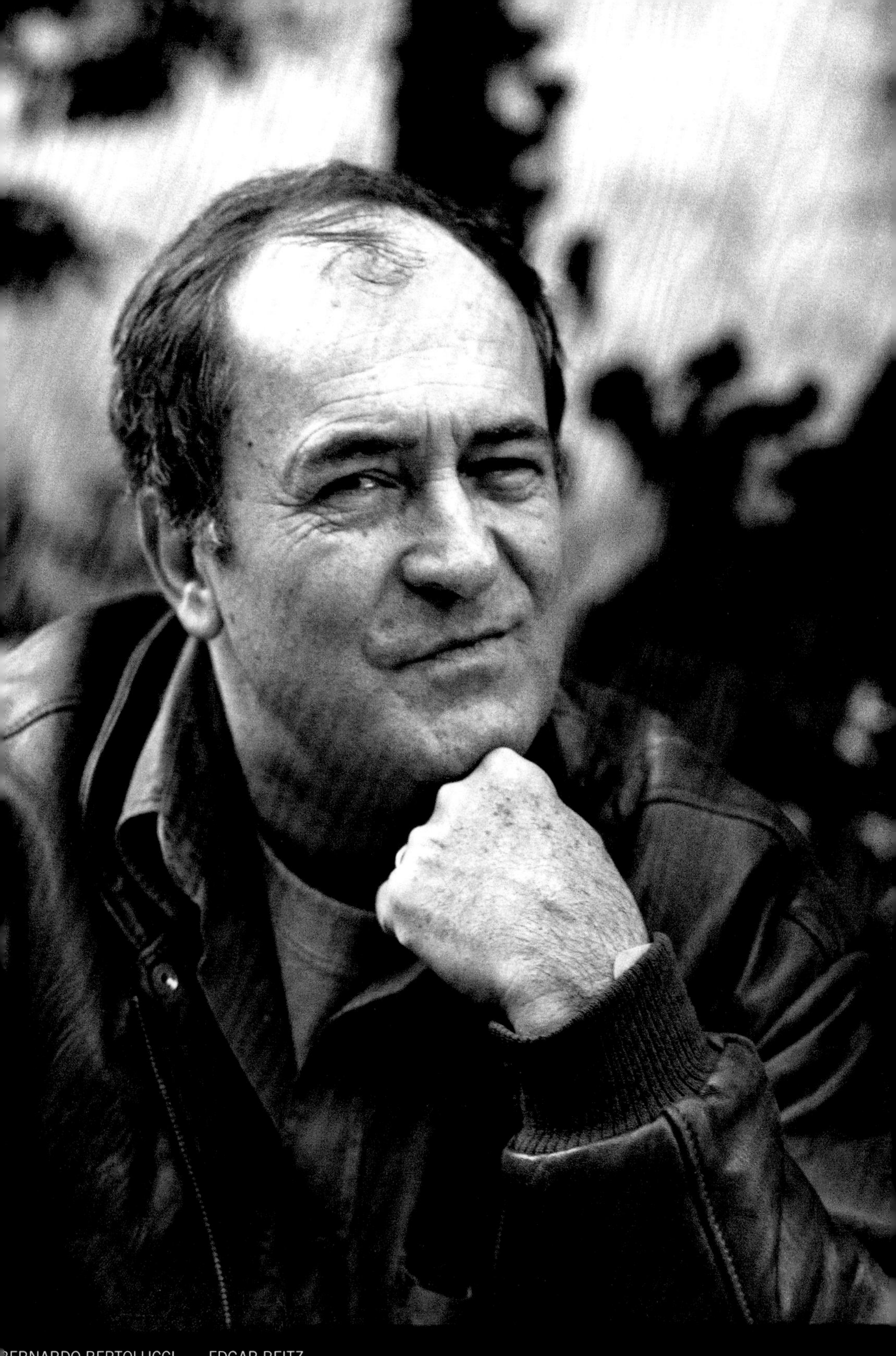

BERNARDO BERTOLUCCI — EDGAR REITZ

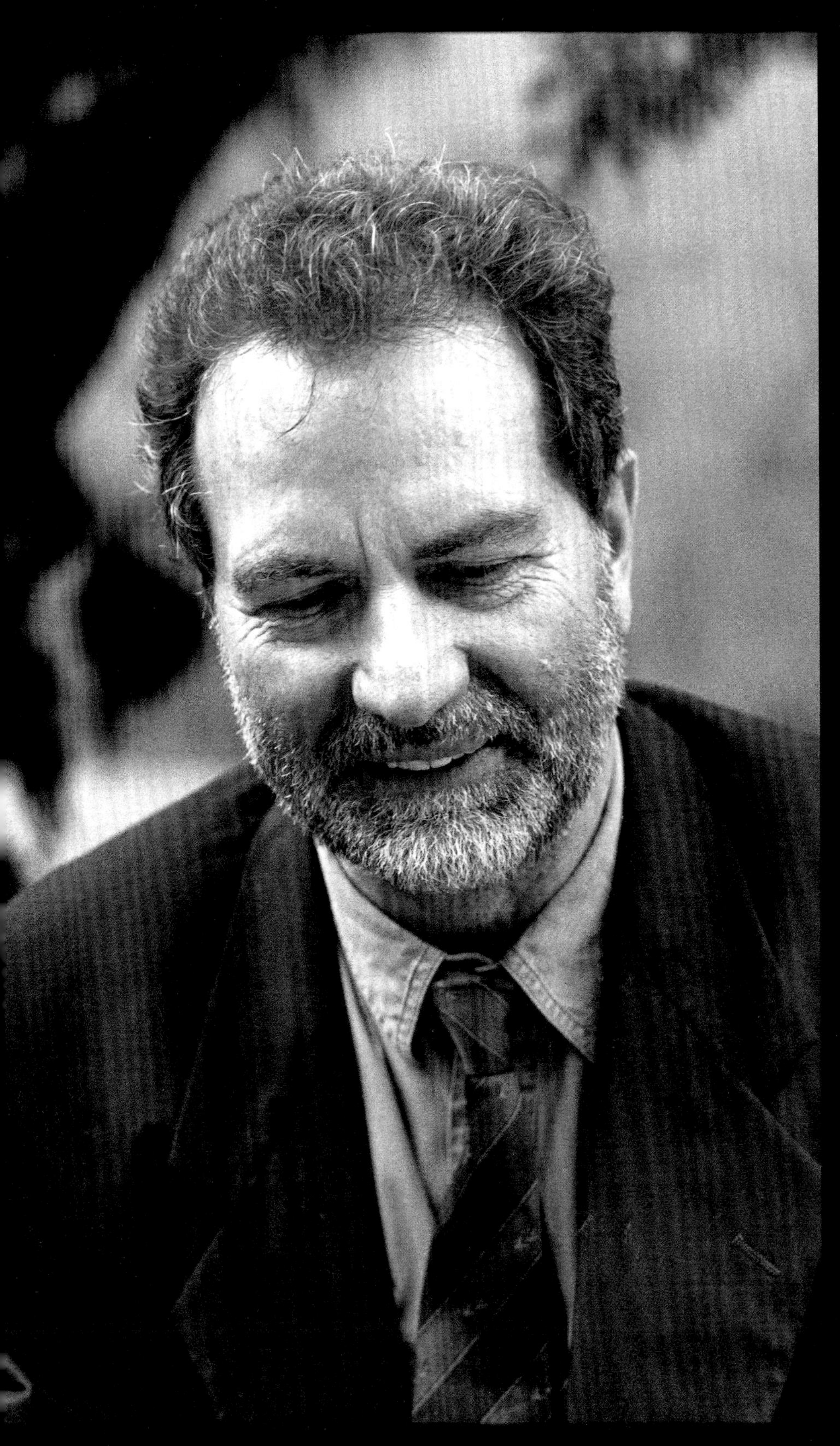

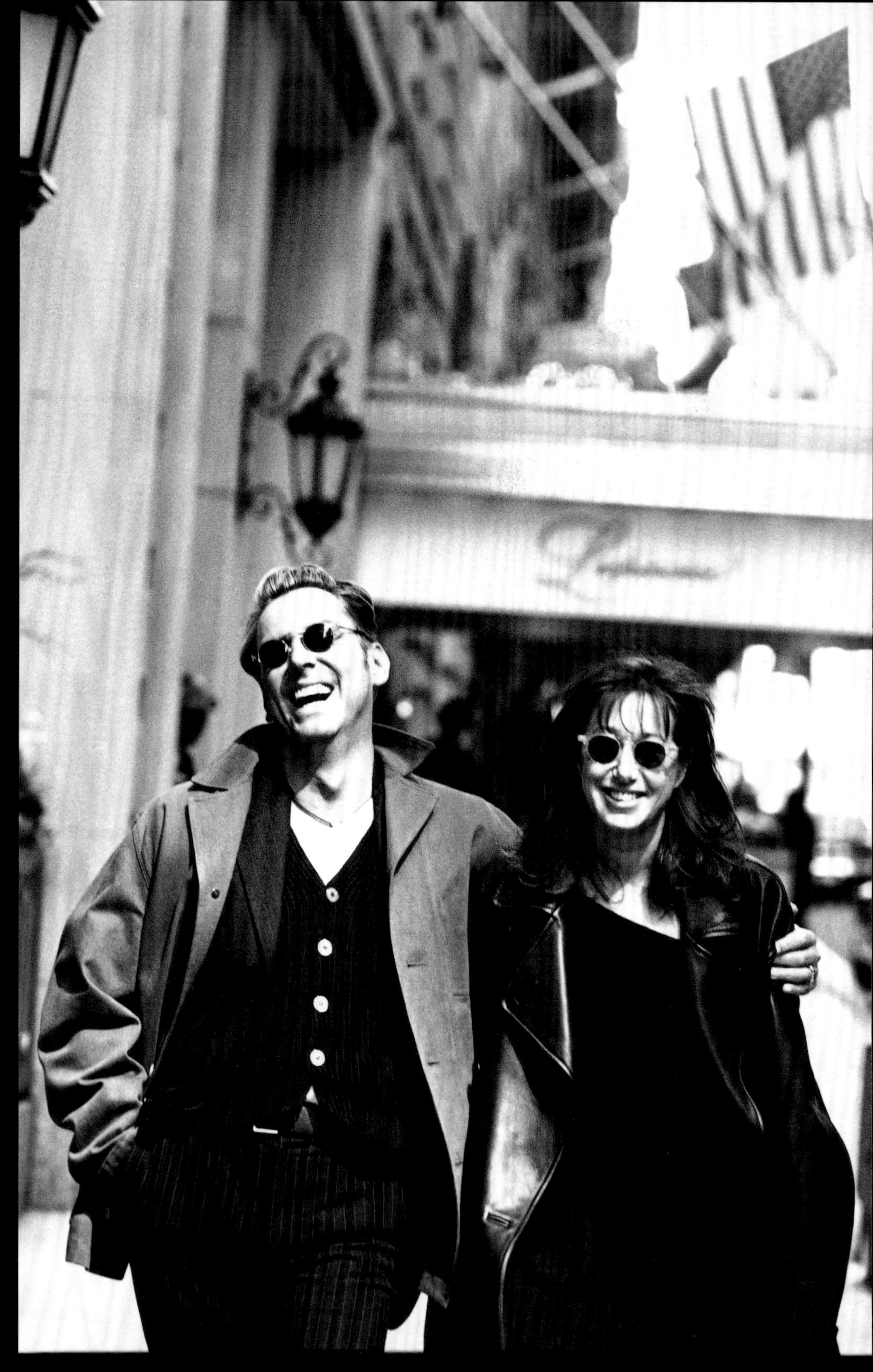

WOLFGANG JOOP — DONNA KARAN

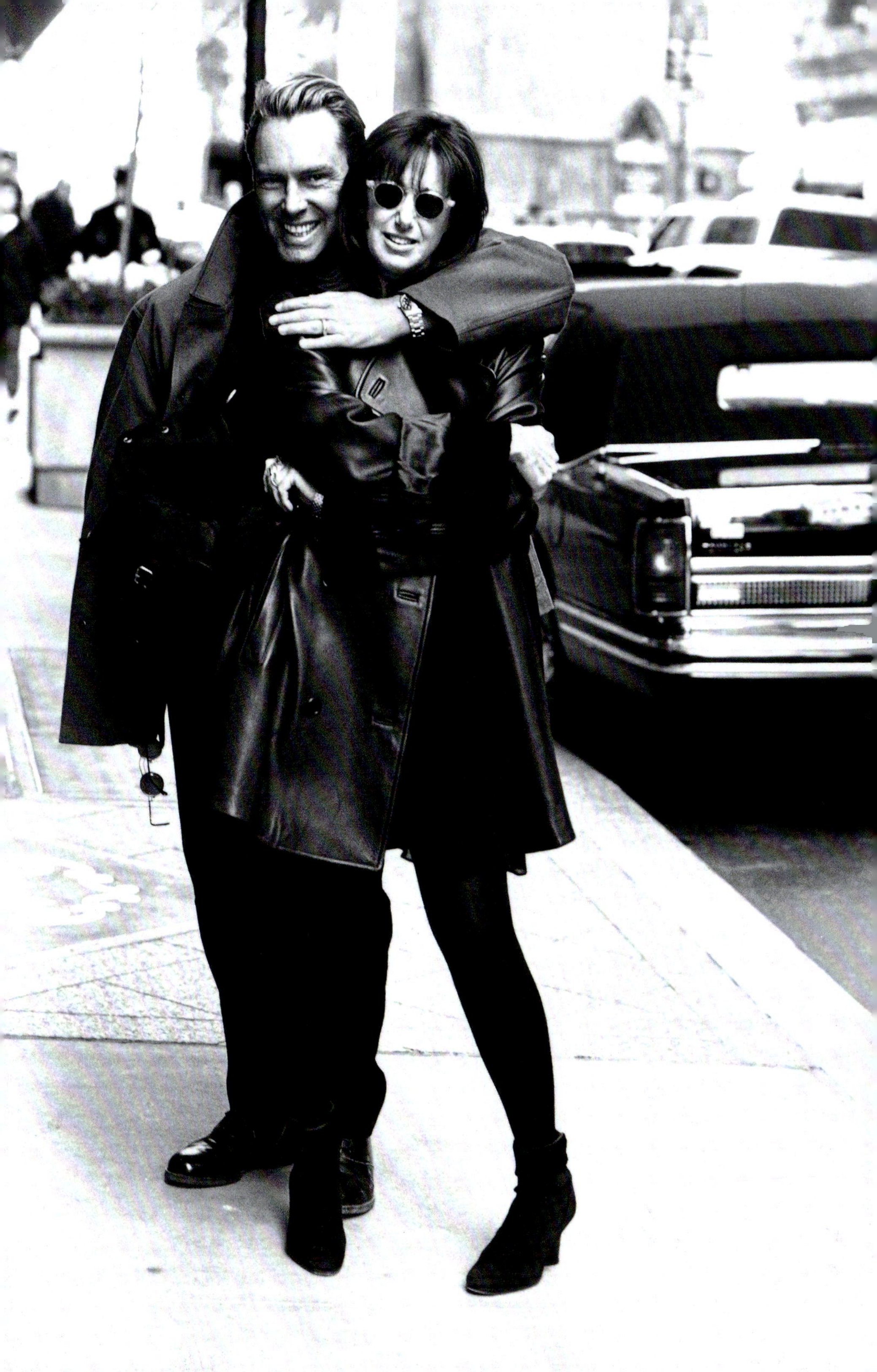

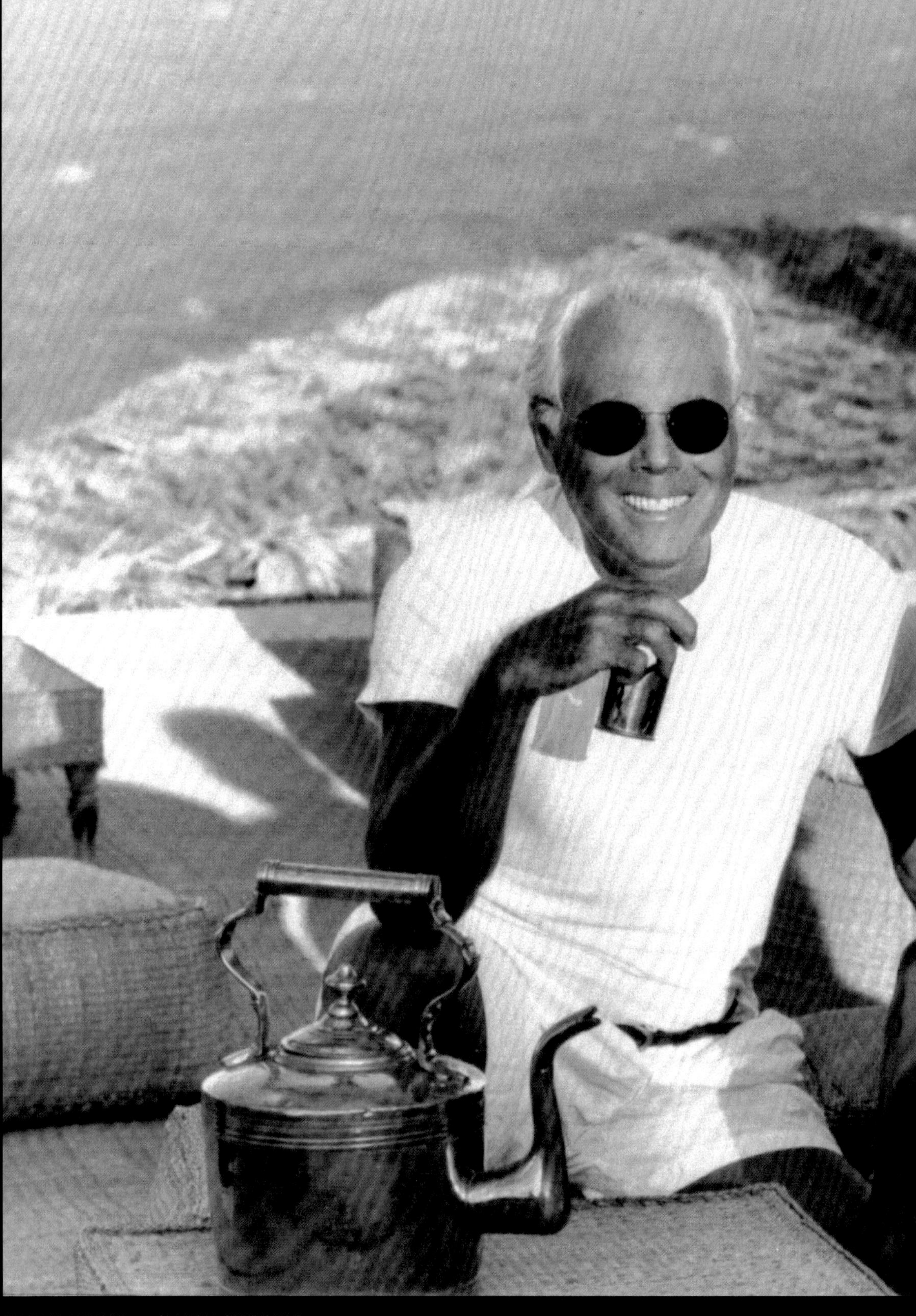

GIORGIO ARMANI — CLAUDIA CARDINALE

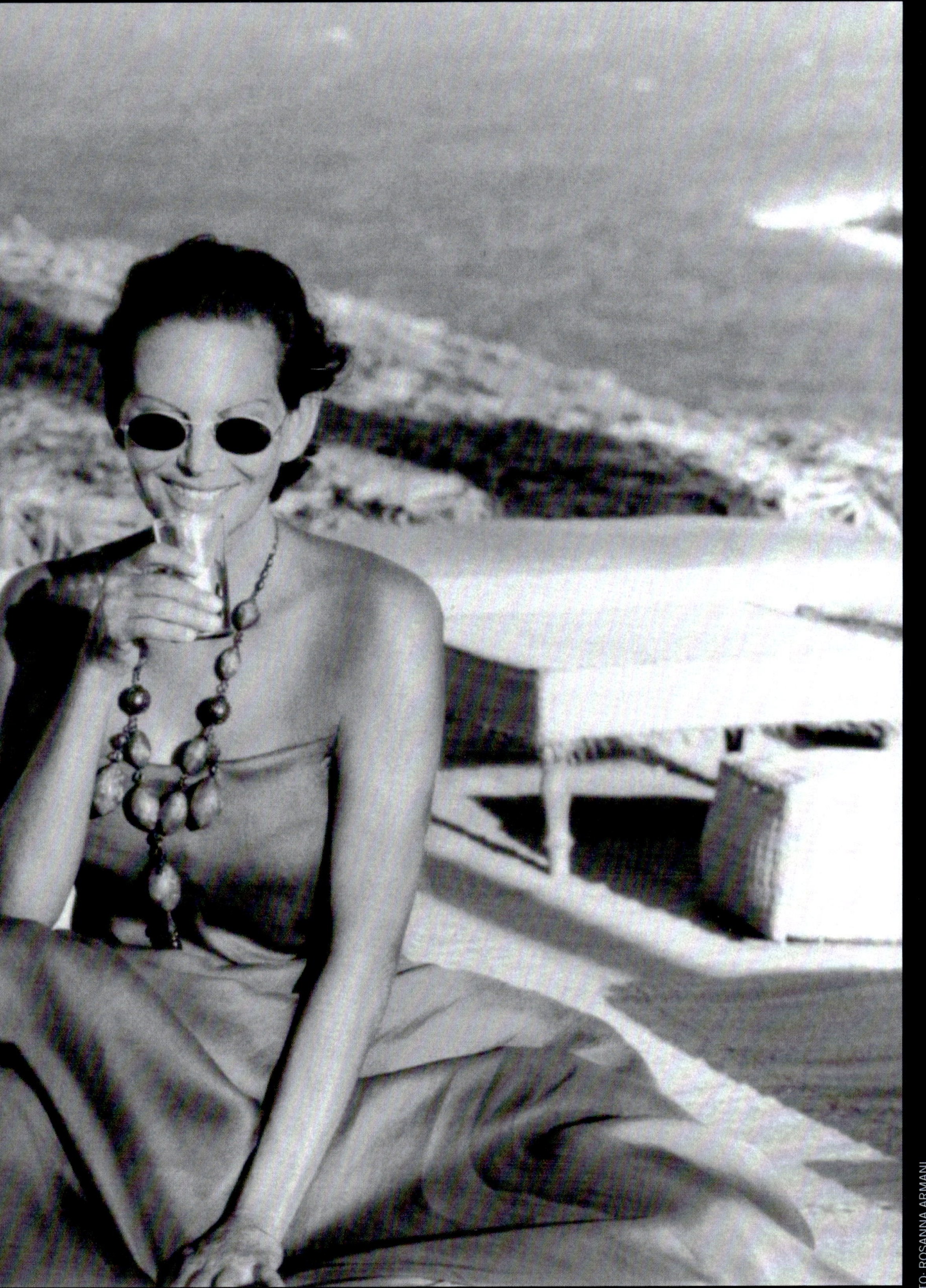
O: ROSANNA ARMANI

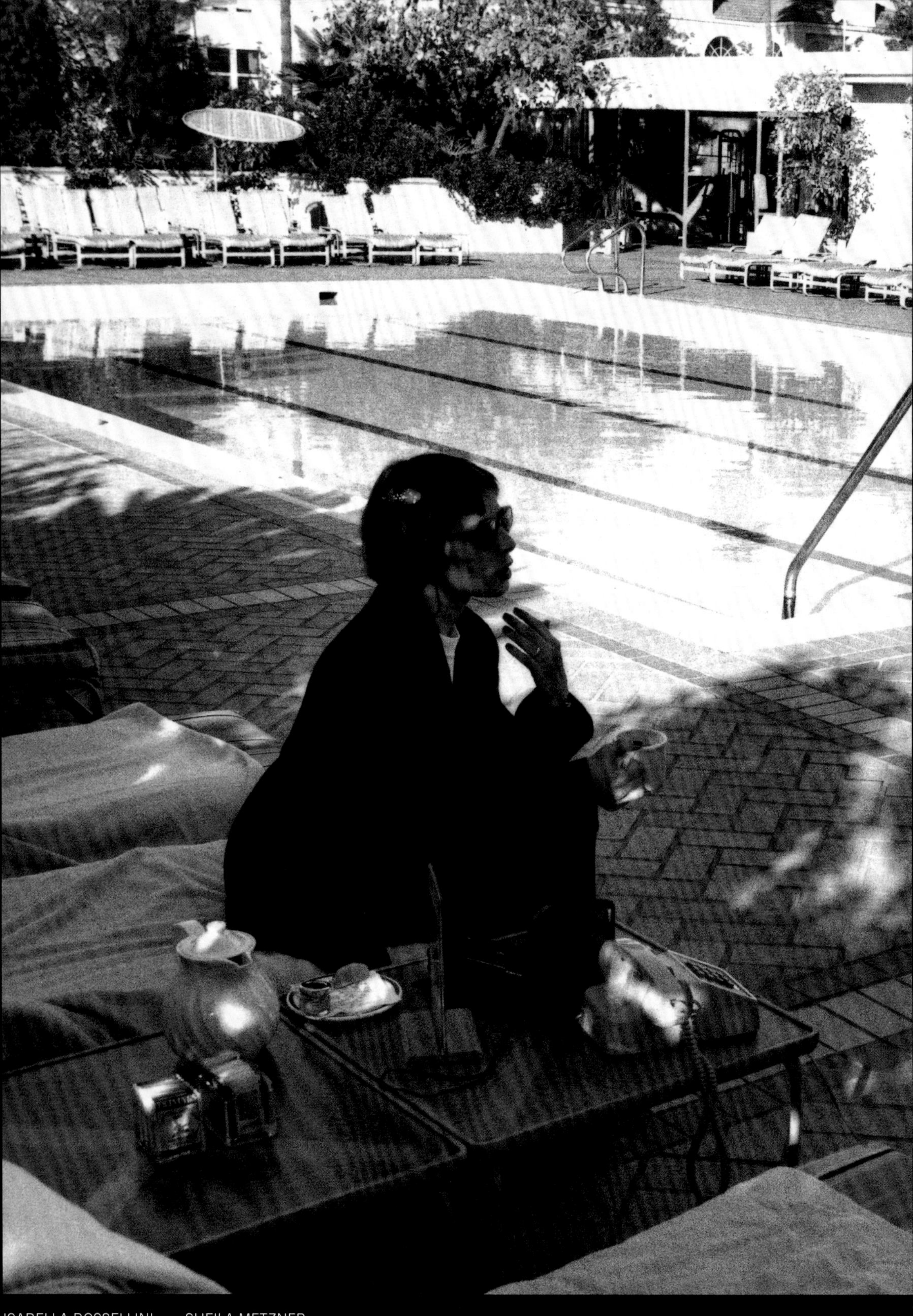

ISABELLA ROSSELLINI — SHEILA METZNER

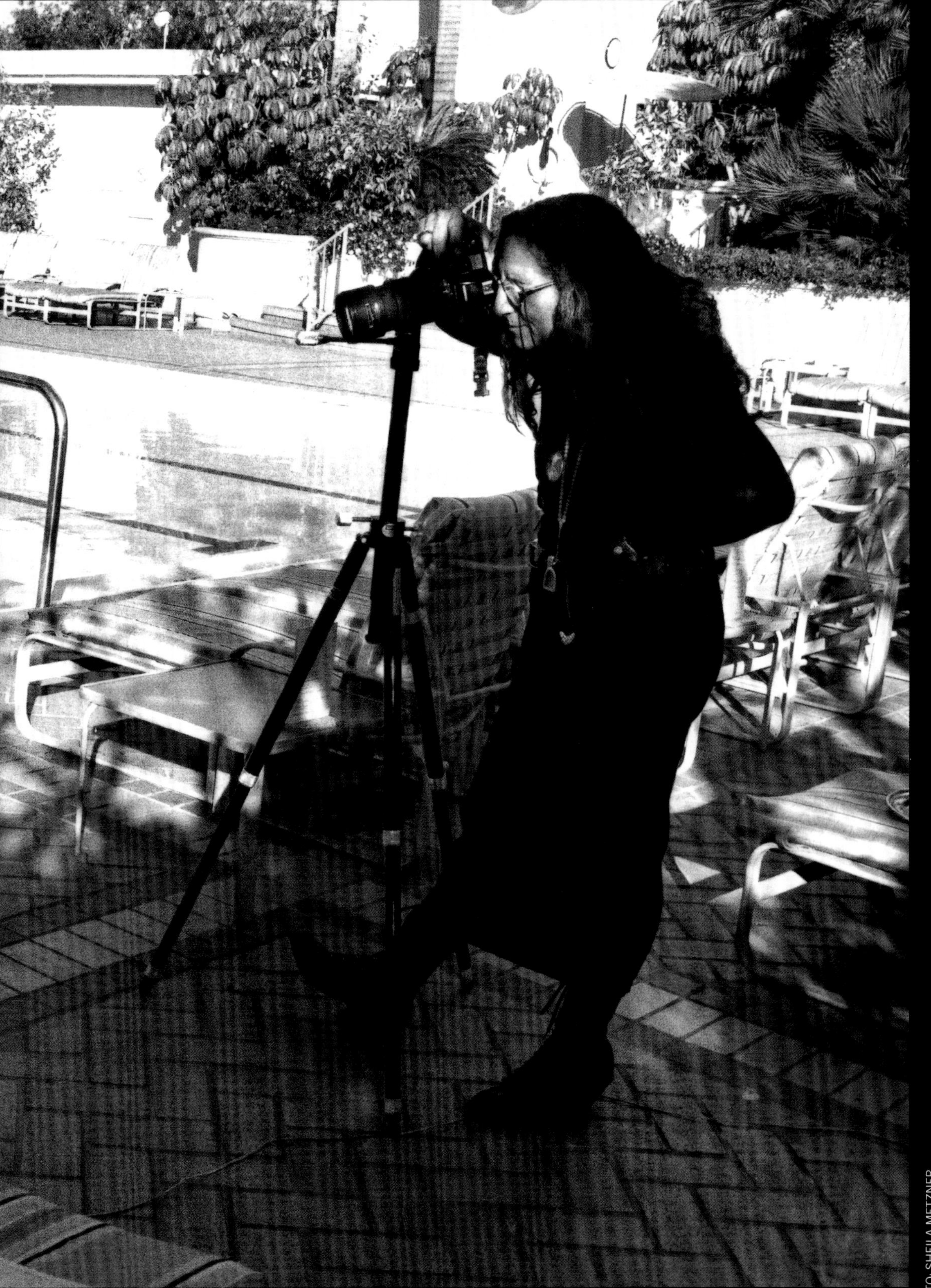
PHOTO: SHEILA METZNER

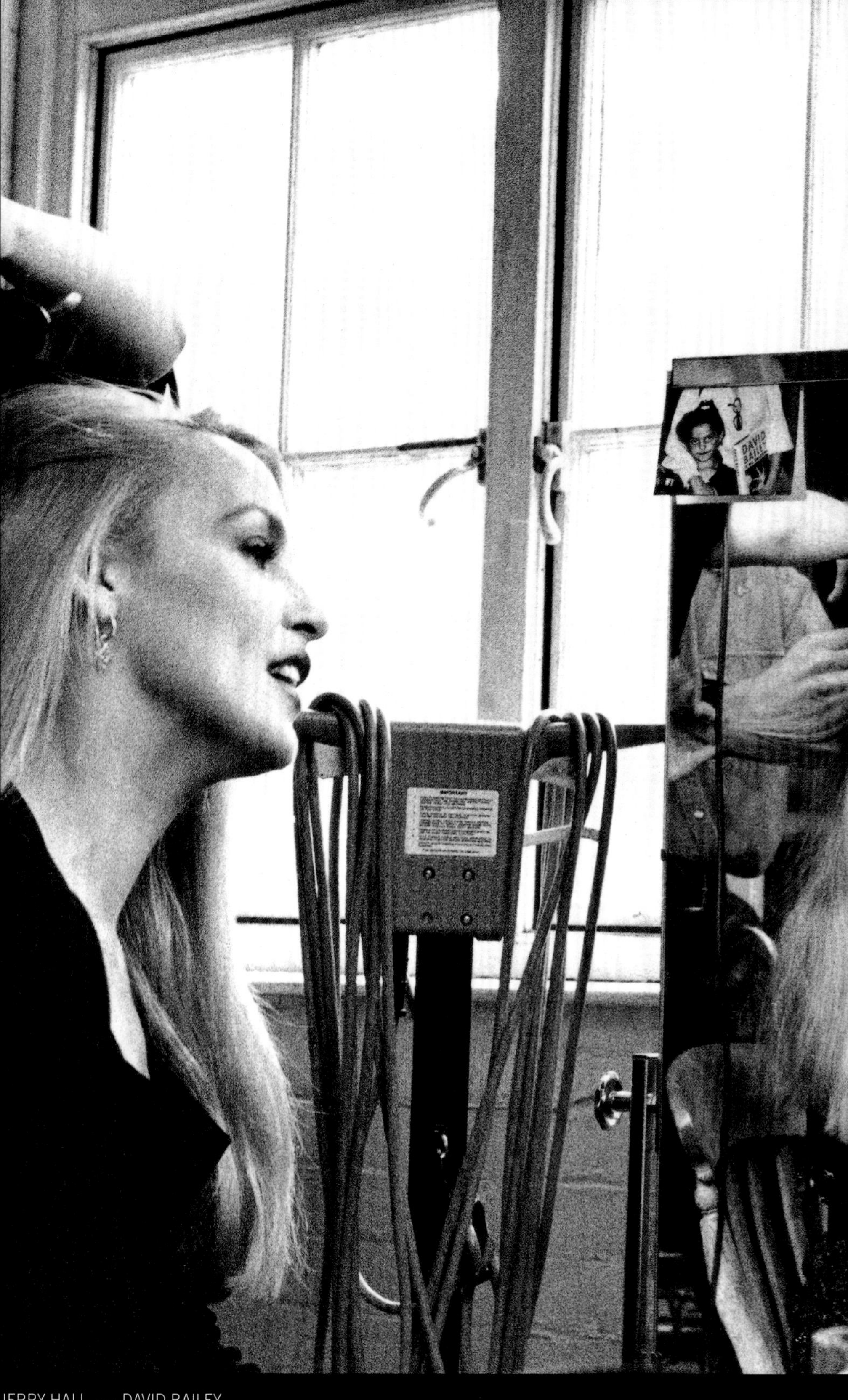

JERRY HALL — DAVID BAILEY

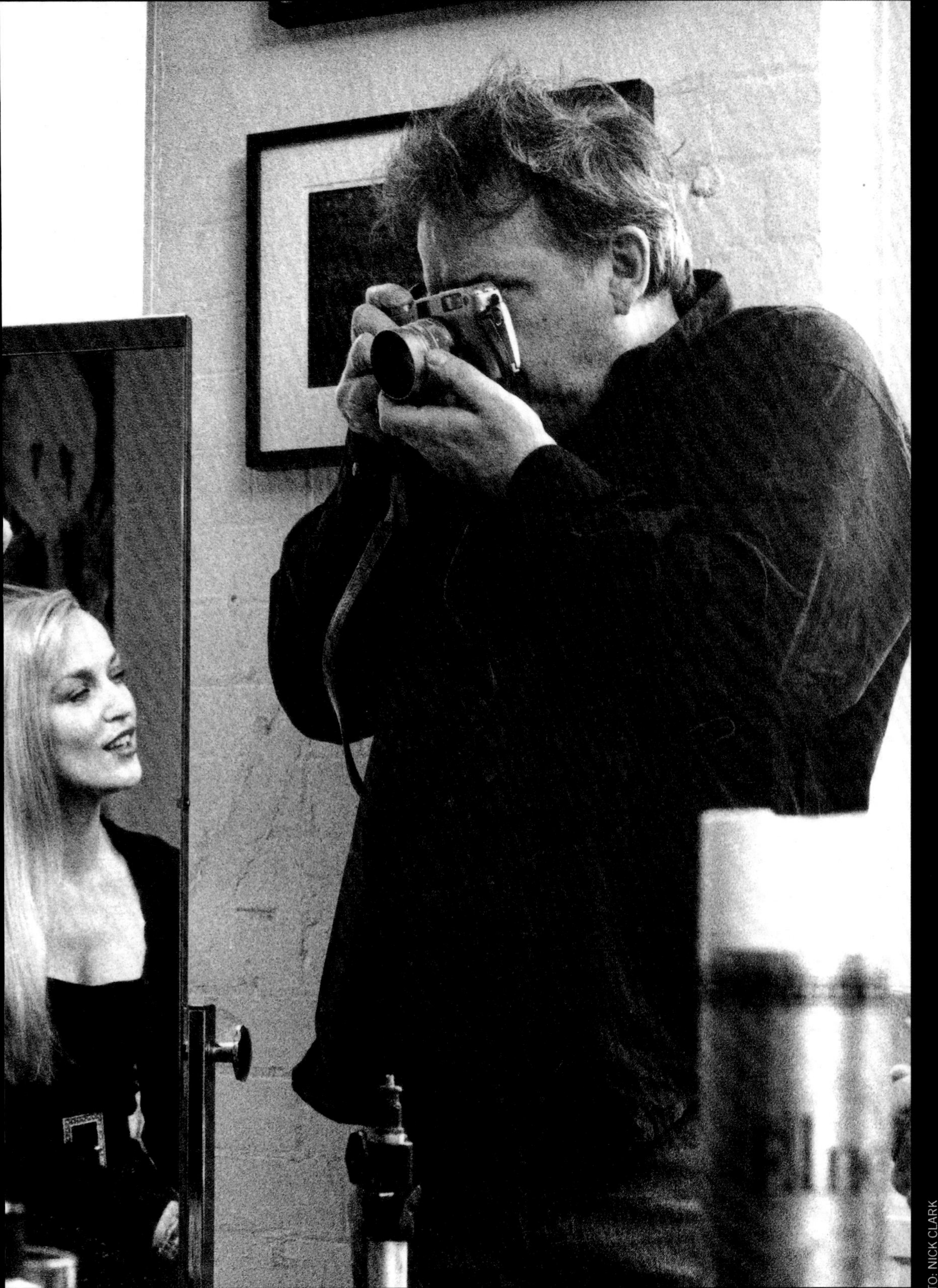

PHOTO: NICK CLARK

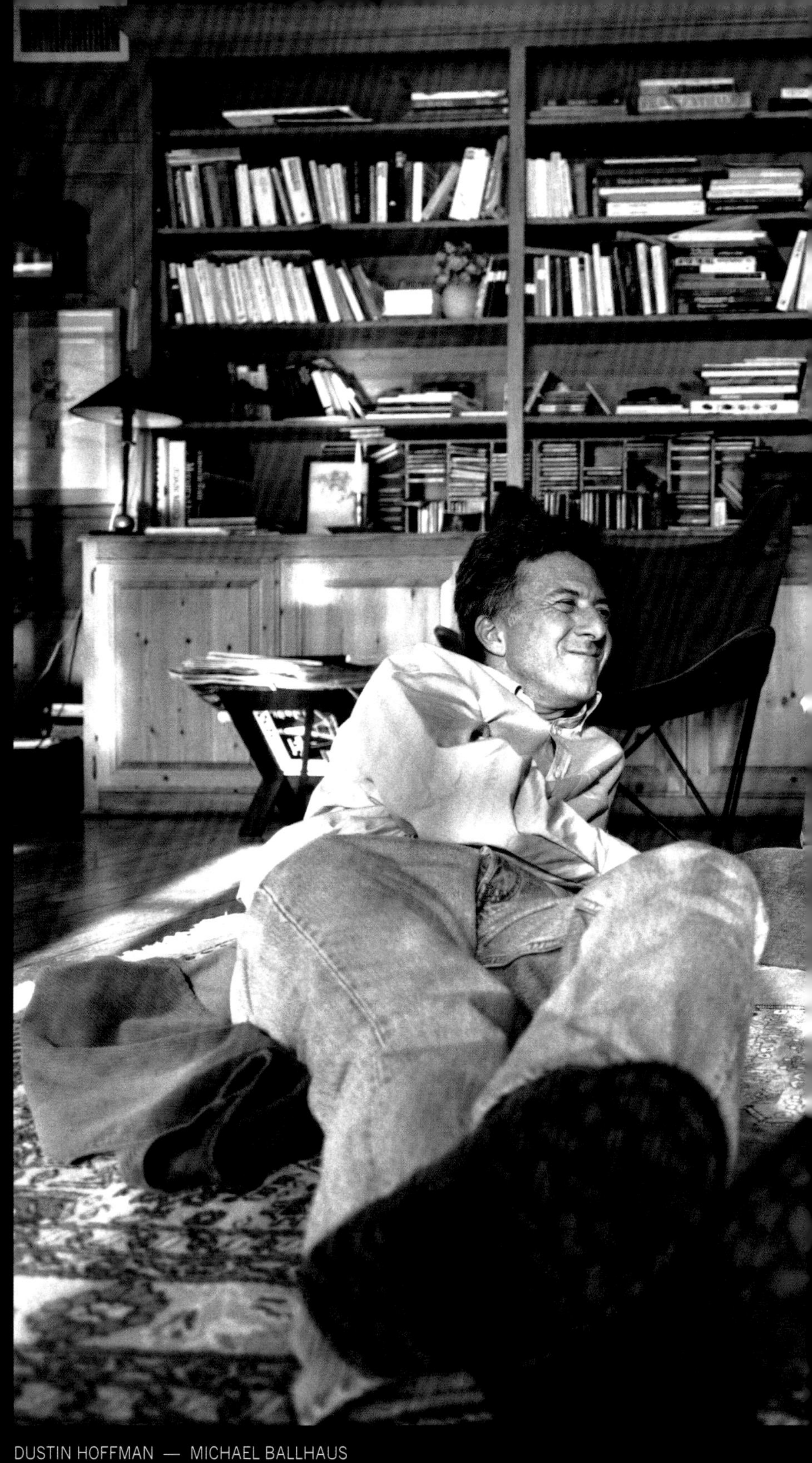

DUSTIN HOFFMAN — MICHAEL BALLHAUS

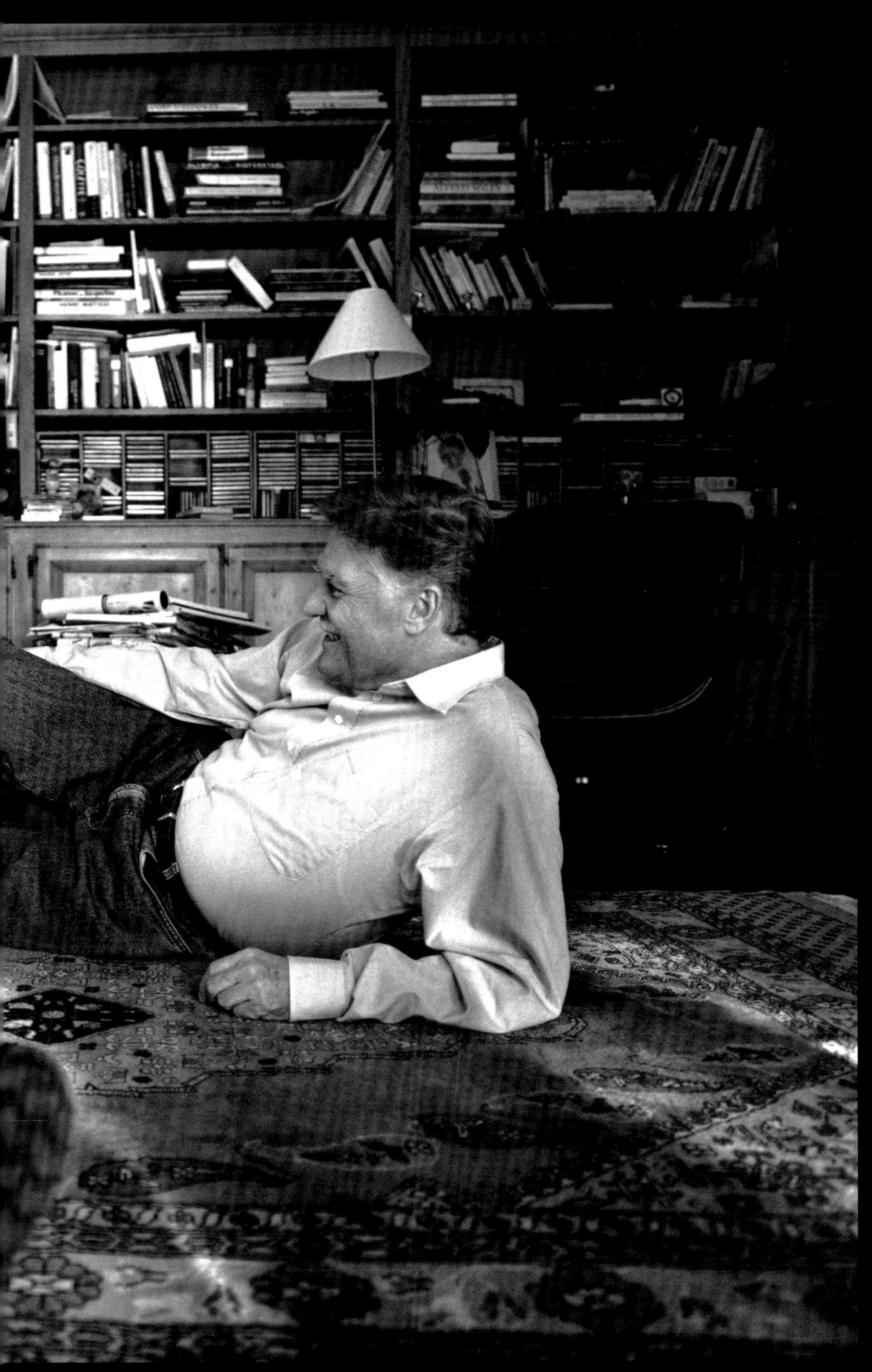

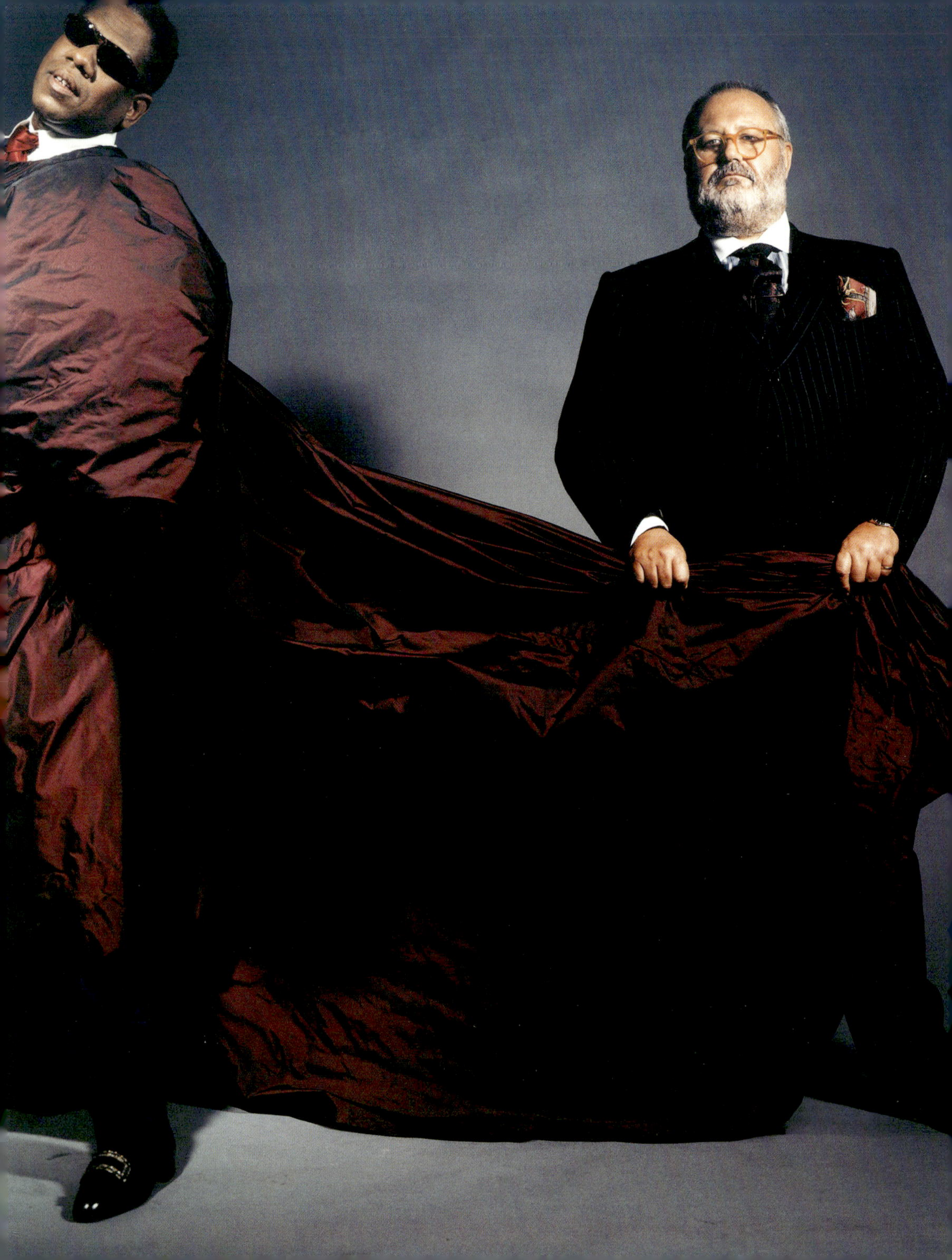

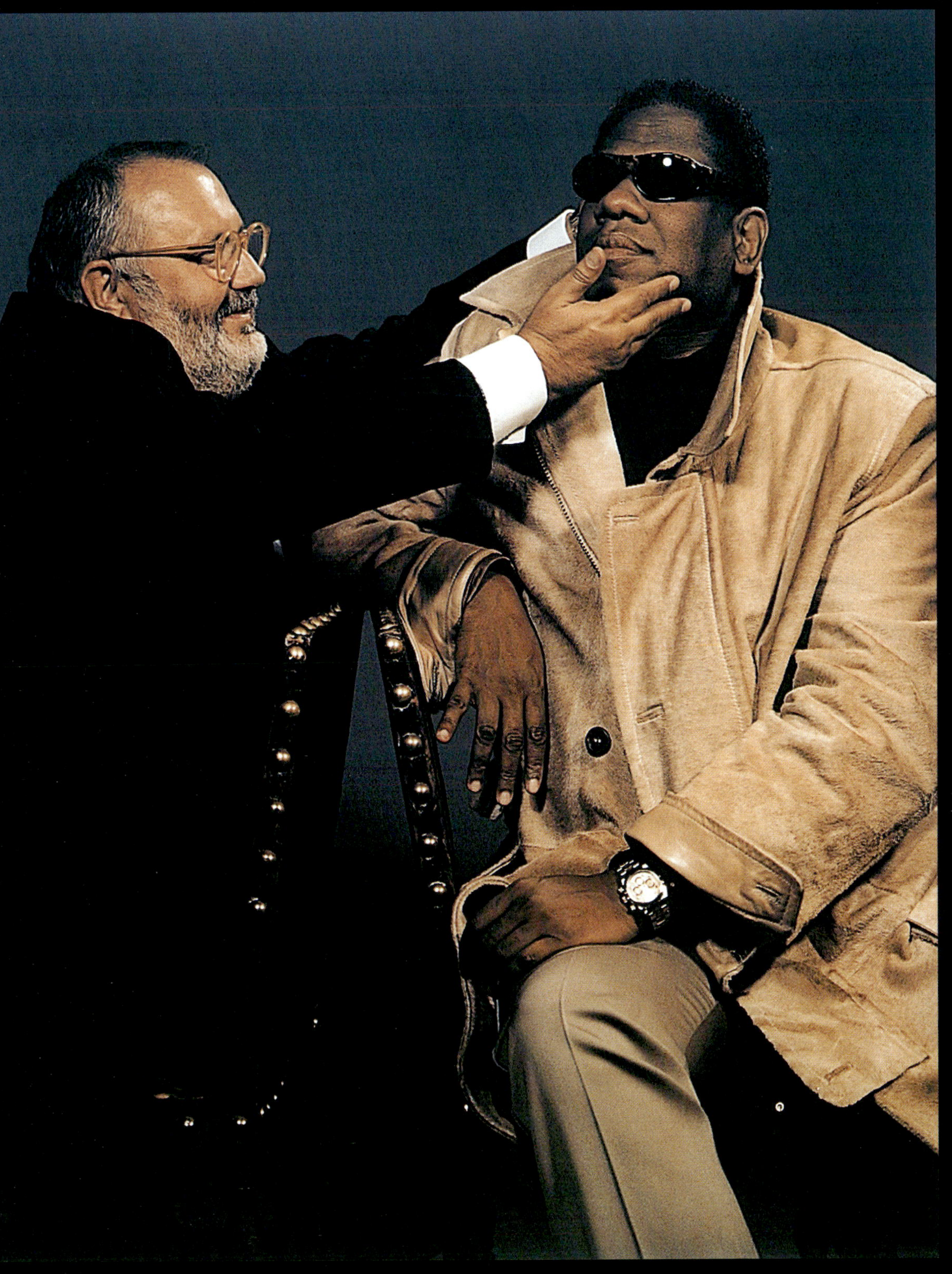

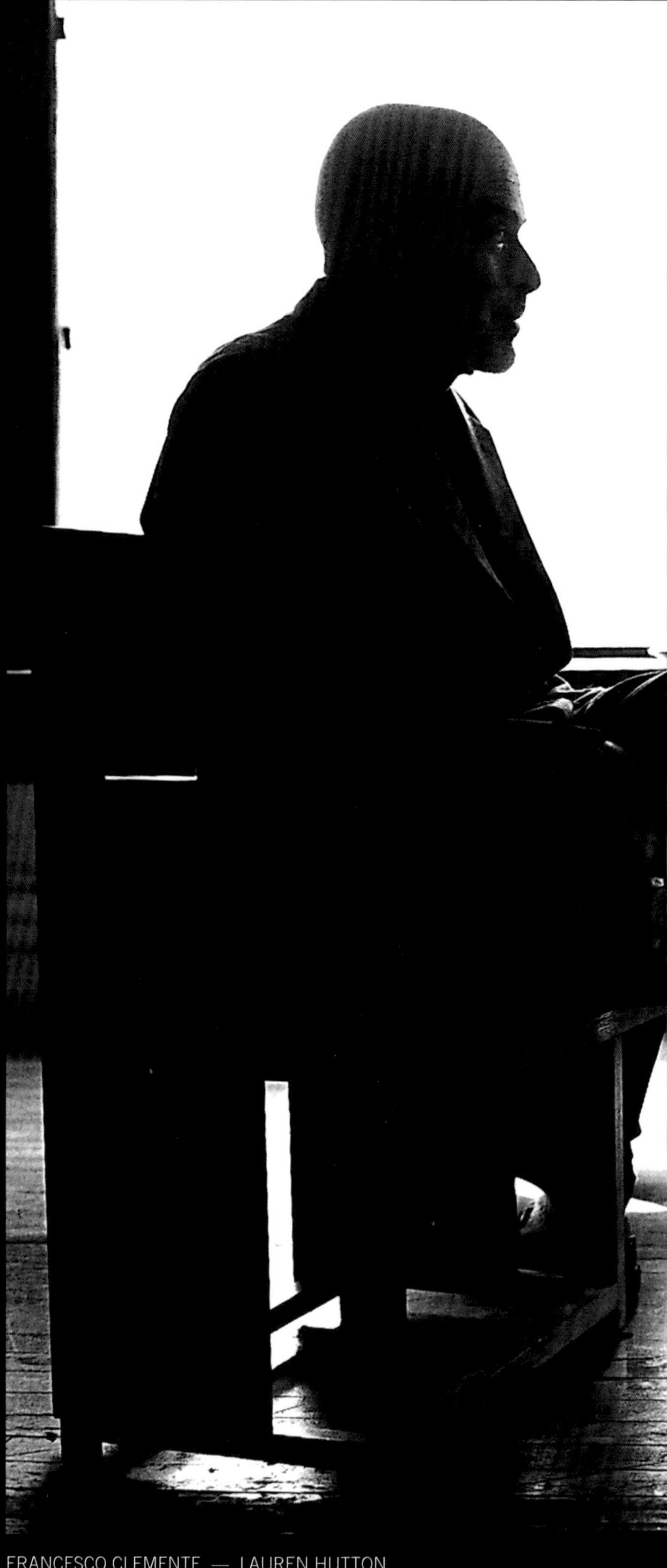

FRANCESCO CLEMENTE — LAUREN HUTTON

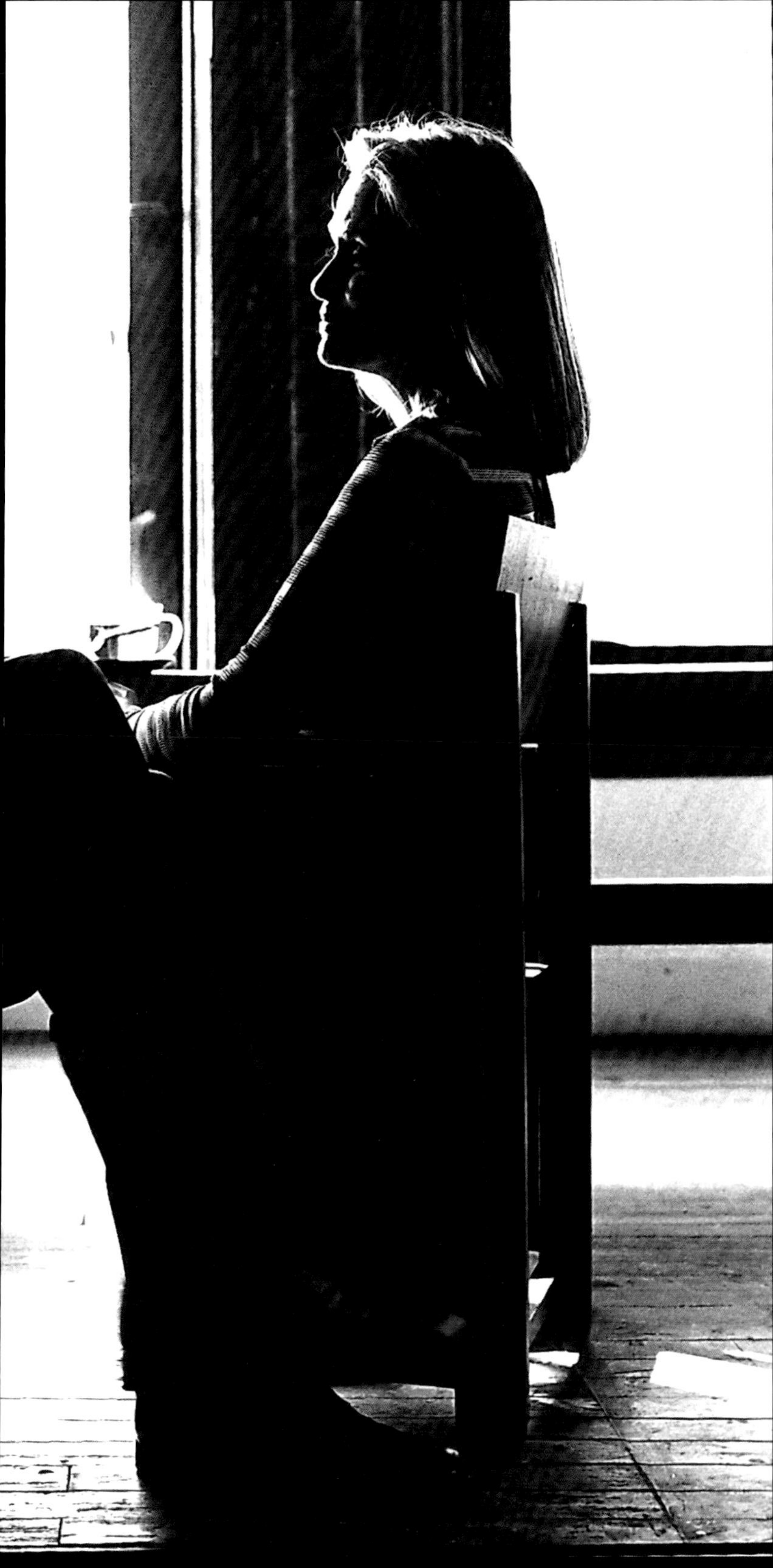

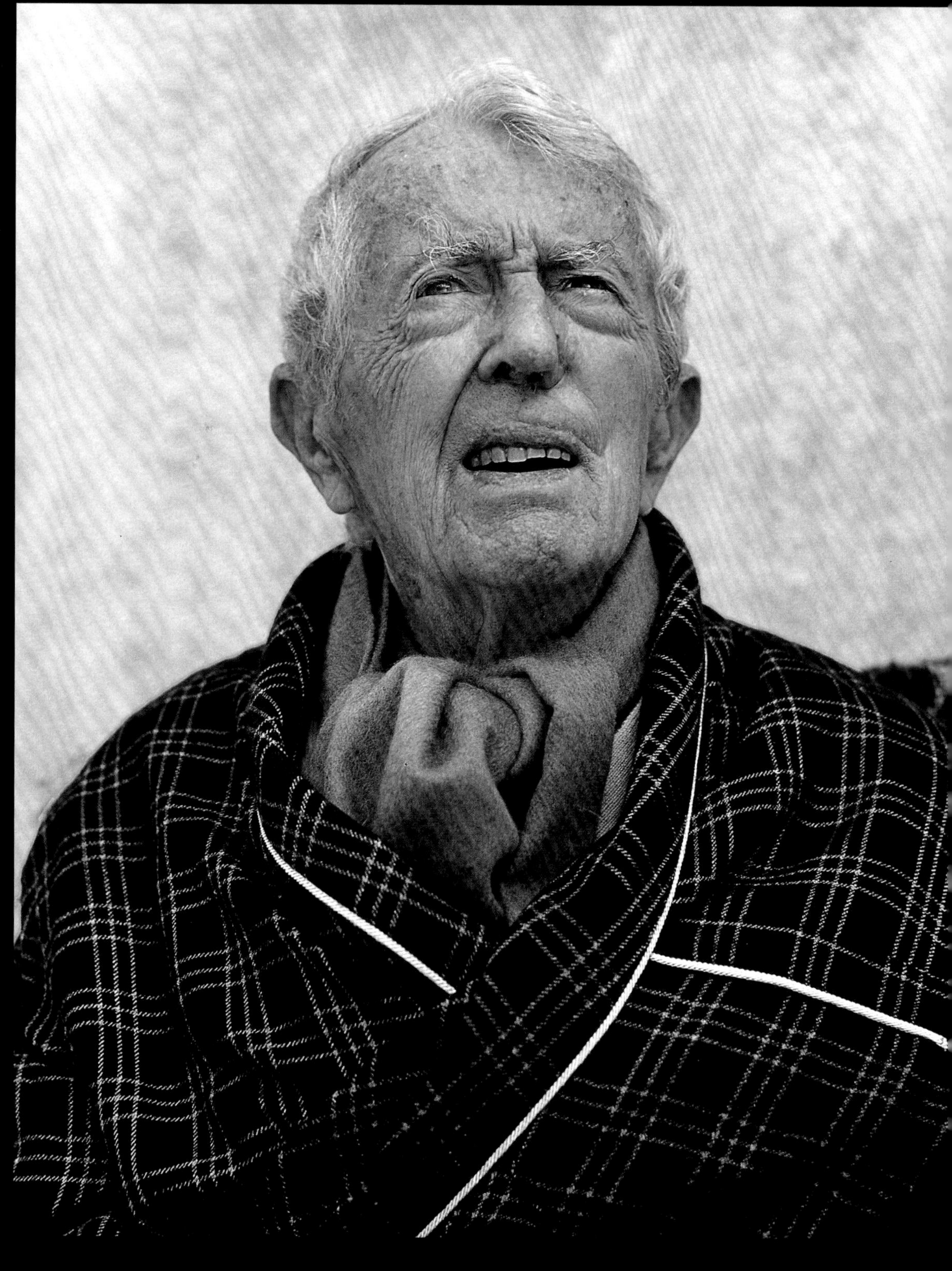

PAUL BOWLES — PATTI SMITH

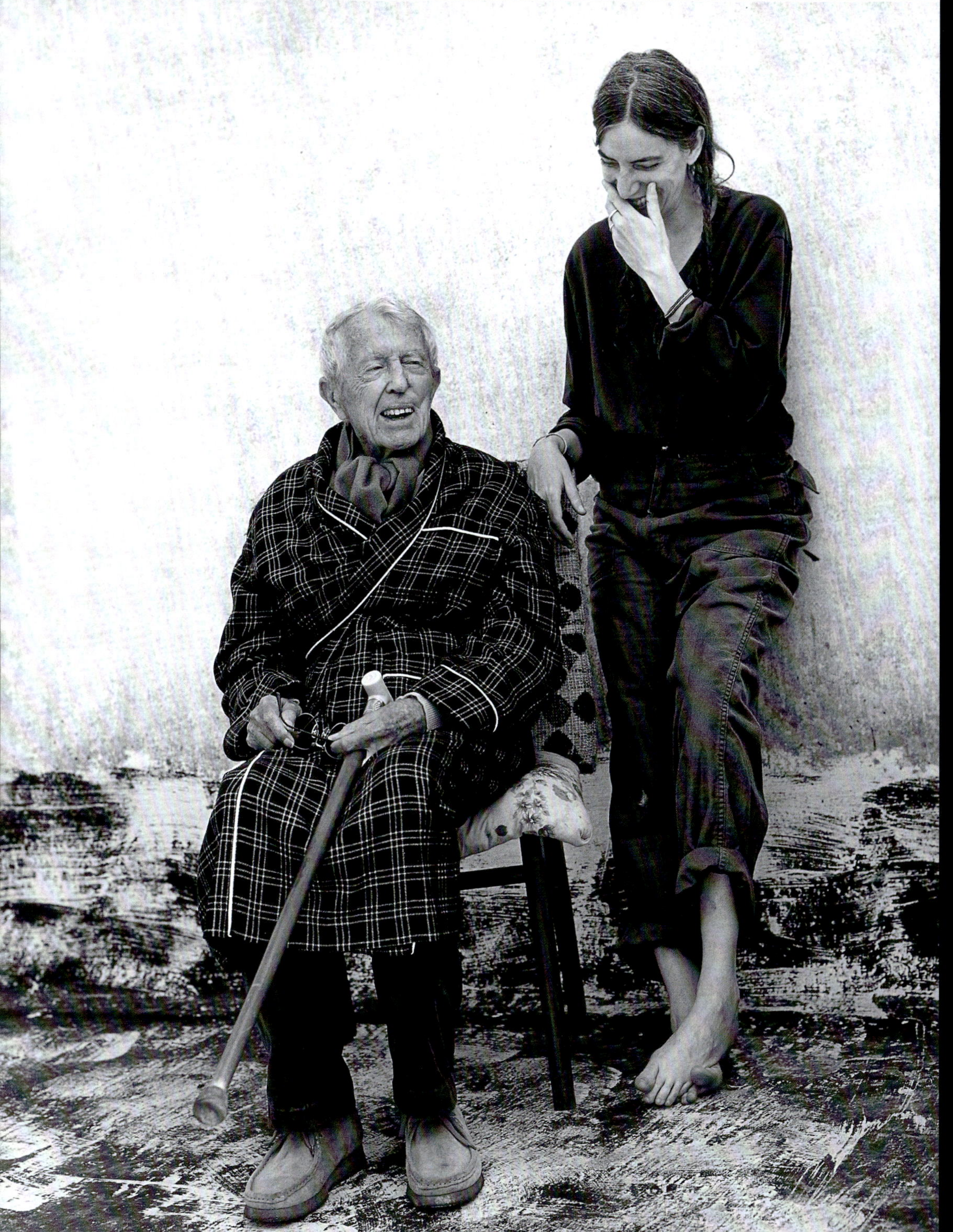

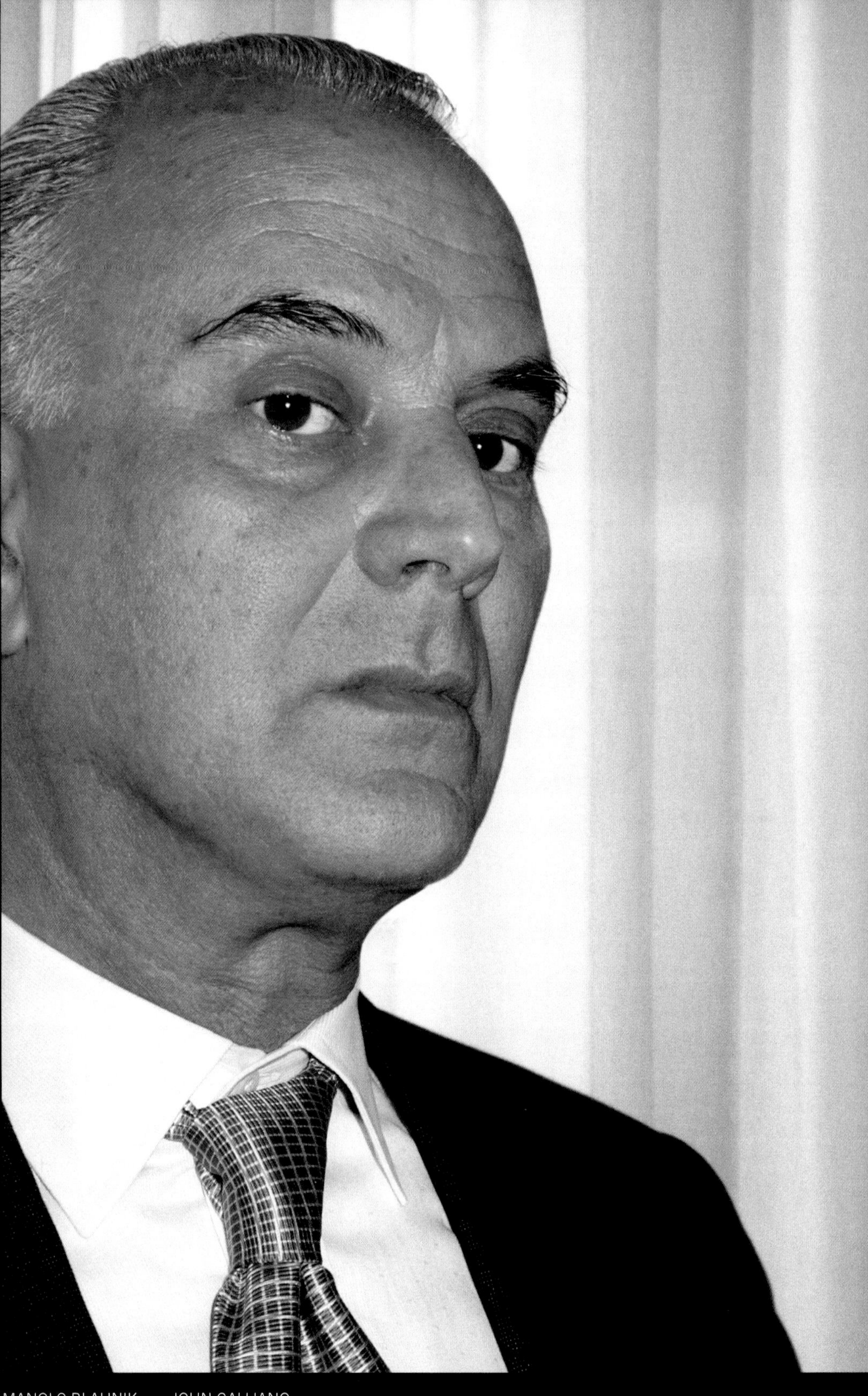

MANOLO BLAHNIK — JOHN GALLIANO

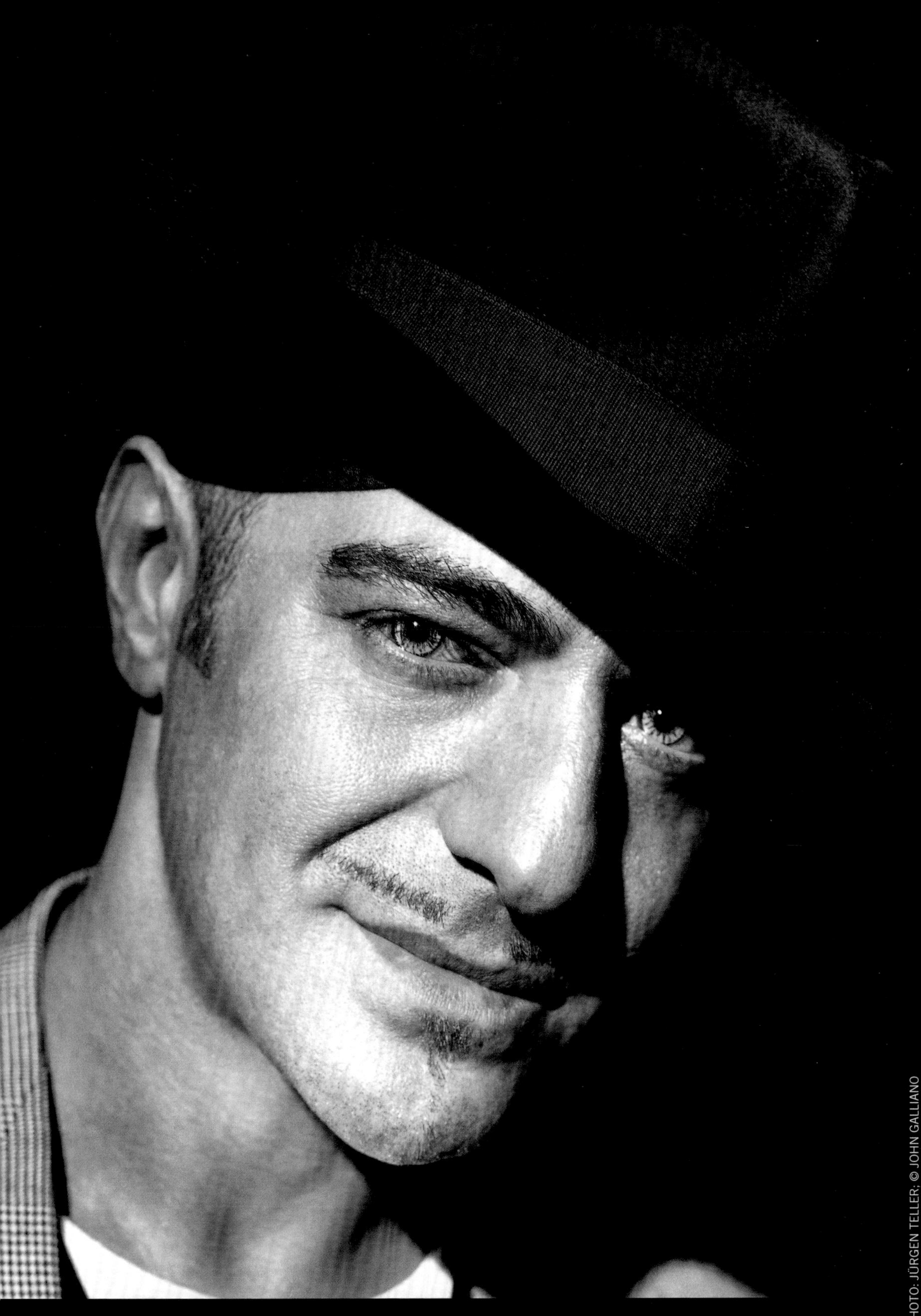

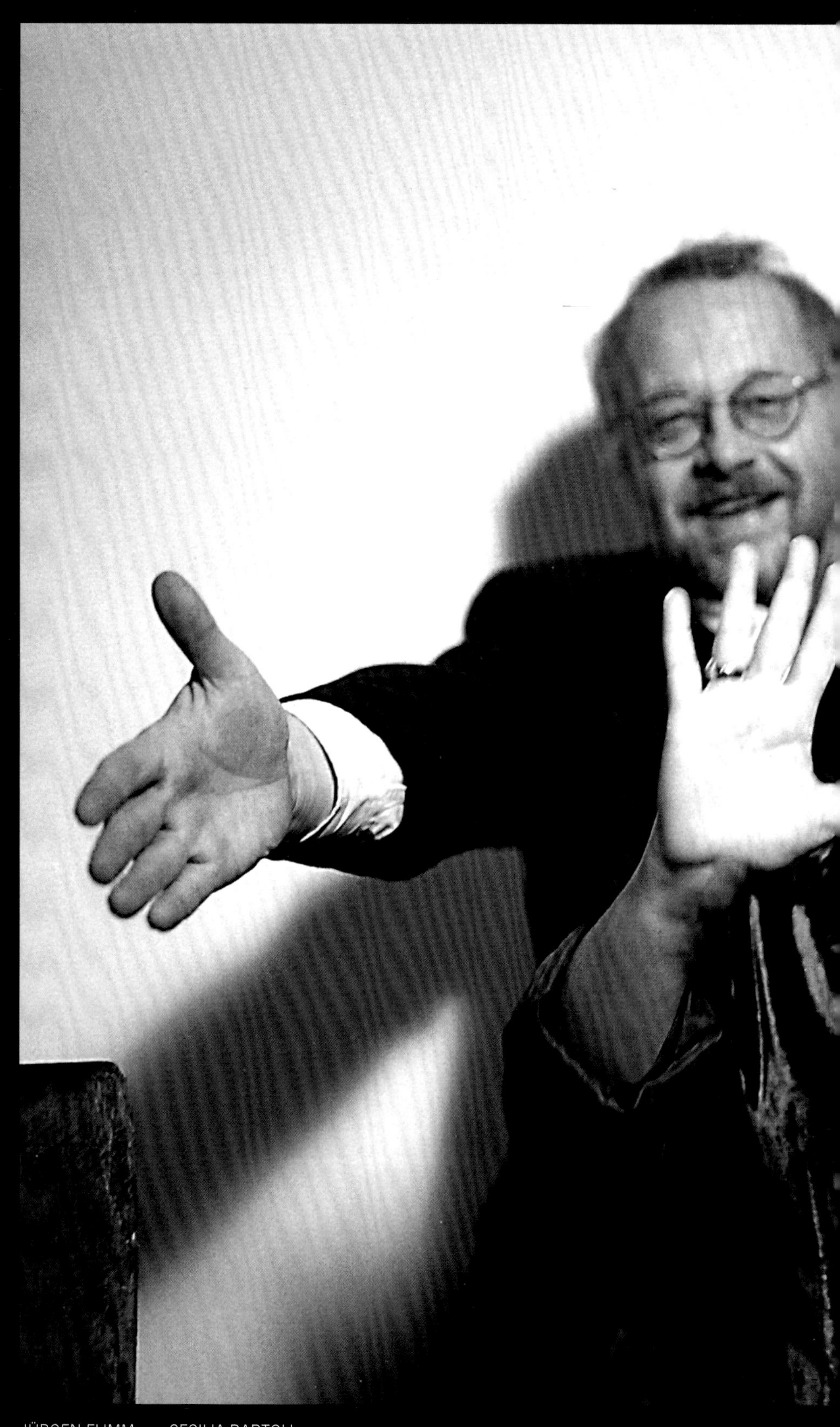

JÜRGEN FLIMM — CECILIA BARTOLI

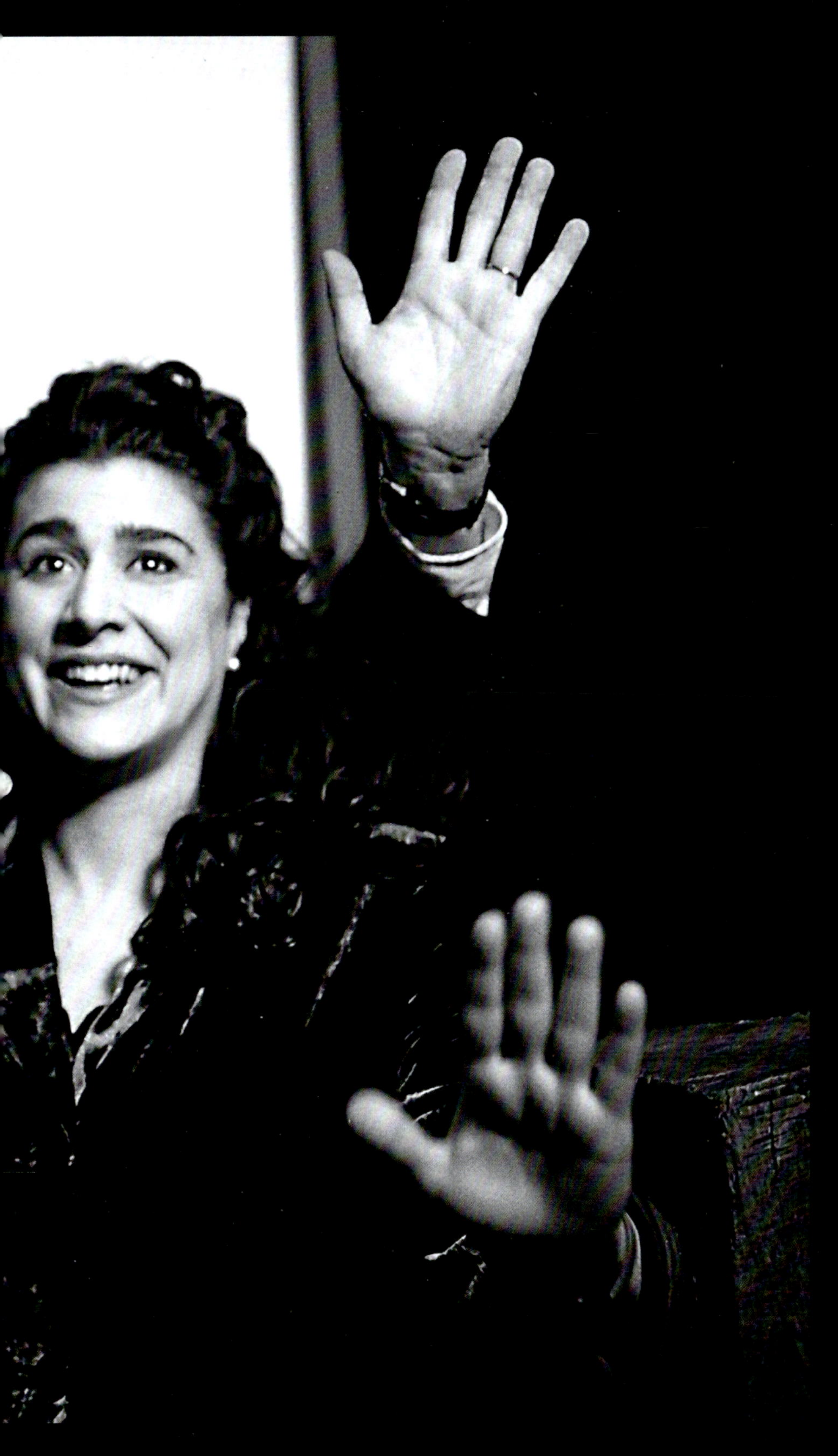

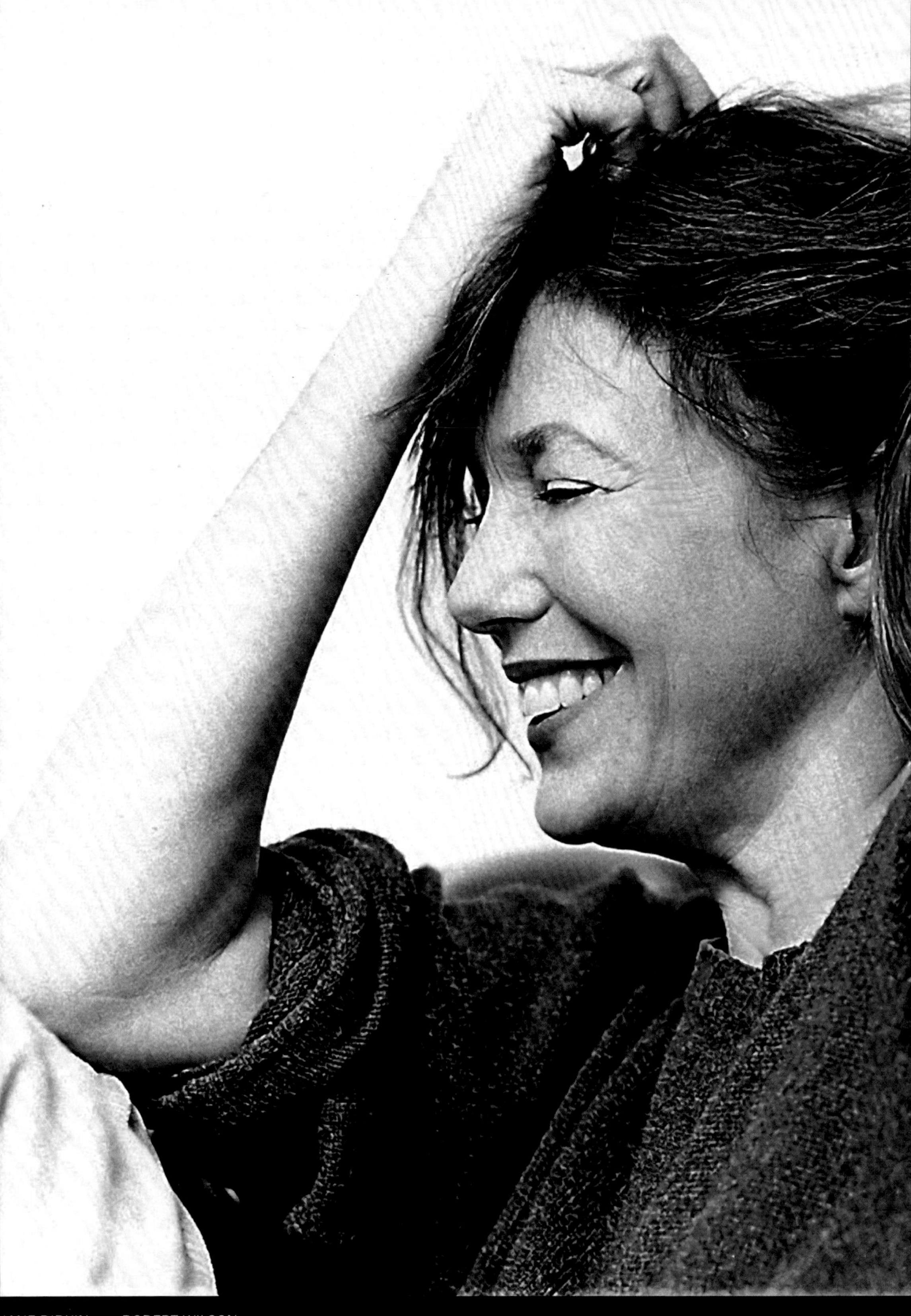

JANE BIRKIN — ROBERT WILSON

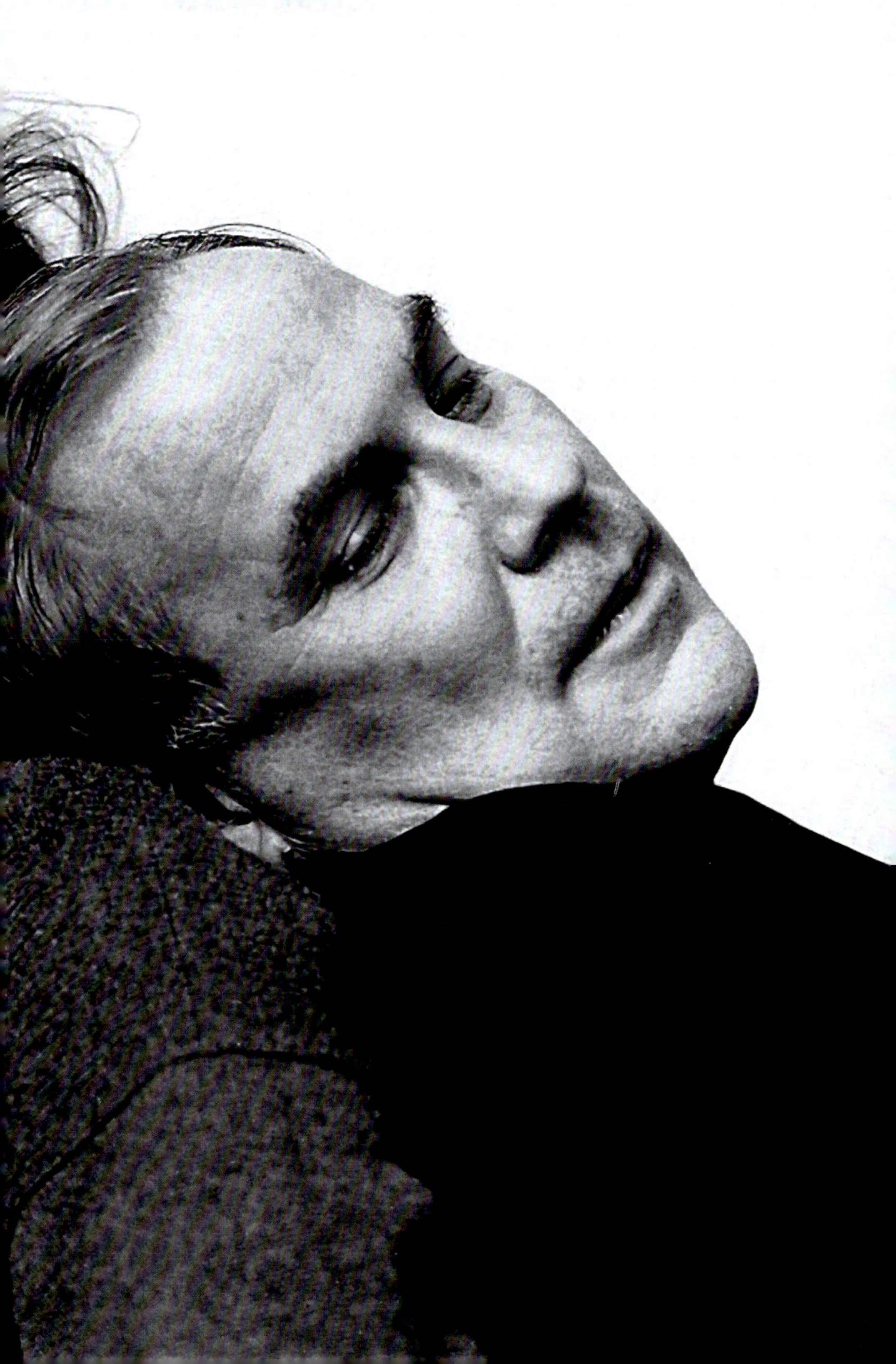

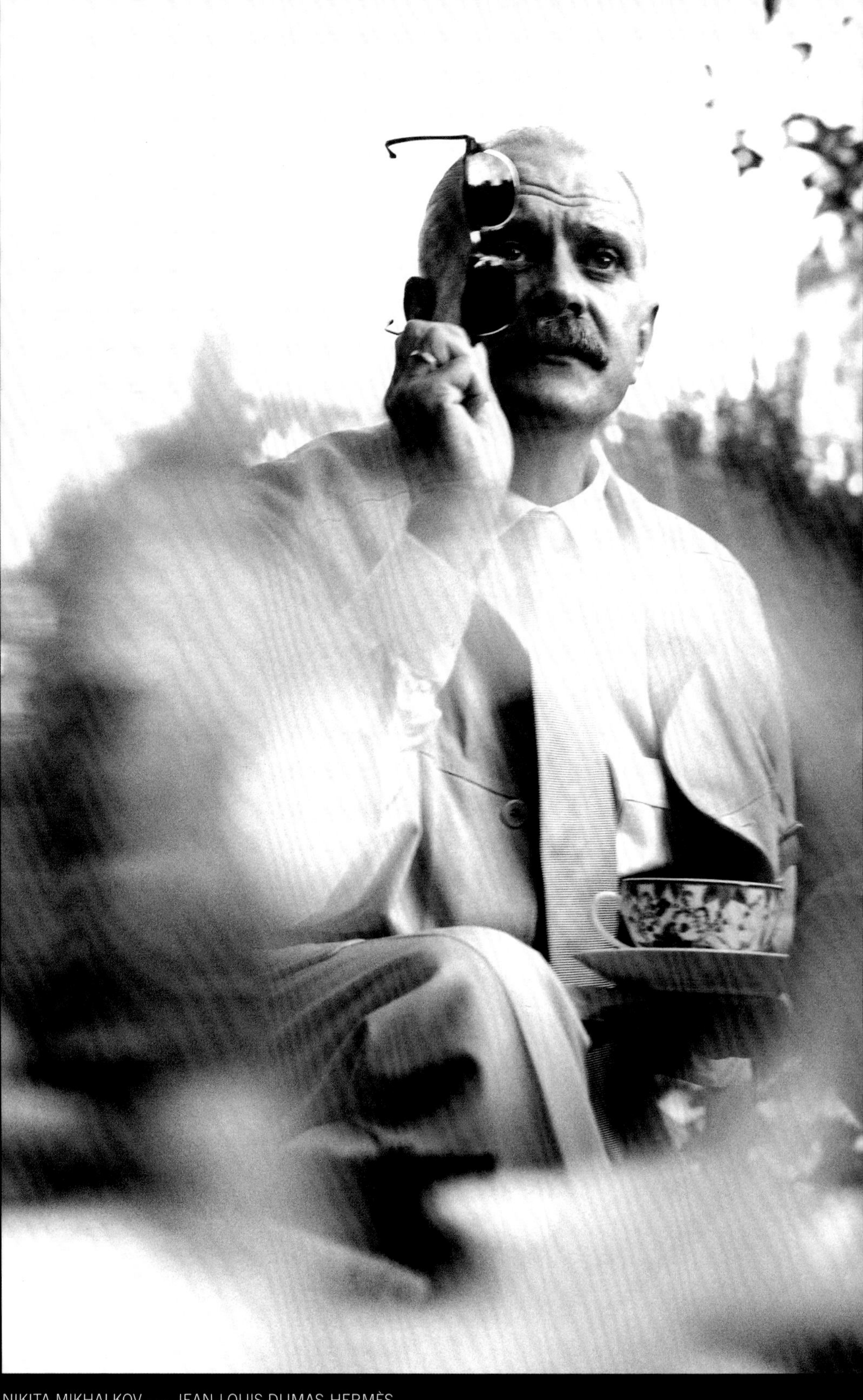

NIKITA MIKHALKOV — JEAN-LOUIS DUMAS-HERMÈS

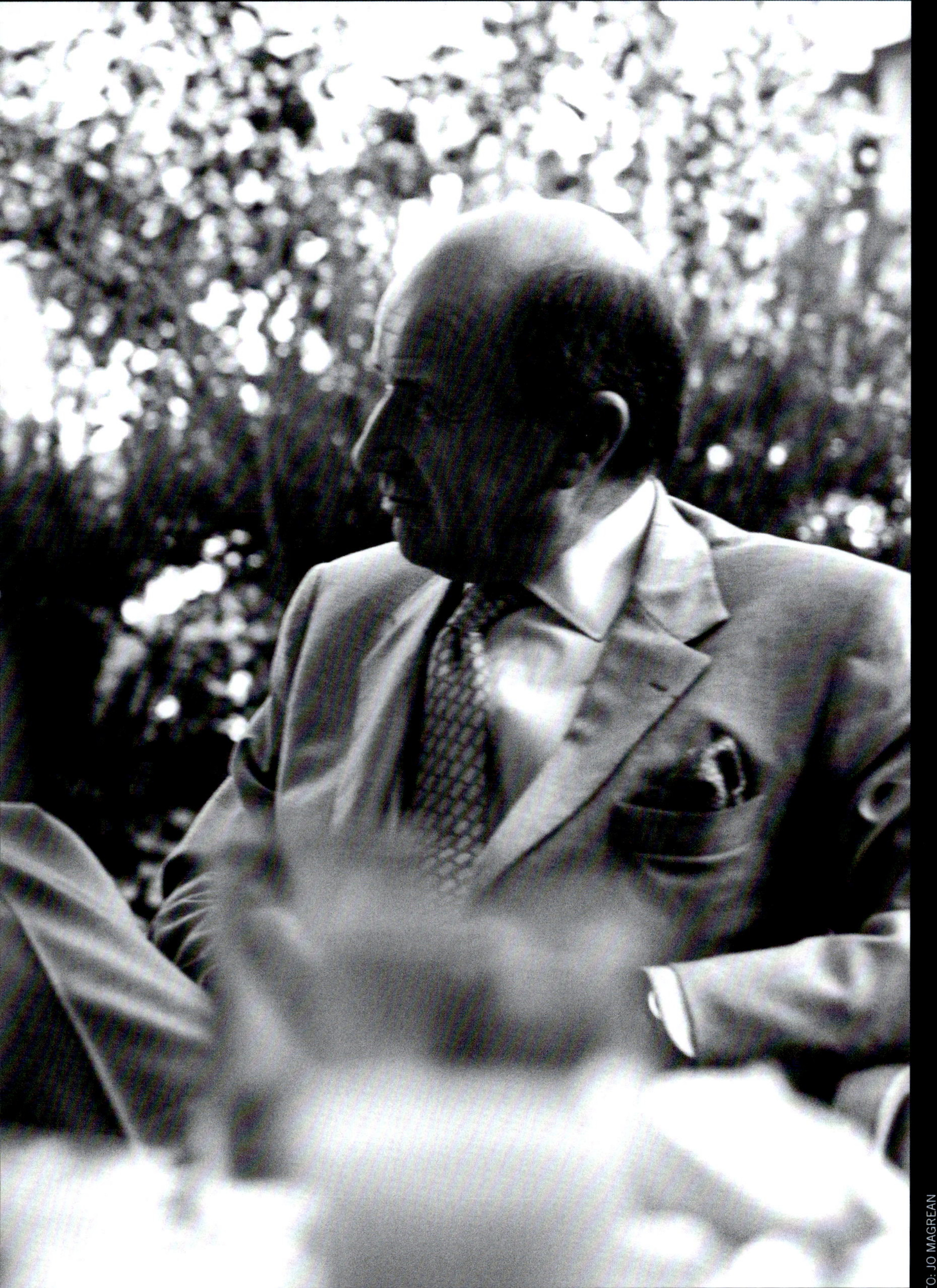
O: JO MAGREAN

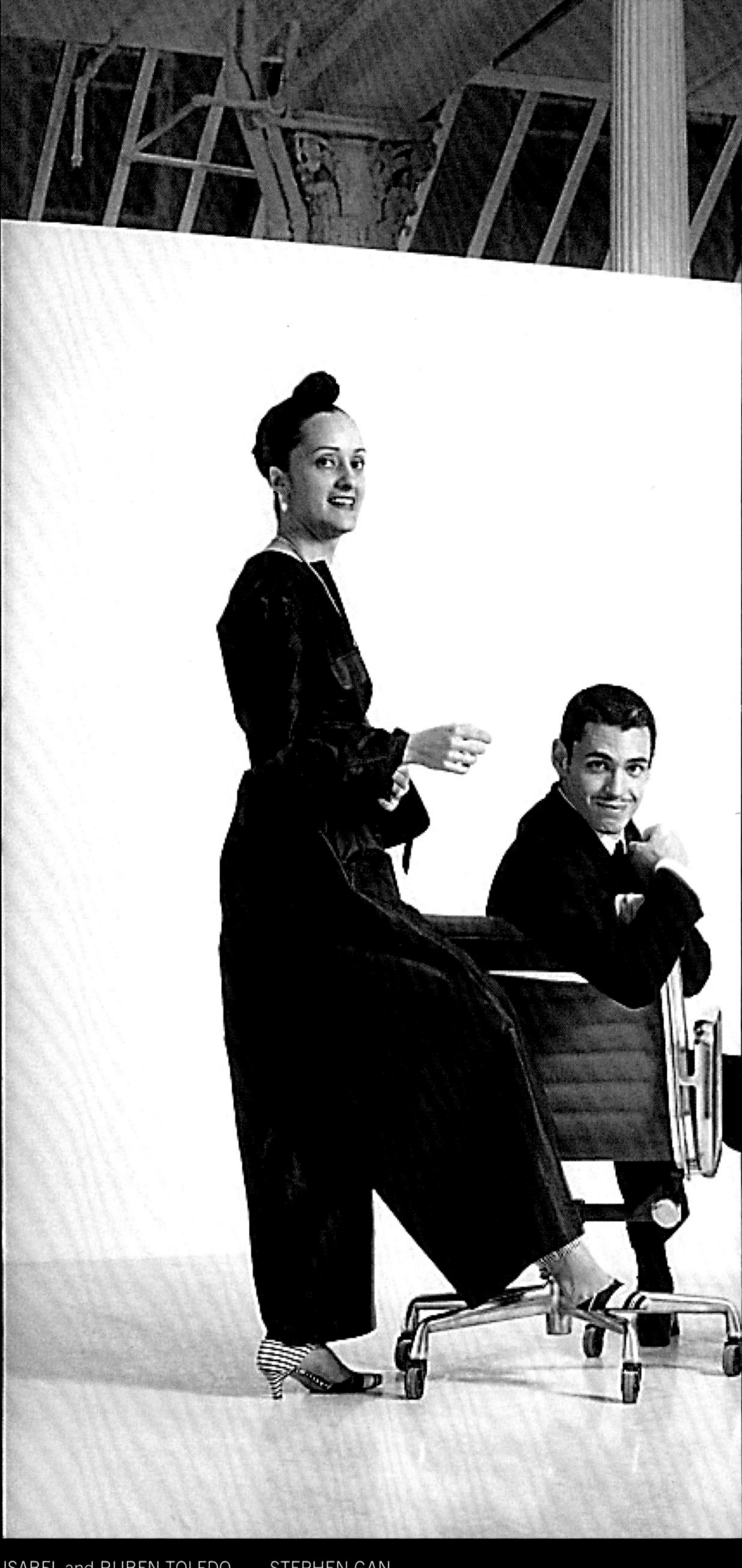

ISABEL and RUBEN TOLEDO — STEPHEN GAN

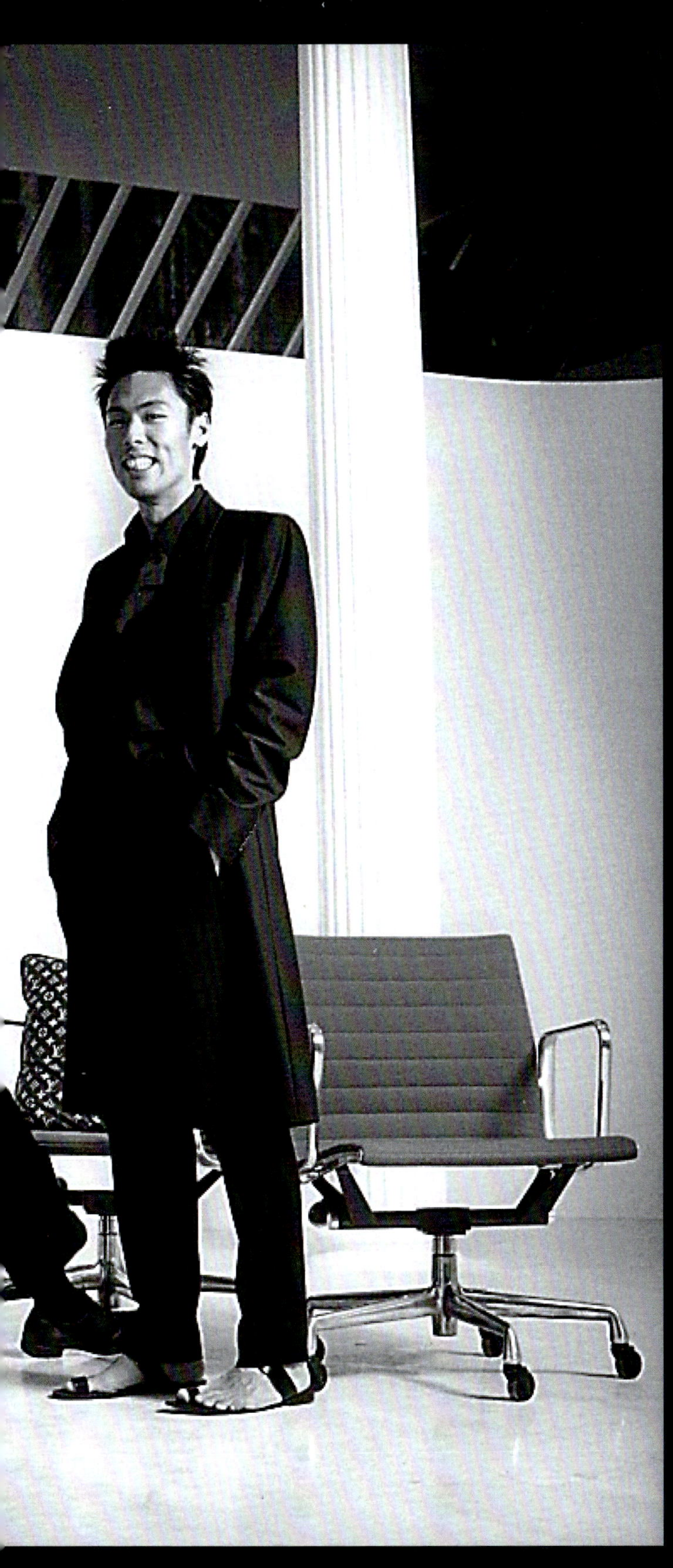

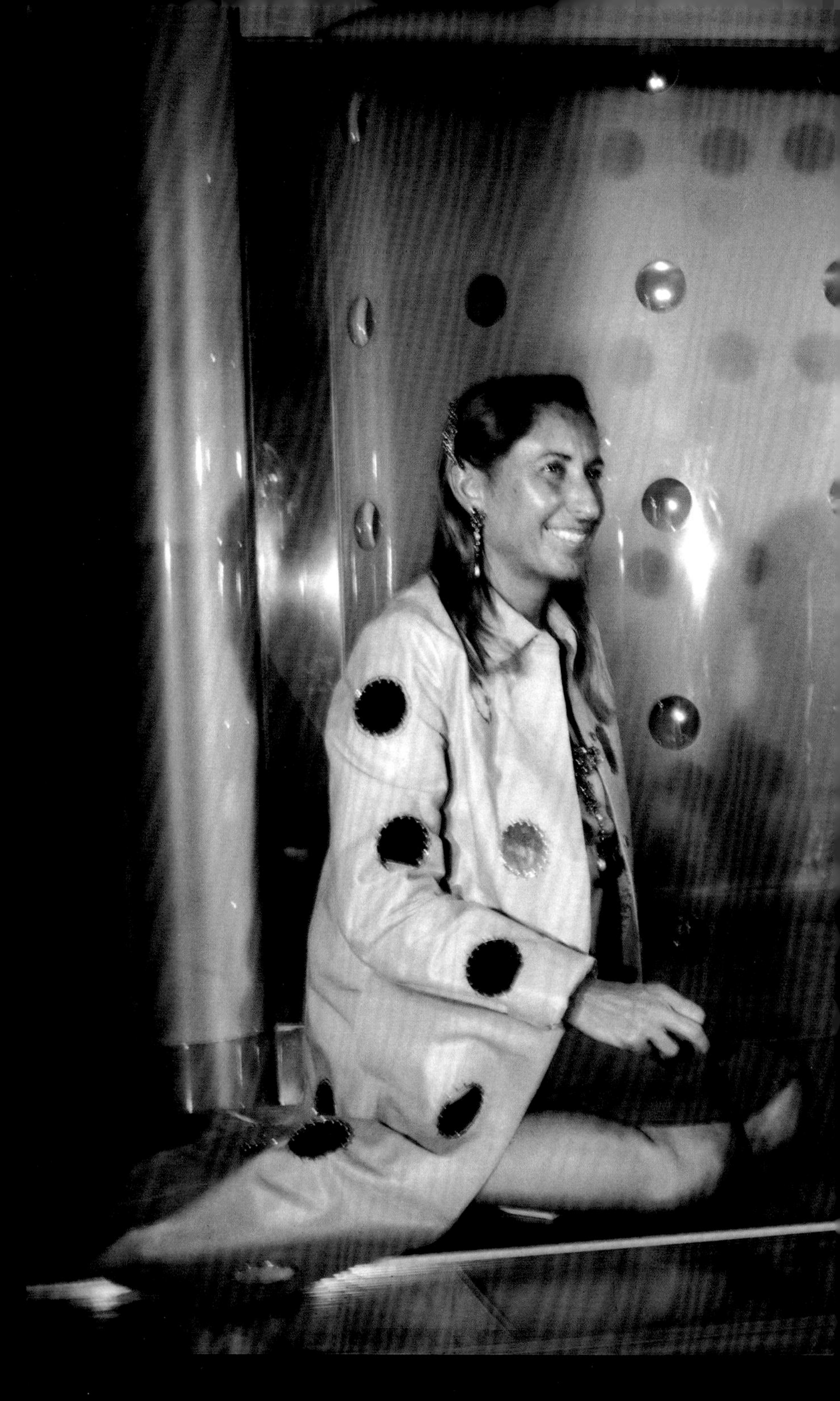

MIUCCIA PRADA — MARIKO MORI

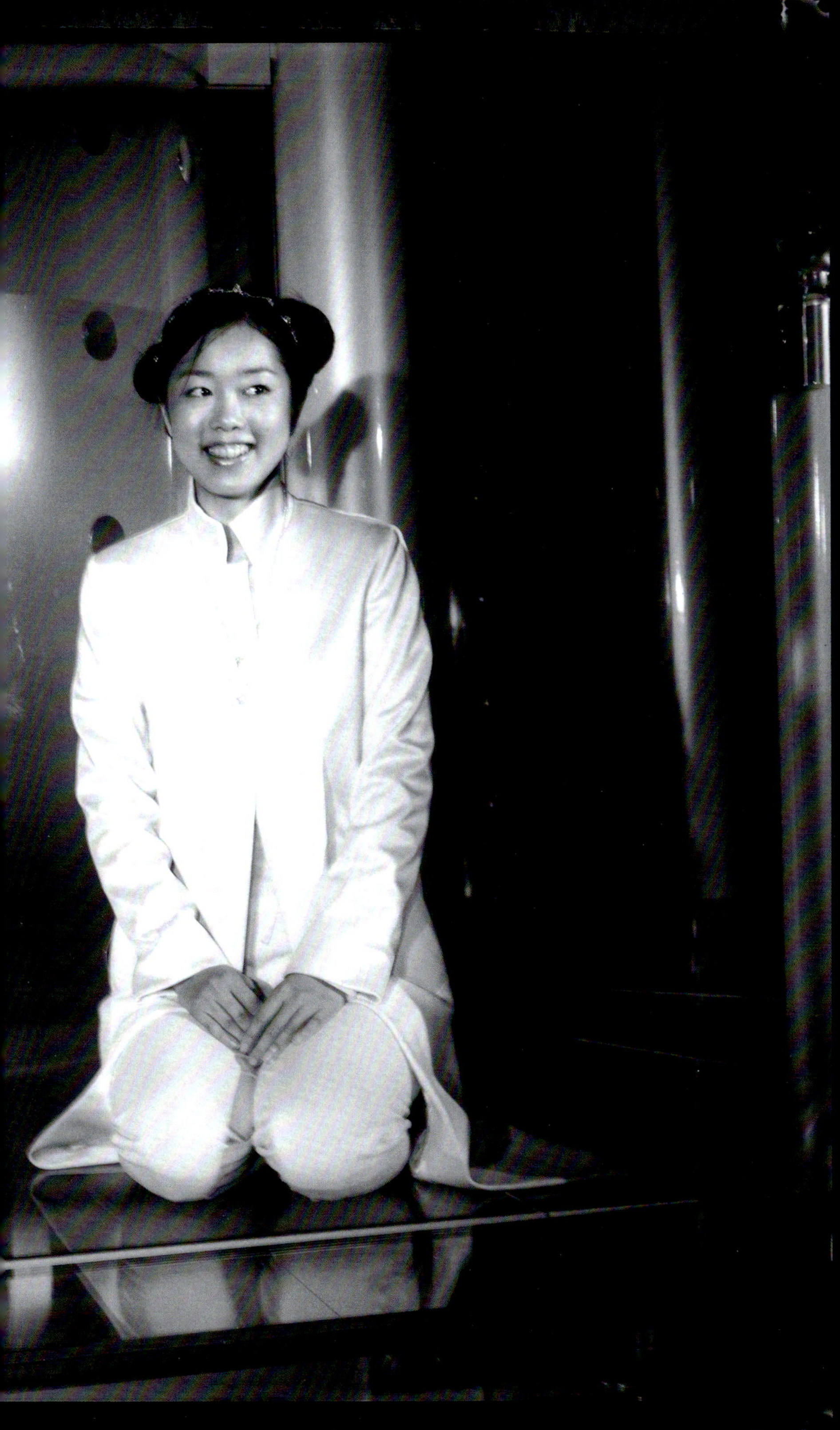

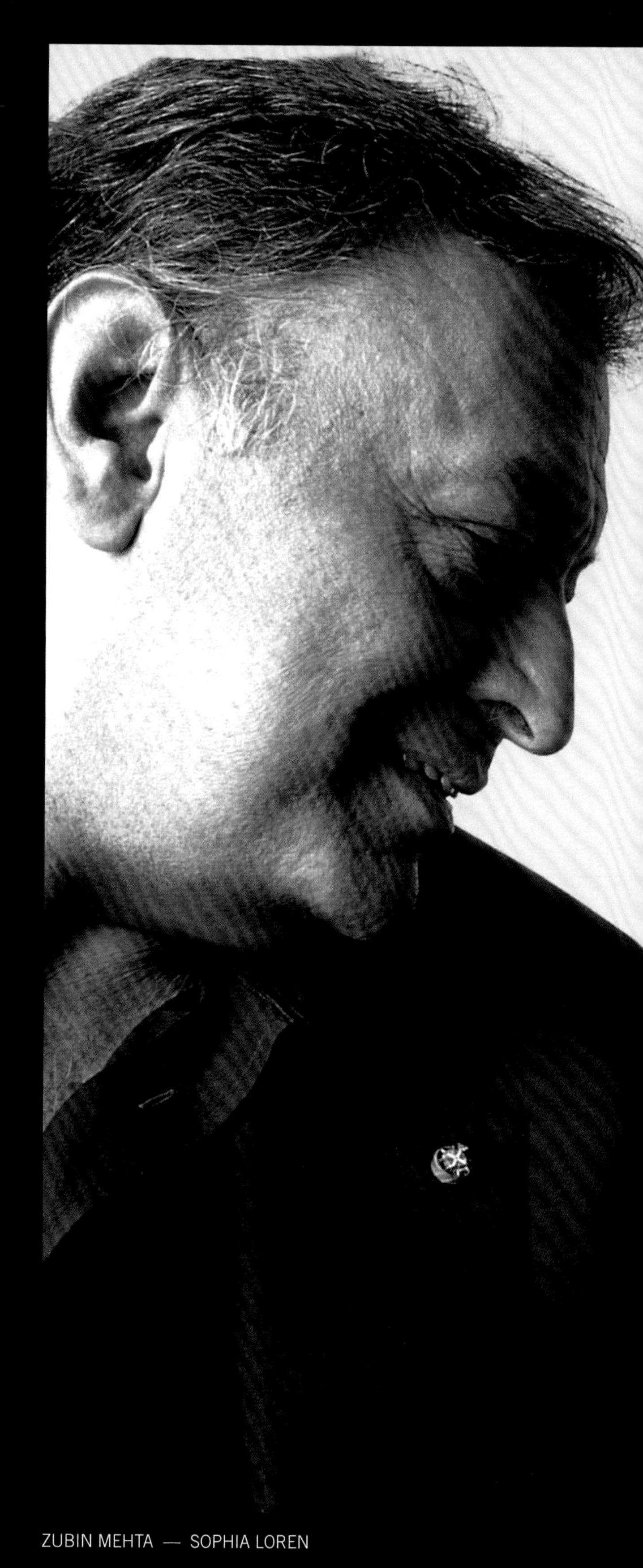

ZUBIN MEHTA — SOPHIA LOREN

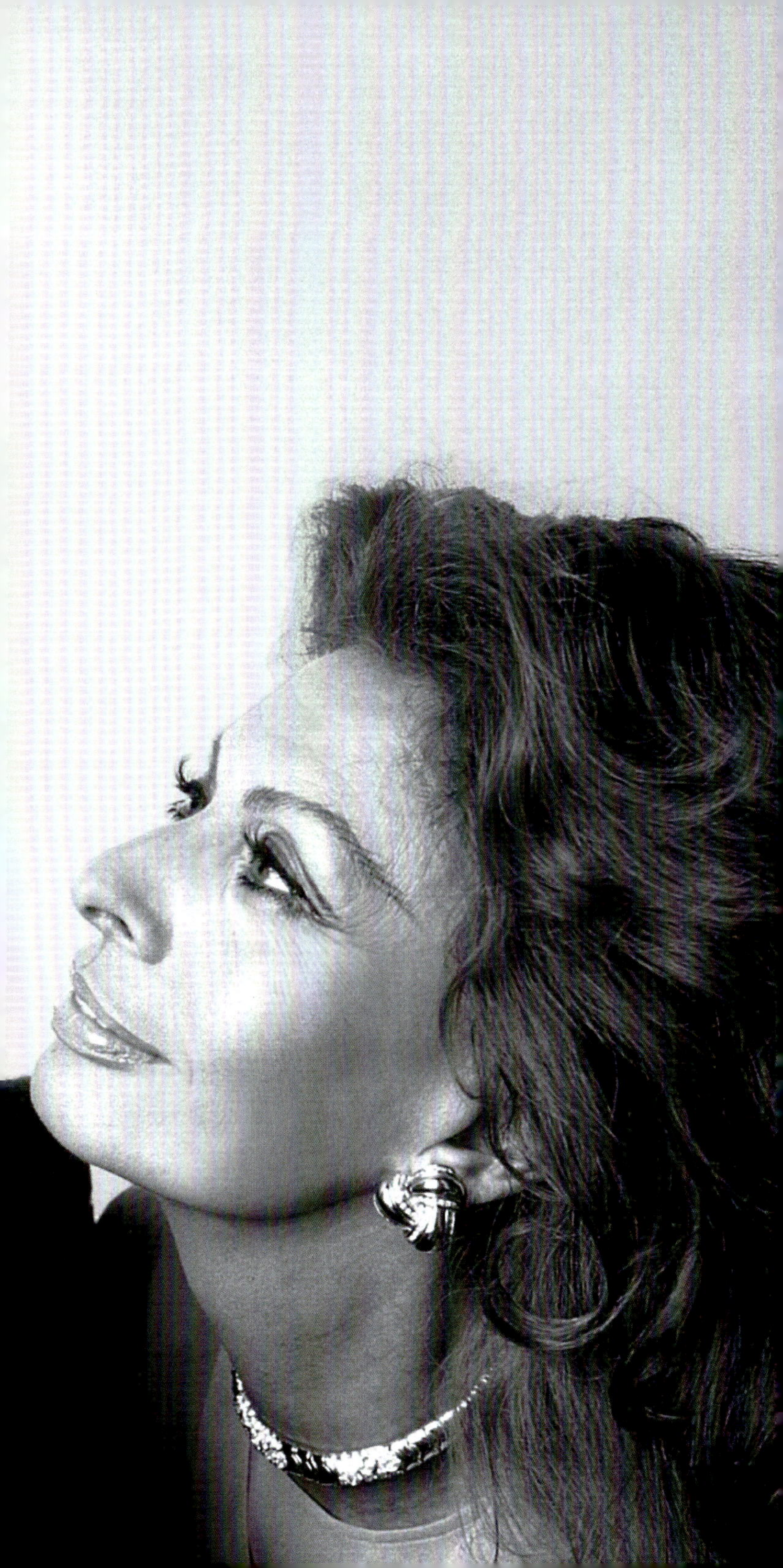

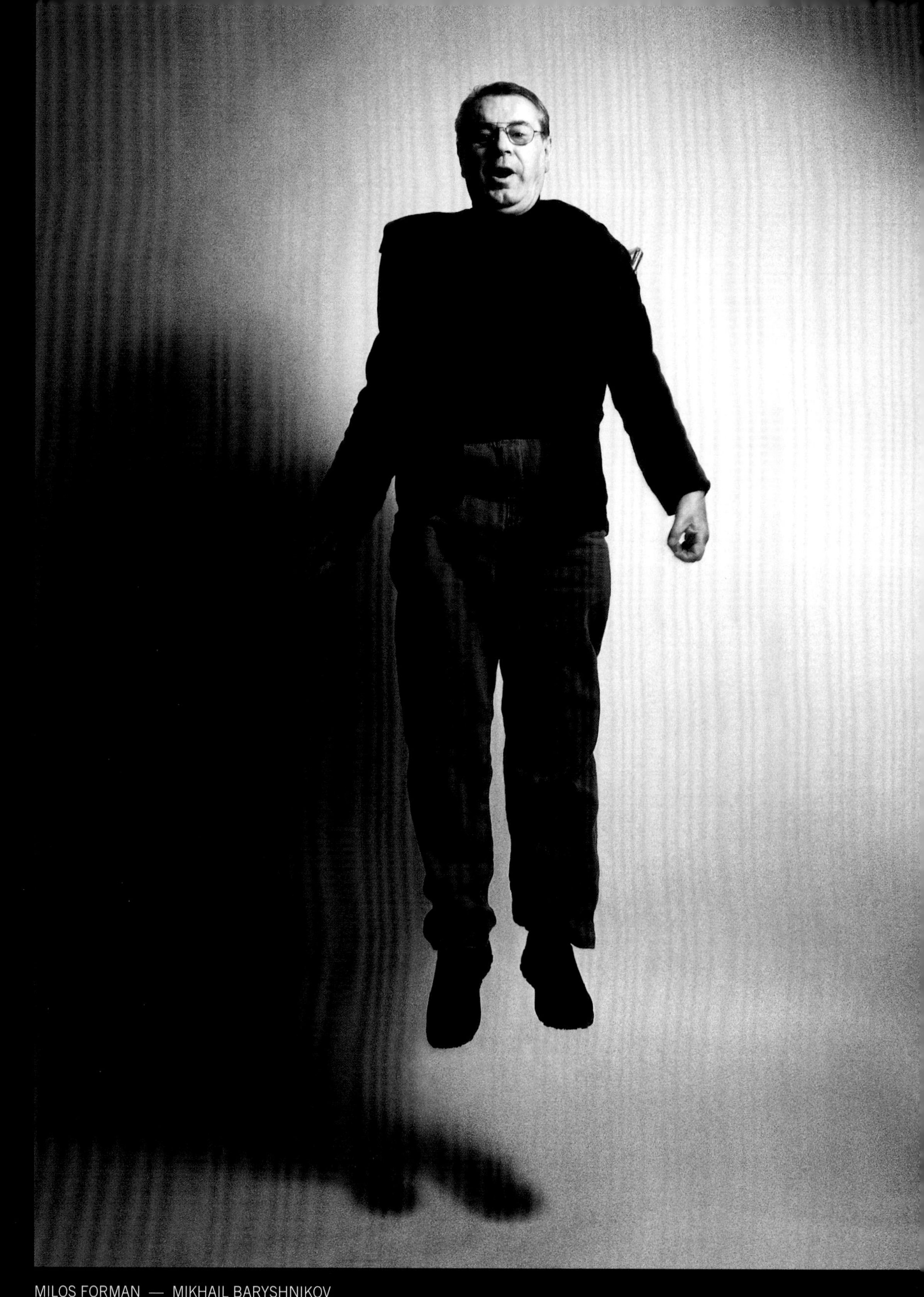

MILOS FORMAN — MIKHAIL BARYSHNIKOV

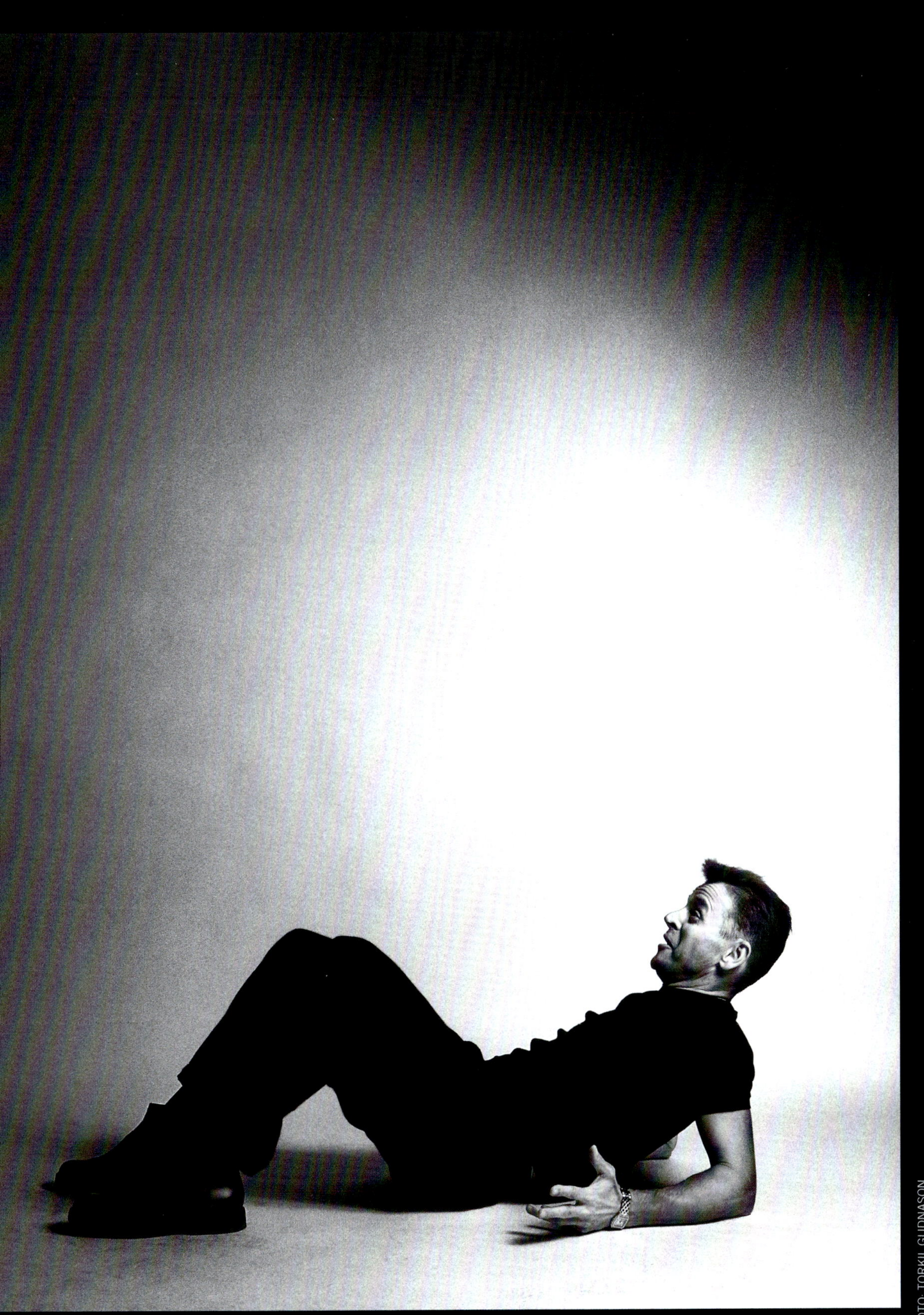

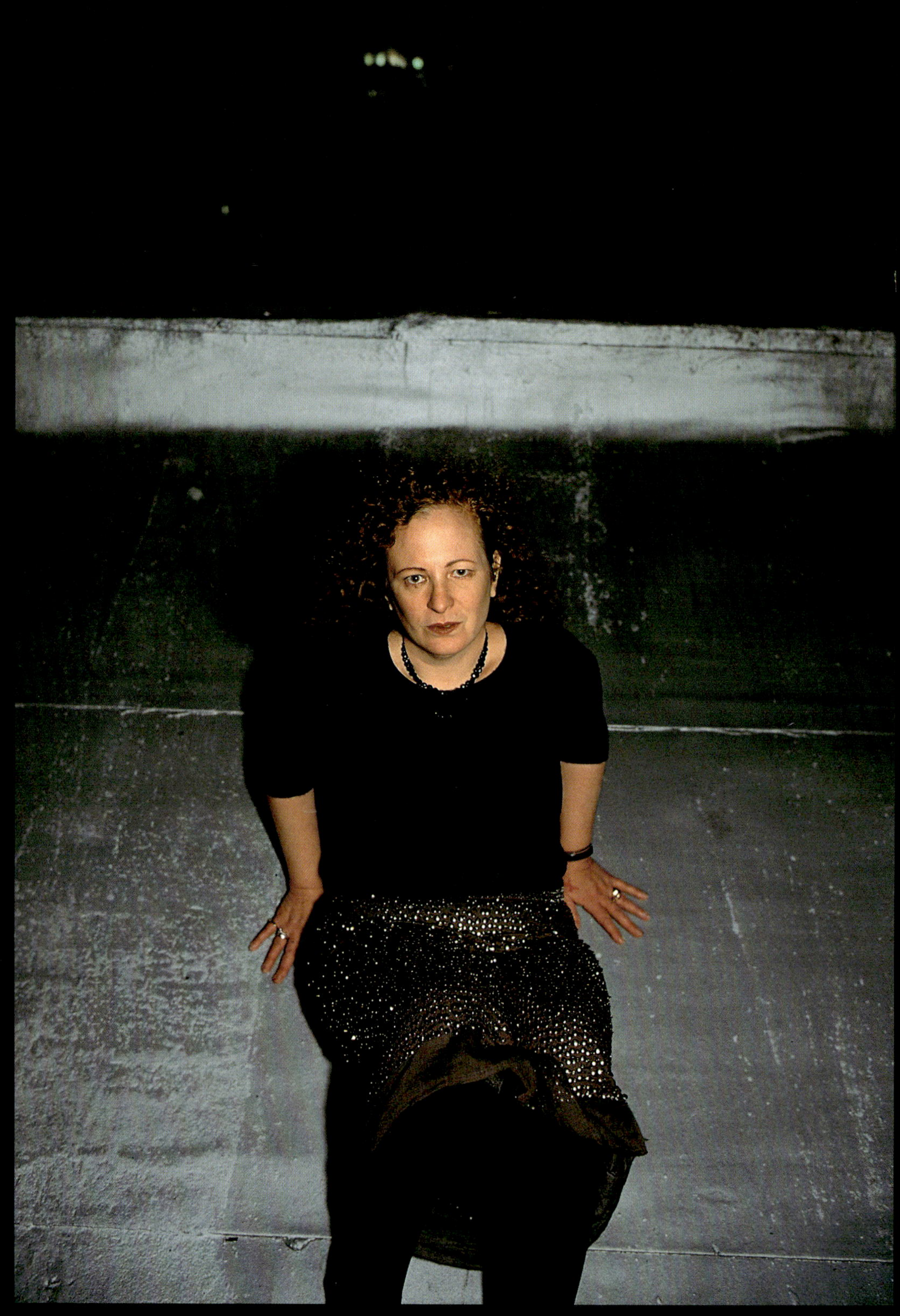

NAN GOLDIN — BJÖRK

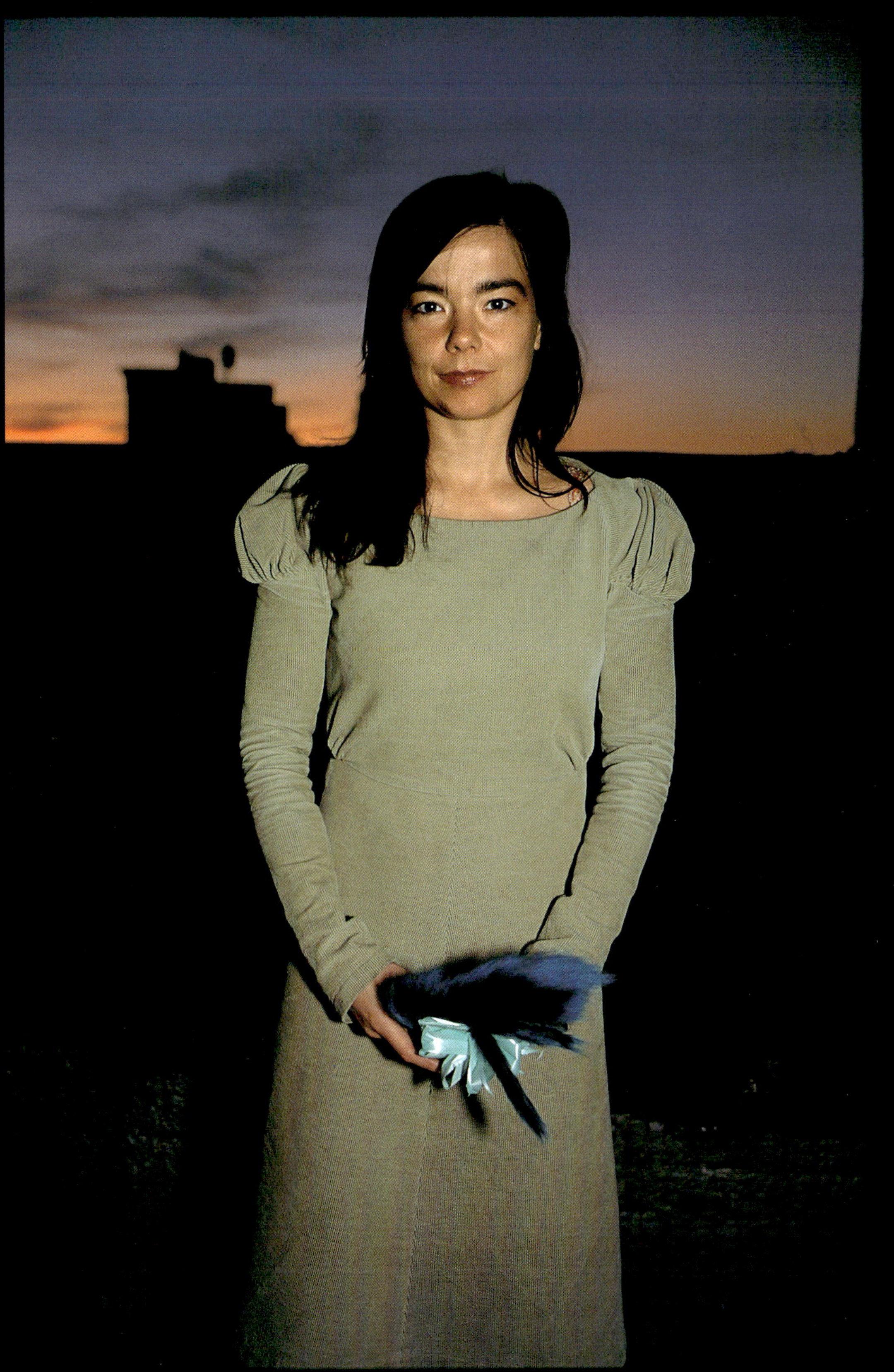

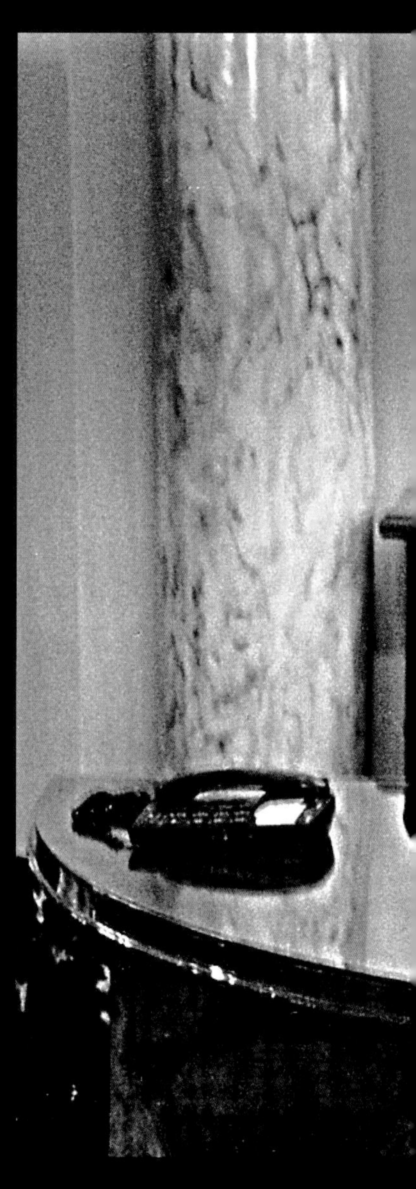

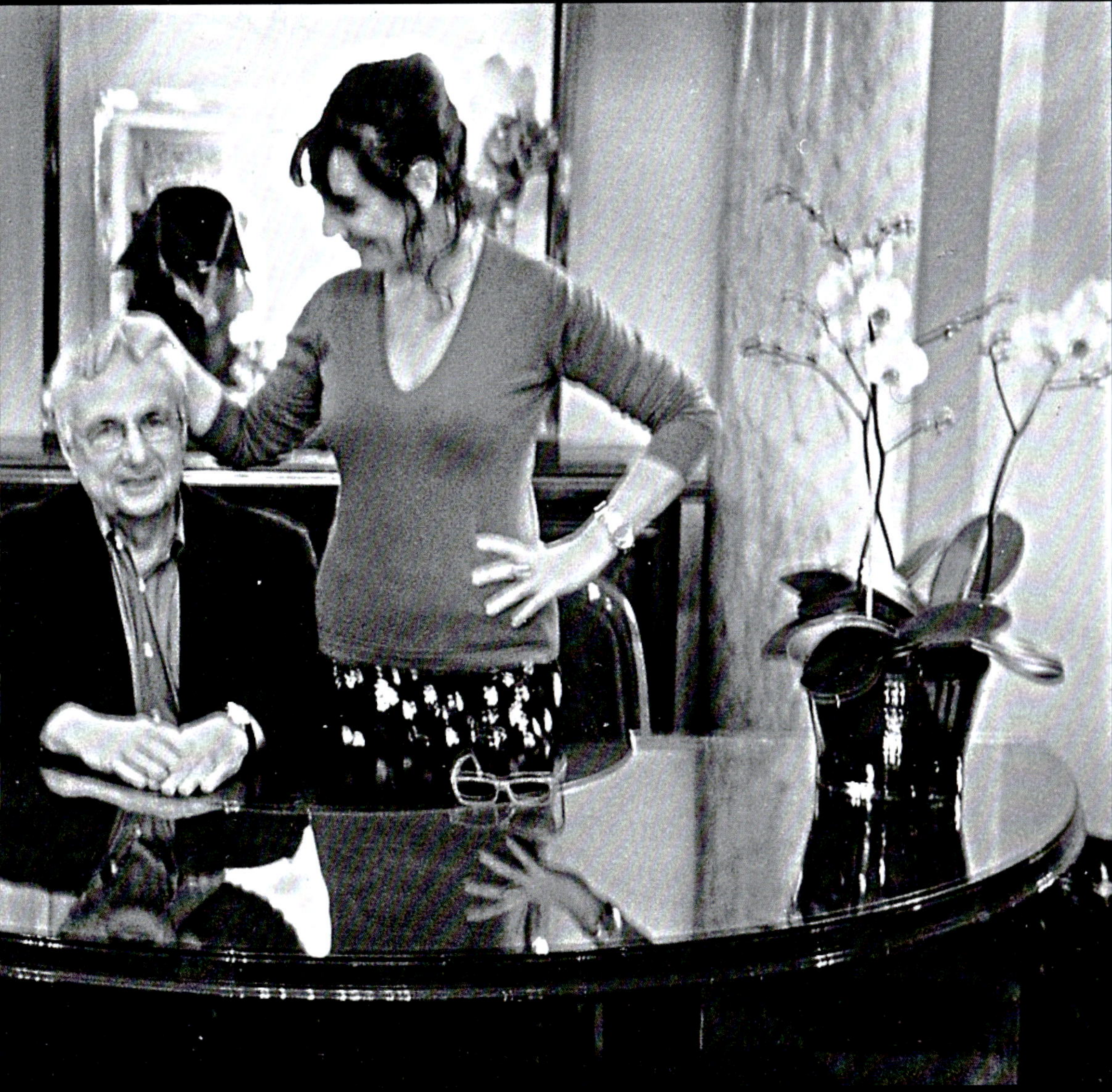

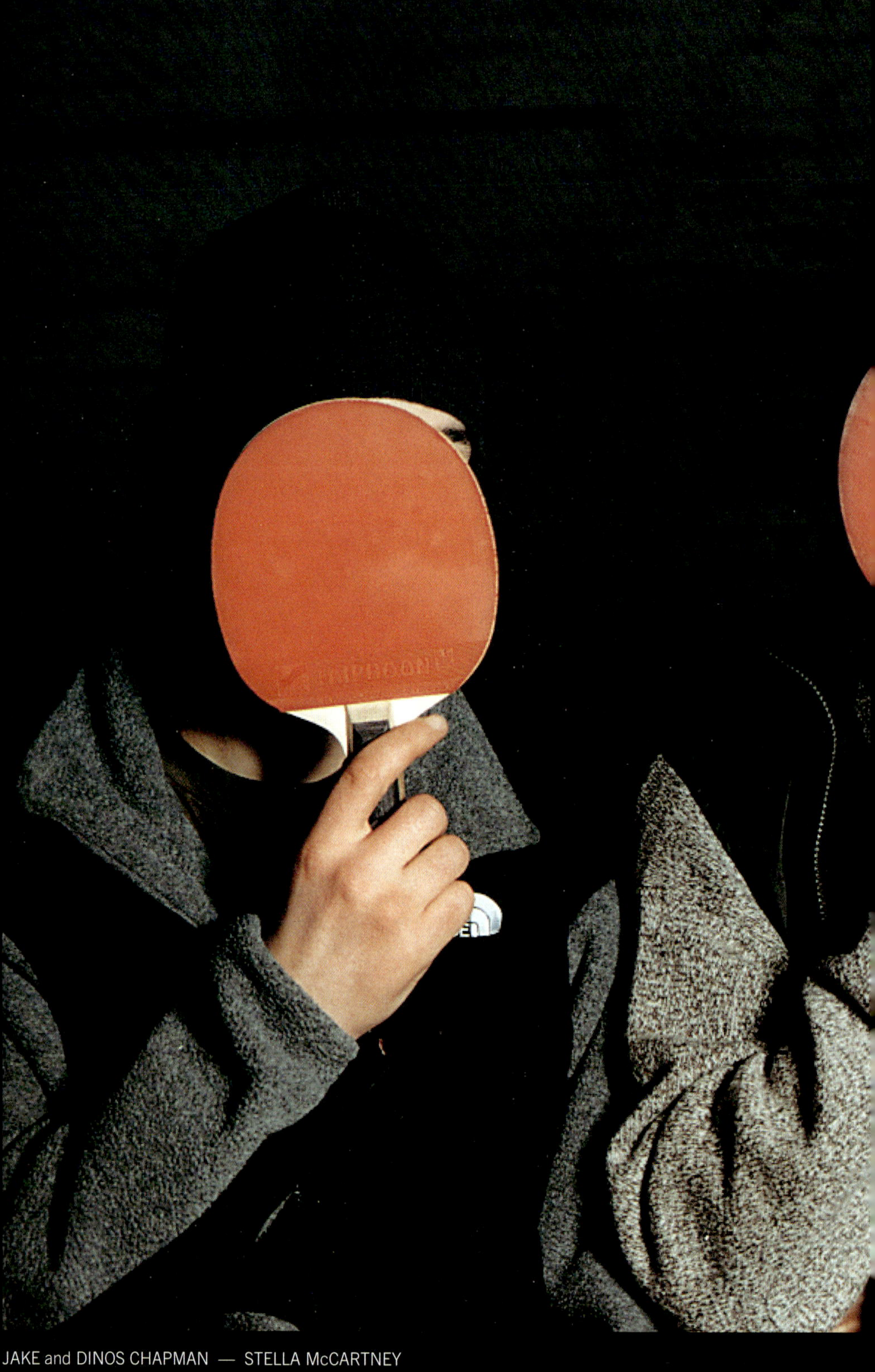

JAKE and DINOS CHAPMAN — STELLA McCARTNEY

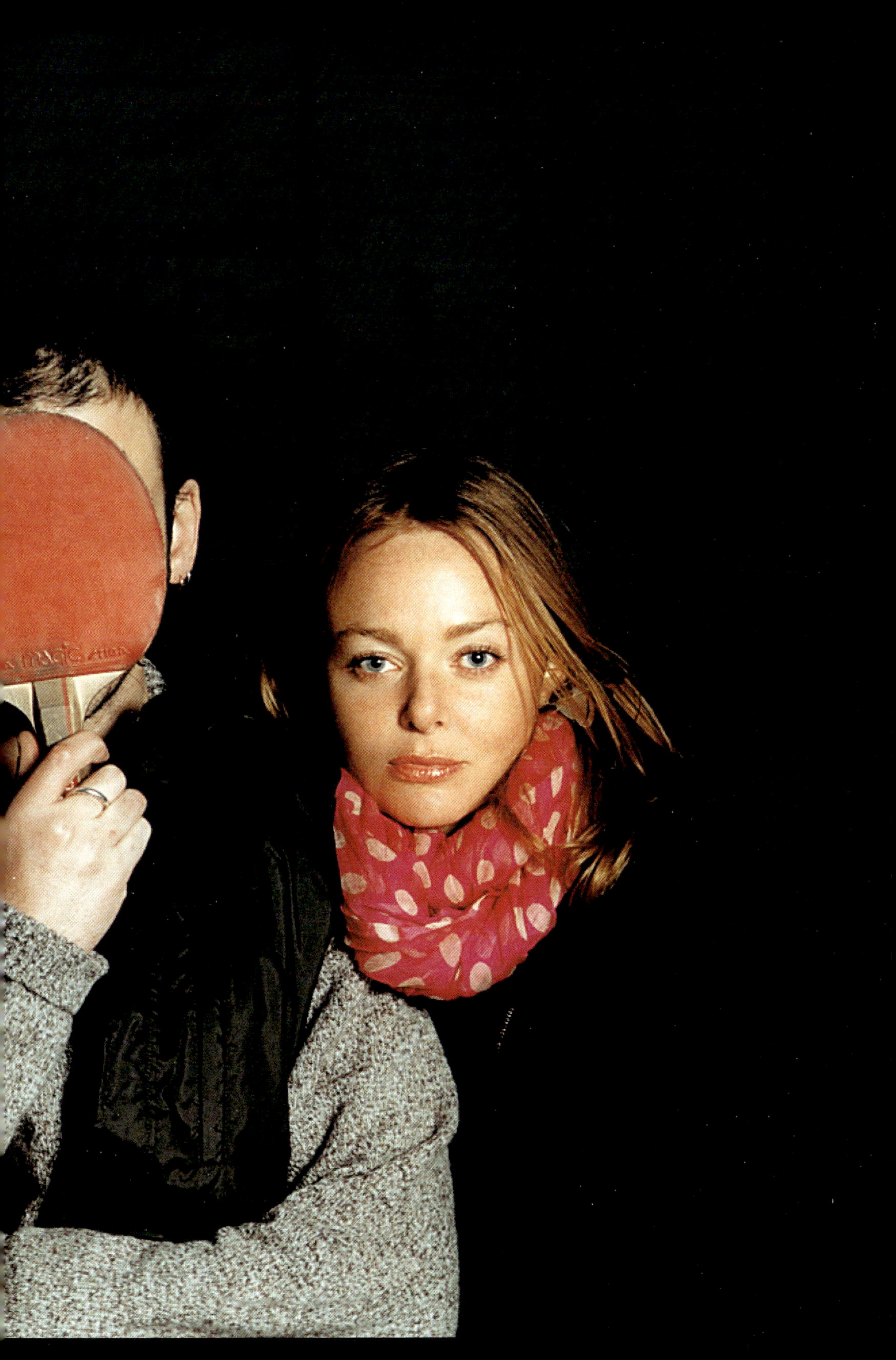

PHOTO: KIM ANDREOLLI

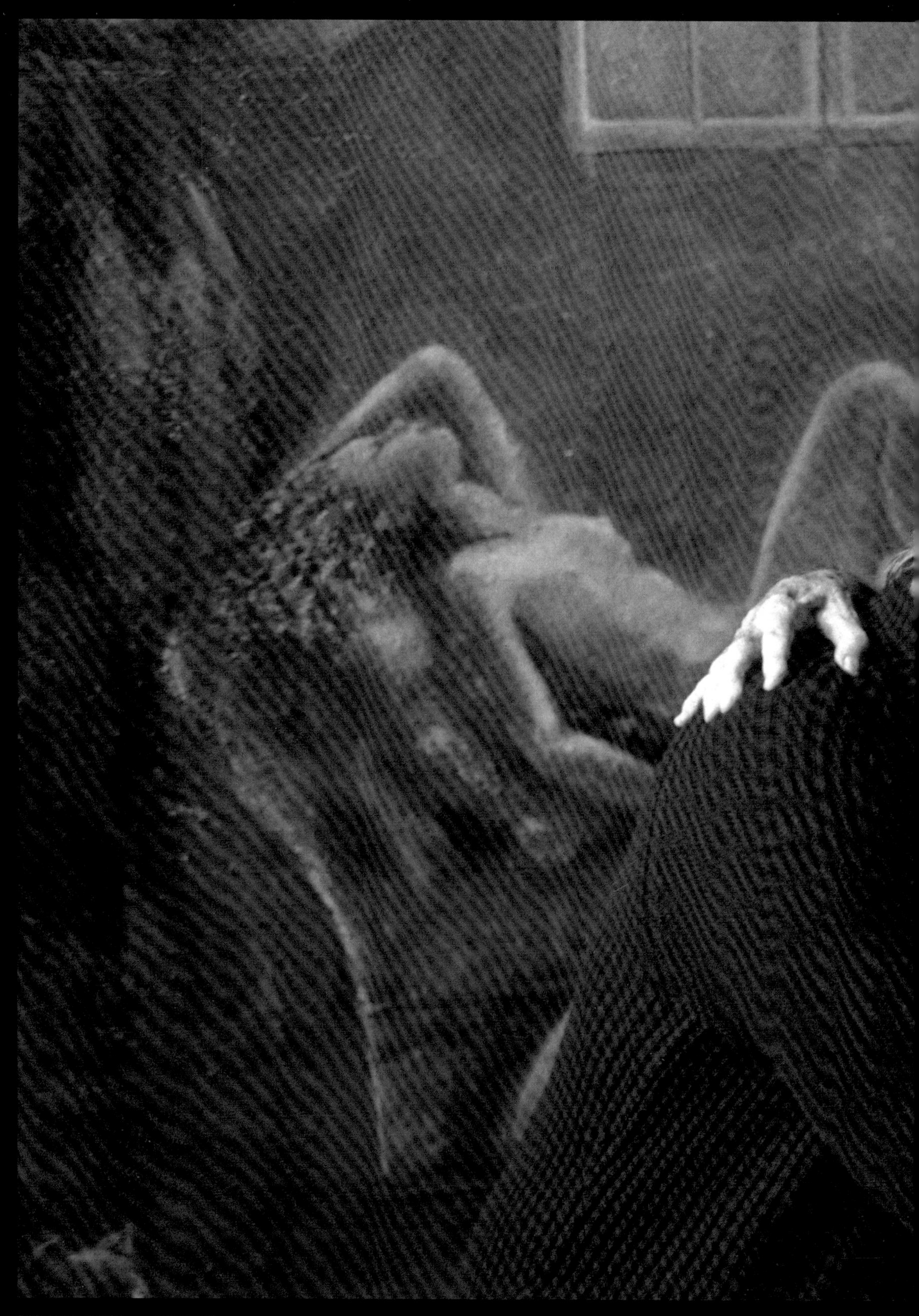

RICHARD GERE — BALTHUS

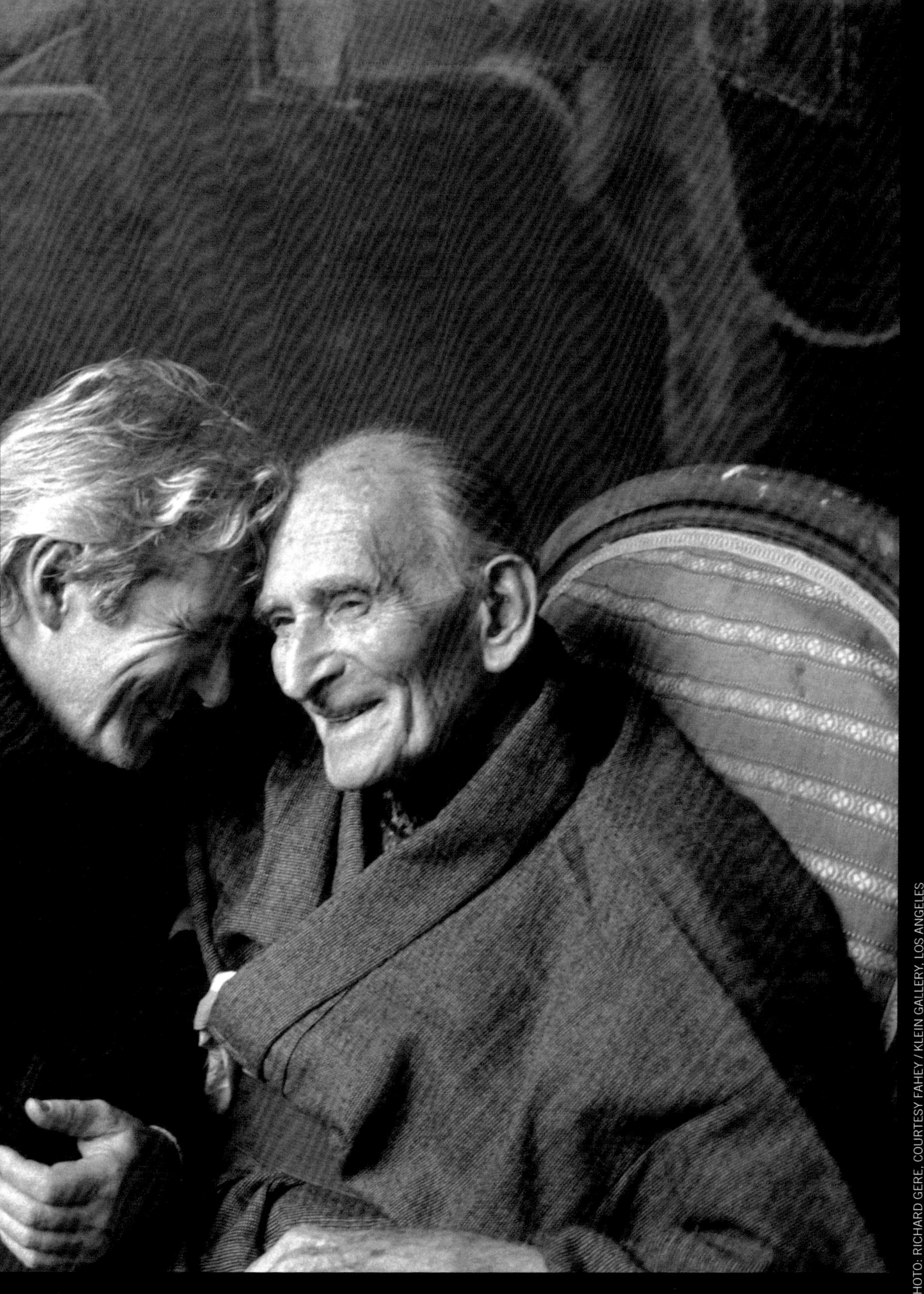
PHOTO: RICHARD GERE, COURTESY FAHEY / KLEIN GALLERY, LOS ANGELES

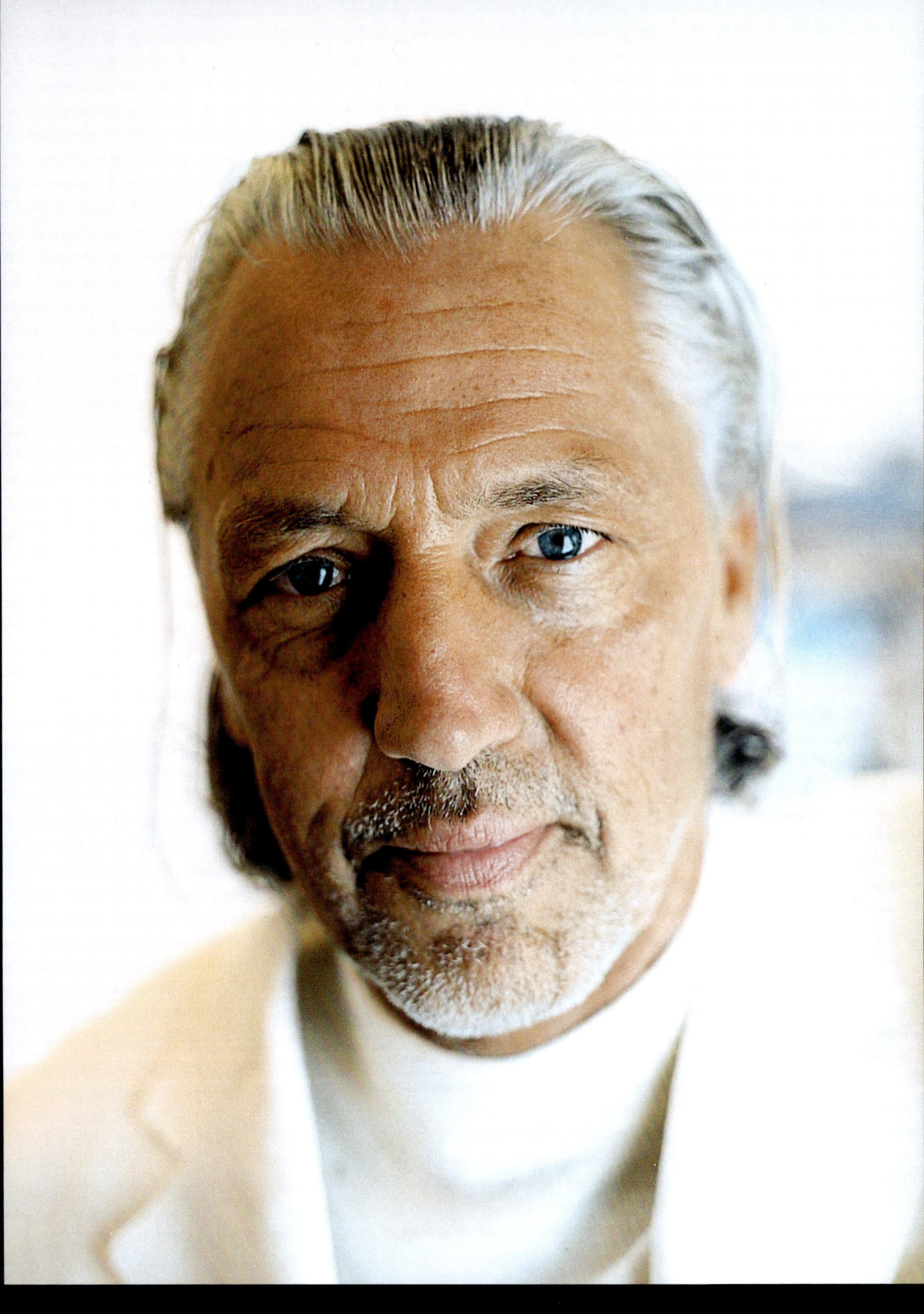

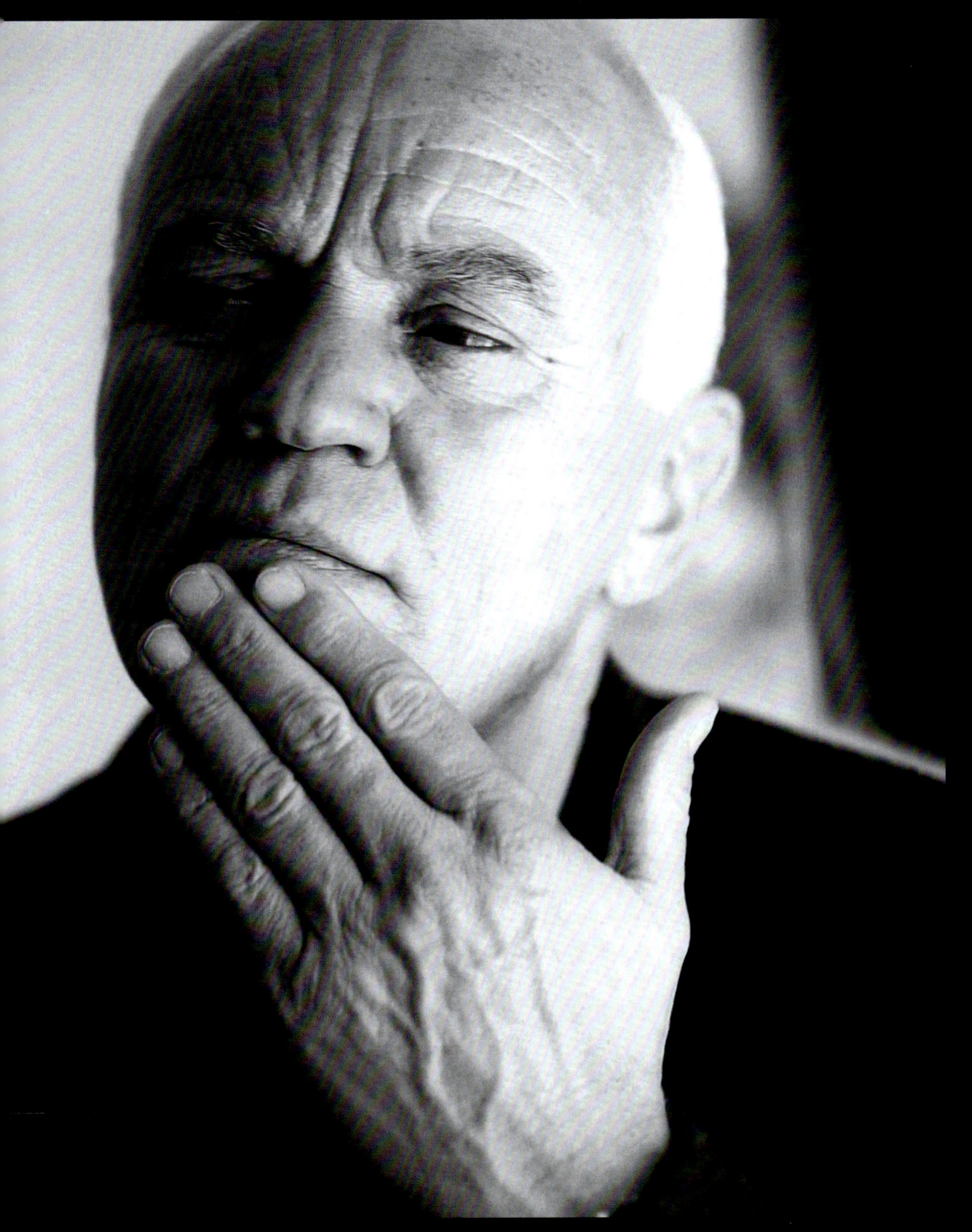

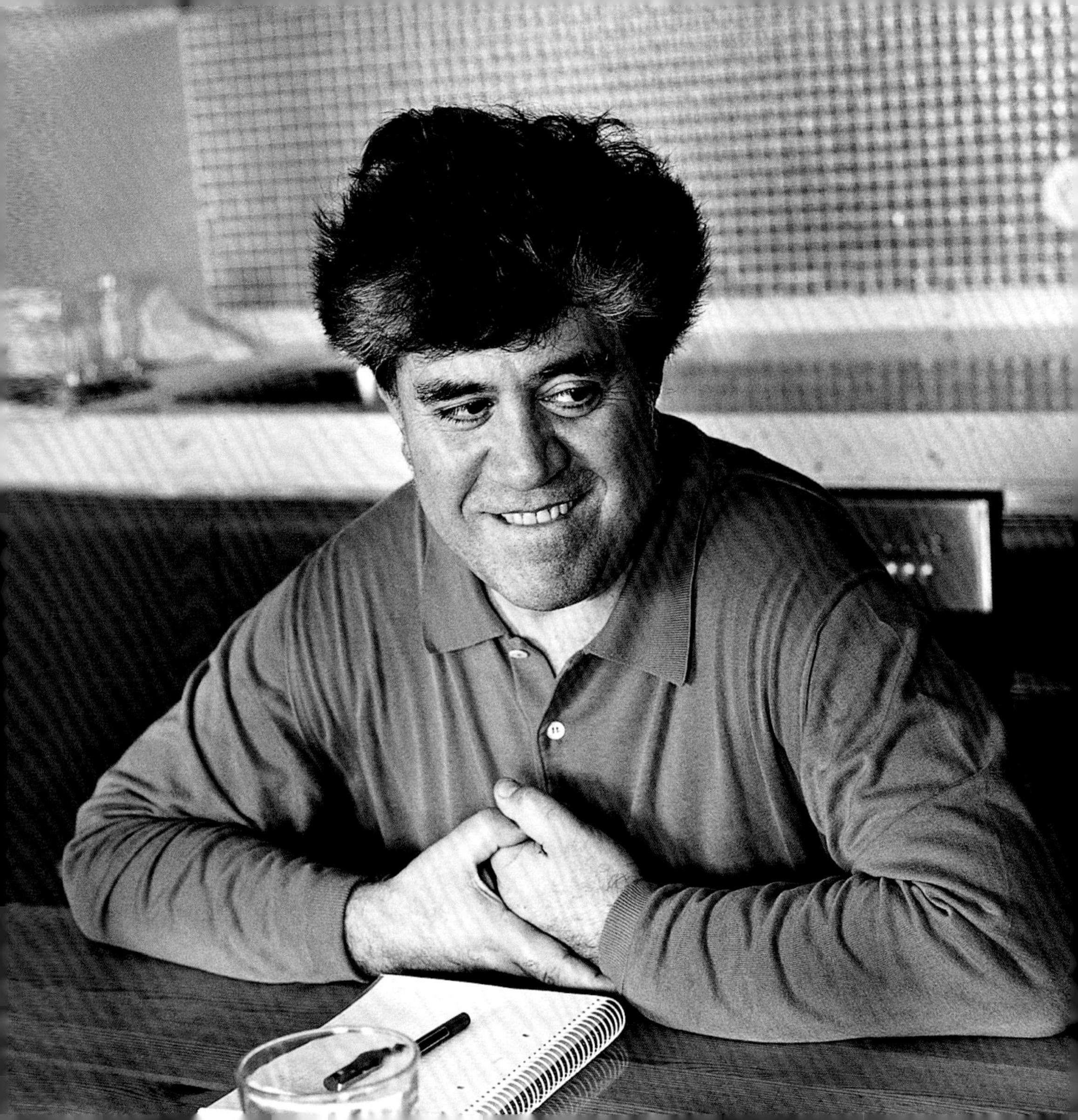

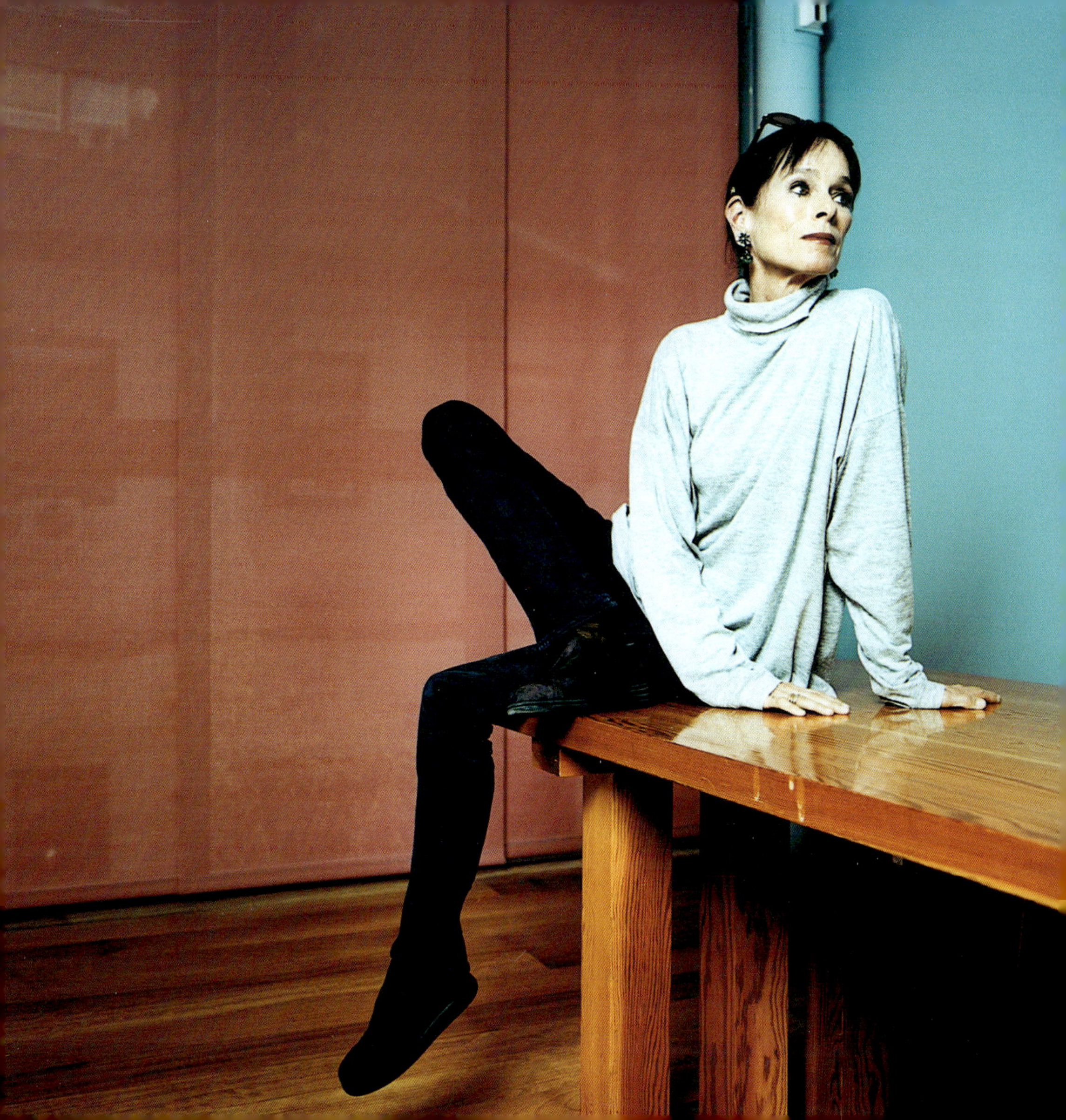

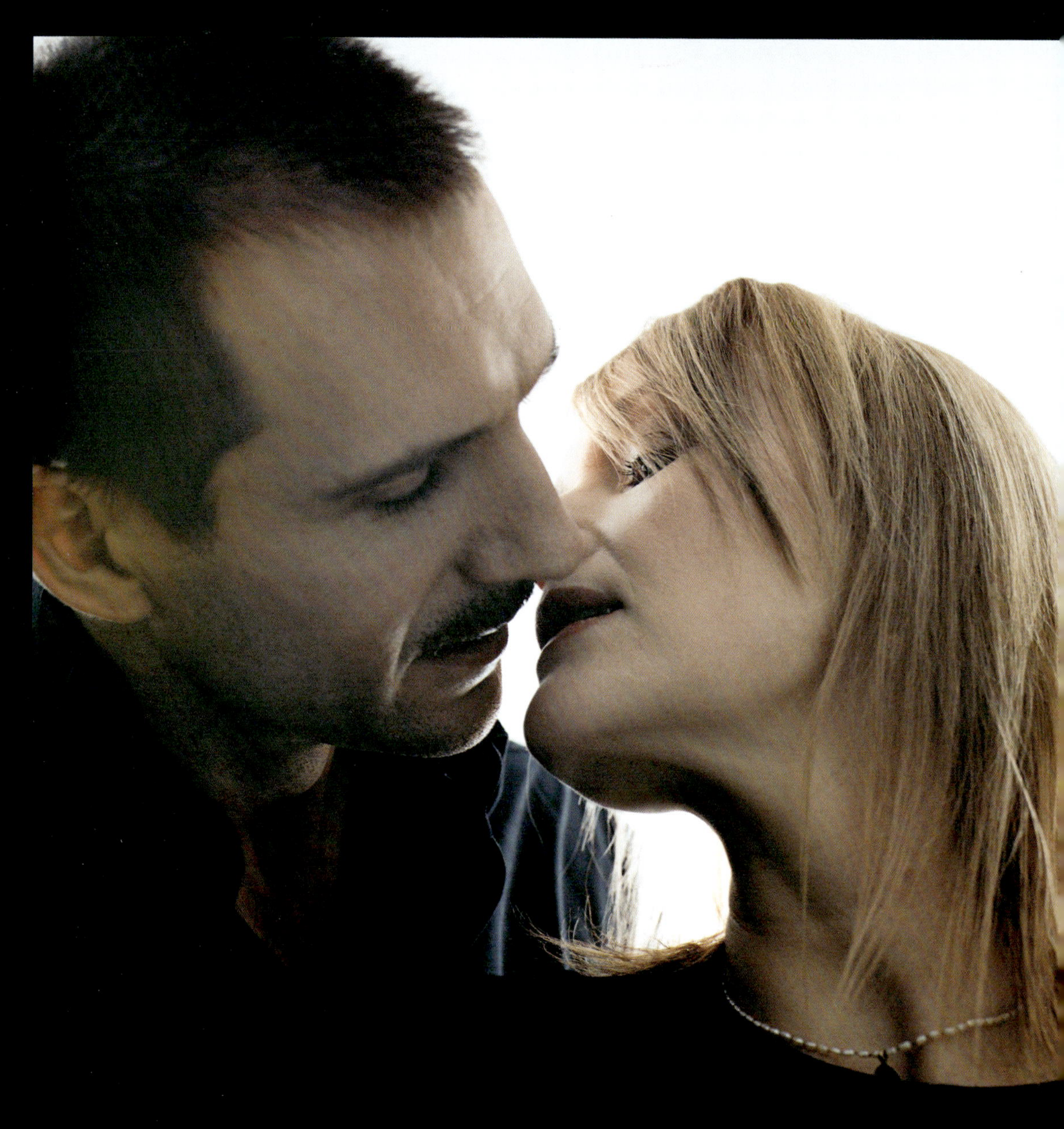

RALPH FIENNES — MIRANDA RICHARDSON

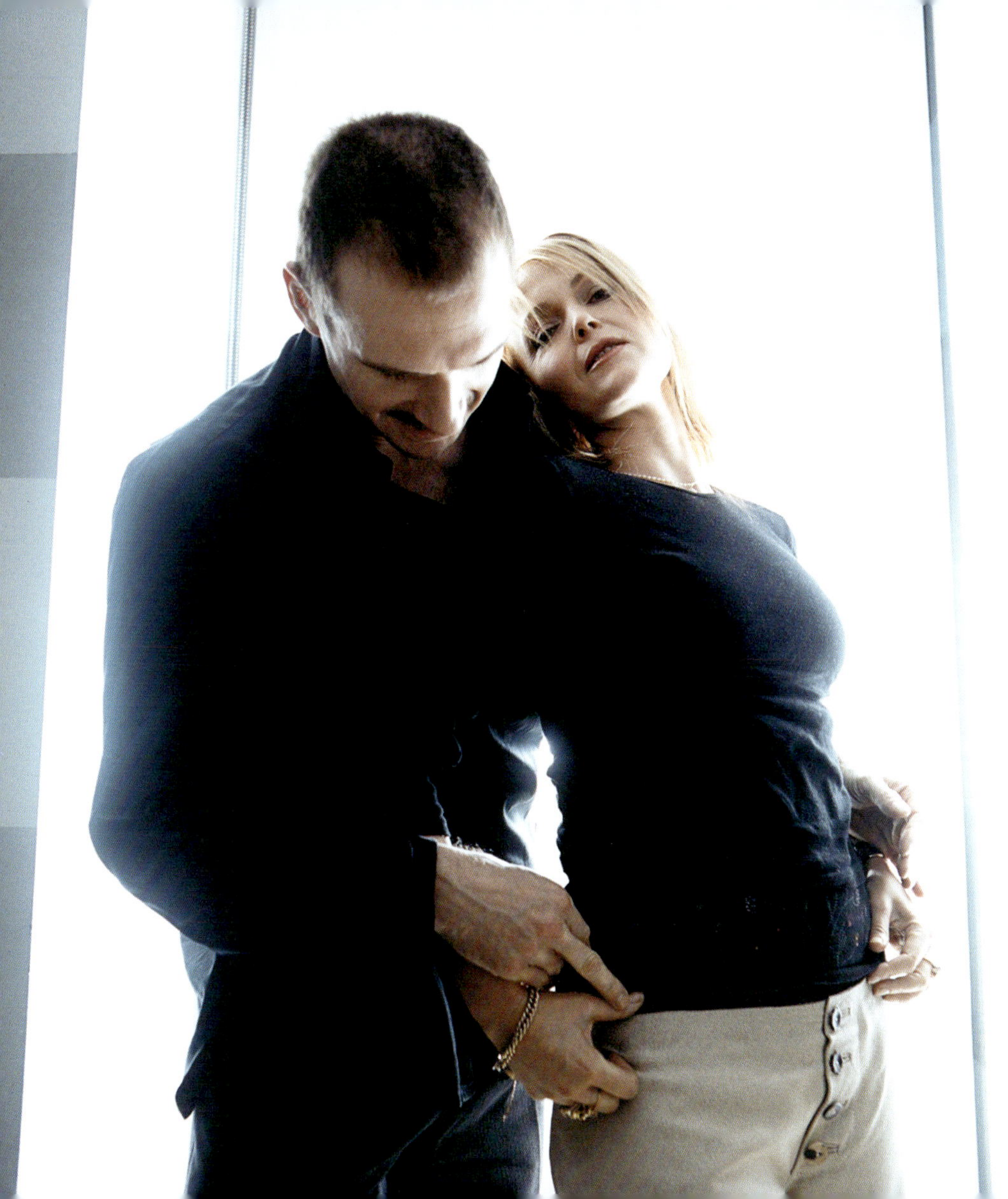

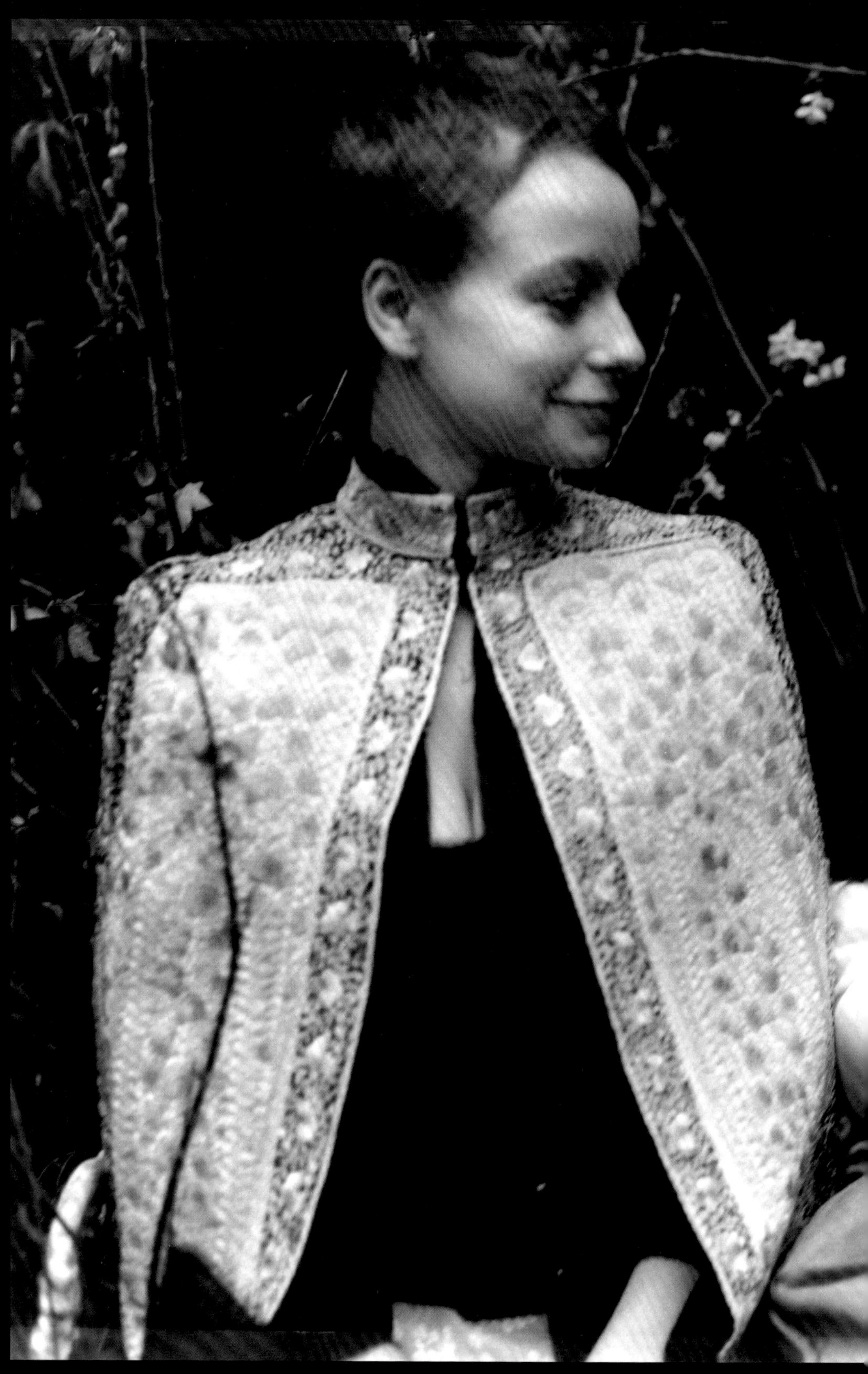

SAMANTHA MORTON — ALEXANDER McQUEEN

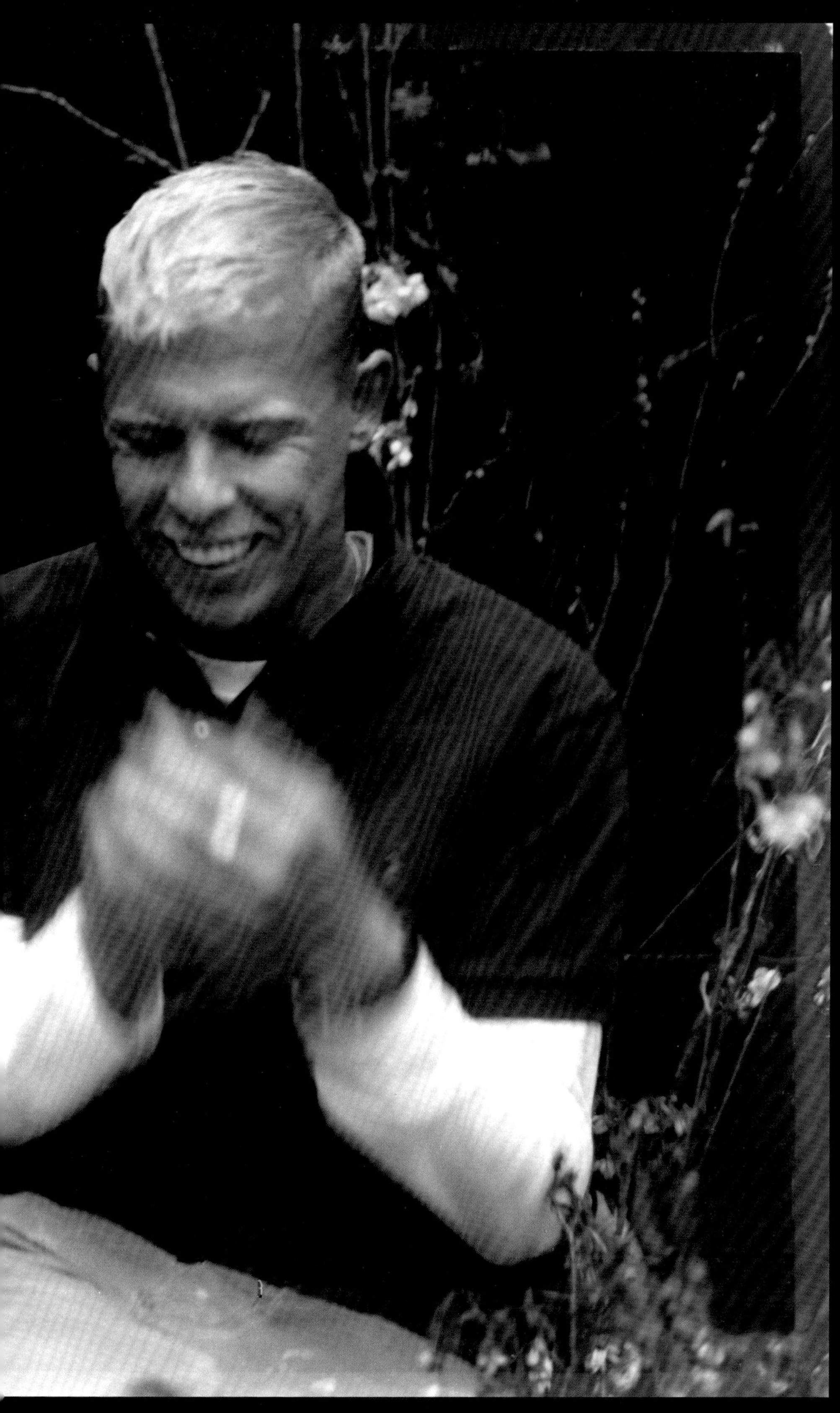

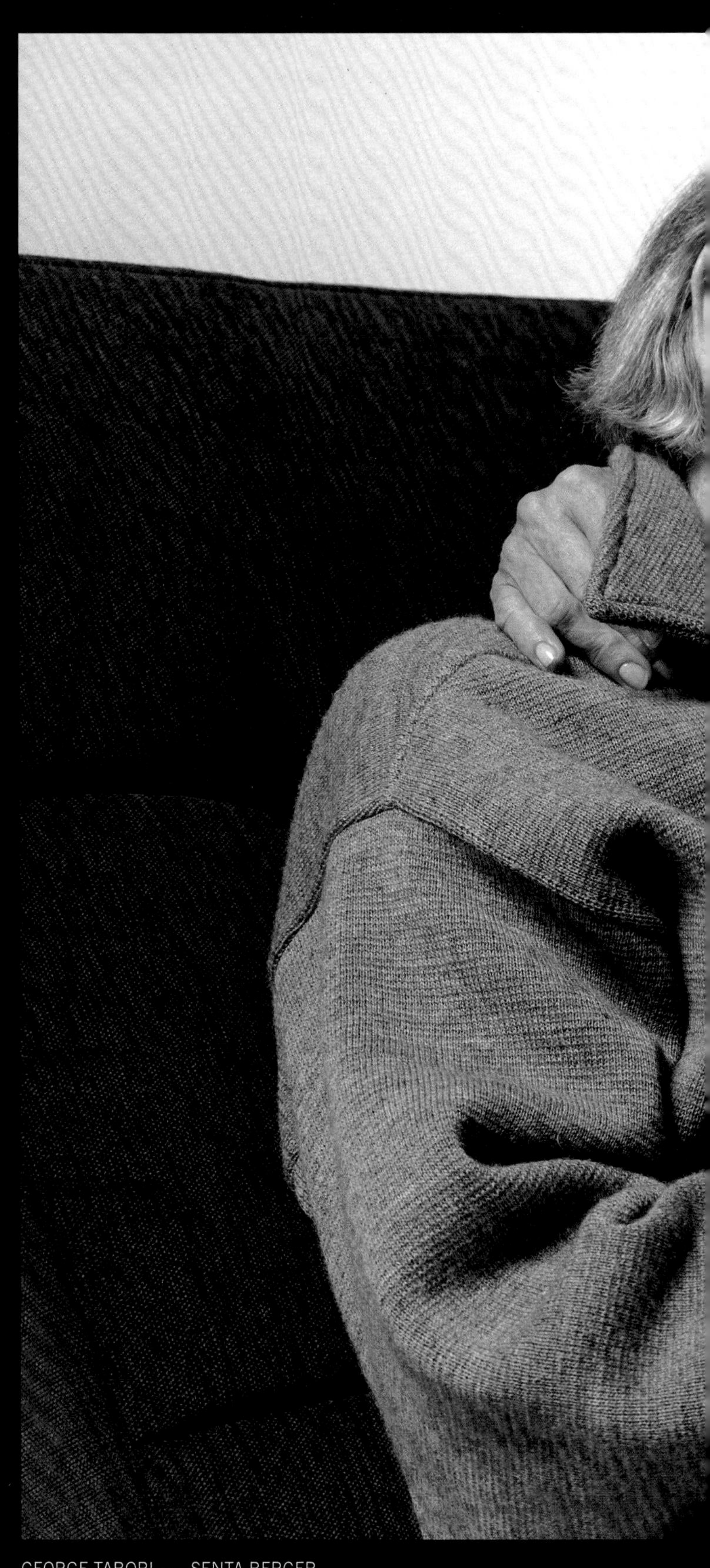

GEORGE TABORI — SENTA BERGER

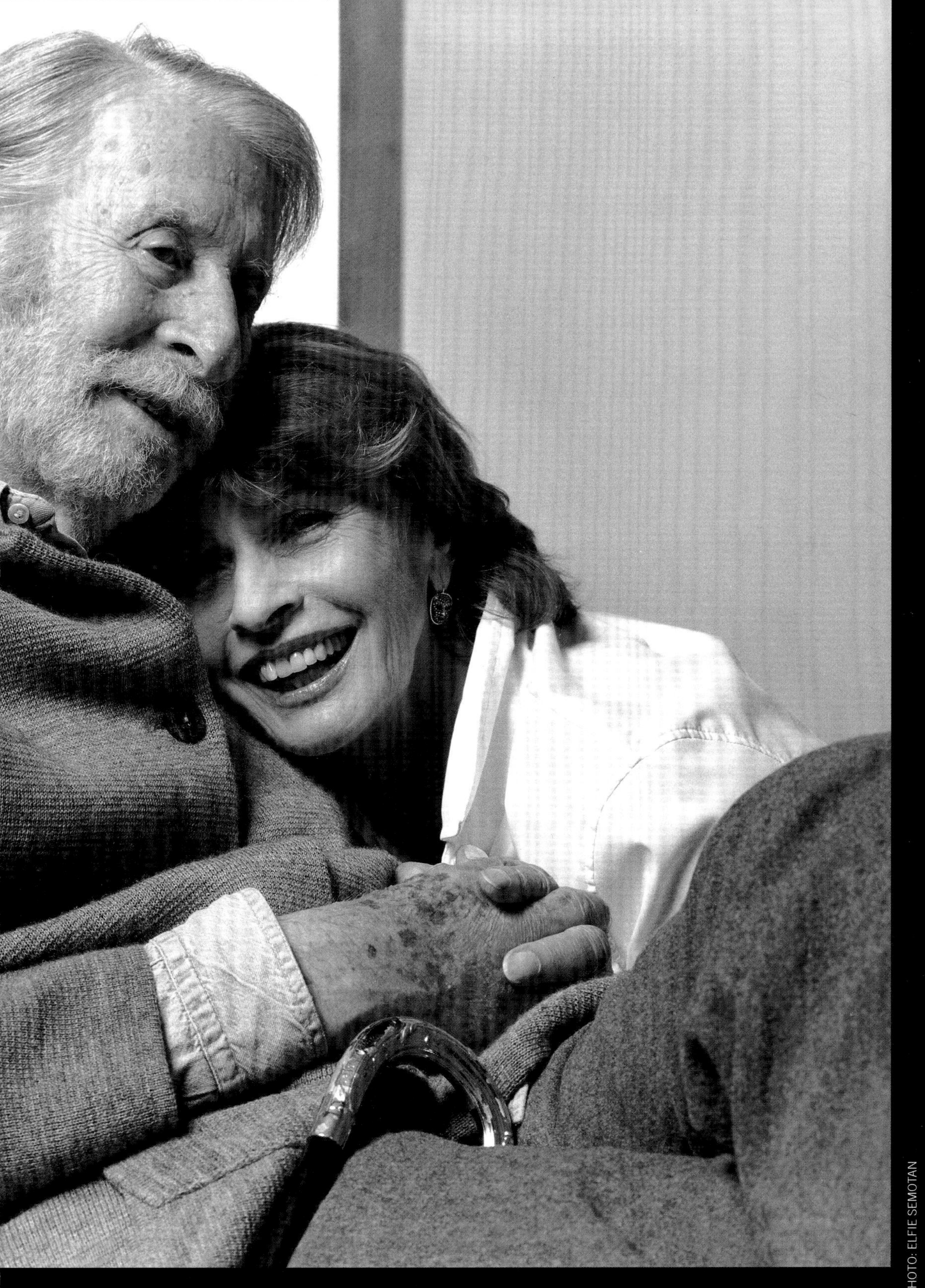

VOGUE DEUTSCH DIALOGUES

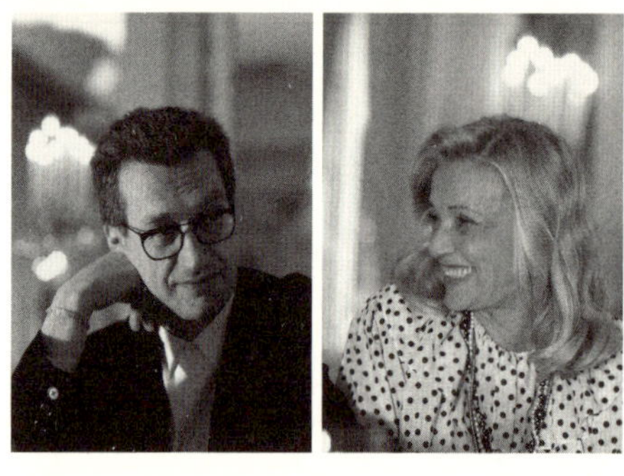

TRAVELERS' TALES

JEANNE MOREAU and WIM WENDERS swap stories
from their travels *Until the End of the World*, and note it all down
for their own pleasure and to indulge VOGUE readers.

They sauntered into the lounge of the Palais Montgelas in Munich a good half hour late, the goddess of the *Nouvelle Vague* and the cult director of the New German Cinema. She looked up at him—she hardly reaches his shoulders. He looked up to her—he was a fan of hers even as a young man. They looked apprehensive. They acted apprehensive. Finally they settled in a mainly white and gold room with lots of large tables and empty mirrors, drank mineral water, edged up close to each other and started whispering:

JEANNE MOREAU We've never talked about films, have we?
(*Wenders looks at her, alert but cautious, and says nothing.*)
JM We could take a walk down memory lane, as my mother would say. We first met in '74.
WIM WENDERS It was in Munich in 1974.
JM You'd just finished editing a film.
WW *The Wrong Move*, written by Peter Handke.
JM That was it.
WW You came with Peter to see the film. It was winter. You almost broke a leg outside my house.
JM My ankle!
WW Your ankle.
JM I didn't break anything.
WW But I've got the X-ray of your ankle.
JM You mean you've still got it?
WW I was so worried at the time that you might have broken your ankle I kept the X-ray. You only needed to sign it for me.
JM (*With a raucous laugh*) Good. (*pause*) You once spent a few days in my house in the South of France.

WW That was the loneliest week of my life. No one was there except your wonderful gardener and your housekeeper. So I took off … I got the heebie-jeebies.

JM From the peace and quiet?

WW No, not the peace and quiet. It was a plague of locusts.

JM A plague?

WW Yes. That summer, a million locusts arrived out of the blue and chomped the garden up in a matter of minutes.

JM Oh my God, and I knew nothing about it.

WW A real biblical plague of them. Billions and trillions of locusts. They came and chomped. The noise was appalling. In the car, you'd crunch over thousands of them. Didn't I ever tell you about it?

JM No.

WW The worst of it was, the living ones fell upon the dead ones and gobbled them up.

JM Heavens above. But at least they're clean beasts.

WW Yes, they cleaned up all right. It was the noise that bugged me. They came into the house, even though I shut all the windows and doors, of course. They still got in—it was a nightmare. Up to then it'd been paradise.

(Jeanne Moreau sighs and bends over, as if expecting another plague of locusts. They're into their parts now. Wim Wenders's voice runs on—quiet, slow, soft, expressionless. Jeanne Moreau sets it to music with countless yeses, noes, mmms, rasping cackles, flattering murmurs, occasional giggles and faint sighs, accompanying every sentence he utters. But you couldn't say she's just following his lead.)

JM The first time you first talked to me about your film *Until the End of the World* was in Cannes. We never discussed the film. I never asked for the screenplay. All you said was, I should play William Hurt's mother and Max von Sydow's wife.

WW … and that you were blind.

JM You came and told me about this blind woman.

WW I told you that she was someone with a lot of my aunt, my father's sister, in her.

JM The story of that woman fascinated me. She'd been blind since fourteen. She got married and brought up children, she traveled …

WW Yes, she traveled a lot. She wrote letters. She stuck paper in the typewriter and wrote. She ran the household without help. She knew people in lots of countries because she traveled so much. Her husband was also blind. He was a teacher.

JM They lived together without ever having seen each other.

WW They never saw each other. They had two children who could see. I was very impressed by this woman. That's why I began to write the story of the doctor who wants to restore his wife's eyesight.

JM How did Solveig Dommartin (*Wenders' partner and colleague, also the star of the film*) and you come up with the plot of *Until the End of the World*? On your travels?

WW It started out as two completely separate ideas for films, which I then combined. We'd begun to write a story about Penelope.

JM … waiting for Odysseus.

WW No. Setting off to follow Odysseus and find him. We wrote the story of a Penelope who was fed up with waiting at home. While we were working on the story, we went to Australia. On a previous occasion I'd started work there outlining the other story, about the blind woman.

When we were there again, it came to me all at once that the two stories together would make the real story. So we tried to mesh the two stories together, the love story, the road movie and the science-fiction story of the man who gives his wife her sight back. The thing was, the more the stories came together, the more they both grew. Which is why you came to Australia, Jeanne.

JM How was it at the last Australian location, when I wasn't there any more? You know, the place with the big stones that looked like sponges.

WW The bungle-bungles. That was the most exciting part of the whole trip. We needed a special permit to film there—it's a sacred site for the Aboriginals. It's also one of the oldest geological formations in the world. Seventy million years ago the terrain was under water.

JM Did the stones look like huge old corals?

WW They are corals. If you stick your fingers in them, you can peel off bits of them. If tourists were allowed there, it would all disappear in a few years. They're trying to protect the area.

JM Does bangle-bangles mean anything?

WW It's an English corruption of an aboriginal name. It means a kind of dream or a way of dreaming. To some extent, the landscape is the embodiment of a dream like that.

JM But you bought pictures in Australia?

WW Yes, several aboriginal paintings.

JM Do you have them at home?

WW Yes. They're the only paintings I have in my apartment. Exporting pictures like that is banned now.

JM You were lucky there.

WW I started collecting these pictures ten years ago. The Aboriginals mostly paint on canvas, sometimes on oak, or sometimes even on thick wrapping paper.

JM The fascinating thing is you think you can see these paintings when you fly over Australia quite low. They paint as if they could fly over their country.

WW They're maps that tell many stories. They're not allowed to tell complete stories. There must always be a secret left. (*pause*) You've just done a film with the New Zealand director Vincent Ward, haven't you? I think it's really great.

JM I only have a small part. I agreed to do it as a favor to myself and him. To be in one of his films. I've known you for sixteen years, Wim. But with you, being in one of your films meant for me discovering a secret link between the two of us. Everyone is the center of a world of her own and likes to think everything revolves around her. That's what's so fantastic about films— when different suns come together, you suddenly feel so good being the planet of another sun.

WW And how do you feel when a film's finished?

JM That's all over quickly for me. While you're working like crazy on your film, I'll have done two, three or four other films. Did you expect editing your film to take so long?

WW I realized from the start it would be a monster. I was rather relieved that it wouldn't be ready for the Cannes festival.

JM If I had time, I'd love to fly to Japan with you. I like even the idea of packing and unpacking a suitcase.

WW Not my scene, unpacking.

(*At which they both laugh—rather too loudly in the circumstances. The chronicler, on whom goddess and cult director had imposed the role of eavesdropper with their concentrated whispering, was definitely getting the impression the two stars were making up a dialogue from a screenplay.*)

JM Packing and unpacking a suitcase forces me to keep my thoughts neat and tidy.

WW I find myself surrounded by more and more unpacked suitcases. I always get a new suitcase for every trip. When I get back, I don't open that suitcase.

JM Amazing. How does it work, if you never unpack?

WW Well, of course, I do unpack a case at some point, but never immediately after a trip. I find unpacking a waste of time. After all, I've come back—that's the important thing. (*laughter*) I've brought myself back.

JM So you unpack yourself but not your case?

WW The things that matter I probably have on me, not in the suitcases. Though I do often buy presents on the way. But because I don't open my cases, a really incredible collection of presents built up.

JM Great. So you could really play Santa?

WW No. For that I'd need to open the cases. But it's true, I'm never at a loss when I suddenly discover it's someone's birthday.

JM (*Laughs. Then suddenly, very seriously*) I love traveling alone. A stewardess I've flown with several times recently said: "You're always alone." (*drops her voice dramatically*) Sitting alone in a plane—for me, that's adventure. (*She breathes the next words, as if remembering making love.*) I love it … in a plane … (*suddenly continuing in a normal voice*) I travel with lots of cases. After all, you never know which will get there. There's always someone to carry my cases. When the chauffeur in Glasgow a while back took my cases out to the Rolls Royce, he asked: "That yer piano, lady? Bin clearing the flat out, then?"

WW (*Without appearing in the least impressed by this performance*) I really like the fact things are getting smaller and smaller. For years I've been working at perfecting the art of Zen packing.

JM Everything *is* getting smaller—even clothes for women. You used to need a full-size bag for an evening dress. Now you just fold it up, like that. (*gestures appropriately*) But shoes aren't getting smaller. I love shoes and books. I travel with lots of shoes and books.

WW Books are the heaviest things you carry about while traveling.

JM And what's annoying about books is they multiply en route. The nice thing about moving recently was, I had a chance to get rid of some books.

WW You actually got rid of books?

JM Yes. Ones I'll never read again.

WW But you don't keep books to read again. You keep them because you've read them.

JM A lot of them were part of my life for a while, but others.… I give them away. Incidentally, I have the impression I shall never read Freud again.

WW Don't throw him away. Call me!

JM (*Laughs*) Okay, I'll send you a parcel, and you won't open it.

WW But I'd have it.

JM I've also got a collection of very old records. Jazz …

WW I'd never say no to those. I throw lots of things away. But books and records—music— I couldn't give those away.

JM I like looking at what books other people have at home. You discover a whole new world. Don't you find?

WW I don't usually go to parties. But if I find myself in a party-type situation, there's only one salvation—I look for the books. That's the only place people don't bother you. Then I sit down and look what this person reads … and then I can go home.

JM Yes … Shouldn't we go and eat?

WW What's the time?

JM Twenty to nine.

WW What shall we have? Kangaroo steak?

JM Of course. Tastes a bit like rabbit.

WW You know what I'd fancy? Honey ants!

JM Honey ants … no! But I've eaten worms.

WW You've eaten worms?

JM Yes. And I've eaten snakes. They're really delicious.

WW Boiled or roasted?

JM Straight from the fire.

WW Are we never going to go and eat?

From VOGUE 11/1991; The conversation was recorded by Marianne Schmidt

JEANNE MOREAU — WIM WENDERS

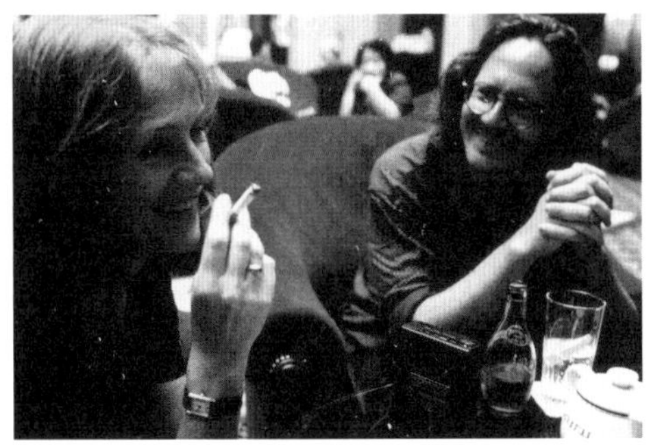

DO YOU OFTEN HATE?

ISABELLE HUPPERT and PETER HANDKE talk about
the difficulties of proximity, about passion and aggression,
and about mozzarella and tomato salad.

One afternoon, Isabelle Huppert and Peter Handke meet for a conversation in the bar of the hotel Ms. Huppert currently favors, the Lutetia in the Boulevard Raspail in Paris. Peter Handke occupies a rather unusual position in modern German literature. Even a quarter century after his brilliant appearance in front of the *Gruppe 47* in Princeton, he still evokes violent reactions. For some, his *Story of the Pencil* (1982) may be a narcissistic expression of psycho-pathological confusion of the senses, while for others this particular work was a benchmark for the best literature of those years. At any rate, the master of the edgy fragment is wearing a wonderful eggplant-colored shirt with white dots and designer trousers. Isabelle Huppert, who has been called a "tragic tear-machine" and "Europe's Meryl Streep," arrives completely without makeup. On the street, you would take the petite figure in a parka, carrying a cheap, ordinary plastic rucksack with her daughter's name on it, for an older daughter or a student who just missed the bus to the university.

Against a backdrop of Japanese hotel guests, the pair embarks on a quiet probing conversation full of unfinished and later resumed thoughts. Contrary to expectations, the two stars have a highly developed, rapid-fire sense of comedy.

ISABELLE HUPPERT You're about to become a father again?
PETER HANDKE Yes, in two or three weeks.
IH Your second child?
PH My daughter's already twenty-three.
IH I'd never have thought it. In some of your books you talk about her, but as if she were a little girl.
PH She's at art college in Vienna. Occasionally she works for the theater.

IH How do you feel as a budding father?

PH There's something unreal about it.

IH Are you nervous?

PH Yes, very.

IH But aren't children the best thing in the world?

PH Yes. They're reality. Children are the soul of man. Reality is getting more and more invisible. As children have so much reality before they're born because of technological achievements, you get the impression they're unreal. The more you know, the less real it is. I tell myself I have to prepare for it, but inside I can't manage it. The woman's belly is reality, of course! And perhaps it's also just a problem for me or anyone getting older. Everything happens so quickly. I still remember when my daughter was born. It all seemed to take such a long time. Now it's still nine months, but it seems much quicker.

IH It's the same with me, since I've had the two children. And it does have something to do with getting older.

PH It was always my great ambition to have a lot of time. I do indeed have a lot of time, but I almost always arrive too late. I tell myself I still have time to go and meet someone. And suddenly I don't have time any more and it's a rush. Then I get annoyed with myself and the others.

IH It's the same with me. When I'm alone, which is very rare, it always happens. When I work, my time is structured. But as soon as I'm alone, I have the feeling of having an infinite amount of time, and then it slips through my fingers.

PH Perhaps it would be important to be alone more—not just a day. Did you interrupt your holiday in Brittany for this conversation? Were you with your children until the day before yesterday?

IH Yes, I had things to do in Paris.

PH And then you left the children by themselves. Do you like being alone?

IH I don't find it easy to leave them alone. At the same time, I like being alone. It's complicated.

PH What's complicated about it?

IH I often want to be alone, but I am extremely dependent on my children.

PH You only have to call them. This being alone, this absence, creates great poetry in children.

IH Do you really believe children like one's absence?

PH Yes, because it's an absence full of warm-heartedness. With adults, that's somewhat perverse. I find it difficult to live in harmony with anyone else, hence the separations. As soon as we're separated, I feel harmony.

IH That's certainly true of many relationships, but we don't like to admit it. It can be a very unpleasant feeling. Absence and separation are all too often identified with unhappiness and despair.

PH It's odd. A separation can be fine for three days, then suddenly an hour is too long. It all tips over into the opposite. That's why forms of communication like the phone are very good, though I don't like talking on the phone. Aren't your children actually alone when you're filming?

IH No, not very often, because I nearly always take them with me.

PH How old are your children?

IH Three and seven. I can't be away from them long because time passes so quickly. They're growing up so quickly. I really want to be part of it during this time.

  PH Is someone looking after them?

IH Yes, a young girl.

PH … who cooks for them.

IH No, in the holidays I organize things differently.

PH Do you cook yourself?

IH No, I don't.

PH But mozzarella and tomatoes at least?

IH That's about it. Something simple.

PH Classic. Do you shop?

IH Not very often actually. Sometimes I cook for them, of course. But I don't bake cakes and pastry. I don't look after them the way I should. One always has this idea, this illusion of an ideal mother, which one can't live up to.

PH It was much the same for me. The word "father" has a certain meaning, and I always had the impression I wasn't doing justice to that meaning. Now that I don't live with my daughter any more, I can really identify myself as a father.

IH It's these wretched ideals, these phantoms, we're always chasing but never live up to.

PH I used to feel just like a guardian, I couldn't call myself "father." But when my daughter left home to go to Vienna, she began to call me father. She wrote little letters to me, very short, but even so she still wrote "Dear Father" in them. It rather embarrassed me. I was never part of that movement, but in the 1960s it was normal for children to call their parents by their Christian names. That time, my daughter used to call me by my Christian name in front of her friends. But now she always says "my father" in front of other people. And that's why I now try to behave like a father.

IH Perhaps it's also so difficult to live up to these ideals because we have other identities, in our cases a writer and an actress.

PH I think that's a problem with many seriously committed occupations. On the other hand, as an actress you have a greater opportunity to live up to the ideal. If you can't act a mother as an actress, you're in the wrong job. You have to try to combine the two forms of existence. On the other hand, you can't be a good writer if you can't manage the daily round. We have, for example, a lot more opportunities than most people. Our occupations make it easier to get closer to everyday life.

IH It constantly amazes me that people ask how I can combine private life and career. You don't ask a sales assistant anything like that. It's taken for granted.

PH Do you find it difficult to be open to these different "realities" when you're filming?

IH Yes and no. You pick it up. Perhaps it's just a particular capacity I have for living on different levels.

PH How do you manage that? I can't do it.

IH For example, when we were filming *Malina,* I cried during lots of scenes, then I turned around and played ball with my son. Then I went off to cry again.

PH In my profession, the relationship is more vampirish, that's my big problem. When I write, I lose my bearings in the world. That's an almost unheard of feeling of guilt vis-à-vis the world. I find it difficult to talk to people or be with them. Have you read the poems of Ingeborg Bachmann? I've never met a man who liked *Malina*, but lots of women do.

IH I've read her poems, and of course *Malina,* too. I like the way she speaks of this inner disorderliness, pushing back frontiers, madness.

PH The book focuses on men so much, it rather gets on my nerves.

IH Certainly, but she's mainly obsessed with herself. It's a book gasping for air. There's something claustrophobic about it.

PH From time to time I like to read books in which nothing happens—a book that lets me breathe. In *Malina*, you're always at the point of suffocation. You're sucked up, like in Thomas Bernhard's books, which also go on and on about the same thing.

IH But it's not hysteria.

PH No, Bachmann wasn't in the least hysterical. She was just very severe.

IH Did you know her?

PH Yes, I did get to know her. We once danced together in a disco. I was very young. That was quite something, I was really intimidated. I think she despised most people. But she was quite witty.

IH Was she stern?

PH No, just severe. And rather unjust.

IH Like all severe people.

PH She was precious, unique. People like that are often hard, full of rage, full of hate and cruelty. Are you satisfied with the film? Proud of it?

IH Yes.

PH Really?

IH Yes. Shouldn't one say that?

PH The phrase "proud of" always surprises me, because I hardly ever am. Only sometimes when I translate a book.

IH I was just thinking how strange it must be to live in a writer's skin.

PH There's a degree of danger in it, too. I often wonder before or after work what it all has to do with this—this table, these shoes, this leaf in the woods. It's all an abyss and a deliverance. It makes my head spin. Sometimes inner and outer worlds coincide, sometimes they don't. That's why I can't work very long, otherwise I'd go mad. Or it becomes routine. That's a kind of madness, too.

IH Sometimes you just have to change your madness.

PH Sometimes you have to be able to just put it all aside, even thinking about writing.

IH Can you do that?

PH Yes, that's always a moment of great joy. Then I have conversations or go for a walk.

IH So you're not always in a state where you're thinking about converting reality in words?

PH No, that's rare, extraordinary, in fact. If a book hasn't yet grown in me, I don't have any inclination to write. But when I write, that's my existence. Then you even feel better than others. But it's also irritating. When I travel by metro, I look at people and want to slap their faces. Just to get something going. But people are what they are.

IH You say you always only write for two or three months. Can you keep up that condition so long?

PH It's madness when I think this stuff. I suffer if I think like a cultural fascist. I don't like it at all.

IH Sometimes I think people really are monsters!

PH It's very difficult to preserve an even keel, keep a distance, one's inviolability. One can live with that, but you need passion, too. Probably you have to go through hate and fear to overcome them. You have to be very easily aroused to be able to achieve anything.

  IH Do you often hate? Or less often as you grow older?

PH Nothing's changed there. But I wonder why it doesn't stop. You know what I mean. I always convinced myself that it would ease with age or detachment. The best cure is ultimately distance. That's the secret. If I find the right distance, I like everything. Then I become a happy idiot.

IH And when you get close to someone, do you hate or love?

PH Then I begin to hate.

IH And if you go away, you begin to love.

PH Yes.

IH Bizarre.

PH Distance is the price you have to pay for harmony and intimacy.

IH So distance is harmony.

PH At any rate, I've often crossed a frontier after which it became clear to me I'd breached someone else's zone of intimacy.

IH And then you regretted it.

PH Yes, always. But I always do that with more and more irony towards myself. Because you can't help breaching that sphere of intimacy. If I've learnt anything in my life, it's what's known as gallows humor. You have to make mistakes, if you can call something like that a mistake. I lived for three years with no permanent home. I traveled. I had a small rucksack, a bit bigger than yours. I got used to this freedom, of being able to leave any time.

IH My dream was always to go to an airport, look at the departures board and simply catch the next plane somewhere.

PH Do you like traveling?

IH Yes, but I'm always rather afraid of it. You discover that the promise of a journey is never fulfilled. You want to go back to paradise, but that's not how it works.

PH If I feel an urge to travel nowadays, it's only within Europe. I hardly know Europe. I like Greece and Yugoslavia.

IH What did you last read?

PH When I traveled, I read the Bible every morning, to feel at home. Only a sentence or a verse. And a few months ago, I stopped at the Apocalypse of St John the Divine. Now I'm looking for something new to get me dreaming the same way, something that repels me, stirs me up, makes me see.

IH Have you never felt an urge to write a "great" novel, a social novel? You go in more and more for small formats. You'll finish up with haikus!

PH Social novels are not my thing. That's up to others to do, if they still exist.

IH People only talk about themselves in literature now.

PH I think you have to talk about yourself. The more you think about yourself, the more novelistic it actually becomes. You have to begin with "I." The more you extend the I, the more world it becomes. After all, how can I know who you are? We have to leave others in peace, describe them like passers-by.

IH This absorption in the self is brave, but it can be dangerous. You never know what you'll come across there. Maybe nothing at all!

PH But you have to try. Otherwise literature has no point.

IH In your book *Versuch über die Müdigkeit* (*Essay on Fatigue*) there's a paragraph I found very relevant. You're sitting on the terrace of a café watching people and thinking yourself into their heads. I love that situation. It's like a kind of trance.

PH I always look like a mongoloid. I prefer to sit on a terrace rather than go to the cinema.

I only get depressed there. These traumata, the violence, oppress me more and more. There's a lot of aggression in the street as well, especially in Paris, but I don't imagine anything. It's enough just to watch people going past me.

IH It's a modern phenomenon, that abstract gaze. In earlier centuries, a look had consequences. I'm always a little isolated if I look. I'm the one looking, but people don't look back. That's always a situation of power and alienation.

PH It's like a series of sculptures, like the Duchamp nude coming down the steps. It's not always funny. But if it is funny, it's as beautiful as a film by Jacques Tati. Nothing happens. Sometimes I even feel like getting involved in this life.

IH And you do?

PH Yes, you have to get up at some point.

From VOGUE 12/1991; The conversation was recorded by Egbert Hörmann

ISABELLE HUPPERT — PETER HANDKE

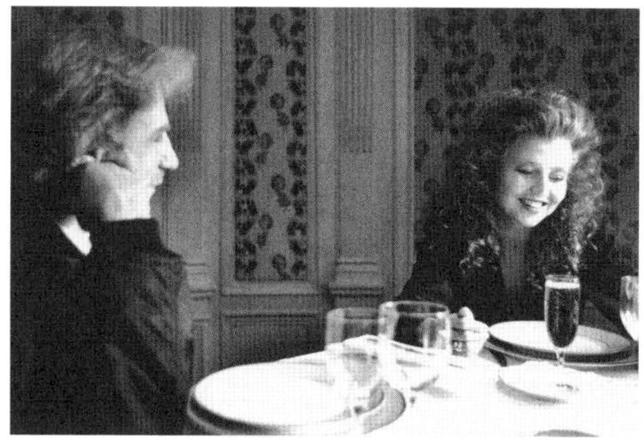

LOVE, LEATHER AND PARADOX

French star designer CLAUDE MONTANA and Germany's film
diva HANNA SCHYGULLA reveal how they became who they are.
And what it is they dream of.

She was still feeling a bit jet-lagged, two days after returning from filming in Cuba. She was totally fascinated by the Cuban people, whose poetic charm brightens their otherwise difficult everyday lives. Hanna Schygulla herself seemed like an angel from some distant star. For years now she has lived along the Seine, first in Montmartre, today in the Marais. She learned French at nineteen, when she worked in Paris as an au pair. The Paris restaurant that Claude Montana, son of a German mother and a Spanish father, has chosen for their meeting reflects the charm of the past century. This wood-paneled temple of the palate on Place de la Madeleine would lead one to believe that the two shy conversationalists are sitting on a film set.

Hanna Schygulla Did you choose me to have a talk with me because I'm German?

Claude Montana No. Or perhaps I did, unconsciously. I love the movies. There aren't many truly fascinating actresses who have charisma. To me, you are one of them. I love voices that evoke something in me.

HS I'm not so sure. In the beginning, everything was always tied to Fassbinder, who surely would have liked you; he also liked to wear leather.

CM He and I actually crossed paths once, briefly.

HS The two of you definitely would have gotten along well. It's strange. I find so many things paradoxical today. I don't seem to fit well into any category, whether it's a religious or ideological one or a matter of style. I reject rigidity. At the same time, I'm discovering more and more the meaning of paradox in life. Leather, for example. Earlier I found it horrible, would never have imagined that I would wear it. Then I met Fassbinder and submerged myself completely in this world of leather. His leather vest was absolutely indispensable to him. Today, I really like leather. It's the same with the things one avoids as it is with those one really wants—you

93

end up wearing both of them. I've read a few articles about you, and one thing that struck me was the sentence that you aren't at all fashionable.

CM That's absolutely right.

HS But fashion, after all, is for …

CM … the frivolous.

HS For the outer appearance. When I read that, I felt an immediate connection to you. When I'm out in public I immediately become shy. I don't feel comfortable in a crowd. And yet I've chosen a profession …

CM … that lives from contact with the public.

HS There's a paradox. Do you speak German, by the way?

CM Unfortunately, no. My mother came to France right after the war and she had terrible problems each time she had to present her German passport. And that was still the case even when I was fifteen, in the 1960s. Whenever she went to some official agency or other and presented her papers, which showed that she was born in Germany, something awful happened. And that's why she never spoke German with us, her children. She didn't want to bring these difficulties upon us. We only heard German when she spoke with her family. I regret that today, because it's an important language. I'd love to be able to read German literature in the original. But now it's too late.

HS I, like the rest of my generation, have a hard time identifying myself as a German. Because of National Socialism. I was born in Katowice, near the Polish border. Everything there is a mix of Slavic and German. But what does it mean, really—homeland? Does that mean something to you?

CM No, not much.

HS I adjust very quickly to a new environment. Even as a small child I enjoyed being a foreigner wherever I was. That strikes a chord in me that isn't my own.

CM It gives you the feeling of being exotic. And yet, I've always remained in Paris, with the exception of a short time in London, for family reasons.

HS Escape from the family?

CM Yes. Even today my relationship with my family is unnatural, somehow. When I started in fashion my parents took it very badly. We had, for all intents and purposes, no contact at all with each other. Today, now that I'm "successful," I just find it too simpleminded that they accept me. It's no longer a problem for me, but it pains me to speak of the past. I have no interest in explaining to them what it is that I do. It's a foreign world to them. They come to my fashion shows now and then.

HS But you work with your sister, don't you?

CM Yes, and that's something wonderful, something very special. We're very close, also in terms of age. We have an older brother, seven years older, against whom we always presented a united front. We fought with him all the time. Because he was older, his interests were completely different from ours. I'd invent games for my sister and myself; I had dreams, plans for her life. But one day she fell in love with a man, whom she later married and with whom she lives happily to this day. I was left alone with my dreams. That was a very difficult separation for me. But then, much later, she joined my studio— not because she had to work, but to help me before each of the major fashion shows. I'm a dreamer; her sign is Virgo, so she's very realistic. My sister has both feet planted firmly on the ground.

HS I'm realistic as well, but I dream a lot. I'm fascinated by the secret laws of life. I believe in chance, in something that is stronger than the rational. It's not that I want to penetrate these secrets or to reveal them, but I want to become familiar with them. Chance has always played a great role in my life.

CM To your disadvantage?

HS Yes, but that is precisely what's wonderful about life, because then you have to reshape it. And in doing so, you reshape yourself. I'm increasingly discovering that there's not a big difference between my own thoughts and reality, because one's own reality is the result of one's own imagination, one's dreams and wishes. I often have—as do many other people—negative thoughts. My life began with the negative, so to speak.

CM In disadvantage?

HS With misfortune. And according to everything I've read about you, it's exactly the same with you. I'm very careful now not to have negative thoughts, because they automatically attract ...

CM ... bad things.

HS And I've discovered that I'm a creature of flexible boundaries, of the *zeitgeist*. I have different currents of thought flowing through me. I can function like a radio, choosing different stations and turning off those that ...

CM ... cause pain?

HS Yes, it's a kind of freedom for me, I find. And since I discovered that things have gone well for me. Because I'm the type of person who takes great pleasure in spending my time daydreaming, I'm often very happy. And it's a secure kind of happiness, for otherwise this emotion depends on so much that is imponderable. I'm sometimes just satisfied with imagining what it is that I want. Of course, much of my fulfillment comes from my second life, in film. I've discovered in fantasy something that is very powerful. It also helps me with my problems.... Did you always want to be a fashion designer?

CM No.

HS Not even secretly? I say secretly because once I was a very good student, in philology. But academia didn't particularly excite me. I didn't want to admit to myself at the time that what I wanted was a life in which I never knew what would happen the next day, not even professionally. And chance played a role in this discovery as well.

CM How?

HS I had a student job as a waitress at a trade show for craftsmen, which was being held in Munich. Another young woman there was carrying on quite enthusiastically about an evening course she was taking. On impulse I decided to go with her. It was there that I met Fassbinder for the first time. But I didn't stay in the group for long. For me, it was too ...

CM ... rigid, ideologically.

HS Yes. Then Fassbinder left too. But we met again later, by chance. That's another reason I believe in chance and in what one wishes for oneself.

CM Absolutely.

HS Actually, as a child I wanted to be a dancer. But as I came from a family that was completely inartistic, in which art was considered a superfluous luxury, I would never have dared to make this known.

CM It was exactly the same with me. I felt myself caught up in a current that was totally different, that ran counter to the way my family lived. But I never would have been able to formulate exactly what it was, namely, that I wanted to design clothes. And yet I had the feeling that every-thing was possible. But I didn't make the final decision until quite late, when I was twenty-five or twenty-six.

HS The same with me, I was twenty-four. And that saved me from having to prove myself, from having to knock on doors. I never had to audition. And I have chance, Fassbinder, and my first appearance at a rehearsal to thank for that. I had to jump right in, replace someone who'd had an accident. And it worked.

CM In your roles you always give the impression of being so …

HS … ambiguous?

CM Yes. One never knows what else it is you're concealing. I like the seriousness with which, on screen, you bear the most horrible things. You go through terrible events and stay calm and collected.

HS It's easier to get through life with a smile on your face. They also always say that clothes are something external, but the way you dress also has an affect on your inner life. And in that, too, one can always choose between seeing things rigidly or with a cheerful calmness. The clothes themselves remain the same, but they're nevertheless a mirror of the soul. I've been thinking a lot lately about death. It may seem to be a bit early for that, but these thoughts have accompanied me throughout my life. Even as a little girl I was fascinated by old people, and by children. If you compare life's daily little adversities with the inevitability of death, it changes your perspective.

CM Yes, that's true.

HS And for that reason as well I can now cope better with the terrible things that happen.… Would you like to do costume design for films?

CM Yes, very much. Actually, I've designed costumes for Jeanne Moreau for several of her films, and once for Charlotte Rampling.

HS I'll make an effort to wear your designs in a film soon.

CM I'd like to work on a science-fiction movie.

HS I was just thinking the same thing.

CM Not on films that are set in the everyday, that wouldn't be any fun. Someone recently suggested such a sci-fi project to me, but everything's still very vague, so I don't want to talk about it. If it works, I'll be delighted. If I talk about it too soon, I'm afraid it won't happen. Have you ever been offered a role in a science-fiction film?

HS No, they're always casting me in roles that take place in the past. Would you like to do a period piece?

CM Yes, of course. I see certain parallels there, for the past also has much that is imaginary about it. I don't find the present as exciting in comparison. That would merely call for designing something ordinary.

HS I appreciate other time periods just as I appreciate other languages. It sounds wonderful when someone sings in French, like Piaf, for example.

CM Though her lyrics are quite simple, in fact. But Piaf was able to express even simple thoughts quite powerfully. The love songs that are sung in Paris are always about a love that has failed.

HS Without love you're nothing. One needs time for love, and no one has time here. Love needs the advantage of time. Here, the pace of life is too fast.

CM One could get the impression that you could live without love. But then, when it suddenly catches up with you, you see that love changes your life. So you give it another try, take the risk. But it's not easy, in any case.

HS It's hard to let love grow. To be in love …

CM … is a favor, a gift.

HS But then …

CM … love requires a lot of work.

From VOGUE 03/1192; The conversation was recorded by Sabine Rollberg

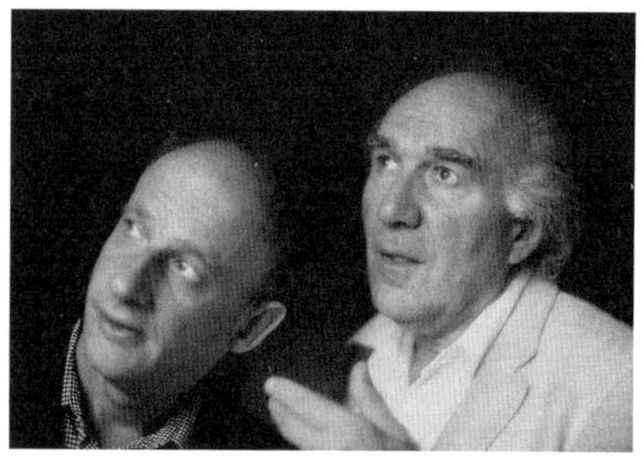

LOVE IS LIKE A NEWSPAPER

Actor MICHEL PICCOLI and director LUC BONDY have been friends now for many years. And they share common passions: charm, Eros and the power of women.

The theatrical cult of the female comes to ultimate fruition in Paris. It is therefore more than fitting that Michel Piccoli and Luc Bondy, meeting for lunch in a *séparée* at the Madeleine, should choose to discuss woman and women. Michel Piccoli, with Philippe Noiret the greatest actors of their generation, is a man of many facets. He is both actor and star, a Grand Bourgeois, knight of the Legion d'Honneur and bearer of the National Order of Merit, but also an intellectual nonconformist of the left with plans for a forthcoming short film for Amnesty International. His appearance has been described as a quintessential Gallic seducer: "A man with depths, behind whose erotic actions and attraction it is almost always possible to perceive a dubious network of social, political, financial and familial entanglement, something which, in turn, forms part of the social facade of the French bourgeoisie."

Luc Bondy, alongside Stein, Brook, Chéreau, Zadek, Grüber, Peymann, Strehler, Mnouchkine and Langhoff, is one of the top ten names in international theater. In 1973, barely twenty-five years old, the director conquered the hearts and minds of audience and critics alike with his performance of Goethe's *Stella* in Darmstadt. His themes? *Le désir*—desire, longing, lust. His dream? To use the magical space of the theater to create a utopian moment, manifested through "the absolute implicitness and musicality of breathing, body movement, tones and voices." His dogma? "For me, Eros is the driving force of communication." When asked to describe the ideal actor, Bondy replied: "That's Piccoli." Together, they have staged Bondy's favorite play, *Das weite Land* by Arthur Schnitzler, and Shakespeare's *The Winter's Tale*.

MICHEL PICCOLI You got married for the second time last November?

LUC BONDY Yes, that's right.

MP Let's talk about woman. I can only say this: she is *ein weites Land* (uncharted territory).

LB Schnitzler says: The soul is uncharted territory. And the French title of this esoteric play is *Terre étrangère*. Freud considered woman to be "the unknown continent."

MP He was like a submarine of the human soul, and was still asking, as his life drew to a close: what does woman want? But I don't like *Terre étrangère*. It's too restrictive in French. Maybe the German "*weit*" carries more associations with it.

LB So should we say that woman is an unknown continent?

MP For men, certainly. And for herself? Yes, I think that she is also an unknown continent to herself.

LB I have always been of the opinion that the soul of a woman places her in closer proximity to the metaphysical than men.

MP Are you talking about the creative aspect—the ability to bring children into the world?

LB Not only that. Because throughout history women were tied to the house, they didn't lose their character through public activity. They had time to dream, to worry, to explore their consciousness.

MP To restrict themselves. But isn't that a compulsive situation?

LB Yes, but that reduction generates energy. I believe that women are more instinctive than men. That's a marvelous quality.

MP It's more than instinctive. They have energies that are stronger than ours. Not only due to their ability to give birth. There is this generalization of women as the "weaker sex." But what's the real purpose of that statement? That the man can be creative. He can found a company or become a sculptor. The general public views a sculptress as somewhat suspect. A woman founding a company is dubious.

LB Or a female orchestra conductor. They don't exist.

MP That's why it's the men that are creative, isn't it? People call women "the weaker sex" because their social role isn't so prominent. When it comes to children, which, after all, are the future of the species, then they are much stronger than men. I don't know how it is in Germany, but in France the power of the woman is manifested very subtly in the private sphere. Here they say: "The woman holds the purse strings."

LB Women have administrative control over the entire private sector. They aren't at all weak. That is a very real power. I believe that they've remained within this cliché that we forced them into for such a long time in order to gather their strength—so that they can finish us off. (*laughs*) Don't you think?

MP I think that we're afraid of women. Maybe we still see them as Amazons, a potential Joan of Arc.... Don't you smoke anymore?

LB Not since last March.

MP You've changed a lot since the last time I saw you. I almost didn't recognize you. And a woman is behind all that? You see, you've become a different person because of a woman.

LB Thanks to a woman. In any case, I now treat my body and my health better than I used to. I let myself go before. I don't mean sexually, I mean the medication, the drugs, the alcohol, the nicotine. I've stopped all that now. Of course, I still have a drink in the evenings. I can't stand fanatical health and fitness gurus. They're usually really boring people.

MP You've beaten cancer twice.

LB While you sit here, drinking champagne and smoking cigarillos! But what we have in common is the ability to be stupid, to fool around, tell each other stupid, dirty jokes, like in boarding school. Our friendship is based on our living out a childhood we never had.

MP That we never had together.

LB Exactly. There's nobody with whom I can sink to such stupidity as with you.

MP The level isn't stupid, it's just low!

(*Both Piccoli and Bondy each cheerfully tell a joke. We shall spare* VOGUE *readers the details.*)

LB We like the fooling around, the lunacy, the joking. I've never had a friend that I could do all of that with. It's very liberating.

MP Because you don't hold yourself back, you're open. Maybe it's the fact that we've worked together, that there were tense moments, most of which I was responsible for. This kind of humor is like a breath of fresh air. You're open—you don't just talk about your private life, and you've led a very vibrant life …

LB But not sexually!

MP No, that isn't the point. Anyone can have a vibrant sex life. At least I hope they can. You also talk about your illness, your women, your parents, but you even talk about the life of Arthur Schnitzler.

LB What I've always liked about you is that you are willing to try anything on the stage. That's very rare. The problem that a lot of actors have is that they have inhibitions—they're shy, bashful. You could say that …

MP … I'm a bit like your wife. When we're working, I mean.

LB Maybe your narcissism is greater than your pride.

MP Maybe. You just said, very flatteringly, that there was a "small" age gap between us. In fact, it's a big age gap: not in the sense that I'm much older than you, but the only advantage that men have over women is that they don't encounter so many problems with getting old. Age is not kind to women.

LB Especially not to actresses.

MP No, there aren't many roles. A man might have a spare tire and wrinkles, he's attractive or not, but it can still be a pleasant experience to see him on the stage. These characteristics may become emblematic.

LB Because the man can still represent power in the stories told on the stage. That means that he can still be loved as well. The woman tends to represent beauty, grace, eroticism. When you lose that, it becomes difficult. I've always been moved by the photo of the old Edith Piaf with her young husband Theo. It's beautiful. But what "normal" woman can do that, without being a laughing stock? She was a star, she didn't have to pay attention to all that. And if an old man has a young wife, then that's more of a sign of his virility. I find that in France and Italy, in contrast to Germany, the age of the actor is much too significant.

MP Why is that?

LB In Germany there is more theater, theater that has better funding, but also a different approach to acting. When I talk to an agent here they always ask: "Don't you want younger people? Younger women?" I think that it's important to mature, especially as a stage actor. Young actors are rarely particularly good. But good actors get better and better over time.

MP If they aren't corrupted or burned out.

LB I recently saw an old Cassavetes film *Minnie and Moskowitz*, a film about loneliness, a close-up love story. The wonderful Gena Rowlands plays a cultured blonde, somewhat sophisticated, she works in a museum. She falls in love with a man who works in a car park and looks awful. What do they have in common? They're both shy, awkward, injured, lonely. By normal standards Gena Rowlands is no longer a beautiful woman, but I find her incredibly fascinating and erotic. She has lived. Some actresses handle growing old better than others.

MP Simone Signoret or Jeanne Moreau, for example. Women are accepted again when they're really old, because then they regain their seductiveness.

LB The time between forty and sixty is very hard for an actress. Lots of plays deal with the "so-called" battle of the sexes, and people expect the performers to be not too old.

MP It's the same in painting and sculpture. You rarely see a picture or sculpture of older women.

LB One of the most famous pictures of an old woman is the allegoric depiction of death by Hodler.

MP You see—*la mort*, death!

LB There are pictures of older ladies in the royal court by Goya as well.

MP But for Goya, the Spanish court is an awful place. The ancient Greeks or the art of the eighteenth century depicted only young women.

LB Even Rubens's women, who we find very attractive today, were young. There are scarcely any older or old women in paintings. Jacques Rivette's last film, *La Belle Noiseuse*, in which you played the leading role, looks at the relationship between artist, model and canvas, a relationship that often has violent aspects. Do you think that painters have sexual relationships with their models?

MP No, I spoke to a painter about it. He told me that the difficult thing about this particular relationship is that the woman is naked and the painter clothed. This means that the insecurity is often far greater than any possible sexual longing.

LB Is the insecurity due to sexual longing?

MP No, it derives from an artistic question. How do I re-create this woman on the canvas? The insecurity of the model comes from the question: what is he going to make of me? Of course, there are artists who have sexual relations with their models, but they are the exception. The distance stimulates the erotic imagination. The eroticism of the creative act is an imaginary one. Nothing is more real than the body that I imagine. Sexuality would only have a disruptive effect in that situation. Even if the painter used his own wife as a model, the insecurity would still be there.

LB Sexuality is contact and divulgence, lust is a form of consumption. The chaste beauty of the creative act, however, only incorporates waiting and dreaming.

MP And the relationship between director and actors? I assume that sometimes directors sleep with actresses. But surely that isn't the most beautiful moment of her creation.

LB No, I think that that can do a lot of damage. If I'm out walking and see a beautiful woman …

MP … You mean a woman that you find beautiful …

LB Yes, exactly. Sometimes I even see one after another. I feel drawn to her body, her legs, her face, her neck. We are divided from one another by the street. The distance is what triggers this image. As soon as I hear her voice, see a gesture, then my image of her changes. That is also the difference between the silence and the word.

MP It's a wonderful transcendental experience, a kind of daydream. Baudelaire described it in a poem, *A une passante*.

LB It's a dream-like situation, one which favors the creative process. My problem is that I'm always torn between the desire to bring the image to life and leave it as it is. When I see a woman that I find attractive she isn't a part of my life. She's an idea. At the same time, I want

to cross that divide. For a split second I create a fantasy of love: I want to love that which
I cannot love.

MP Sometimes I enjoy observing my wife on the street purely by chance, or when she comes
home. I see her, she doesn't see me. I find it incredibly amusing to ask myself whether I would
still be attracted to her if she were not my wife. Sometimes I pretend that I don't know her,
look at her with the eyes of a stranger.

LB And then what do you think?

MP Damn it, she's nice!

LB So it's a question of distance, of respect?

MP Yes, it's the ultimate thing; that's the art of love. That's why I often ask myself whether
you should perhaps address the woman that you sleep with the formal *Sie* form in public.

LB Yes, I can understand that very well. Most couples fail to clear the hurdle of proximity and
distance. Whenever I was in love with a woman, we argued and then I would see her in a
restaurant with other people and often thought that she was a completely different woman: a
stranger, with another life. Then I was always frustrated to find her so beautiful and charming.

MP Sometimes I think that the prerequisite for getting along well with one another is that
each couple has two bathrooms, two toilets and two bedrooms. The marital bed is a poor
institution.

LB That depends.

MP I'm certain of it.

LB Do you sleep in the same bed as your wife?

MP Yes. I just mean that there should be the choice of choosing your own bed or the marital
bed. People always say: ah, they sleep in separate beds, they don't get along anymore. That
sounds derogatory. It can be great, sleeping alone. You need promiscuousness from time to
time because promiscuousness is a very agreeable thing—promiscuousness with intimacy.

LB What do you consider to be the routine of intimacy?

MP It has nothing to do with dining together. Children sometimes like to eat alone with
their little friends, I think that they find that much more fun. Once more, it's important
not to have a marital bed. That can be the intimacy trap. You should have the freedom to
choose when to make use of that arrangement. Of course, it's also a question of space
and money.

LB Isn't every couple a unique experiment? I'm knocking on wood here, because everybody
naturally hopes that they'll manage to pull it off. It's a very complex, complicated and fragile
experience.

MP Every relationship should be seen as work. Love is like a newspaper: it has to be printed
anew every day.

LB You have to find a balance between the controllable and the uncontrollable. A couple
should consciously set aside time for themselves. I think it's dangerous to entangle yourself in
groups of friends and acquaintances. There's a kind of labyrinth of social contacts. Sometimes
it can be very hard to just have each other to look at when you're suddenly on your own.
Heterosexual couples received the support of society, but that often gives a false sense of
security, which increases the feeling of emptiness when it becomes fossilized.

MP This couple business is a funny thing. I'm now married for the third time, you've got
married, and yet we are still a pair as well, without being homosexual. What I want to say is:
the way in which a couple is formed is a very complex process. It has nothing to do with

sexuality, it's more complex. But I don't only form a couple with you, I also form a couple with Patrice Chéreau. I lead a double life.

LB Maybe it's because we both like the same plays. You don't get that very often.

MP And you said that I was the ideal actor for you. Is there such a thing?

LB For me, the actor is the instrument that I use to express myself. But he should also possess a reality outside of the theater—a personal reality, not a theatrical reality or one drawn from films. I look for an actor with character. I need that, because I see myself as a realistic director. And not many actors have their own reality beyond the stage.

MP The word "realistic" can be misunderstood.

LB Of course, I don't mean it in a naturalistic sense. I mean it in the same way as you could say that Flaubert's *Madame Bovary* is a realistic novel. It concerns a deeper, poetic reality. How do you see your relationship with the director?

MP Well, the director explains the play, the psychology of the person or his individual vision of the whole. What I personally find amusing about this work is that I can represent the director, a person who—consciously or unconsciously—is present in all characters in the play. He himself could never be on the stage. I am a projection of his personality.

LB How do you develop a role? What path do you follow? When does the role open up? Is there some kind of central theorem?

MP I try to sense the inner relationship that the director has with the character that I am playing, whether in cinema or theater. It took me a long time to understand that. In rehearsals, the director reveals himself—not just his talent. That's why I have a very passionate relationship with my directors. I'm sure it would be no different with female directors. This is why director and actor form a couple that never settles down. There are peaceful couples, and that's great, but we certainly aren't peaceful when working together. Of course, the calmness, the peacefulness, the stability may also be a passion.

LB Is that the passion of age?

MP No, that may also come earlier. Have you seen Chéreau's performance of *Die Zeit und das Zimmer*, which you first performed on the Schaubühne in Berlin?

LB No, not yet, what's it like?

MP Really sensational: funny, light and cheerful. The audience smiles, and that to a so-called avant-garde play. But watch out, I know what you're like. You'll be pleased to find that this is just as great, and if you think that, it's even better—*ah, quelle catastrophe!*

From VOGUE 06/1992; The conversation was recorded by Egbert Hörmann in April 1992

MICHEL PICCOLI — LUC BONDY

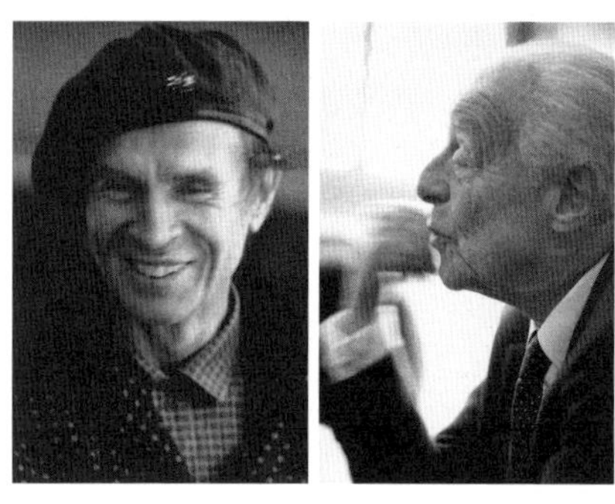

THE RUSSIAN SOUL

The eminent dancer and choreographer RUDOLF NUREYEV
and BARON GUY DE ROTHSCHILD, epitome of social elegance,
on their countries, customs and their love of art.

When the high, heavy gate on the Ile Saint-Louis closes behind you, for a brief moment you are transported to the world of Balzac and Proust, the fabled world of immense fortunes. This is the sublime Hôtel Lambert, a spacious seventeenth-century building that has been in the hands of Guy and Marie-Hélène de Rothschild since 1975. The Baron, unobtrusive in his gray flannels and accompanied by his dachshund, is meeting his friend Rudolf Nureyev. The private salon, with its antique books, exudes an air of tastefulness. It would be all too easy here to break into that childish admiration of the wealthy that Paul Morand once found so amusing in Jean Cocteau.

Nureyev, too, exudes elegance. After all, this renowned exile, together with Vaslav Nijinsky, is the greatest dancer of the century: "The human creature in a lyrical state," as a critic once passionately stated. The Tartar, born 1938 near Irkutsk in a wagon of the Trans-Siberian Railway, defected to the West in 1961, with a quasi *entrechat dix*. Although cosmopolitan, he also personifies the drama of certain Russian artists: heavily molded by their backgrounds, yet at the same time uprooted.

BARON GUY DE ROTHSCHILD Where is Russia today? What paths lead to the future?
RUDOLF NUREYEV I was still skeptical even after *Perestroika*. A system like that which had existed, one that even generated its own psychological structure, cannot simply be changed overnight. The government made all of the decisions; there was no individual initiative. However, when I was in Russia a few months ago, I changed my mind. *Glasnost* has created an incredible degree of openness. It will be difficult to transform the economy into a free-market one, as the society is not prepared for it, but the people have both the energy and the will to do so. The entrepreneurial spirit is there. And at the moment, the most important resources are the human ones.

  BGDR But will that be enough? The economy is in a desperate situation.

RN The people have to be aroused, inspired. There will be a power vacuum all of a sudden, more criminality, more anti-Semitism, more national conflicts. The redefinition of my country is no easy process, of course, but people are moving in the right direction. The decline of the Soviet empire also released positive energy. And secure economic conditions are also the prerequisite for a more stable world order. That's why the role of the West is such an important one.

BGDR The greatest difficulty in the transition to a free-market economy is almost certainly the fact that over the past fifty years the people have lost the feeling of taking responsibility for themselves. The best example here is the farmer. A French farmer has to take multifaceted, complex decisions, even if he is a completely normal person. The Russian has had the freedom of decision-making taken away from him.

RN Television plays a very important role in such a big country. There are lots of open discussions of social problems. And there is complete freedom of the press.

BGDR Before the Soviet system was imposed, there was a very unique Russian culture. What kind of contribution could the new Russia make to world culture?

RN Bolshevism destroyed parts of it. For example, the great culture of the Russian peasantry. There is also a crisis of cultural identity. On the other hand, this tradition was never completely suppressed. I'm thinking of literature in particular: Pasternak, Brodsky, Bulgakov, Solzhenitsyn. Even a cosmopolitan author like Nabokov still remained indebted to the classical Russian literature of the nineteenth century. So the cultural contribution was always there. Suppression does not eliminate artistic performance. At the moment, I would say that the decisive contribution will come from literature.

BGDR How is the art scene in Russia today?

RN The Russians love music above everything else. There are a huge number of orchestras; there are fantastic music academies.

BGDR So there is a lot of talent?

RN A lot of outstanding talent. Even under the Soviet regime, musical talent was promoted. There is also continued interest in theater, even if there is no Chéreau, no Brook, no Strehler. But the know-how required for staging performances is not very well developed.

BGDR Could you imagine a new dictatorship arising?

RN No one knows. No one can predict that. The Russian character is one marked by ambivalence. At the moment, there is a crisis of national identity and self-respect; people are easily manipulated in times like that.

BGDR The economic conditions have to be reinforced. Experience has shown that a currency has to be convertible. If a currency is stable enough, then it can also be converted. A currency can be convertible from a technical point of view, but without a stable economy there's no point. That is the problem with the ECU (*European Currency Unit, predecessor of the Euro*) as well.

RN What is actually the point of a European currency?

BGDR It's the idea of the Eurocrats: one country, one currency, one passport. The problem is that this house of European is seen as requiring only the right management. Nothing grows together naturally; it's all done by decree.

RN I find European unity frightening. To me it sounds like a party of unity, a wiping out and deletion of the differences that are so vital and creative.

BGDR You have an Austrian passport. You have homes around the world and even own your own island. What's your cultural identity?

RN A passport alone does not create an identity. I consider myself to be European. You've read *Madame Bovary*, so have I. We both love the same Mozart, the same Beethoven. That creates ties that establish cultural identity.

BGDR Not so long ago, before 1914, if you wanted to travel to Russia, for example, you didn't need papers, just cash in the form of gold coins. No passport! You traveled, you arrived, that was Europe!

RN Do you believe that Russia is a part of Europe? In Russia there has always been a strong Slavophile faction, and groupings that were more Western-oriented.

BGDR If you speak about Europe in a political context, that is, the countries of the European Community, then Russia is clearly not a part, and that isn't going to change in the near future. It's a world of its own, not in a hostile sense, but as a neighbor. Russia is not part of the West.

RN There are different notions of that.

BGDR I find it hard to imagine a Europe of the next century, with one government, in which Russia is included. Such a Europe would be difficult to manage.

RN That's what I think, too. The country is too large. I find the idea of a united Europe a very strange one. Why join countries together? That idea failed in the USSR as well.

BGDR I find the idea very childish; it's like a poorly-made salad. You cannot create a united Europe by decree, something like that has to grow. I know that the success of the EC is remarkable from an economic point of view, even if that success is hopelessly exaggerated by the Eurocrats. Politically they can't agree on anything, the Gulf War proved that, as did Yugoslavia. And Germany takes a back seat due to its history and policy of not interfering, which is understandable. What do you think of the two most famous Russian ballet groups, the Kirov and the Bolshoi?

RN I have to be careful what I say. The Kirov was recently in New York with *Swan Lake*, the reviews were really bad. It was described as being completely vulgar and outmoded. And yet this is a company that often tours in the West, so they should have known about new developments. But they always want to perform their standard repertoire for a state theater audience. And the Bolshoi has done nothing of significance for quite a while now. They wanted to include my *Cinderella* in their repertoire, but I wouldn't let them have it.

BGDR Is innovation in dance found primarily in New York now?

RN Yes, New York is the international center of the dance scene. A new classical dance movement is being created there. Just think of Martha Graham, who rejected classical dance completely and thereby created an entirely new classical dance. In the USA dance is now one of the most important art forms. It's appreciated more there than in Europe. America has always been good to me. In Europe, I was thanked for my efforts by being fired from the Opéra Garnier.

BGDR What about your career as a conductor?

RN At the moment, I'm something of a curiosity, but they will accept me in the end. I recently conducted *Romeo and Juliet* at the Metropolitan Opera and a Haydn symphony in Vienna. But you don't just become a conductor from one moment to the next. It comes with the accumulation of experience with different works. It takes time. You have to provoke, convince, prove yourself. Yes, I'm a musician, yes, I have talent, give me a chance! I'm just a man who wants to learn to do something else.

  BGDR And what about dancing?

RN I've finished with that. I have a physical affliction that prevents me from dancing, and it's not likely that I will ever dance again. Here in the West, we live in a consumer society, one determined by supply and demand. If someone is willing to pay for a performance, then you perform. If no one wants you, you retire.

BGDR And the teaching?

RN Of course that's important as well, but most dancers are egoistic, narcissistic. They want to protect themselves and their secrets. Fonteyn and Ulanova were open on stage, vulnerable. This aura, this ability to radiate—you can't learn that. The muse is capricious, inspiration is random. Real beauty cannot be forced. I think that teaching would be too tiring for me. But if I had an offer …

BGDR And what does the comparison with Nijinsky mean to you?

RN It doesn't bother me, and it isn't a burden. He was always my role model, because he was a dancing actor. He gave the roles depth, psychology, profile. That was due to his illness. It's the key to his art. His schizophrenia was his fortune and his tragedy. Without it we wouldn't have had the genius Nijinsky. But who said that all thereafter had to follow that course? You have to read the original diaries, not those published by his wife, Romola. His wife was hopeless, she destroyed his opportunities. And Diaghilev was guilty of not allowing him to perform more. In his diaries, Nijinsky talks of not being able to dance, and that destroyed his soul. Did you have a central figure in your life, a Diaghilev?

BGDR Not everyone has a guru, but some people have idols that they worship; my mother, for example. She was surrounded by gurus: philosophers, painters, writers. Whoever happened to be there. The natural result of such an upbringing: I myself never had gurus. I don't think much of them; I trust my own intellect. But I was impressed by de Gaulle, historically speaking, not as a private individual.

RN Two people were decisive for me: Margot Fonteyn and Nigel Gosling. They were my first friends in the West. I was nothing, and they taught me everything: style, taste, social skills, *savoir vivre*, but also toughness.

BGDR Did Nigel Gosling, who was an art historian for the *Observer* in London, also give you professional advice?

RN With regard to dancing? No, he only gave me cultural advice. To come back to de Gaulle: He once said that France was nothing without its grandeur. Now, at the end of this century, France could be seen as a country that still harks back to its lost power, but no longer has the means to exercise it. Can the French deal with that? Is the indignity too much?

BGDR The French are in love with themselves, but not without humor. They really do believe that they represent something in the world that goes beyond wealth and power. They have managed to create an aura around themselves and their country, and this aura is accepted both in France and abroad. France stands for certain things: lifestyle, culture, living life to the full. All of those things that are fun, that give life that extra gloss. Compared to those fineries, power appears to be too loutish, cloddish. Pure physical power appears ridiculous when compared to these artistes of the good life. In that respect, they are superior to the Americans, for example. Aren't you in the process of leaving Paris? I hear that you want to live in New York for a while?

RN I think that my Paris phase is over for the time being. But you're French, so of course you're hopelessly devoted to Paris.

BGDR America has New York and Washington, but no city in the world has the prestige and aura of a European metropolis like Paris or Rome. Paris is the focal point in a very concentrated land. Paris alone stands for all things that we consider French. Being a Parisian means assuming an identity that transcends social class and economic differences. It's a qualitative difference, an essential cosmopolitan character, an intensive *élan vital.*

RN Well, anyway, Paris is no longer the art metropolis of the world. It used to be a melting pot of art. Art was defined here—not necessarily by the French, by the way! Foreigners were always welcome, even if I can't say for how long, in my particular case.

BGDR And what is your favorite city in Russia?

RN Petersburg. It's Russian and Western simultaneously. But it isn't the Petersburg the tourists are familiar with, just the facades of the palaces. It's true to say that Russian literature began with the foundation of Petersburg: Pushkin, Gogol, Dostoyevsky, the city became the center of the earth for them. The city has something that frees the imagination. But for me, Petersburg is basically now no more than an idea. It was a caprice when I danced *La Sylphide* at the Kirov Theater at the end of 1989. It didn't mean that much to me, too much space and time stood between us.

BGDR And what is the much-fabled "Russian soul"? Is it possible to speak of a national character at all in such an enormous country? Is the literary hero Oblomov a model of the Russian soul?

RN There is the Russian soul, the Russian cosmos, the Russia within, but it's something mystical. You can see it in the lyrics of Yessenin, for example, and in the work of Chekhov. Maybe the mystical proximity to the land and eternal lonesomeness are characteristics of the Russian soul. Solzhenitsyn and his texts are typical of the Slavic separatism that is found in every part of society. The Russian identity is somewhat battered at the moment.

BGDR What does perfection mean to you? Are you a perfectionist?

RN Perfection is not an easy thing to define. Is it the harmony of technology and vision? Is it creativity? Is it the intensity of expression? I don't think that perfection is creative. Of course it is a praiseworthy element, but perfection always has something conclusive, final about it, but also something sterile and repelling. I would like to have the same qualities as a conductor as I did as a dancer. But that requires time and experience. And humor, courage and modesty. (*Inevitably, the conversation turns to the wife of the Baron, currently recovering from bronchitis, and their "magic circle" of close friends, to which Nureyev also belongs. All of Paris knows the Baroness simply as "Marie-Hélène." She is unmistakable. Especially since her legendary Proust Ball of 1971 and the Surrealist Ball a year later, the star choreographer of the "beau monde" is the undisputed society queen.*)

RN If ever there was a perfectionist then it's Marie-Hélène.

BGDR But that's something different. If she organizes a dinner or a social event, she takes care of every detail. That is the artistic pleasure of my wife. She has a creative talent, and she's professional. At the moment, she's working to restore the Opéra Comique.

RN You once said that she was more of a Rothschild than you are yourself.

BGDR I didn't mean it seriously. But she loves living in the tradition of the Rothschilds of the nineteenth century.

RN So do I!

BGDR We would both like to do that, but it's no longer possible.

RN Does high society have a purpose, as far as art is concerned?

BGDR Think of the Renaissance: art has always been supported by the upper classes. The artist as a social outsider, as a "worker," that's a creation of this century. Since the end of the First

World War the relationship between artists and the *beau monde* has been slowly transforming again. Artists have become part of the *beau monde* again. Between 1920 and 1930 there was a very creative mixture of artistic avant-garde, aristocracy and the wealthy in Parisian society. Today, industry and the government take on many of these tasks. You can argue about whether that is a good or a bad thing.

RN And they dictate their conditions.

BGDR Not always, no. You worked in Germany at the beginning of the year, what were you doing there?

RN I visited Germany for the first time in 1960. We toured East Germany, traveled through the country by bus. I recall beautiful gardens in Rostock. The East German landscape is very beautiful. I liked Dresden very much. Now I've done a new production of *Sleeping Beauty* at the Deutsche Staatsoper in Berlin. The theaters in Berlin are excellent, very international. Soloists and *corps de ballet* at the Staatsoper are outstanding. It was a great success. I will always be around—I haven't exhausted my potential yet!

From VOGUE 10/19992; The conversation was recorded by Egbert Hörmann

RUDOLF NUREYEV — BARON GUY DE ROTHSCHILD

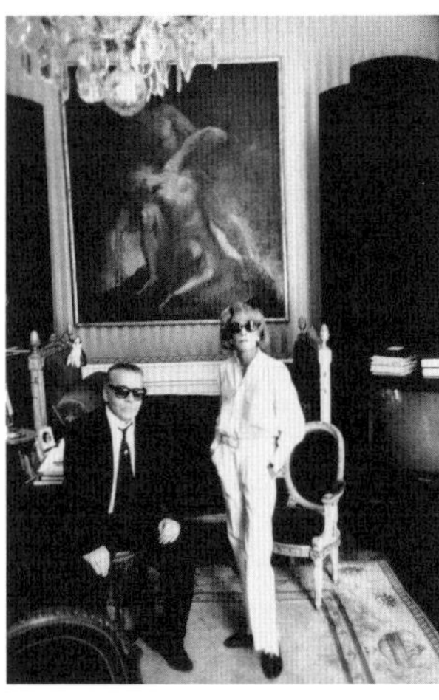

CAMOUFLAGE, CAMOUFLAGE

Voyeur KARL LAGERFELD in conversation with his friend
GABRIELE HENKEL, an expert in the stage management of life.

Gabriele Henkel and Karl Lagerfeld have known each other for many years.
In 1985 the university professor gave a memorable dinner in honor of the
fashion guru at her home in Düsseldorf. On entering, he was greeted by an
armada of old irons, heading towards an art deco doll in a taffeta dress. A dis-
membered tailor's dummy lay on the dining table, with black wool and white
thread spilling out. The designer reacted to the still life amusedly with a laconic: "Well, that's
a good start!"

For this meeting with his friend Gabriele ("She needs a PR person like me to present her
in the proper light"), King Karl even went so far as to open the doors to his painstakingly
restored Parisian mansion, where he resides in the style of a Rococo prince, tended by a
generous staff. The mood of the conversation swings between the relaxed and the meaningful.
The conversation of the two cosmopolitan individuals is sprinkled with French expressions,
a quote from Goethe here, from Heine there, as well as the occasional Americanism, for
simplicity's sake. As the differing temperament of the two would suggest, the conversation
has a tendency to allow the one to speak more than the other.

GABRIELE HENKEL Karl, we stood in front of that enormous urn in front of your desk, somewhat
frivolously, and talked of obituaries and oblivion. Balzac said: "Fame is the sun of death …"
KARL LAGERFELD I love frivolousness. I know a lot of people who would have disappeared long
ago had they not been frivolous.
GH That's part of the art of life. Let's come back to the urn: do you think that your work belongs
to the ephemeral arts? Ashes to ashes?

KL I hope so. I hate it when the gentlemen with their taffeta and scissors take themselves too seriously. I love everything that is transient. You should never anchor yourself in an epoch. The tale of Romeo and Juliet lasted only one night, and now it's the symbol of eternal love.

GH A story like in a film. Do you go to the cinema often?

KL Not very often. The webs that I have spun around the world mean that I get new films quite quickly, and then I can watch them at home on cassette in peace and quiet. Sometimes I even like to watch bad films; I like to see just how far they can take it.

GH I often notice that I spend more time on things that I don't like than with things that are perfect. Is it the same with you?

KL No, I can free my mind of everything that I don't like. But I prefer to watch a bad film than a pretentious intellectual one that bores me to tears. And anyway, I prefer extracts, much more interesting than the film itself. They're often too long for my liking. I'm too fast-paced. Life is too short. And I find average films and plays pretty boring.

GH I think that's a pleonasm: everything average is boring.

KL Exactly. That's why I prefer pictures, because they allow me to imagine something else. I like *fumettis*, for example. Otherwise, I have my favorites: Stroheim's *Foolish Wives*, for example, *Dames du Bois de Boulogne* by Bresson. If I ever make another film then I want it to be like that.

GH I'm afraid that my tastes are too Catholic for the film business. Whatever that means.

KL You can't argue with that. I'm more afraid of a Protestant taste. If I had to describe my religious views, I would say: Calvinist, with a little Port Royale and a touch of quietism.

GH Calvinist sounds so inhuman, strict and dour.

KL Maybe I am too.

GH Well you've hidden it very well, camouflage, camouflage!

KL I've hidden a lot of things well. And anyway, I only apply it to myself. I'm very rigid towards myself.

GH And how is that expressed?

KL That question is almost indiscreet!

(By way of opera and museum culture [Karl Lagerfeld: "A spectator civilization: stand around like sheep and want to see something."], the two cover more modern fields, arriving at a—for both parties surprising—mutual admiration for the dramatist Robert Wilson, songwriter Tom Waits and their joint project, The Black Rider.)

KL I thought that Bob Wilson's work was great, and that of Tom Waits—the best thing I've seen in theater for years.

GH I found the German-English text funny as well, things like "It's easily said *und schwer getan*." That mixture of entertainment and highbrow is rare in Germany, something for all tastes, not just intellectual. Karl, people often say that you derive inspiration from the street. But you never go for walks?!

KL I can't. If I do then people always come up to me: "You haven't got a job for my daughter-in-law, have you? She recently got divorced and she loves fashion," and other such nonsense!

GH So where do you get the inspiration for your work, as an innovative fashion designer—to use that awful word?

KL I read all of the papers, and I have my spies. And anyway, my creativity may come more from that which I consider to be reality, not that which actually is.

GH That's a thought: the *palais* as an ivory tower. Then the world outside doesn't have to be perfect, just the view.

KL How did your book *Tafelbilder* come about?

GH From my friendship with artists. When I entertain they are the most attentive guests; they see the pictures, the others just see the other guests and the food. And it was Joseph Beuys who said one day: "You should have your tables signed."

KL Quite right, too. He did the same thing.

GH He did a lot more, and significant things. Beuys was a great pedagogue. It was fascinating to see how he encouraged students and artists, nurtured and strengthened them.

KL Well, unlike you, I place no importance on meeting artists personally. Pop singers, for example, are often very talented people, but I really don't want anything to do with them: they are ill-mannered, boring, egocentric.

GH Clichés always have some truth to them. The worst thing about artists is that they're always too late.

KL I prefer to imagine how something might be rather than to know how it is. I think that that is the secret of happiness. I live as a recluse. I'm socially unambitious. If I go out three evenings in a row, then I suffer a mini-*dépression nerveuse*.

GH I'm interested in people and their work, I'm a journalist, and journalists are curious. I see my invitations as more of a visual offer. The way that I am seen by the public has something to do with the German penchant for pigeon-holing: "hostess," "industrious woman"—Why does she still teach, why does she still have to write? And now she does shop windows and installations, artistic spaces. I don't just stick to one thing.

KL That's right, if you thought any differently you wouldn't do anything at all any more.

GH Only one thing for it: carry on! I've just come from Potsdam, I saw Schinkel's *Roman Baths*. I was invited to do an exhibition entitled *Fragments of Desire*. That's a very interesting task, of course, filling these spaces with associations and pictures. For me this work is always more important than standing about at private viewings.

KL I have the feeling that all of these receptions and social events are a bit outdated. And anyway, I only ever see people that I've already known for a long time. It's not that I'm not interested in people, but I prefer to do it the same way as the researcher Rostand studied insects: from a distance, through a microscope. I'm a voyeur.

(*After a short discussion of means of communicating with friends and acquaintances [faxes, handwritten letters, telephone calls] the conversation turns to the advantages and disadvantages of various international metropolises and the outsider status that cosmopolitanism inevitably brings with it.*)

KL Paris is not really your favorite stomping ground, Gabriele, is it?

GH I think that you need to live in Paris to have friends here. A visit shouldn't be an event, it should be something everyday, normal. In Paris, I'm happy when I can drive along the *quais* of the Seine at night, go to the Louvre, stroll around the 7th Arrondissement. And when I see you!

KL Even I'm exotic in Paris. But that's how I want it: I want to be a stranger everywhere, the nonintegrated migrant. Even in Germany I'm a migrant. Even in Germany I'm a foreigner. As my mother said: "I take myself everywhere I go."

GH Who doesn't? I think that there is better "quarry" to be had in New York, but you have often said that you don't find the city interesting.

KL There's nothing there for me. I'm from the old continent.

GH For me, New York has a fascination that I don't find in Düsseldorf, although it's my hometown.

KL Well, I don't live in Düsseldorf.

(*The pros and cons of various bookshops and building styles of the various metropolises are discussed, before the maître reveals a secret wish.*)

KL I would like to build a house once in my life, a modern version of a castle with a moat, where you raise the drawbridge every evening, with an enormous photo studio, an enormous workshop, an enormous library, rooms for all of my staff and on top of it all a penthouse for me.

GH A house with everything in it, where you don't have to search for things, a pair of glasses in each room—an autarchic realm, one that you never have to leave. How do you manage to handle the enormous workload that you have, the eleven or more collections a year?

KL Appetite comes with eating. You should never stop.

GH Then you should be fatter, because if you look at it like that, you eat very often.

KL I tend to be overweight. But that only came with age. My famous fortune-teller always said: "Everything in your life is slowly looking up." It's like breathing for me. I don't pay any thought to it any more. But I always seem to be completely lazy. I have a guilty conscience if I stay in bed an hour longer than normal. It's been like that since I was told as a child: "The early bird catches the worm."

GH You can only manage it with Prussian discipline and perfect organization. Are you well organized?

KL Internally, probably, yes, but externally it could be better.

GH But whatever you do professionally, you're always in the vanguard, never too late.

KL Otherwise I would have to choose another profession.

GH But aren't you under intense pressure, always having to look to the future, in summer at autumn, in winter at spring?

KL No, I don't have that feeling. You see, my father was still working at eighty-three without ever even hearing the word "stress." Today people are always "under pressure." I think we shouldn't exaggerate things too much.

GH Talking of stress—even my students refer to it already. But stress is also something positive.

KL My dear Gabriele, like you, I was once a professor at the College of Applied Art in Vienna. In the short period in which I lectured, I realized that I had absolutely no educational fiber whatsoever, that I wasn't interested in my students. Without being egotistical, what I do is make things. Explaining it to others is not my thing at all. I'm a battlefield person. And generals don't necessarily make a good minister of war.

GH I don't understand. You have a lot of contact with young people: models, stylists, assistants, photographers, staff, people that you have to teach to see things with your eyes.

KL And I get on with them very well. I don't have a generational problem. But those students at the time acted as if they were victims of an establishment that they were powerless to oppose. I can't stand that. Do you sometimes have that feeling?

GH Yes, I often think about how time-consuming teaching is, hard work as well. But then when we've done an installation together on an interesting topic I'm really pleased with the results. What I have to offer the students is inspiration, imagination.

KL You see, there are only a few exceptions among students. And you spot those straight away, pick them out and put them somewhere else. It was really a joke having someone like me as a professor; I haven't even got A-levels.

GH But we have that wonderful term "general education," important for the puzzle pages in magazines, for example. Have you ever done crossword puzzles?

KL Never. I hate crosswords. I find them unnecessary. If you don't have something positive at the end, then I'm not interested in it. If I do a drawing, for example, then I have at least done something. Even if I tear it up afterwards.

GH And what you do should never look like work, either. I'm always slightly irritated when people say: "That must have been a lot of work." Did you ever feel that you had wasted your time?

KL No. I'm not that pretentious. I have no concept of my valuable time. For me, wasting time is the ultimate luxury. For example, if I'm lying on the couch and reading an interesting book when I should be doing something else, maybe that's wasting time. But the stimulation of a guilty conscience is extremely creative. It's the spice of life.

From VOGUE 11/1992; The conversation was recorded by Peter Rogalewski

KARL LAGERFELD — GABRIELE HENKEL

114

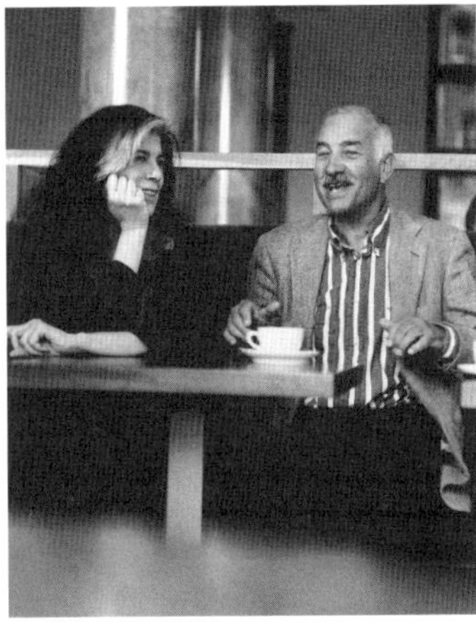

TAKING HEART

Two characteristics of SUSAN SONTAG, diva of the New York intelligentsia, and ARMIN MUELLER-STAHL, the actor who left Berlin for a belated career in Hollywood: critical awareness and serene humor.

A stone's throw from the Gendarmenmarkt, the most attractive square in Berlin, Susan Sontag and Armin Mueller-Stahl meet for Sunday lunch in Borchardt, the latest star of the fickle restaurant scene. While ordering a steak (*très saignant*) and french fries, Ms. Sontag reflects with amusement that during the war Goering often lunched here. The essays of Susan Sontag outline extremely sensitive, skeptical analyses of modern consciousness, rich in associations, and at the same time helped to form that consciousness. The *Volcano Lover*, her first novel in twenty-five years, is a sensation: a historical romance, the turbulent story of the *ménage à trois* between Emma and William Hamilton and Admiral Nelson, but also a meditation on passion, travel, melancholia, art collections, feminism, history and love.

Armin Mueller-Stahl is a phenomenon of international cinema, one of the few European actors to achieve a breakthrough in Hollywood, where he has made his best films to date. The actor shares a number of decisive traits with the author: the courage to question and a talent for innovation. Their cool intelligence is combined with courage and a tranquil humor.

ARMIN MUELLER-STAHL I still have a strange feeling in this part of the city, even after all the years.

SUSAN SONTAG Well, that's understandable, although I'm neither from Berlin nor a German. As I arrived with the S-Bahn I saw this "American Circus" which isn't American at all, it's from Italy.

AM-S Where is it?

SS In the middle of no-man's-land, on the former death strip. Seeing that gives you a strange feeling: this gaping wound in the middle of the city, with that stupid, second-rate circus on it.

AM-S My wife and I have just read my Stasi file (*information collected by the former East German state police*). My heart was in my mouth as I opened the folder. Then I thought that I wouldn't be able to stop laughing. The depths of that perfidious stupidity! We laughed, but at the end there was just a feeling of horror. Orderliness and thoroughness are dangerous things. I found a plan of my old house, for example, with twelve arrows indicating the best vantage points to observe it from. We also found the names of friends who had worked for the Stasi. That hurts. Some of them were even honest in their statements, but the sum of those statements was no longer honest and truthful.

SS When did you leave the GDR?

AM-S Signing the Biermann petition (*a petition in support of the East German songwriter Wolf Biermann*) resulted in difficulties for me, I couldn't get work. After three years I was given permission to go to the West.

SS Did you have any idea of the scope of the surveillance you were under when you still lived in the GDR? I have friends in Russia, Poland and Hungary, and people knew about the observation, but in the case of the GDR it was shocking to discover the extent of it. Husbands reporting on their wives and vice versa. That manner of political paranoia was unexpected in that degree.

AM-S Yes, we knew about the surveillance. But you had the feeling that it was something you just had to put up with. Reading that nonsense, what time I left the house to go to the baker's! After reading my file it was clear to me that this government could never survive.

SS And then you began a second career in the West. That was quite late, wasn't it?

AM-S Yes, I was already fifty and relatively unknown. Last night I had a dream that I want to tell you about: I dreamt that I had turned sixty. It was a real shock! We can't celebrate, I said to my wife, I'm not ready and not serious enough to be sixty. Turning sixty was something that hurt, but then you forget it again. The end comes sooner or later, whatever happens. That's why I think it's important to always have plans, always be on the move.

SS Do you have children?

AM-S Yes, I have a son.

SS Having children means that you can accept the ageing process. You're simply happy to watch them grow up. The fact that they exist makes you very happy. Your son is eighteen? Men are so lucky! It must be wonderful to have a child of that age.

AM-S At the moment he's struggling with himself and with us, that's normal at that age. At the moment he's discovering that he can live on his own. He's a talented painter and has a distinctive character.

SS As far as the age difference is concerned your son could be your grandson. He's two generations away from you. My son is forty years old.

AM-S Well, you're much cleverer than I am!

SS Well, I just did it earlier. But I would like to have younger children, but it's no longer possible. Our sons are spared our struggles and problems. Yours just has to cope with having a famous father. Your struggle was far more complex, related to a historical situation. Your son probably won't have to face that.

  AM-S Yes, history changes.

SS Young people today have the feeling that history is disappearing. History really is disappearing. The only problem that the youth of today have is how to have a good time, how to develop into a significant individual. We're from the same generation, although I grew up in the USA and you in the GDR we have an awful lot in common. We grew up with a sense of the seriousness of the situation, and that no longer exists. Young people today don't know what that is.

AM-S Do you really think that seriousness is disappearing?

SS Yes, or at least in the sense that it had twenty or forty years ago. Maybe there is a new definition of seriousness today. But a particular sense of idealism is certainly disappearing. Today everyone just thinks of personal or group situations and interests.

AM-S My son, for example, reads both Bulgakov and Bukowski.

SS That's modern, that's new. That would have been impossible for you and me. If you liked Bulgakov, you couldn't read Bukowski. I hate Bukowski, and I love Bulgakov. The one excludes the other, but young people today are able to like both writers. What does that mean? I can't imagine what that would be like, liking both.

AM-S Why not? People begin life as communists and then become conservatives. That's human development.

SS For some people, yes! For me, Bulgakov is full of passion, full of responsibility. In that universe human actions have consequences, Bukowski is just an id, a voice, constantly saying "me, me, me." There is no world in his books, just a little ego, and a cynical one at that. There is nothing to learn with Bukowski, except the permission to be selfish. Or permission to whine and complain.

AM-S There is no vision with Bukowski.

SS There is one, but it's very cynical: that we are all nothing but dirt. With Bulgakov you are in touch with feelings the whole time, a world of longings beyond yourself. And with modesty.

AM-S But couldn't you see Bukowski as a contemporary Villon?

SS I wish that I could. He was unknown in America for a long time, he was discovered in Germany.

AM-S How do you explain that?

SS Because the Europeans like to see the Americans as barbarians. If I ask my German friends what they like about America, they say: the absence of culture. This is a kind of relief for Europeans. Europeans also use America as a kind of barbaric playground. It's Disneyland, the fantastic countryside, the naive, friendly spirit, the picturesque violence. The European love of America is really a very patronizing one. It's a kind of selfishness that can't be experienced in European high culture, and there is no expression of it there.

AM-S We live very close together in our small states. You're always treading on someone else's foot! What I like about America is the sheer expanse of the continent, the open space.

SS But you can get lost in it as well.

AM-S In Paris, for example, I always have the feeling that a football match has just finished. It's a condition that can be enjoyable, but sometimes it is also very tiring. You're always trying to get away from people. In New York it must be the same.

SS But as we know, New York is as typical of America as Berlin is of Germany. Do you spend much time in the USA?

AM-S No, otherwise my English would be better! I like the fact that my film work takes me there sometimes. It was always a dream of mine to be able to soar across borders like a bird.

SS Did you know Brecht personally?

AM-S I can tell you a funny anecdote about that. I was a young actor and I wanted to meet Brecht. When the time came, he died. That was his mistake.

SS When you played Utz from the novel by Bruce Chatwin, did you identify yourself with that character?

AM-S No, never. There was nothing of me in that figure. I never played myself, always just the character, although I use my body for it, of course. I serve the figure, subordinate myself to it. But I know what it's like to live in such a system, of course.

SS Were you allowed to leave the GDR? Did you travel? I met Heiner Müller in Rome many years ago, for instance.

AM-S I know him. He once had a play with my brother, John Reed's *Ten Days that Shook the World*, in which I played. And he always asked me for money.

SS Then you signed the Biermann petition and fell out of favor. Did writers like Heiner Müller and Christa Wolf sign that petition?

AM-S Christa Wolf certainly did. But writers were more important for the system than actors. Being against the system as a writer was lucrative. It meant you were published in the West— that generated foreign currency.

SS One thing that interests me very much is the question of what the collapse of the Soviet Union meant to Europe. All those tribal conflicts! The enmity towards everything unknown. I don't know if the Germans are aware that the riots against foreigners were on the front pages of the papers around the world. I find it astonishing that your government does nothing about it.

AM-S This government doesn't exist. It isn't in a position to react, never mind to act. It thinks that it is helpless.

SS I don't believe that it's helpless. It's a bad mistake to think that.

AM-S Sometimes I really have the urge to leave Germany. Are you in Berlin very often?

SS I've been here often since 1989. I have an apartment that I can rent on a monthly basis. I should have bought an apartment here a few years back, when they were really cheap. It's too late now. I'm a really bad businesswoman, and I think that I want to stay that way! I have a very intensive relationship to Berlin, it's hard for me to understand it. It's an incredible city, unique, like New York. Of course, Berlin has become more German since the passing of the period of "splendid isolation." For me it's the place to experience history. That can be experienced here better than any other place in Europe. And it's a destroyed city.

AM-S But it's also a boom town. Cranes and building sites everywhere!

SS What do we see when we look out of the window? A cheap bar with a bright neon sign. Two years ago, it didn't even exist. Next to it is an enormous construction site and a crane. That's very typical of Berlin at the moment. Berlin is especially interesting for the future of Europe, and I'm not that optimistic as far as that is concerned. Because the people here think more about the past than about the future. Their idea of the future is a very superficial one. United Europe, for example! Did anyone actually understand what Maastricht means? Did nobody think that this represents the loss of state sovereignty? A single European currency means a clear loss of sovereignty for every country. Nobody has understood what the collapse of the Soviet Union meant: it's as if we've been thrown back to 1911. Look at what is happening in the Balkans!

AM-S The existence of two superpowers constantly flexing their muscles seems to have stabilized the world political situation. I recently spoke to Billy Wilder; he said that the world needs to have a war every thirty years. Otherwise it doesn't work.

SS He's a fine one to talk.

AM-S That's what I said. And anyway, it's too expensive.

SS There will be civil wars. What's happening in Bosnia is typical. The Serbs will win. In my opinion the Germans should have intervened.

AM-S The whole world should have intervened.

(*The conversation is disrupted by a telephone call for Mr. Mueller-Stahl, which he takes on the restaurant's cordless telephone. Ms. Sontag is impressed with the practicality of the device, stating that this the first time she has seen such a small telephone.*)

SS We are all in constant contact with one another, yet have less and less to say. Where do you live?

AM-S Near Hamburg. Whereas you still live in the middle of the city. You're that type of person.

SS I like cities, the distractions of a city: operas, concerts, cafés. And I enjoy going to different restaurants. I like being a stranger.

AM-S Does that stimulate your literary productivity?

SS No. I could write in a broom closet. I just need peace and quiet, to concentrate. Being in a strange place gives me a feeling of being able to lead a different life. It should be possible for people to slip out of a life like a glove.

AM-S I think so, too. Maybe we should do something different every three years. Unfortunately that is rarely possible.

SS Waking up in a strange city is wonderful. I'm no hermit, but sometimes it's important to be alone, to listen to what is in your head. The telephone doesn't ring, no one bothers you.

AM-S People say that your essay on Canetti contributed to his receiving the Nobel Prize for literature.

SS People say that, I know. But I was never a critic. I like to admire, to celebrate another person or their work if I can. The thing I always liked about Canetti is that he himself has such a capacity for enthusiasm and admiration. There's something very rigorous about him, but when he admires, then he admires with a passion.

AM-S Like Fassbinder. Lots of people were envious of his enthusiasm.

SS His films convey the same feeling. I didn't know him and I didn't wish to know him personally, but I found a film like *Berlin Alexanderplatz* extremely moving. Maybe our ideas of art and literature are already so sophisticated that we no longer think about simple things that can be achieved by a work of art.

AM-S Fassbinder was more Kafka than Döblin. That was the other side of his character: his humor was almost Jewish. Isn't it true that nothing binds people together more than a similar sense of humor? Humor is the fingerprint of character.

SS That film managed to make me sympathetic towards people that I would not normally be sympathetic towards; tramps, for example. I found I could even identify with them. I don't see myself as particularly heartless, but up till then I found the people in the Bowery in New York irritating.

AM-S People like that were always my best roles.

SS Before I read Döblin and saw the film by Fassbinder I just thought "how awful" when I saw those tramps. But suddenly I could recognize Franz Biberkopf in them, their humanity. That is what a great work of art manages to achieve: it enables you to identify yourself with other people. It forms the heart. Another great thing about Fassbinder is that he breached the standard concept of what beauty was.

AM-S He wasn't interested in the classical idea of beauty. He was my most important director in the sense that he needed the risk. Other people might like risk, for him it was a requirement. Are you happy with your new book? After all, it's your first novel in twenty-five years.

SS Of course, I've asked myself why I didn't write *The Volcano Lover* earlier. Wouldn't it be great if it were my first book?

AM-S Consider yourself lucky. I think it's better to develop slowly. And it's a great pleasure to make your mistakes at the very beginning.

SS For me it wasn't as much a question of mistakes, I just didn't know enough about human nature. And I didn't have enough time for it either. Today I'm much freer than I was, free to express myself, freer to be more direct.

AM-S That's another advantage of growing older. You know that competition among writers in Germany is very fierce.

SS I never feel injured by the artistic success of other writers. Quite the opposite, it even encourages me. The public has to be fed, has to have a broad selection of different voices. It would be a catastrophe if I were the only good author!

AM-S Do you never have doubts about your work? Or do you sometimes stand in front of the mirror and tell yourself that you're a great author?

SS No, but I think that I'm getting better. That is important. And who is the greatest writer anyway? Who decides? And when? Criteria like that are pointless. But some writers were more important for me than others: Calvino and Thomas Bernhard. I admire Canetti more for his life's work: the crazy project of being Canetti.

AM-S What do you want to achieve with your novel? What was your goal?

SS With *The Volcano Lover* I wanted to create my own world, not just a single voice, anger or destruction. Because I don't believe my consciousness to be identical to the world. I would like to expand my consciousness, let in more reality. Writing is not a form of revenge for me. At the end of the novel there are four monologues by four different women. They talk from beyond the grave, and the entire book actually leads up to those monologues. Literature has to be direct, and it has to move people. I cried as I wrote the monologues, and readers have told me that they sometimes cried as well. To achieve that is the ultimate accolade for a book.

AM-S Or if they make you laugh. That's why I love clowns so much, because they are both laughter and tears. And they have their own poetry.

SS It's important to be moved, and it's important to surprise yourself. I surprised myself when I wrote this book.

(*Two ladies rush past our table, loaded with shopping bags. Where have they come from on a Sunday with those bags? Where are they going? We will never know. Half an hour later a taxi whisks them away.*)

SS Do you never feel the urge to simply go and buy something?

AM-S Only when it's rainy and I'm depressed.

SS Do you also find it consoling to go and buy things? I'm no collector, but sometimes I feel the desire to fill the world with objects, when I feel an inner emptiness. I've been alone a lot in recent weeks and noted that I've been buying CDs, although they're much cheaper in New York. The CDs kept me company. The impulse that I modestly follow is probably the driving force behind the great collections. And collections are also an attempt at endlessness, at eternity. People want to create a world because they feel empty. Collecting is a passion, an obsession. Bruce Chatwin, who I was very close to, was typical of that. He was already very ill, but he still had someone push him to an auction in his wheelchair in the days before his death.

AM-S Do you know that I find it strangely easier to act in the English language than in German? That's one reason why I enjoyed filming in the USA The German language is very aggressive.

SS You are the first actor I've met who finds a strength in another idiom. Jeanne Moreau, who I was friendly with, had an English mother, but her talent didn't translate into English. Max von Sydow is a similar case. German and American are both stressed when spoken. American is expressive, although it tends to be spoken in a very slovenly way, as if the mouth is full of mashed potatoes. But that isn't your problem. You're very successful in Hollywood. How do you feel?

AM-S It took a long time to become genuine. It's very important to be genuine in this profession—but only to a certain degree. I was lucky, I wanted to have the best part of life at the end.

SS I had no idea of growing old. The idea of being almost sixty years old is like the other side of the moon to me. You become aware of the fact that you no longer have so much time left. For decades now we have been saying that we are living at the end of civilization. I think that this time it really is true. It's the end of civilization as we know it. The next century will have a different civilization, but one that we don't particularly like.

AM-S Do you ever think of something like immortality?

SS No, never.

AM-S But it would be nice to at least be a footnote of history?

SS Long before he wrote *The Name of the Rose*, Umberto Eco told me that he writes in order to be immortal. He writes in the belief that in one or two centuries' time someone will read one of his books. I have never had that idea, I even find it embarrassing. I want to pay tribute to certain things in the present that are under threat, such as literature. It's important to protect this project, it's been around for 2,000 years—a certain idea of intellect, of gravity and human depth. Most of the things admired by people will disappear, little will remain.

From VOGUE 01 / 1993; The conversation was recorded by Egbert Hörmann

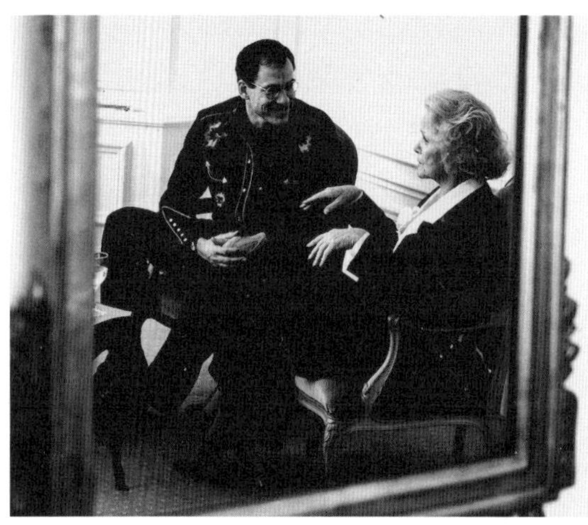

GODDESSES AND MORTALS

ROSA VON PRAUNHEIM, Germany's most aggressive homosexual, and MARIA RIVA, the daughter of the screen diva Marlene Dietrich, on the Sagittarian zeal for commitment, the charm of the androgynous and, naturally, the secret behind the myth of Marlene.

The scene: The Meurice, a luxury hotel in the heart of Paris. The daughter flew here from New York, the fan from Berlin. Of course, there is only one topic: Marlene—the myth and reality. Maria Riva, clothed in refined elegance, the picture of a lady, only emerged from her mother's shadow at a late stage. She explains one of their differences in the statement: "My mother would have never put up with this," when we do not find the room that has been reserved for the photo session immediately and roam helplessly through the corridors. "This is additional proof that I am not a star!"

Rosa von Praunheim, alert, enthusiastic, reminds one, in his dark suit, that this is the day when, for the second time within a short period, a national funeral is going to take place. Today, so soon after Marlene's funeral, Willy Brandt will be laid to rest. "Wasn't that the 'sweet' politician Dietrich had an affair with, but whose name she left out of her memoirs?" He was the one. Then, coffee and mineral water are served; the official part of the conversation can begin.

ROSA VON PRAUNHEIM My dear Maria Riva, maybe it should be mentioned that this meeting, here in Paris, is our second encounter. We met each other in New York, through your longtime friend Dolly Haas …

MARIA RIVA … my neighbor for forty years …

RVP … who was famous in the UFA (*a major German studio*) comedies in "pants parts," and through her husband, Al Hirschfeld, who is now being feted everywhere as an icon of theatrical history. He chronicled every Broadway premiere for *The New York Times*, for I don't know how many decades—in the form of a caricature. Several generations grew up with his drawings; he is a classic. Didn't he also draw camouflage games?

MR Yes, during the Second World War. That was a kind of picture puzzle where the name of his daughter Nina was always hidden. These puzzles were so visually complex that the American bomber pilots used them in their training. Only when they could find all the "Ninas" within a reasonable period did they know that they could rely on their eyes. In any case, Dolly and Al convinced me to meet you here and have this talk. Dolly said: "Praunheim is a nice man, I'm sure he won't do you any harm." That's why I'm also prepared to talk to you in German; it was my mother's first language, but is not my mother tongue. In everyday life, I speak English. Unfortunately, there are often misunderstandings on such occasions. I was really annoyed at a Hamburg magazine when they claimed that I had said that I was merely an "object" for my mother. I had actually explained that she was a queen and I was her "subject," her subordinate. It's a question of hierarchy, a description, but not a negative evaluation.

RVP What is your zodiac sign?

MR Sagittarius.

RVP The same as me! People say that we Sagittarians can develop a considerable zeal for commitment, that we are sometimes almost fanatical about truth. If I'm not mistaken, when we met in America you were wearing a pin from an AIDS support organization?

MR Yes the red ribbon on my lapel. The only reason I don't have it on now is because it is hardly known in Europe and the appeal for solidarity would get nowhere.

RVP Can we go back to the zodiac, please? You are a Sagittarian, Marlene Dietrich was Capricorn: both dominant, independent signs—together they form a volatile combination. Weren't conflicts preprogrammed?

MR Of course. My mother knew that one day I would get around to writing my book. I assured her: "I'm not going to do that because I can't lie," and she replied: "Yes, you will. Wait until I'm dead, then you can tell everything." There was no question that it could have been published before. There were various offers for those kinds of revelations—and I could have used the money, because I am not rich—but why should I hurt an old woman who had always lived in a self-made dream world! Marlene Dietrich was always something special and that is how she saw herself. Even as a child, her mother and sister saw her as a queen; nobody close to her had any doubts that she was one. You have to remember that most actresses—particularly those who make it in Hollywood—come from simple backgrounds and have only one desire: to get to the top and dive into this fairy-tale world of money and jewels. This was never an issue for my mother, she had experienced that already. That's why my book begins in 1898: to shed some light on her origins, an officer's family in Schöneberg in the era of Wilhelm II. Actresses don't suddenly appear like Pallas Athena from the head of Zeus, they have roots.

RVP But, Maria, your very existence seems to be proof enough that goddesses and people have at least procreation in common.

MR Yes. Look, I don't want to give the impression that I was shocked when another *ersatz* father showed up. My mother's lovers became my friends and I felt only pity for those sweet men.

RVP But wasn't there also talk about relationships with women?

MR How can a person like me who never went to school and never had school friends judge what is "normal" or not? My mother was in love with a man, with a woman, later with a song, after that a painting or maybe a city. She had the same feelings for Brian Aherne and Jean Gabin as she had for Vienna or Paris. I thought, that's how grown-ups are.

RVP But, in later years, Marlene's attitude became much harder, if we can believe her own account. Her animosity to sex was quite pronounced.

MR My mother was not particularly interested in sex. Holding hands, a stroll in the Bois de Boulogne—yes. But "the other thing" didn't satisfy her at all. "We have to take part in that disgusting activity to keep men happy, so they won't run away," is how she put it once. If my mother had found sex more fun, I would have been disgusted with her frivolous way of life. But she only played along in bed because she had to. Or at least she thought she had to.

RVP Werner Schroeter was originally mentioned to direct a documentary film about Marlene Dietrich. Maximilan Schell finally made it. It is said that in the initial stages of preparation Dietrich made a homophobic statement, something like she didn't want to get too close to faggots. If this is true, then it is astonishing when you consider that she has a huge group of fans in gay circles, above all. Many fans, particularly gay ones, were disappointed that Marlene, the sex symbol, showed herself as being so prudish in Schell's film and in her autobiography. That was a complete break with the image which had made Marlene so famous. Gay people, in particular, have no problems in identifying themselves with your mother, because she was such a strong, sexually independent woman, and not a simple housewife like one's own mother usually is. I can still remember how hypnotized I was when I saw you mother in the Queen's Theatre in London in 1972. I almost fainted when she gave me, and some others, her hand at the final curtain. Every gay person would like to see himself in the role of your mother, driving all the men in the world crazy with her legs and her furs.

MR And this adoration is completely understandable. Long before entertainers like David Bowie and Michael Jackson, Marlene was the "ultimate sexual cross-over," a model of androgyny. This gave Josef von Sternberg the idea of dashing the audience's expectations in *Morocco*, her first American film. Everybody wanted Marlene's legs, and they got them—in tails! Apropos: I'm not joking, complete strangers have sometimes lifted up my skirt, on the street, to see if I inherited my mother's legendary legs. Unfortunately, a generation was skipped over: my sons inherited them but they passed me by! But I have to come to Maximilan Schell's defense. It was his idea that Marlene Dietrich should only be heard and not seen. She had thrown him out and he made the best of a bad situation.

RVP I found it a stroke of genius. On the one hand, she is so present and, on the other, the mystery which always surrounded her remains intact. I noticed while you were standing over there in the hotel lobby, that you have perfect posture, you exude grace and charm: did you ever want to be a dancer?

MR Good heavens, no! Acting, which I did until 1956, was more than enough. I think it's terrible to have to struggle as hard as many young women do today. If what you say about me is really true, then it is through no help of my own. It must be the genes! And, of course, the body, the hands, the eyes all reveal whether one is content with oneself or dissatisfied.

RVP It is not only the eyes and hands but, also—let's call a spade a spade—a sexy body, tits and ass which impress me. In addition there is the psychic aura. In your mother's case it was

  dominance, the man-eating vamp, who many wanted to submit to. Men are usually expected to be strong and, so often, want to be weak from time to time. For the first time in ages, I've let a strong man come into my life. So far, they were usually quite harmless chaps who submitted themselves to me. Now, I think I've found the man I've been waiting for because he's not only sexy, he has a personality. What about you?

MR I found a wonderful man, have four wonderful children, and you can probably see that. Women who are as strong as my mother are forced to find men who give in to their ideas and are subordinate. My husband would never have done that, and so I gave up my career—with no regrets, I must add. In the fifties, I was a television star and the movie industry offered me a long-term contract, with a villa with a swimming pool in Beverly Hills or Bel Air as bait. I was about to follow in my mother's footsteps—a step I would have certainly regretted bitterly. Instead of that, I've now been happily married for forty-five years—with one and the same man, don't forget that!

RVP That sounds like a miracle.

MR It's not a miracle at all, but a lot of hard work. And you need a certain amount of patience …

RVP … which you brought into the marriage?

MR Yes, I guess so. Marlene could be terribly disciplined when it was called for professionally.

RVP There is something American in the way you are—maybe that's the difference between you and Marlene—which we would probably describe as "tough." I mean that the harsh environment, particularly in New York, the battle to survive has rubbed off on you a little. I'm thinking about the scene in the subway which you described to me at our first meeting: how you were attacked and threatened and instinctively turned so that the knife wouldn't injure any vital organs. This presence of mind is typical of New Yorkers. I also lived and worked in New York for a long time and was always fascinated by the creativity of the jungle. I met the most exciting people in New York. In comparison, Germany is boring. Now, with AIDS, so many of my friends in New York have died, I am afraid to go back. Then, there is the economic recession, which has made New York even tougher. A lot of my friends have had to take on three jobs just to be able to survive. Very few have time for their private lives, much less their friends. In spite of it all, I am still homesick.

MR You know the Frank Sinatra song: "If you can make it there, you'll make it anywhere." The USA still has the traditions of a pioneer country, where monarchs, even constitutional ones, have no real place. That's why I found it right that my mother spent her last years in Paris, even though it was complicated and uncomfortable for me. In Europe, a particular form of reverence for queens has endured up to today, and along with that, a kind of respectful distance. I could protect her better here. It was absolutely necessary to protect her. We had to keep her alcoholism, which was a problem for more than fifteen years, secret or, at least, carefully prepare her colleagues on the stage and in the orchestra for it. If you know that somebody drinks, you are more likely to make concessions, to put up with bad behavior, to excuse other faults as coming from the addiction, than if you know nothing about it and think that the problems are just a result of a bad temper. There's more to the dark side than that: when you think about how many people pray every day for health, then it's really disgraceful that Marlene Dietrich brought on herself the handicap which kept her in a wheelchair. And, with her own stubbornness, she finally managed to convince herself that she had been dealt a fatal blow. Even worse, she convinced

David Niven that she had the same illness. And the poor man, who was really in miserable shape, then thought he had to take care of her. Or, another example: my son Paul was born with a handicap and my mother liked people who were weak. Then, she could play Florence Nightingale—which was one of the few positive aspects of her personality. In any case, she hoped that he would never be able to live his life alone, and that would probably have happened if I had left him to her. My mother wanted to possess people, not to allow them the strength to become independent. She loved it when people were dependent on her.

RVP You were more or less trained in self-sacrifice. My parents, on the other hand, were amazingly tolerant. What I admire about them is that they accepted me, without understanding me, my gayness or my art. One can only dream of so much generosity. I don't think I could ever accept a square. And, my parents were middle-class and not really interested in the arts. Perhaps it's because I always had to struggle that I've become so strong. If I'd had an artistic home, I might have been more passive.

MR I only became aware of my lost childhood when I was going through puberty. I was fat and not very attractive, the complete opposite of the "cute angels" à la Shirley Temple my mother's entourage had in mind. Acting helped me in my despair as a kind of shock therapy: to present myself to an audience in my abominable condition was the worst thing I could imagine. And, it worked. As you can tell, the scars from a childhood like mine are there. It has no sense pretending otherwise.

RVP Today, you seem to be the personification of tranquility and balance. You obviously found the antidote. What was it?

MR Real love. Something my mother never experienced. It makes you think about the other person first of all, instead of yourself, and respect him as an individual. I know, it all sounds terribly kitschy …

RVP No, not at all. At the moment, I'm reading Erich Fromm's *The Art of Loving* and this little volume has helped me a lot, after all, I have just fallen in love. When a person like me directs, it leads to a certain kind of solitude, and then, suddenly, somebody comes and, with his very presence, puts your very existence to the test. It's a completely new experience for me to look at the world through the eyes of another man. I have to question my ego, something I hardly did before. It has to do not only with my own advantages and my wish that everybody submit himself to my art and genius, but that I finally comprehend that others think and feel differently and that it is more important to love than to be loved. I'm only fifty, maybe it's not too late to learn.

MR It was similar with me and my husband. When we first met I just stared at him as if he were a creature from a fairy tale; he was infinitely kind-hearted and naïve and discovered something positive in everyone he met. For me, who came from—let's be honest—an ugly environment, full of lies, this giant baby, who is now seventy-two—absolutely incredible— was a liberation.

RVP I'm sure that his kind of innocence is contagious. The leading actress in my film *Überleben in New York* was walking, like Little Red Riding Hood, through Central Park one day when somebody ran across her path and screamed "I hate women, I hate women!" "Oh, that's really interesting", she replied "unfortunately I don't have any time now. See you later." The guy was utterly speechless and—at least for the moment—cured. But, please let me know: after Marlene Dietrich's death—how will life be for Maria Riva?

MR I am happy and proud that friends and acquaintances have told me that this is an exceptional book—independent of the fact that Marlene Dietrich appears in it. There will be a second one—without my mother. I have the great fortune of having found a second profession at sixty-seven which I can do sitting down! Just imagine if somebody had discovered that I have a talent for running, steeplechase or something like that!

From VOGUE 03/1993; The conversation was recorded by Stefan Dornuf

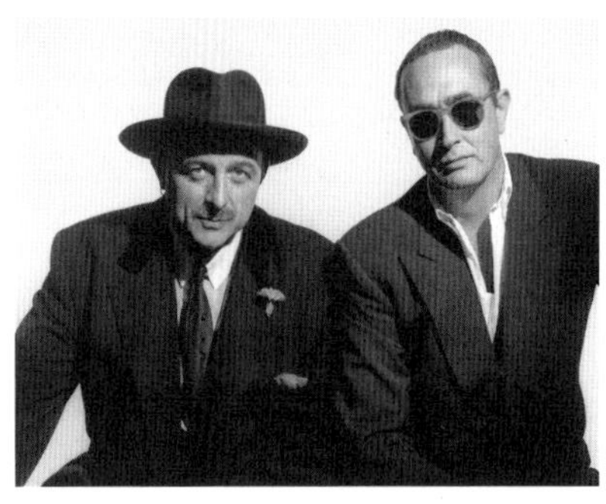

ENTRANCE TO ETERNITY

BERND EICHINGER and MARKUS LÜPERTZ agree: art must be successful, women have to be beautiful, and eternity can be bought.

The painter Markus Lüpertz and the film producer Bernd Eichinger meet in a salon, under a faded Tiepolo sky, in the Hotel Kempinski in Berlin for this conversation. The artist Lüpertz leaves no leeway for indifference—you either like him or you don't. He cultivates his appearance as an aristocratic, artistic dandy, who asserts his genius with nonchalant sovereignty. Massive gold bracelet, exquisite shoes and his bald head might appear confusingly provocative; the fact remains that this spiritual foster-father of the "*Junge Wilden*," who is today director of the Düsseldorf Art Academy, belongs, along with Beuys, Baselitz, Immendorff and Kiefer, to Germany's artistic elite. Bernd Eichinger, Germany's sole film producer of international standing, has maintained his dream of wonderful-life cinema. Who else would have taken the risk of bringing *Last Exit to Brooklyn*—that so-American cult novel, full of fear and rage—to the screen? Eichinger's love of literature films remains unbroken. He secured the rights to Isabel Allende's *House of the Spirits* and cast Meryl Streep, Glenn Close, Winona Ryder and Jeremy Irons in the main roles.

MARKUS LÜPERTZ Seeing that we are in Berlin, one of the places where East and West meet, I would like to ask whether the East is an attractive market. Will it influence the cinema landscape?

BERND EICHINGER Of course, the enlargement to the East means an increased market. In the case of the new states this will amount to about ten percent.

ML And what about the adjustment to the West? This is something in the visual arts which I criticize a great deal. In a flash, the East discovered a visual, Western language which is already well known over here.

BE It's clear that the will to adapt is enormous. An additional problem for German cinema is that there is no functioning film industry in this country in which they can be integrated. We only have a functioning television industry.

 ML Isn't that a general trend?

BE No. In America there is a functioning film industry.

ML Isn't it supported by television?

BE No. In the USA, a film project is conceived on the assumption that the movie will be as successful as possible in the cinemas. That is where the most money is made on a film. The money from television and video is purely a sideline.

ML I just can't watch films on television, because a film is conceived in a completely different way. A commercial break makes a film impossible for me. I'm a passionate enemy of television. I have noticed that it ruins taste.

BE One can think what one wants, but television has become a central part of our culture. But, it is also my opinion that this medium, which permanently brings images into the living room, has an effect on people which leads to the wasting away of various gifts.

ML Its permanent presence and the infinite ugliness which this medium delivers! Nowhere else, have I seen such ugly and undemanding human portraits as on television. It is perfidious and lowbrow.

BE But it is a good medium for live broadcasting, news and sporting events. I find that great.

ML That's a small benefit considering the terror it exercises. And exactly what information is transmitted? Do you watch much television?

BE No, I'm not a television fan.

ML I never watch television. I only turn it on in a hotel when I am traveling. That is part of the image; a bit like whiskey. I only drink whiskey in hotels, nowhere else. Part of my early memories of Mickey Spillane is that you have a bottle of whiskey in your hotel room.

BE Americans and Germans watch television differently. Over there, the television is often on all day long. As early as in the sixties, Marshall McLuhan coined the phrase: "The medium is the message." What comes out of the apparatus is not as important as the simple fact that it is there; the basic possibility of being able to receive images from all over the world in the home. That changes people's lives enormously. I'd like to ask you something. It's fairly easy for me to say how much artistic quality a film has. But what are the criteria for evaluating modern painting? I listen to a lot of music but have no connection to atonality. And, for me, it's the same with completely abstract painting. My understanding stops with Kandinsky, at the latest.

ML Do you understand experimental films?

BE No. I don't understand them either.

ML Is it a total block against all abstract things or do they simply not appeal to you sensually? I'm sure you have no problems with Richard Strauss!

BE Of course, but he continued in the tradition of the nineteenth century. But my understanding stops where harmony, in the classical sense, stops. That's the way I also feel about modern painting.

ML In all disciplines, there are really no quality standards any more. What I mean is that all these things rely on something which is dependent on engagement and experience. You have to be trained to look at paintings. With the flood of visual images today, art has had to withdraw in order to remain art, to not become an everyday thing. This withdrawal is naturally a form of negation, of encapsulation. Today, you have to have more self-confidence, be more experienced when you look at art, than was the case 100 years ago. Maybe you simply don't want to participate in this kind of rejection. Maybe you're not willing to cross the threshold of "not understanding." You don't think that the difficulty involved in reaching that point is worth it. You don't want to believe.

BE Quite simply, these works don't touch me, don't make me a better person, as some music does. For me, they are not a concentration of life.

ML But isn't it the case that the criteria which are applied to films today, which are material on the surface, only exist as abstractions when one goes deeper?

BE No matter what, the film has to touch you. The entire composition must follow a curve. I have to leave the cinema with the feeling that I have seen something whole.

ML But you can only be touched by something you understand. If you listen to Beethoven without any experience it might appear to be only loud, too complicated. Any appreciation of art requires a certain amount of experience, a certain education.

BE Of course. It's not that I don't have a certain amount of experience. Film music is sometimes written by extremely artistic people.

ML Precisely! Film music is extremely atonal, even in completely normal films.

BE I understand film music as a musical accompaniment to the images, which tries to conjure up emotions in the audience, along with the flow of those images. A film which has any emotional power needs leitmotifs and they are usually tonal. Think of the themes from *The Godfather* and *Doctor Zhivago*. Is art produced today only for an audience of specialists?

ML The artist is a specialist in our society. He is dependent on a highly qualified, extremely sophisticated audience. The everyday consumer who finds it easier to deal with Mozart doesn't exist for us. Understanding art requires serious work on one's own part. It could be that the sensitiveness for a further development in these fields of belief and sacrifice is lacking. They are two decisive aspects for experiencing art.

BE And just who do you think is the audience for modern art?

ML There is not a large audience for art. Even a mass medium like cinema has only a limited audience. It might sound provocative, but I think that everybody is equal in respect to what can be demanded and expected of them. I believe that we must force ourselves to demand the utmost and best from ourselves. That is the only educational aspect of a work of art that I permit: that it always shows the way, is a provocation and a desire with a goal. This "showing the way" is the most noble and important duty of art.

BE There are simply some things which do not interest me. It is the same as with a woman. You could be attracted to a woman who doesn't interest me at all.

ML But precisely you, as a filmmaker, should be interested. I, for example, am very interested in films because I come from an area which implies a certain tolerance and logic which I can apply to all existing phenomena. In the same way that one can watch a film excessively, one can also look at a picture, because one has the system of thought for it. If somebody asked you what you liked about painting, what would you reply?

BE The totally representational. The modern American realists, for example, but also photo-realistic painting. Isn't art a dreamed part of life? And, these paintings are very poetic.

ML You love epic films, which are your trademark, so to speak. I'm not a psychologist, but you seem to have constructed a world which can be experienced concretely, and have dramatized it. And, I feel that this understanding of film could also survive if it were constructed on abstract mechanisms. A film like *Nosferatu*, for example, is one of the high points of abstraction. It's like a moving Mondrian.

BE We seem to agree on that—a tremendous film.

ML Today, the question of abstract or material no longer interests me. The abstract has become a part of our consciousness, has become mundane.

BE I can go along with abstracting, but not with abstraction.

ML And how do you find the state of cinema?

BE I no longer like Godard, and I no longer like Fellini. You can watch *La Dolce Vita* time and time again, but in *Città delle Donne* I only see his weariness, his craftsmanship.

ML Then you understand me; I have the same mixed feelings. But I see film purely as a *métier*, as opposed to fine arts because they alone provide the content and spiritual framework for all visual imagination. I think that Fellini made the mistake of trying to make something static out of something mobile.

BE I don't want to offend Mr. Fellini but, in my opinion, he has lost the strength of being able to hold a film together artistically. He has become selective, only creating individual moments. He doesn't create an artistic totality any more. He has became totally private and, for me, totally boring. He is genius enough to be able to make a film interesting but, all in all, only he understands himself. On the other hand, Bergman, who I really admire, went in another direction. He started with abstract films and ended up with something as gossamer and understandable as the brilliant *Fanny and Alexander*.

ML Concerning Fellini, I tend towards the explanation that he simply became more and more a painter. He left the medium of film and became a painter. He became an artist. In a film like *Casanova* he combines this magnificently in the tracking shot over the water which is really a sheet of plastic. In spite of that, the film is real.

BE A provocative question—could you paint a portrait of me where I would be recognizable?

ML Of course. I didn't turn abstract out of frustration. It was an intention, not an incapacity. I am one of those artists who can do everything. I can give proof of my craftsmanship at any time. Talent no longer plays a role in art.

BE What do you mean by that?

ML Of course, it's not easy for me to say something like that. I have friends who produce wonderful paintings, and I would still insist on saying that they have no talent. Because, at the most, they have introduced something new, a weight, a specific gesture, a specific ground, into painting. In art, I always differentiate between termination and doors. Cézanne was a door, leading to a specific form of painting through reduction. Matisse also, who led to the monochrome, the pure color, the pure line. And then there are the "terminators," the revolutionaries who drive art to its limits so that one really asks oneself: "Is that profound, or am I being taken for a ride?"

BE And what is the problem with art today?

ML One problem is that there is now a form of visual art which entertains. That is the worst thing that could happen to it—that it abandons noble art. And, if it is no longer noble it is no longer free.

BE And what function does art fulfill today?

ML In no case should art have a social function in the sense of entertainment because then it would no longer be critical—contrary to society.

BE You consider yourself to be one of the greatest of all. Why is this notion so important for you?

ML I am absolutely possessed by this idea. The simple reason is that my existence is absolutely singular. What do we see today? Never before have so many people gone to exhibitions. That can only mean something negative. Basically, it could be good, but it could also mean that something is afoot which has nothing to do with art.

BE Why? Because, in your opinion, they are not advanced enough, that they don't understand it? I am thinking about my favorite Buñuel film *Belle de Jour*, where he uses an extremely avant-garde aesthetic in a way which I can still understand. Do you think that film is an art form?

ML I consider film art; for example, Cocteau's films. On the other hand, for me, after *Bullit* there were no more films in this sense. After that, technology took over, as in Spielberg's films. Before that, all directors had a connection with the fine arts. Now film has become its own *métier* with its own criteria. And maybe it would be hurtful if film were art, because I consider it to be its own discipline. Previously, film orientated itself completely towards art. We have a similar situation with photography.

BE I don't think that I'd hire you for one of my productions! Is photography art?

ML Photography can never be art for me because I don't think it is possible using this technology. But I think that the *métier* itself is wonderful, with its own wonderful, specific criteria. Directors and photographers have always had the strange desire of wanting to create art!

BE Only the second-rate ones! After Orson Welles started seeing himself as an artist he only produced garbage.

ML But there is his magnificent *Falstaff* film …

BE You're the only one who could say that! To make a film you have to be extremely disciplined but, at the same time, you need to have wild ideas in your head. The same would seem to apply to painting.

ML Isn't the production of art always instinctive, based on intense practice, experience, and knowledge? You have to lose control but still remain capable of maintaining a certain distance, of knowing when to stop. Each painting has its own strategy, but the only reason I paint is because I am a painter. I don't need any inspiration to paint. In the creation of a painting there are many long phases of work and only a few short phases of genius.

(*The conversation moves onto Coppola's film* The Godfather, *to Beuys' little boxes, yearning for Arte, the relationship between Wagner and Strauss, the mechanics of the New York art market and art in its function as a replacement for money for some artists.*)

ML Art has to be successful, must have quite high prices, to survive. Everything which was expensive at one time has usually survived. I would much prefer to give paintings away or swap them, but experience has shown that people don't value something which they have been given, or purchased at a reasonable price, as much as something which cost 500,000 marks. That might sound cynical, but …

BE It does sound cynical, but it's hard to disagree with you.

ML The price of 500,000 marks is a work of art's entry into eternity. That is essential and of elementary importance.

BE I'm sure that we all dream of this aspect of eternity.

ML Yes, it is the sole mission of art. Art is nothing else than the conquest of death. If you live one second longer than your death, it is worthwhile staking your whole life on it, with all tricks and ruses.

BE Do you think that there are people who not only admire your paintings but also love them?

ML I think it's only possible to love them. And, I don't think it's possible to understand art in its time. That was the starting point of our conversation: in order to understand or live with art today, you must be prepared to believe, even at the risk of being lied to. You must decide for yourself if you are prepared to play the game. It's just like love—if you understand a woman, you will no longer be able to love her.

BE Seeing that we are comparing paintings and women: you would never take an ugly woman!

ML You don't have any idea about what I find beautiful or ugly. Something you find ugly could be beautiful in my eyes. And real beauty is also produced over a moment of ugliness.

BE I would be very surprised if our tastes were different on this point!

ML For me, a woman is attractive to the extent that I don't comprehend her.

BE I understand that. But there must be a certain amount of comprehension which binds you to your lack of comprehension. If I understand nothing at all, I go home.

ML That is also a possibility. In love, I think that understanding nothing at all makes it even more beautiful. In love, you are prepared to make a fool of yourself, to ignore things you don't understand.

BE But in bed you have to get a grip on the woman!

ML Grip? I think you should love her in bed. People see me as a chauvinist, a macho, but …

BE You're certainly not a macho!

ML No, but I have that reputation, because every kind of self-assured, masculine statement is interpreted in that way. I only believe that man and woman are two different species. I don't believe in the unisex.

From VOGUE 05/1993; The conversation was recorded by Egbert Hörmann

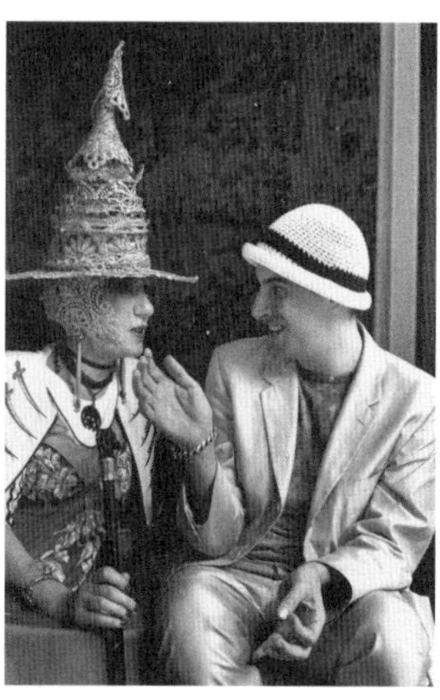

TWO OF A KIND

When the designer RIFAT OZBEK and the lady-dandy ANNA PIAGGI meet, the only topics are: fashion, fashion, and fashion.

A woman who does not shy away from being a theater critic and actress in the same person: Anna Piaggi. She has written, taught and judged competitions, and, as her main profession, designed pages in major fashion magazines. She has overseen their graphic and textual layout, and embellished them with carefully chosen words, like a poet, for over twenty years. In spite of all this, she communicates most directly through her appearance. She mixes individual creations with elements from her giant stock of flea-market purchases, which would be worthy of a museum and which Anna uses every day to create her ensembles, crossing all stylistic borders. Nobody has ever seen her in the same outfit twice.

The first impression one has of Rifat Ozbek—in spite of the fact that, in 1992, he was voted best English fashion designer for the second time in his young career—is of absolute simplicity. A simple suit, the greenish-beige barely recognizable as a color, a faded T-shirt and as the single personal touch, a pert knitted cap that he pulls down over his ears from time to time—that's all.

With his hands, he conjures up female bodies, like ballet dancers, in the air. He dresses them with words, as if his conversation were a fashion show. Even though he has obviously noticed that Anna Piaggi is wearing pieces from his most recent collections, he doesn't mention it.

ANNA PIAGGI I fell, slowly but surely, into the fashion world. I come from writing—I still do that—but my interest in clothes, and the magic and theatricality of fashion, have somehow become part of my being, my brain. It's a way of coming into contact with people. I communicate with people through fashion. The way I dress produces reactions which are extremely helpful to me in my work for fashion magazines. In a way, it's an expression of attention, on my part, towards others: I'm not very good at talking and for me that's a better means of communication. As far as I'm concerned, the visual is the most important element, but when I'm preparing my pages, I keep reducing and refining—searching for the essence in pictures and words. It's like a filter: in the end, I have a small selection of words in front of me, like a row of hats or shoes or dresses. I don't like to use the word to refer to my work, but it's possible that my method—a great deal of research, preparation, little talking—is similar to that of a poet. I call it synthesis.

RIFAT OZBECK The visual is also the most important aspect for me. I had a very elegant mother who had a great influence on me, even though I was more interested in architecture at first. It was only after I left Turkey and came to England that I stopped studying architecture and switched to fashion design. But I find it difficult to explain that; I actually find it difficult to talk a lot about my work at all. For me, things should explain themselves. When people ask me after a fashion show, what that all meant, I throw my arms up in the air and groan. Wasn't it clear enough on the catwalk?

AP Talking is not really my thing either. And I often get asked to do it. Not long ago, I was supposed to take part in a symposium about Coco Chanel, with a lot of important participants, at the University of Urbino. I asked a young Basque woman to do research into the time Chanel spent in Biarritz, I put on a Chanel dress from 1920, took a suitcase with a dozen Chanel hats, and asked Karl Lagerfeld to lend me some of his sketchbooks. This provided the students with a tangible experience, instead of a dry speech. Now, I'm supposed to give an encore at the University of Bologna.

RO I am not opposed to words, and my mother gave me a lot of encouragement with the help of the large library in our house on the Bosporus, although I only fully appreciated it later. I don't like to philosophize. Even with my mother, there was hardly any significant communication on the conversational level. The influences on my work came from elsewhere: my many travels in exotic countries and the history of fashion itself, for which I have enormous respect. Today, I try to let fewer historical elements flow into my designs. Until three or four years ago, I was stuck in my retro-period. As a young person, you can't help being in love with the twenties—or with the fifties, when women looked so glamorous. But then you have to look forward, to develop yourself. Today, I'm particularly interested in the clothing of people who don't change their style every six months like we do—nomads, tribes, ethnic cultures. On the catwalk, this style never appears to be retro. In Thailand and Morocco, these patterns are worn just as they were many years ago. It seems to me that the nineties haven't developed an individual style. If, in twenty years' time, we look back at the late eighties and early nineties, what will there be? In the seventies, when we hunted down clothes from the twenties at flea markets, we only wore them when we had added something from our own fashion era: a dress from the twenties with a bit of rock'n'roll, a touch of glam rock—it was only then that it became a statement of our own time. I think people take things too lightly these days. We adopt things from the twenties without mixing them with much from today.

AP I think that that's only partially true. On the level of proportions there has been a funda-mental change. In my opinion, that's what really brings about changes in fashion. I have cases and cases full of clothing from the sixties and seventies, but only a few pieces can be worn today, even though they are modern again. For example, I wanted to wear an Ossie Clark jacket today—then decided on your uniform tails—and it would have fit. English fashion survives time quite well. But, today, most things are only conceivable in other proportions, even if there is a certain repetition in the design. Today, fashion is created for a completely different female body. We live differently today, eat differently, do more exercise; we are more aware of our bodies, not to mention that there are many more mixed races, particularly in the USA and England. All that makes a difference. That's why I believe that every age finds its own, ideal fashion—like jeans in the seventies.

RO I still find that nothing very original develops today. Sometimes I look through the current fashion magazines with Manolo (*Blahnik, the London shoe designer*), and I can't believe my eyes. The stories and photographs could have been by Avedon. I hardly see anything new. I'm afraid that, one day, we'll have to look back on our time as one of retrospectives of various eras. Single designers will always be exceptions, of course. For myself, I prefer to make things which don't give me the impression that I'm stealing from the past. Also, the distance between us and the eras which we look back on so nostalgically is decreasing all the time. The economic situation is preventing a lot of people from being really creative.

AP But you must admit that there are new influences. Just take the Japanese, their influence has played an enormous role in recent times. And there, one doesn't feel any love for retro. It's not a fashion which tries to flatter; it's more anarchic, newly discovered, deconstructive. Only people who aren't interested in trends, but want to penetrate with their own ideas, can produce something like that. I also don't have a feeling of standstill in your work, quite the opposite. Leaving aside the fact that you integrate your own experiences, your travels, into your fashion, I can identify something else which is extremely important: a truly modern lightness, a freedom in your mixing of influences. Wearing something by Rifat Ozbek is a true reflection of the spontaneity of life in contemporary London.

RO That must have to do with the fact that I don't design any matching combinations. All of my clothes are designed independent of each other and can be worn in any number of combinations. I design fabrics, design this or that, and then, two or three days before the show, I somehow put the individual pieces together. I never have a preconceived idea about how a model should be dressed from top to bottom. I also don't make any sketches, as other designers do. It's not so well thought out. I might see some Indonesian fabric over there, a European jacket over here, and then I simply put them together. Many find that nerve-racking, and I am also sometimes worried and ask myself if everything will really match. But somehow it always works.

AP Your show was really refreshing. You sit there after days and days of fashion shows and along comes Rifat, and you immediately have the feeling of something genuine. It is almost as if the models had just got up and put on the first things they laid their hands on. It has atmosphere, it's a complete way of life.

RO I know how it happens. But if I had to have six fashion shows in a row, each one would be different from the one before, because all of my pieces of clothing are interchangeable. That's the way people dress themselves. Everybody mixes his clothes differently every day; even if you wear the same jacket, you will definitely wear a different shirt and different pair of trousers every day. That's probably typical today. There are no rules; you can wear what you want—more or less—and in any combination. Men are often not so adventurous in what they wear, so I don't design for them. It would be an uphill battle trying to change men, I think, and I'm not going to try to. Women are much more used to changes in fashion. But I occasionally take a garment, such as a sarong, which is worn by both men and women in

Indonesia, and turn it into something for women. I also adore the masculine touch of military jackets and have often designed them for women, just like the jacket you're wearing. I was inspired by the uniforms of the American Civil War. I also like to mix different cultures. The row of longish bones sown onto your jacket come from an old Indian necklace. This turns the jacket into a political statement. On the other hand, it's a piece of clothing from today, with a zipper like a sports jacket and with the pep that suits contemporary women.

AP What I've noticed is that your things always fit with each other even if they're not from the same collection. This little vest, for example, is from last year's collection. But still, it goes with this jacket. This style shows the personality of the designer. But every year there is something extra, something in the air, a general feeling, which you recognize and use. It's difficult to explain; there are waves, and you recognize the wavelength.

RO The whole question about changes in fashion is also a question about the strength of character of the female wearer. Many woman would say: "I can't wear that, it's last year's." But somebody like you recognizes the enduring quality of each piece, can mix the vintages and create something new each time. Of course, I consider my 1993 pieces as progress on 1992. We all try to improve ourselves. I always imagine a woman when I'm designing, without knowing the specific woman who will finally buy the clothing, without knowing her cultural background, the films she has seen, her circle of acquaintances, her criteria and reasons for doing things. What leads to new fashion is not primarily our attempt, but the constant pressure to sell new things. There are always changes in the air.

AP Change is renewal, and we can only accept or reject it. It's not only a question of the time and spirit, but also of competition, the influence of other designers and cultures. Designers are all chameleons and are very cannibalistic. It's completely natural and cannot be avoided. In addition, they all want to create something new, hope for a new social image from a new fashion, and that women will compete against each other. Today, fashion is not deigned by the woman herself with some help from a "seamstress," but from people in this new profession, which has only existed since the nineties, the fashion designer. Today, "status" is a benchmark and people are measured against it. One achieves status through the car one drives, the house one owns and through fashion. Fashion has become a social quantity. Clothes change people, but people also change clothes through their character, body shape, their willingness to appear more natural. We are probably living in a period where the body is changing more than at any other time in history. And in addition to what we've already mentioned, there's plastic surgery.

RO You recognize new freedoms everywhere. For about five years now, fashion has been very body-tight, maybe that's why exercising and body styling are so popular. Azzedine Alaia really started a revolution, which has now gone further with transparent materials. In my opinion, Alaia is the new Dior; he gave women this new freedom. Sex can never be avoided in fashion; it all started with Adam and Eve. A man, a woman, they attract each other and fashion is a function of the mutual attraction of the sexes. My attitude to my designs is quite sexual; they must flatter the woman and correspond to how a man imagines the woman. Naturally, there are also a lot of emotional elements, a lot of decoration. A dress can be very sexy and still feminine. On the other hand, there are also political influences. The sensitization from the feminist movement of today has led to the rejection of a specifically feminine image. That goes so far that women often don't want to be immediately identified as women, and sometimes would even prefer to look like men. But my feeling is that these are trends like all the others, such as the puritan trend in the eighties or the mania of wanting to look like a cardinal. They come and go.

AP One influence on modern fashion is new and it needs to be mentioned: that of fashion students. The educational possibilities for fashion designers, which exist worldwide, have increased tremendously. The students don't just get their impressions from everyday life. They know the history of fashion and often see it as an impulse for their work. You notice this throughout the world. Fashion, like so many other professions, used to be a skilled trade, a craft. Today, it's a university subject.

From VOGUE 08/1993; The conversation was recorded by Gideon Bachmann

RIFAT OZBEK — ANNA PIAGGI

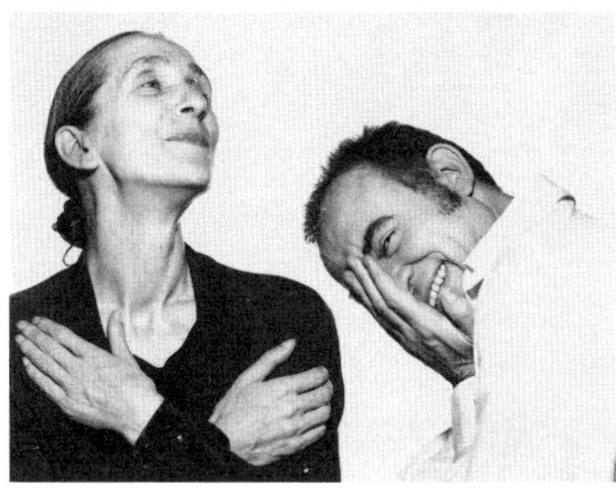

PINA, MON AMOUR

Germany—for CHRISTIAN LACROIX, that means one person:
the choreographer PINA BAUSCH. The couturier met his idol
for the first time in a Parisian working-class bistro.

The first arrive as early as 7:00 p.m., even though the performance does not begin until 8.30. By eight o'clock the foyer of the Théâtre de la Ville in Paris, where Pina Bausch, from Wuppertal, Germany, is presenting her *Tanzabend II*, is full. They are the hopeful—the countless Bausch admirers without tickets. They stand there, downcast, holding their little paper signs wistfully in front of them: "I will buy any ticket" or "I only need one" or even just "Please! Please!!!!!!!!!" They have hardly a chance as the performances of the Tanztheater Wuppertal were sold out weeks in advance. For a long time, Christian Lacroix, the forty-two-year-old Parisian fashion designer, has been in the audience at the Théâtre de la Ville whenever Pina Bausch appears there with her company. His most longed-for wish—to meet Germany's great choreographer personally—was fulfilled this summer. Lacroix invited Pina Bausch and VOGUE to lunch in a secluded, working-class bistro in Paris' twentieth arrondissement. We eavesdropped on the slow process of getting to know one another over *boeuf en gelée* and *rôti de pintade* against the hubbub of rattling dishes and the uproar of the beer-drinking workmen at the bar.

CHRISTIAN LACROIX I feel much more comfortable here than I do at the Ritz or in a chic apartment. The genuine Paris is in the process of disappearing, but in this district I can still feel its spirit. When I was asked with whom I would most like to have this VOGUE conversation, who held a special place in my life, a person who moved me, who made me laugh, cry and love, somebody who touched my innermost being, someone really quite exceptional, I immediately thought of Pina Bausch. I've only been to Germany four times and have never had any real contact with average Germans, have never had the feeling of German everyday life. Over the past ten years, my idea of Germany has been formed entirely by your dance performances. I first became acquainted with you through a television film made by Chantal Akerman. And, I wept during it. That's something I do not do everyday. That was in 1982. Since then, I've seen your troupe three times at the Théâtre de la Ville and, each time, I was overcome by the emotions you produced in me. It's difficult to explain the reasons. I feel an inner attachment, a perfect chemistry, which unites me with the world I am aware of, through another person. It could be that this meeting is not even necessary, seeing that I have the feeling that we have already met on another level, on the level of images, gestures, words, pieces of music and feelings. I can't come up with a better analysis than this: I feel that I have, in some way, been recognized. Each of us sometimes has the feeling that he or she has experienced things before and everything which you show appears to belong to the most profound depths of my personality. You work with gestures, with movement, aspects to which I have absolutely no access. I cannot even dance. I know that I cannot find an outward expression for my inner self.

PINA BAUSCH But you do express yourself through your work.

CL Fashion also destroys a lot of things. I don't feel guilty, because I'm not really planning to fly too high. But I hate fashion that exists merely for the sake of fashion. Fashion without roots, with no origin, which only exists to change something which does not need changing—like this district of Paris, the last honest corner.... Fashion, which exists only to take money out of people's pockets. I tell a story through my creations which cannot be written down. A little bit like the story of this conversation … just why did you agree to it?

PB I was surprised that you wanted to talk to me. I found it quite beautiful, a truly warm gesture, your wanting to talk with me.

CL You played a role in making my work more difficult and, at the same time, more stimulating. The movement you give to the clothes which you use was always a source of envy for me. For example, I wanted to ask you about the importance that clothing has in your work. I feel that the articles from the twenties and thirties which you use have retained their vitality through your work. They still exist today—through you. It would be impossible for some designers to imitate the impulse which you give your costumes. We lack the chemical contact between the wearer of the piece and the piece itself. A piece of clothing can never be as alive as it becomes through your work. I wish that, once in my life, my models on the catwalk could demonstrate the same sense of vivacity which you produce on the stage. How important are the costumes for your work? Who selects them—you or the dancers?

PB It's a bit more complicated. When I start working on a new piece I have no ideas, and therefore cannot say which pieces of clothing will be appropriate. Sometimes we have new costumes made, but usually I just let these things develop. In the first weeks of rehearsal, I ask questions which my dancers answer in words, gestures or scenes—and they often choose a costume which helps them to show the answer. It sometimes happens that they all choose the same costume or that they just stay in their rehearsal dress. It's important for me that the dancers are able to move in their costumes, that they feel comfortable in them. I don't pressure them into anything.

CL The "inner life" of pieces of clothing has always been a major problem for fashion designers, if I can say it that way. The dress lives from being worn. That's why I don't like fashion museums. There, everything is dead. There, we can't experience the movements, the feelings, the gestures of the wearer. I myself can't wear anything which is new. This is one of my father's shirts, the trousers belonged to somebody I can't remember any more, I bought the jacket at a flea market. I don't feel comfortable in perfect, new things. In one of my collections, I attempted to introduce the movements of your dancers into some of my designs—naturally without any success. But it was a good idea.

PB Of course, a lot depends on the person who ultimately wears the clothes—both in my ideas and in your work.

CL How far is Wuppertal, where you work, from Solingen, where you were born.

PB They are right next to each other.

CL I really must visit Germany and get to know it; I have the impression that something is lacking, that I'm possibly missing something. I can imagine how much fun it would be to speak German, not to mention the literature. I have a few German friends and am fascinated by their language. England also fascinates me. I love contrasts and it's a part of French culture to love English things. When you're young, you're sent to London. I was there in a very romantic period, in the sixties. You've worked a great deal in America; why not in England?

PB We have appeared in London and Edinburgh, but I studied and worked in New York. There are so many different things which come from New York that I just can't avoid being influenced by them. I'm talking about New York and not the USA. Today, there are so many good schools and so many good dancers, but the problem is that there aren't enough good choreographers. It's exceedingly difficult to learn choreography. You can learn a great many things, but fantasy is not one of them, just as an inner desire cannot be learned. There are no limits to fantasy; it shows its face here and then there. There are no rules.

CL It has become very modern to divide the world into nationalities. As we are speaking about Solingen: I met one of your dancers, Antonio, by chance and he told me about the city and the horror that occurred there. (*In 1993, four German youths set fire to the house of a Turkish family in Solingen. Five persons died in the flames.*) When I went home that day and opened the newspaper I had to cry again. It was not crying like a child, but crying out of anger. I'm always confronted with the question of how I can continue making my expensive clothes, safe and sound in my studio, assisted by a fine staff, good craftspeople who embroider and weave, completely isolated from the world. I wake up every morning, and go to bed every evening, with the same question—how can one remain normal in this world? The media and television have turned this into a trite question, but it's by no means trite. We have to fight, but how? I don't know if it's possible to fight through dance, but I do know that it is not possible to fight through fashion.

PB Why are you so sure about that?

CL Solingen made me think a great deal about this question. There are so many things happening at the same time, in Africa, Sarajevo, and I am sitting here in Paris starting work on my next collection …

PB But what happened in Solingen was nothing new. It wasn't the first time. The problem has existed for a long time and, naturally, has made a strong impression on us. I have also asked myself whether it's possible to keep on working when one fears that everything one does is senseless. Sometimes, I ask myself where I find the strength. I often feel depressed and helpless but, at the same time, I know that we are a company of dancers of many nationalities and that we all get on fantastically well with each other. If there are problems, they are always personal or artistic, never problems of race and nationality.

CL It's the same with us in the fashion house. We have very few French people; our staff comes from many countries. There is something very strong between us.

PB It's also important that other people in Germany recognize the cooperation in the company. So many horrible things happen in Germany, I think that generalization is dangerous. But it's very common. What do people expect of me, that I commit suicide? What can I do? I think that in these terrible times one has the duty to be optimistic.

CL Of course …

PB Flowers will continue to bloom every spring. I think that we simply must not give up, we must keep on trying, there is no alternative.

CL I don't want to make any comparisons, but it seems to me that it's much more selfish to be involved with fashion, it's much more difficult to say: we're doing something. On the other hand, your work is helpful and useful to so many, even if you're sometimes in despair. But the pictures which you conjure up are so poetical. I believe that no other audience is as involved as yours. The audience becomes a part of what is taking place on the stage.

PB The pieces have a life of their own. I can only attempt to come closer to my real feelings every time … It happens that our brain tries to understand things that our feelings have already comprehended.

CL How do you bring your people to express themselves purely through their feelings?

PB Precisely by asking them questions, often very many—whatever occurs to me, sometimes personal things. Over the weeks, the material grows into a new piece. It's extremely gripping to observe how much the individual risks in exposing himself. Some hide themselves behind clichés because they're afraid of opening up, especially in the group, seeing that they are not alone with me in a room. There is also a difference between men and women; women are usually more courageous. Men often attempt to protect themselves by taking things somewhat humorously. For me, that is a kind of escape.

CL What kind of questions do you ask your artists?

PB What was Christmas dinner like when you were young? Your first love? What do you do when you feel affectionate, embarrassed? And then I watch how the dancers move. I also watch how they move in everyday situations. It's interesting that, in specific situations, we often use the same gestures to express our feelings. Sometimes, I think that we're like a battery which loads or discharges electricity under specific circumstances. Gestures are an incredible language if you know how to interpret them.

CL Sometimes I think that, in a time like today, when so few read poetry, people like you are the real poets. Poetry is embodied in gestures, images, movement, in the theater—hardly in words.

PB I also think that feelings which certain clothes convey when they are worn play an important role.

CL For me, eroticism is only one element among many in fashion, such as the color and weave of the cloth. As a southerner, I have no difficulties with that, nor have I ever had any. Happily, I belong to a generation that had no problems with sex; it is our sixth sense. On the other hand, I believe that today, most people don't have enough inner freedom to be really what they want to be in our world. The nineteenth century, with its bourgeois, moralistic restrictions, is still very much a part of us. I see that in the male attitude towards fashion. Men are very modest; they refuse to dress colorfully, to give greater expression to their own feelings through their clothes. I'd love to be able to rediscover that former freedom which also used to determine what men wear. I don't make any clothes for men, mainly for economic reasons, because that would be a completely different industry with other rules and markets. Sometimes, I would like to clothe myself in pink, red and green, with embroidery up here. Today, everything is ruled by gray and white. We southerners do not make any real differentiation between men and women. With us, there were always people capable of sharing things and experiences with each other and doing—or not doing—certain things; but it was never a question of gender. In French, we suffer greatly from our lack of words when we are talking about such matters. We have difficulties in expressing our emotions. We only have *amour* and *amitié*, but love and friendship are not enough. There are so many feelings which fall between these two expressions. I have different feelings for all the individual people in my circle of friends. The decisive point is not sexuality; sex is unimportant. "Good sex" is like good cheese, good mustard, good wine. The femininity or masculinity within us shouldn't be so clearly defined from sexuality alone. Each man has something feminine in him and each woman something masculine. For me, Pina, you are a man. For example, at this very moment, I find myself much more feminine than you.

PB An acquaintance of mine works with a semi-precious stone which is suspended by a thread over the palm of the hand and begins, by itself, to rotate: with men in one direction, with women in the other. In my case, he discovered that the stone sometimes turned in this direction and sometimes in the opposite … and she told me that in her case, the rotation is in the "masculine" direction, but this changes if she is with a man.

CL My wife is perhaps sometimes more masculine than I am. We had decided not to bring children into this world, but today I regret it. In those days, we didn't want to risk it, maybe out of cowardice or fear. There is quite simply a very personal chemistry between my wife and me.

PB Why and when people have children, or don't have them, is a very interesting theme. It doesn't depend on the parents' intentions; often children come along at precisely the moment when the relationship is on the verge of breaking up. It is a matter of continuity, of keeping going. That's what it's all about. I find it amazing that nature is so powerful—that we are so powerful and haven't been destroyed, so far.

CL My favorite word is "tomorrow"; maybe it's a kind of escape from the present. I still have utopian dreams. That's what young people of today appear to be lacking. They have no dreams, no fantasy, no strong imagination. I would be happy if I could believe in the next generation. The fashion world really doesn't interest me at all—this world of money and superficiality. I love to take hold of things, real things, with a life of their own. We tore out the walls in our apartment just to be able to fit in my grandmother's furniture and bathroom fittings. Even though, now, the water is not always hot enough … I simply can't stand having things around me which have no connection to me personally or with the past.

PB I find it terrible when people throw beautiful old things away, just because they feel they have to be the same as everyone else. But why stay in fashion then?

CL I've sold my soul. And what are your visions for the future?

PB Dancing!

CL Me too! Me too!

From VOGUE 09 / 1993; The conversation was recorded by Gideon Bachmann

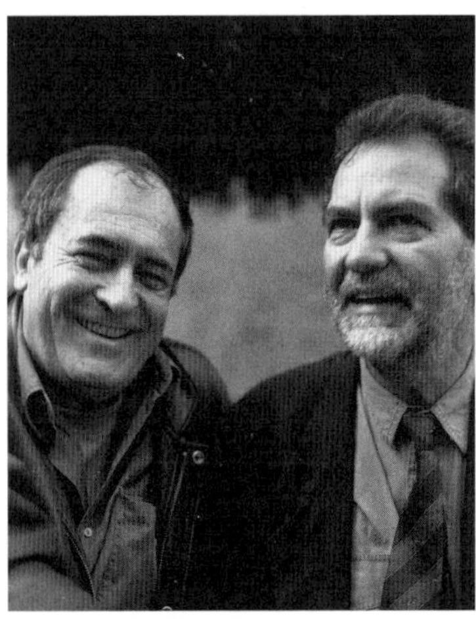

LOVE—A WILD ANIMAL

Buddhism and desire, exorcism and eroticism: The film director
BERNARDO BERTOLUCCI meets the grand master of cinema,
EDGAR REITZ.

There are two famous addresses on Via della Lungara in the old Roman district of Trastevere: the largest prison in the city and the (now closed) film club "Filmstudio." In the seventies, both gave this narrow cobblestoned passage the reputation of being a hideout for the political left. The revolt of the prisoners, who rioted with fire and banners on the prison roof, and the aesthetic revolt of the political films which formed the program of the cinema each played their own part. In those days, nobody paid any attention to the fact that Count Torlonia had his private sculpture museum on this street. Nobody, except the count himself, who then speedily transferred his museum to another storage place and converted the now-free spacious garden into apartments for rich Romans. After some years of haggling with the authorities (of course, the apartments had been built without approval), official blessing was granted and today many famous Romans live here in these magnificent surroundings—among them, Bernardo Bertolucci. His German colleague, Edgar Reitz, who visited him there, had just arrived from Parma, one of the cities in which he had introduced Italian audiences to his film *Die zweite Heimat* (*The Second Homeland*)—an enormous success, by the way. Bertolucci had just arrived from Paris, where he had shown the Dalai Lama—who had never before been to a cinema—his latest film, *Little Buddha.*

EDGAR REITZ How did it actually start—you and Buddhism?
BERNARDO BERTOLUCCI First of all, Elsa Morante, Moravia's wife, gave me the book *Millarepa,* a Tibetan story which, by the way, Liliana Cavani later used for one of her films. In my own second film, *Before the Revolution,* the actress Adriana Asti tells a little story which comes from this book. And then, there were so many other occasions in my life when I came into

144

contact with Buddhists; once, in Hollywood, I went to a friend's place and they were all sitting there on the floor in the lotus position, listening to a lama reading from the *Book of the Dead*. I also experienced an initiation, but it was more like a game, a little bit superficial. Four years ago, I was approached with the idea of filming the life of Buddha, but that didn't interest me. Not the legend, in any case. What did attract me, however, was the confrontation of the ideas of a person who lived 2,500 years ago with today. In my opinion, this kind of confrontation is the only reason for making historical films. The camera only exists in the present.

ER But what about human memory, the memory of things experienced?

BB That is an additional aspect of our work. That which you create out of your memories and put in front of the camera stands in front of the camera today, only today. That's what makes this process erotic—the expression of desire—in this case, the desire for something already experienced.

ER Does that make the camera an erotic instrument? Does it maybe even take the place of touching?

BB Yes, it can be such an instrument. Although what it replaces is more like voyeurism. I have been analyzed by psychiatrists throughout my entire life and have always believed that looking through the lens can be compared with peeking through the keyhole of one's parents' bedroom.

ER Where, of course, you do not see everything—just like when you look through the lens you only see the section within the frame. It's the same as with the people in front of the camera who have aspects, internal aspects, which I can't see. Don't you also think that one never really knows what will happen when one looks through the camera? In spite of all the problems beforehand?

BB That also fascinates me and I think that that is the reason why I like *Heimat* so much. In the film, you left so much space for the unexpected. I've always felt the constant attack of life on that which you attempted. Our colleague Jean Renoir once told me that you should always leave a door open in the studio. Somebody you aren't expecting might come along and that is the most wonderful thing in cinema. The Jews have rituals where a door is left open and there is an empty chair at the table in case the Prophet Elijah should appear.

ER On the other hand, I don't like improvised dialogue at all; I'm more interested in precision in language. Camera movements also don't turn out to be beautiful if they aren't precise and predetermined. It's the same with you, one clearly sees the thoroughness of your work.

BB Of course. I don't just start shooting and hope for miracles from the actors. I simply mean that, particularly when I'm making exact plans, I let myself be inspired by the reality which presents itself. This prevents the audience's preconceived ideas from being fulfilled, so that it becomes vital, unexpected. This openness towards everyday happenings also keeps me fresh, creative, open to new impulses. No mater what one films, one always films reality, even when all the ingredients are artificial. The filmed becomes reality. One always produces that which is often called *cinéma vérité*. Always. I can remember that in my film *Last Tango in Paris* I once told Maria Schneider that she should question Marlon Brando about his childhood. When Brando heard that he said: "Give me half an hour." And in that half hour he thought about his answers and wrote them down. That is how it became reality.

ER You left the door open. I've noticed something in all your films; the stars are not stars but, in some way, themselves. Simply people. In German filmmaking, there is never enough money to work with world-famous actors, but I've always been somewhat afraid of that. This world of international cinema, with all its financial and human calculations, is a cinema of closed doors. Nothing is allowed to remain open. That is the real difference between American and European cinema: the open door—that is what European cinema is about. Any story that deserves being told is an open story, one with an unknown ending—one that has something which surprises us. It's the same in real life, where an experience, with some unexpected aspect, gives us the sensation of being alive. I feel the opposite in American cinema: that one always attempts to control everything, even the outcome. Just imagine: the people who took control of a huge continent discovered things that were unknown to them. They simply needed security, things they knew, moral support, ideas to give them a foothold. How do you get your American actors to deliver this more open impression?

BB You have to drag them out of their shells. I took Burt Lancaster, Donald Sutherland, Robert De Niro, Sterling Hayden and the others to Parma, took them into the country, into the cowshed we used in *1900*. They stepped into cow dung, Lancaster attempted to milk a cow; they discovered new approaches. There are also American directors—Scorsese, for instance—who transform their actors into real people. It's also a question of language, of film language. The American audience sees things differently than the European one; they are accustomed to other forms. For me, a bigger problem today is that European audiences seem to have a longing for this American film language. And, seeing that the perceptions of the world today are, to a large extent, visual as a result of the images we are stuffed with from the screen and television, we are in danger that the world will soon only be seen through American eyes. Wim Wenders said that Europe will disappear because soon there will be no more images of it. It's our way of seeing things which is endangered and, because of this, our notion of ourselves.

ER And what do you think we can do about it?

BB I think that American directors have to help us. They know that we are essential for the survival of their form of cinema; there is a kind of reciprocal dependence. How often has it happened that a European director has done something new only to be copied, ten years later, by Hollywood! American cinema has always absorbed ideas emanating from Europe. There is also an exchange in the other direction: it's false to think that each individual film has an independent identity. By the way, that brings me back to the ideas of Buddhism: it is said that everything in the world is dependent on others. That's like the individual organs of the body which cannot exist alone. That's why Buddhism also says that no person can exist alone. We are all dependent on each other.

ER Even as a filmmaker, I never have the feeling of standing alone: everything I do has a connection with the history of the cinema and with the things other filmmakers do or have done before me. Why do you think that people always demand originality from us?

BB That you evoke other films and other filmmakers and that your work develops in this connection in no way indicates a lack of individuality. It is always your viewpoint, even when you see something, through your own eyes, which somebody else has already seen—through their own eyes. It is all a conglomeration of feelings and thoughts, like waves in the ocean. There were moments when I was tempted to agree with the opinion that cinema is the art of a dying age. Today, I no longer have this impression because it's not true that television has "won." Quite the opposite: in television—in good television—the language of the cinema is becoming more and more obvious. Nothing whets my appetite more for filmmaking than your television production *Heimat*. I know, it was a film, and I saw it on the large screen, but without the structure of television it would never have extended to thirteen episodes. At the most,

it would have been a film lasting five or six hours, instead of fourteen, or twenty-six as was
the case with *Die zweite Heimat*. My "homeland" is the cinema. My memories, my feelings,
my legacy, my life experience is the screen.

ER I feel the same—cinema is today's muse. I am convinced that, if he were alive today, Richard
Wagner would be a filmmaker. He also wanted to unite all art forms, appeal to all our senses.
That was the romantic dream—to unite all art forms and all languages in order to discover
a universal means of communication. In every art form you see a reflection of reality, not its
reproduction. Even cave paintings depict a humanization of reality: the dangerous lion loses
its character by being integrated into our world of experiences. It is still dangerous, but the
threat is no longer random, it has become domesticated, become "human."

BB The lion has now become controllable. However, it would be too simple to say that the lion
has lost its dangerousness through becoming an image. But every picture is a sort of exorcism.
Precisely as it would be too simple to say that the camera is an erotic instrument with which we
could make love "without risk." In spite of this, love stories are also great exorcisms.

ER When I tell a love story in a film, I can survive it. It is the same as with a wild animal:
my instrument is fantasy and, when I think of the danger awaiting me outside, I'm no longer
capable of leaving my cave out of fear of nature. However, the image provides my fantasy
with another solution; the image helps me to enter into nature once again. That's why art is
a medium for my survival. Also being in love. You call it exorcism; for me it's more like magic.
In my life, in my real life, filmmaking acts as a kind of magic which makes it possible for me
to keep on living.

BB Right. If they took filmmaking away from us, we would die of thirst; they would be taking
away the possibility of defending ourselves against life. We are very privileged; we have succeeded
in making people like us—and are paid for it—through the use of our defense mechanisms.
I think that that is mainly a result of people identifying themselves with their self-defense. We use
a means to defend ourselves, of not perishing, and we offer this means to our audiences, who
can participate in our activities. Towards the end of the sixties, we all thought that the camera
was something of a means of attack, that it could be used like a machine gun to improve the
political situation. That was a petit-bourgeois illusion. At that time, all of my friends prostrated
themselves before the Cultural Revolution and, at the beginning, I also regarded this as theater,
which was taking place on the streets with millions of actors unarmed except for a little red
book, attractive. But I quickly found out that the repetition, time and time again, of the same
slogans was much closer to fascism, and I slowly found my way back to the center. That brings
me back to your first question: at that time, Buddhism started to answer my questions. Buddha
sat under a tree and, for years, nourished himself from a single corn of rice each day. His life
was slowly coming to an end and he heard how a musician, drifting by on the river, explained
to his pupils that a string should never be drawn too tight because it would then snap. It should
also never be too slack because then the sound would not be beautiful. That is the golden mean
of Buddhism and that, in a way, is my motto today. I never gave in to the temptation of the
various extremes.

ER At that time, I made a documentary with Alexander Kluge with the title *In Gefahr und
größter Not bringt der Mittelweg den Tod* (In Danger and the Greatest Need the Golden Mean
leads to Death). That was a typical slogan of the time. It was concerned with the occupation
of houses. We filmed a police operation from both perspectives—from inside and outside
the house. A huge machine began to demolish the house as soon as the last student had been

driven out. I was still on the grounds with my camera. I just managed to escape into the apartment of Alexander's sister who lived next door. I began filming small, apparently unrelated objects because I had no idea of how to express myself. In those days—1968—dreaming was forbidden …

BB In those days, one didn't have the right to explain things, everything had to be pressed into an intellectual corset. And we were required to be of use to the revolution. There were a lot of extreme statements at that time, such as: "Poetry has no practical purpose—get rid of it."

ER But being useful is also a dream! Sometimes artists are so desperate that they cherish this dream.

BB In my opinion, this idea of "being useful" is quite new. It has found its confirmation in the ongoing, rampant capitalism of the past forty years. It's a paradox that this idea was picked up, in 1968, by the leftists. That's why I called the use of the camera as a means of attack a petit-bourgeois idea. There was a strong petit-bourgeois dimension to the entire 1968 movement. The whole concept of usefulness only became possible with the birth of capitalism.

ER This concept turns us into instruments; we become the performers of usefulness. And we were threatened with solitude. They told us, if you aren't useful you'll remain alone. That was the terrible demagogy of that period.

BB It was only in China that I learned how the renunciation of our Western idea of individualism—how one can never be happy without being different from the masses—could lead to real contentment, to the sensation of feeling in harmony with the masses. This was a fundamental discovery for me. And I'm not talking about Mao's communism, but 4,000 years of Chinese culture. This discovery was an enormous shock for me.

ER A shock—isn't it also fear? Fear of something which we do not know? Maybe of harmony? What do you feel when you observe this unreachable harmony?

BB Ecstasy and fear, at the same time. Fear, because I can never attain this harmony and because I can never forget who I am—a Western man. Ecstasy, because I have a notion that my ego is my worst enemy. Buddhism does not teach that I should relinquish my pleasures and passions; it teaches that I should give up my selfishness in the perception of these pleasures and passions. Maybe it's an additional paradox for us, seeing that we have no perception of ourselves, not to mention our lusts and passions, without self-deception. Of course, I cannot claim that I'm capable of giving up my ego, but I am beginning to understand that many of the problems I experience in my life are the result of my selfishness.

ER This perception, that selfishness is an enemy, is something that every artist experiences and the ecstasy is something an artist senses when he feels united with another. In my work, I always feel these moments of utter joy when I sense the greatest harmony between myself and my crew, my actors and my staff.

BB And, on the screen, this feeling of harmony produces beauty!

ER It goes beyond the screen. This form of very long films is a social event. If you see an episode of a film every day—or every week as is the case in Italy—you always encounter the same people and, sooner or later, it becomes irresistible to talk to them. For this reason, you need a cinema with a lobby suitable for discussions. In Munich, we sold tickets which included dinner and beer and it was only the premature broadcasting in television which forced us, after six months, to stop this kind of presentation. And, seeing that each film represents a stage in my life, its presentation is also personally important to me. I had the most wonderful experiences in Italy, where people in the cinema identified so closely with the film that they smothered me with genuine love after the showing. And, as you know, Italy has the most beautiful women, so you can imagine how that felt to me as a sixty-year-old man. In Milan, the audience collected money in order to be able to rent the cinema for an extra day and the 500 in the audience had their picture taken by a photographer. They sent me the photograph with 500 signatures—can you believe that! When I tried to leave the cinema in Parma, up the center aisle, people pushed their way through to try to touch me!

BB I know that when you're thirty you can still resist the women who look at you that way after a screening, and so on. Now I'm fifty-three, and it's not so easy any more. It's like avoiding death: feeling that a woman finds us attractive. What else happened in Parma? Can you tell me about it?

ER It was a strange feeling. On the one hand, I felt a little embarrassed, because everything was so public, then I can't just …

BB If it had only been one or two …

ER Yes, but 500 are just too many … but I have to admit that the possibility of being loved is a motive for so many things, one of them is filmmaking.

BB It can also be dangerous. You can become addicted. You can imagine what it was like with the *Last Tango* … I was thirty-two years old and the film was not only a success all over the world, it dealt with love, with physical love, with the possibility of sexual attraction without taking anything else into consideration! It was something that one doesn't give up so readily, something that one would like to experience one more time.

ER When you are so young, you think that you can experience and survive all those things. You feel that you have to take advantage of everything life has to offer.

BB Moravia said: "Success is like a good meal: you have to eat it and then throw it up …"

ER I also find that success is, almost always, an erotic experience. But success in Italy is something special. I don't come from Protestant Germany—the land of Bach, Nietzsche and Wagner—but from a Catholic culture. You find it in the south of Germany and along the Rhine—wherever wine is grown. Rome is the center of the universe for me. That's why my success here is so important: it's like a homecoming. It's as though I had roots here. I walk across the Forum and it's like I have memories here, memories of these roots. That is why the erotic feelings I experience here can also be explained on another level: it's a catholic feeling, a feeling of a more powerful expression, of surrendering to the entire universe of emotion. You can understand it if you compare it with the repressive, Protestant Teutonic spirit of the north, where every erotic expression is suppressed and rejected. Even eating must be correct and unerotic. And, there has to be a moral justification for every kind of pleasure. Where Bach sounds erotic it is, at the same time, religious. Each and every erotic expression has to have a justification.

BB We have the same thing here, but with the Catholic church. We find it repressive and restrictive, just as you find the Protestant church.

ER But just look how sensuality thrives here! The colors, the clothes, the cuisine—even sin is more colorful … That's why my success here in Italy has something of my first experience with love, with eroticism, with sin. It's forbidden, but we do it in spite of everything. That's why this success in Italy gives me this feeling of coming home.

From VOGUE 03 / 1994; The conversation was recorded by Gideon Bachmann

BERNARDO BERTOLUCCI — EDGAR REITZ

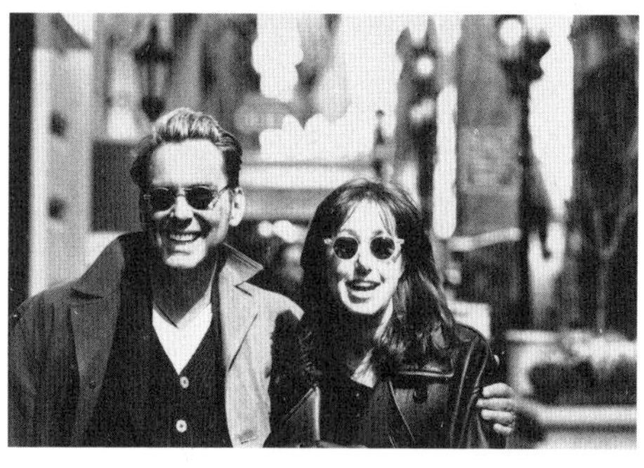

SUMMIT FLIRT

DONNA KARAN and her colleague WOLFGANG JOOP
on the power and machinations of fashion, and the objects and
meandering paths of love.

"You look fantastic," calls Donna Karan, on spotting Wolfgang Joop in the lobby of the St Regis Hotel in New York. The two then embrace in a welcome hug. Donna Karan is the first to let go, but retains a firm grasp on Joop's arm, peering intently at his face. "Absolutely astonishing," she says, "where did you get this tan?" Joop smiles boyishly and explains that he has done a little sunbathing in Monte Carlo. Donna Karan, who has spent the past weeks working intensively on her collection, rolls her eyes. "Why don't I ever have the time for things like that?" she says, before guiding Wolfgang Joop into a quiet corner of Lespinasse—the hotel restaurant.

The two quickly determine that they are not actually hungry, choosing instead to order tea and water (Karan), a Cappuccino (Joop) and a glass of fruit juice each. The VOGUE conversation begins spontaneously, without the usual small talk, with the topic of fur, a controversial fashion point for a number of reasons.

WOLFGANG JOOP You've created some wonderful things with fur.
DONNA KARAN At the moment I'm not doing anything like that anymore. Fur is a very personal matter. Just like leather, or the question whether someone eats meat or not. Everyone should decide for himself on that.
WJ I did designs for fur earlier as well. To be precise, I did designs for everything that came up. As a freelance fashion designer, I was having to support a family and children, so I accepted all orders. At the time, I felt that I was going to be sick at any moment—not because of the moral questions associated with fur, but simply because I saw too many dead animals and not enough beautiful clothes, you know? There's no sense in killing an animal if you just make an ugly fur coat out of it. There's that advertisement by Christy Turlington, where she says she would rather walk around naked than wear fur. And yet she was always walking

about in those Mongolian lambskin trousers. I mean, what's the big difference between a lamb and a mink, as far as the moral aspect is concerned?

DK So you don't do any fur designs now?

WJ I wouldn't accept any more fur coats in my collection—it's too ladylike. I've never lived in a social environment in which I had contact to the nouveau riche. I'm more comfortable with talented beginners, with the avant-garde, with artists, students and my daughter's friends. Fur doesn't fit in with them.

DK I think that you perceive the international fashion business somewhat differently than I do.

WJ Really? I thought that German fashion had a lot in common with American fashion.

DK Are you serious?

WJ Yes. Both are based on purely commercial foundations. If you look at fashion in London or Paris, it's much more eccentric and frivolous than American and German fashion. Someone like Karl Lagerfeld, who comes from Germany, would never have made it in Germany or America. Because the Germans like to be, well, average. And the Americans are sometimes overanxious about standing out too much or being too sexy.

DK It's strange that there are these differences between countries in something with such a global culture as fashion. Paris can still be viewed as something completely different compared with Italy or Germany. For example, when I think of Italy I think of neutral fashion and flat shoes with crepe soles. With Paris I think of colors and pumps, sex and fantasy. And as soon as someone mentions New York, I think of black and an aura of power.

WJ And Germany?

DK For Germany I think of clear lines. Of green.

WJ I think more of beige. Beige and navy blue.

DK And Italy—that's terracotta and neutral stone colors. Or faded colors. But the one universal language, the one we all use today, is the lowest common denominator in youth fashion: blue as in blue jeans. Everyone understands that—jeans, T-shirts and leather. As far as the language of fashion is concerned, the world is really unified by jeans. If you were to put young people from around the world in a room together, all wearing jeans, you wouldn't be able to say where the individuals were from. A fascinating thought.

WJ I thought that whole image was great.

DK So you mean that when my customers buy my clothes they're also getting a piece of New York?

WJ Yes, and then there's the name: Donna. That name really means woman, after all.

DK In Italian. As an American I never really thought about it.

WJ I liked your whole look and your confidence from the first time I met you, at a fabrics fair in the seventies. And now I know why your collections are always such hits. Because they use the concept of a business woman in a world dominated by men, a woman who accepts men. You aren't such a feminist; you're not so grim as to banish men from your world completely.

DK Well, I'm very much in support of women's rights—freedom from oppression, freedom of expression. I hate fashion designers. (*laughs*) No, what I mean is that I don't like it when designers dry to dictate fashion. And that's impossible nowadays anyway. People have become much too independent. For me, fashion means celebrating people's feelings and perceptions, their language, their sensuality and their sexuality, because that's what fashion is about, after all.

WJ You don't shy away from showing your fashions on older women. That makes it easier for potential buyers to identify with it. And that expresses the latest trends in our culture. You only have to look at women like Meryl Streep, Cher, or Tina Turner—all goddesses of our times.

DK That's because we're all young, you too. We were treated as youths when we were young. We didn't grow up in a bourgeois environment, and we reject those values. I never really understood nylon tights, for example. The point of them really escapes me. They're artificial, they're uncomfortable, and I always say that you shouldn't put on anything that you couldn't do gymnastics in. You should only wear things that are comfortable. As simple as it sounds, that philosophy has given women more freedom than almost anything else.

WJ But I'm sure you've noticed that fashion today has a new kind of eccentricity—stiletto heels and the like?

DK Yes, on the other hand I think that the idea is often one of: "I want to play around with my sexuality a bit." It's fun, and that's good. The pomp that the rules of fashion often bring with them doesn't really gel with the image that we have of ourselves—that we're artists. After all, we don't like to be bound by rules, do we?

WJ (*Laughs*) Fixed rules are always awful.

DK Technically, I mean biologically speaking, we are getting older as well, but women today aren't like they were when their parents were young. If we play around with make-up, then it's because it's fun, and we use natural make-up. And we know that there are a few indispensable things that we can't do without, but those are nothing like the masks that women wore for decades in order to meet some expectation or other. We don't want that, and we don't have the time for it either. It's the same with clothes. Everyday I get up at a quarter past seven, do my exercises, take a shower and then throw my clothes on. I'm not interested in any clothes that I can't just slip into.

WJ But there must be a lot of women who are rich, married and don't have to work—who have nothing better to do than worry about their clothes. I don't know any women like that personally, though. At least I've never met any. Neither of us design clothes for women like that. But if I look at the Paris collections, I get the impression that the fashion designers there have lots of customers like that.

DK True. I more or less look to myself for inspiration. My designs are primarily conceived for me.

WJ It's the same with me. I simply design things that I want to wear myself.

DK And that's why I think that anyone can be a fashion designer. I mean there's no one in the world who couldn't design clothes. After all, everyone knows what they like to wear, don't they?

WJ In Germany I often get enquiries from men saying that now that the children have left home their wife would like to be a designer, "and I'm sure she would do a good job of it." And then they say: "because she always dresses impeccably." They really just want to know if I need an assistant.

DK (*Laughs*) And you probably say yes, right away!

WJ Well, it's usually better to have people with experience. I taught in Berlin for six years and some of the stuff that my students produced, well, I don't wish to be mean, but …

DK … you said who the hell is supposed to wear this?

WJ Or I said something like: "I'm sorry, but that's nothing new, it's last week's Gaultier jacket." They were always trying to reinvent the wheel.

DK I get the most motivation from working directly on the body itself. With a draft design it's possible to do anything. You can use the pencil to sketch any lines you want. That's the artistic freedom you have, and it's a great thing in itself. But on the other hand, you need the practical implementation: You need to know just what restrictions you can subject a foot to, and how to make a shoe fit most comfortably, how to make a leg feel at home in a sock, with everything fitting just right. If I have a living model to try my things on, then they can tell me where there's a problem. They do it unprompted, without me having to say anything. How do you work when you're designing women's fashion?

WJ I have assistants who model for me. But first of all I create a concept. To begin with, I don't even have a particular material in mind. I just write down the concept: what I'm trying to do, what my ideas are, what my vision is. Then my assistants and I take the concept to fabric fairs. I'd be lost otherwise, because I like all the materials that I see (*laughs*).

DK I usually tend to begin with the material.

WJ Female fashion designers like you usually have a very practical idea of the female body zones. That's good, but sometimes I like the way my male colleagues look at it. Karl Lagerfeld, for example. Sometimes I have the feeling that he hasn't actually seen a woman for a long time, because his clothes don't appear to be very practical, but on the other hand he manages to completely reinvent woman. That's the surprising and creative thing about him. Sometimes women tell me that they've found their style. That's always a bit sad, because to me it sounds like Ravel's *Bolero*—the same notes over and over again.

DK I understand what you're trying to say. I would get bored very quickly.

WJ What's your zodiac sign?

DK Libra.

WJ I'm a Scorpio. I get bored very easily. Variety is the spice of life, after all. Is it true what they say about you and your husband? That you were married to another man but couldn't forget about your current husband throughout your marriage?

DK (*Smiles*) Yes, that's true.

WJ What an extraordinary love story!

DK Hmm, yes it is. The first man that I married was my best friend, but the one my heart had chosen was a different man altogether.

WJ And why didn't you marry him the first time around?

DK Because he didn't want to marry me.

WJ So how did you change his mind?

DK I'm not so sure myself. I just know that it took ten years. I tend to make a beeline for what I want.

WJ It's just that sometimes you get what you want a bit later—like last season's fabric (*laughs*).

DK Timing was never my strong point.

WJ Librans always take their time.

DK Well, that certainly applies to me. Making decisions is one of the most difficult things for me to do because there's always a risk of triggering a disaster, and all I want is happiness and harmony. I find the fear of making a decision almost unbearable, there's always a chance it's the wrong one.... Every time I say yes, there are millions of dollars and the jobs of thousands of people at stake. Few people can appreciate the pressure that we are under. I bear the responsibility for a turnover of hundreds of millions of dollars. And then, when I see the containers with all of the clothes that I have ordered, I ask myself who is going to buy it all. It's like playing roulette or investing your money on the stock exchange. It can be really nerve-wracking at times.

WJ Yes, those are the bad days. But you must have enough good ones as well, don't you? After all, we've both arranged our lives the way we want. Unlike a lot of people, who never consciously plan one moment of their lives. They're just the puppets of others, with the exception of two or three weeks a year when they're on vacation.

DK Yes, I'd like to be able to live like you, honey. You have everything you could wish for. You're talented, you look good and travel the world. It's enough to make a person really envious.

WJ But you don't live badly either. You're happily married, you have a beautiful daughter, manage a big company and own homes in New York and the Hamptons …

DK … which I never get time to see. I'm just glad that my daughter gets to enjoy it all at least.

WJ It's the same with my house in Potsdam. I inherited a wonderful farmhouse near Sanssouci and had it completely restored. Now the house is so elegant that it's no longer homey. That's why I hardly ever use it.

DK It's probably best if we don't talk about my impoverished lifestyle.

WJ I know, dear, you're terribly poor. I pity you wholeheartedly.

DK It's true, I don't have a cent! People always have this idea of me as a successful business-woman. The truth is that I don't see a single penny of it. All of my money is invested in the business. You only get paid if you work for others.

WJ Don't worry, we'll have a collection for you.

DK (*Smiles*) You should. I've lived in the same apartment for nineteen years now. If you were to see my apartment, the shock would kill you. You would drop dead on the spot. You can't imagine the conditions I live in. I don't even buy furniture. I've got nothing. No paintings, no jewelry, nothing. No possessions whatsoever.

WJ No jewelry? So what's that glinting in your hand?

DK Fashion jewelry from my own production.

WJ You designed that? Great. I'm doing the very same thing. This is a Joop ring, for example.

DK That's nice, I really like that.

WJ I can get you one if you want. What size are you?

DK No idea.

WJ Give me one of yours. (*tries on one of Donna Karan's rings*) You've got very slim fingers.

DK Well yes, you're a man, I'm a woman. What I wanted to ask you was, how have you got on in New York since moving here?

WJ I love New York. It's a city full of foreigners. You can hear hundreds of different languages and accents every day. And then there are all of these fantastic buildings. It's like a science-fiction novel. Beauty and the beast live next door to each other. And everything is so enormous. The bad things are just as enormous as the good ones. And everything is in cinemascope. Do you know what I mean?

DK Is that why you moved here?

WJ I moved here when I launched my perfume. At the same time the press in Germany began to wonder if I had maybe been an East German spy. A couple of journalists came up with this nonsense. They wrote that I had worked for the communists. Absolutely ridiculous. My family suffered so much, first under the Nazis and then the communist regime—that's completely inconceivable. I was glad to be able to get out of the whole situation for a while. I didn't want to go back, either. And that's also due to the tendency of the German press to build you up and then, when you're successful, they lose interest and start to demolish you.

DK Yes, that's really nasty. The problem in my life is that I register all of the negative things and try to do something about them. My persona is characterized by the desire for consolation, harmony, love and solidarity. That is the quintessence of my path in life. For example, I find it really hard to see all of the suffering and misery in the world, and then to think that I do nothing more than design clothes for other people. How could we manage to get this tiny planet into a relatively functional state, what could we contribute to that? For me it's just making fashion—honest, genuine fashion. That gives the world something of a different perspective. These things come at a price, of course. But instead of buying three, four or five blazers, you could just buy one and see it as something special. It's easy too get wound up about price tags if you have no idea of how the thing was created. I know the worry and anxiety that goes into a particular collar or lapel. The fact is, someone has had sleepless nights because of this object. What price can you put on that?

From VOGUE 07/1994; The conversation was recorded by Rogier van Bakel

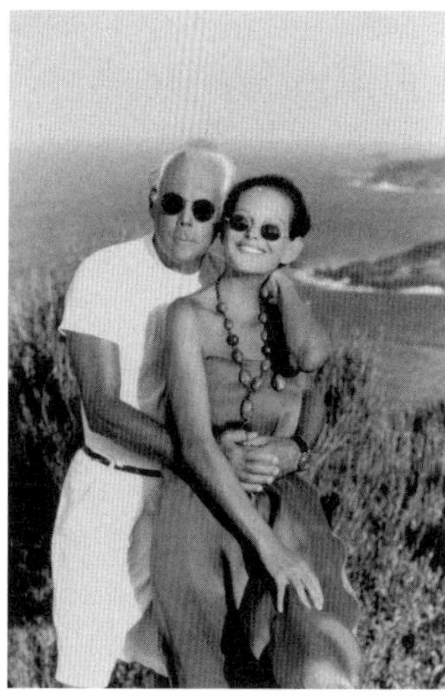

THE SUM OF FRIENDSHIP

CLAUDIA CARDINALE and GIORGIO ARMANI
discuss trouble with the law, getting away from it all, and real life.
The common denominator is fashion.

Years ago, when Claudia Cardinale tried on her first Armani outfit it was immediately clear that the diva and the designer have similar tastes in fashion. Since then, that concurrence has been extended to other areas; the customer has become a good friend. The two meet for a VOGUE conversation in the fashion designer's palazzo in Milan's Via Borgonuovo. The evening before had seen Armani present his 1995 spring/summer collection. A great success—following the awkward situation of a few days before. Like most of his fellow fashion designers, Armani appeared before the fearsome examining magistrate Antonio DiPietro—accused of offering gifts to tax collectors in order to gain their leniency.

Now, however, following the successful show, the taciturn fashion designer is in the best of moods, almost euphoric. Reminiscences of the previous summer are exchanged: the two had spent a holiday together in Armani's house on the island of Pantelleria, near Sicily. (*This is where the VOGUE photos were shot.*) The mood remains upbeat even after Cardinale broaches the current difficulties.

CLAUDIA CARDINALE I remember the first time I wore one of your outfits. It was in Cannes, at the presentation of Werner Herzog's *Fitzcarraldo*, in 1981. I've still got it; it was a blue Faille skirt and a flowing top. I've never swayed from you since. It's as if I found peace and harmony in your style. I tried other things, in Paris, but I can't get used to anything else.

I was really worried when I heard that DiPietro had summoned you. I called straight away, just to say that you were in my thoughts. In France, they really make a meal of what's happening in Italy. But we can talk about something else if you like

GIORGIO ARMANI Well, I may well have preferred to start on a different subject, not get straight to the nitty gritty of this, but while we're on the topic we may as well discuss it. As far as I'm concerned—although I had no hand in it personally—I didn't like this so-called "standard practice," but I was assured that this is how it was dealt with in all companies. You know that I'm more of a strict kind of person, so I didn't just have a guilty conscience. I was also annoyed at having to pay. I should have put up more resistance, but it looks like none of the other companies did either. As far as politics are concerned, all I can say is that I expected a lot more from the present government. Maybe our hopes were too high. I assume that you're better off living in France.

CC We all hoped for more. People voted for this government because they had had enough, they had had their fill of the squalor and corruption that you found at all levels of society. I was in Rome at the time of the election, and I recall the atmosphere well. Now, I get the impression that everything is in a state of confusion; politics—at least what we read of politics in the newspapers—is more like a football tournament. I'm still Italian and it's the events in Italy that I get wound up about, not those in France. Your colleagues—how did they react in this bribery thing? I saw a lot of them at your show yesterday. It seems to me that people show a lot more solidarity than they used to.

GA They probably realized that we're all in the same boat. But not all of them. Actually a couple of them weren't there yesterday, although all of them were invited. Versace wasn't there, Valentino and Ferré weren't either. Recently, at La Scala, one of them even walked passed me without greeting me. By the way, I have to confess to being a little envious of some of them. I find them better, freer, less pinned down. I saw the Dolce & Gabbana collection, and I'm envious of them. They have fun and can make what they want. If I decided to design basques or bodies or bizarre bathing suits, then the managers of the Armani boutiques around the world would gang up and lynch me. I can make the whole system start to topple just by making a skirt shorter or longer. I bear responsibility. I'm the emperor, but being emperor is no fun. That's what I said to them: "Don't let them put you on a pedestal, you'll never be allowed to get off it." And your colleagues, Claudia? My impression is that they're less malicious and aggressive than mine.

CC I was never envious of my colleagues. I watch them, observe them like a spectator. Some of them I admire very much, like Jeanne Moreau or Fanny Ardant. I like to converse with them, discuss things. I have a more superficial relationship with others. I'm not great friends with any of the Italians, also due to the fact that I stay with my family when I'm in Rome. Of my colleagues that dress in your clothes, I only know Ornella Muti, a nice girl; I know Sophia Loren, our national diva. Of course, sometimes someone ignores me and lets me know that they see themselves as something better. But that's not important if you are secure in yourself.

GA And where does that security come from?

CC Maybe from what I've done, from the directors I've worked with—especially Visconti. It may seem trivial, but he taught me how to move, how to walk. He thought that I was taking too small steps; he made me increase my stride. You have to measure the space. He was right: beauty comes from things like that. Gestures, movements—they're almost more important than the face or the body. That doesn't change the fact that I'm extremely hard on myself.

I inspect myself very closely before putting on a bathing suit. I don't know how women who aren't one hundred percent find the courage to get into a bikini. I wouldn't dare.

GA I saw you on the beach this summer and I can assure you, you don't need to worry about that at all. But I think that this perfectionism is part of the respect that you have for other people.

CC Yes, I'm a perfectionist, I can't stand slovenly people. When I lived in Hollywood it used to really irritate me to see women on the street with curlers in their hair and face masks on. Beauty care should be a very intimate ritual. I have to be alone; I need absolute quiet. The presence of someone else would disturb me.

GA I know it's banal, but in my opinion beauty is a question of what's within, a demeanor, a manner of being. Do you agree? There are no set rules, measurements, hairstyles or colors. But that doesn't mean that I don't need a particular type of woman to present my clothes: tall, slim, broad-shouldered and with a radiant smile. You have all of those characteristics …

CC But before—you may not remember—I was fat, I had broad hips and a big bust, and I was constantly dieting and suffering from it. Now that I eat what I want—pasta, of course, sometimes even sweets, always Italian cuisine—I no longer get fat. There must have been a certain point when something changed in my life.

GA As you know, for me the ritual of eating is more important than the food itself. I especially like certain northern Italian dishes that are traditional in my family—agnelotti and tortellini, homemade—but I have to eat them with company, sitting at a well-laid table. Even when I eat alone, I never make do with just a panino. And I don't trust restaurants where the chef interferes with everything—and that's the case with most of them! I like simple, unadulterated things. I never diet, I'm naturally moderate, we're very similar in that, don't you think?

CC If I were to listen to you without knowing you, I would think that you had no faults whatsoever, that you were balanced, confident and moderate. But I know that you're tough and demanding—if someone leaves you there's no going back.

GA And I'm jealous as well: of my family, of my staff, my friends. I'm possessive, hard, that's true. I never give praise and get angry when things don't work out. But my staff knows that if I say nothing then I'm satisfied, everything is okay. It used to be worse. The turning point for me was the death of Sergio Galeotti. I will never forget that, quite the contrary, I consciously recall it so that I don't get accustomed to a life without him, without the pain. Since he's been gone, I've become much calmer, more sociable, I think of others a bit more. For example, now I would take the time to ask an employee why she looks sad.

CC Somehow or other I've been spared a lot of pain, I seem to have managed to avoid it up until now. I know that I have it all before me, and I'm afraid of it. I have family, brothers and sisters, and my parents are still alive. Yes, I'm afraid of suffering. Maybe that's why I never go to the doctor, like some kind of wild savage. And anyway, I believe in fate, that everything is predetermined, that it's useless to resist it. I'm afraid of growing old as well, like everyone, but the fact that I had a daughter at forty has extended my youth, put my body-clock back a bit. I worry about my daughter, that's normal. I'm like all mothers, I stay up until she comes home, I can't sleep before she comes in. I'm not afraid of anything in particular, just everything, and it's also because she isn't afraid of anything—she's fearless.

GA The only thing I'm afraid of, as you know, is surprises. That's why I try to plan everything in advance, for today, tomorrow, the day after tomorrow. If I knew that I was going to die next week, I would accept it. Everything would be under control, there would be no surprises. I simply can't bear surprises. But for the time being, I still see myself as being immortal, and I read the passing of time in the faces of my loved ones more than anything else. One of them turns gray, another is getting wearier and slower—the aging of the people around me frightens me more than my own. Sometimes I have my own moments of weakness though, and then I take stock of things: I'm sixty, what have I done, what can I still do in the time I have left?

CC And afterwards?

GA I believe that there's something afterwards. We can't just be met with a black hole. It would be too horrific for us, as intelligent beings, to have to think that there was nothing waiting for us on the other side. And then there's something that gives me hope, almost certainty even: I often have the feeling that Sergio is there in some form.

CC I have hope as well. I couldn't live without it. I need hope for my children, for the people close to me. I can't accept the idea that nothing comes afterwards any more than you can. But I must confess to thinking of the future as little as possible. I dislike thinking of the past just as much, to be honest. I love the present, my life here and now at this moment. There's a lot to do right now, a lot to be considered. Because I hate being afraid, I stop myself from contemplating on what has passed, and especially about what is to come. I have wonderful memories, especially of work, but I don't wallow in them. And then of the people that I have encountered, people who gave me something or simply loved me. I don't know, Visconti, Zurlini and Pasquale Squitieri. Of course, as I'm sure is the case with most women, my fondest memories are of the birth of my children.

GA I have the past within me, but I don't dissect it. The future is different, as I said, I would prefer to plan everything in advance; I already have to think about winter '96. To put it bluntly: as I've achieved all that I wanted to achieve in my work, and a great deal more, I would like to have a more fulfilling private life in the future, more time for my family, my friends. I sense that I can longer stand these superficial relationships, the "Ciao, how are you?" and nothing more. In the future, I would be happy if people said: "Armani? He isn't just good, he's a nice person, too."

CC I know you and I can confirm that, but I suppose that isn't the case with everybody.... With regard to taking stock, I think that I've also achieved what I wanted to achieve, and a lot more. I've made four films a year for thirty years. That's different today, of course, but I can't complain. The times are long gone where directors tailored their films to their actresses, but I'm still working. I read lots of scripts, but as I have the luxury of not having to worry about money, I can wait until a project comes along that really grips me. And anyway, I worked a lot: one hotel after another, one plane after another, and I liked it like that. Then I met Pasquale. I think that now I'm entitled to think of myself a little bit, have some fun …

GA I know what your idea of amusement is, I've seen you. Do you remember that awful discotheque on Pantelleria this summer? I wasn't sure if I should be taking a diva like you into a dive like that, people told me not to. But then you really let your hair down, danced like a fury and would have preferred to stay even longer …

CC That's true. I really like going out, getting done up, the admiration. I just like to live.

GA The only thing that I still enjoy doing is stopping thinking, switching off, letting myself go. That happens in August, when I'm on holiday. I'm in charge the whole year, making decisions, organizing things; in August other people can decide things for me, and I return to a kind of childlike state. And I like it, it's a real pleasure for me, it clears my head. I don't have many other distractions. Ceremonies and the like are a real grind for me. Yesterday, too, with the meal after the show, I was happy when I was greeting six hundred people one after another.

It was nice to have all of those people around me, but it made me feel sorry as well, because there was no opportunity to talk to anyone. In cases like that, I always say, "Thank God that there are three or four people I can count on," family and friends, like you. We don't see each other that often and don't talk about ourselves much, but I know that you are there, a distant friend. I'm happy when you call me from Paris. Maybe we then talk about clothes, but that's okay, isn't it?

CC We're both much too cagey to talk about the things that really matter to us, but that doesn't alter the fact that we're friends. My family is my oasis as well. You know, it must seem like a strange family: with Pasquale in Rome and Claudia in Paris. People talk about it, they always have. They don't know that we see each other practically every week, that we speak to each other every day.

GA Why did you decide to move to Paris five years ago?

CC It was coincidence, really. I had been there a lot with work and felt very comfortable there. And I have some French blood on my mother's side. In Tunis, where I was born and lived for almost twenty years, French was my first language …

GA That's where that accent comes from; it sounds so irresistible to Italians, with your deep voice. Do you think that you'll come back to Italy one day?

CC I don't know. Sometimes, when I see the worst side of Italian actors, I'm glad to be away from it all. At other times, I'm incredibly homesick for Rome …

From VOGUE 01 / 1995; The conversation was recorded by Isabella Bossi Fedrigotti

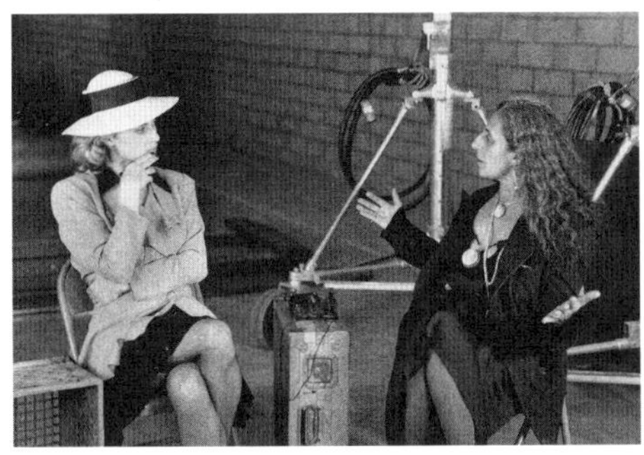

BAD GIRLS, GOOD MOTHERS

ISABELLA ROSSELLINI and the photographer SHEILA METZNER
on passion, men, and a woman's weapons.

Hollywood is used to pampering its stars. We know the stories, we have heard about the limousines, the 600-dollar-a-night suites, gourmet meals and domestic staff. The scene is anything but luxurious on the set of "You, Murderer," the episode of the slapstick television show *Tales from the Crypt*, in which the main role is played by Isabella Rossellini. The giant studio is void of any atmosphere and astonishingly cool. Time and again, director Robert Zemeckis goes through the two scenes that are to be shot today. The whole thing takes a good fourteen hours, during which Isabella Rossellini scarcely has time for an hour's break, eating a small salad from a plastic plate. The fact that she is able to spend her lunch break in the company of her old friend photographer Sheila Metzner, who has so often managed to capture her in particularly seductive poses, helps her to relax. Being beautiful has never been difficult for the daughter of Ingrid Bergman.

Today, however, the similarity between mother and daughter is particularly striking. No coincidence—the script requires her to be dressed and styled like her mother. The conversation between Sheila and Isabella is both lively and relaxed. Isabella enthusiastically agrees to continue the conversation the next day at the swimming pool of the Four Seasons Hotels in Beverly Hills, where she is staying during filming. The result is an open discussion over cappuccino and fruit juice. The towels are fluffy, the service perfect. Hollywood has lost none of its flair.

SHEILA METZNER What I like about you is that you're always so natural.
ISABELLA ROSSELLINI Am I? Thank you. I have to work hard at it. (*laughter*)
SM Wearing your mother's hat—that must be pretty strange for you.
IR I'm only doing it because Bob Zemeckis wants me to. I'm always getting calls from people asking if I'm interested in doing a remake of *Casablanca*. No, I wouldn't dream of it! But this seems to be a nicely surreal idea, and Bob is such a good director—if I do it now and never again, then only for him. I think that my mother would have liked it, too—or she would at least have found it amusing. You want to make films as well, don't you?

SM Well, up till now all I've made is a short, nine-minute film. The dialogue is good and I think that the film is original. It's a homage to Man Ray. I wanted to see if I could manage to bring still photos to life.

IR What if you were to make silent movies?

SM I love dialogue! Beyond a certain point my photos are very complex—I constructed these great scenes. I found it frustrating to have an action and not do anything cinematic with it. That's why I'd like to get into directing more. I've always preferred working with models that wanted to act, and if I come across one with talent, then I advise her to take acting lessons.

IR For me, working as a model is the same as being on the stage. The body language is the same, the expression, the concentration, the feeling that comes over you, and the emotion that you have to show in your face; it's all the same. Unfortunately, film people often say: "Oh, she's a model, that'll never work." You come across that kind of discrimination far less often with photographers. How did you get into photography? Did you just pick up a camera?

SM I've always sketched and painted. Lots of my friends were photographers when I was working as art director for an advertising agency. One of my really good friends happened to be a photographer, he was a kind of mentor to me, and one day he said: "You should take pictures. You live like an artist and you have a good eye." So I thought I would give it a shot.

IR One of the reasons why I never pick up a camera, let alone take pictures, is that I'm in awe of you and Richard Avedon or Bruce Weber. I could never be as good as you are. Well, I got up the courage to act, despite my parents and their great talent, but I didn't start until I was thirty. I think that I needed time to build up my self-confidence.

SM I didn't start taking pictures until I was twenty-nine. When I see some really good Chinese film or other then I get depressed and think: "The world doesn't need you, just drop it." But then I realize that I can't give it up that easily; there are particular stories that interest me. It's not the style, it's the content.

IR That surprises me, because you have such a good eye and your work is always so graphically perfect.

SM The story is what interests me. I love literature. When I was a child I was always going to the library and taking out as many books as I could—and that was thirteen—and then I would read them all in one week. I still do that today. My bed is surrounded by books.

IR I don't read very much. Not novels, anyway. I read biographies. And I like animals, that's why I read books about their behavior. Of course, I try to read up on the characters that I portray, about the times they lived in, their countries. And doing that I realized that everybody comes from the same base—that there's no reason to panic and say: "How on earth am I to play a murderer?" You can do it! (*laughter*) And when you've pushed aside your prejudices or your fears, then the feelings that you want to show just come naturally. Just sit back and allow them to wash over you. After a while you realize that you're filled with this enormous anger or aggression, or whatever the script and the role dictate. It doesn't happen when you read the script for the first time. It has to develop.

SM Well, once I actually felt that I could kill someone. Really and truly kill someone. No kidding.

IR Why? Jealousy?

SM Of course!

IR Yes, of course, (*laughter*) me too. I had a boyfriend who confessed to an affair with another woman. Luckily they were in another city, otherwise I would have shot them.

SM I'm glad you refer to both.

IR Well, I especially wanted to kill him. But maybe her as well. Or maybe even her first. So he could see her suffer and die—and then he would be next. I saw how it's possible to lose control. Especially if you have a gun or something within reach.

SM Darling, you don't need a gun. You can do it with your bare hands. (*laughter*) For my part, I just imagined how it would be to kill the other woman. I wanted to leave him and kill her. I even tried to call her. She wasn't home, luckily. I didn't know where she lived, but I would have asked her on the telephone and then gone there.

IR What ridiculous things we do! After all, at some point in our lives we could be on the other side of the situation, getting a call from a desperate wife telling us to keep our hands off her husband, and then we'd say: "Listen, it has nothing to do with me, talk to him about it!" (*laughter*) I like this viewpoint, looking at things through the eyes of others. It's the fruit of adulthood.

SM But some people just get meaner and meaner.

IR Maybe. In my case, I've noticed that I get more pleasant as I grow older.

SM I would like to think that it's the same with me. More pleasant towards others.

IR When we grow up, reality is so staggering; feelings are so intense, complex and different.

SM My own life has developed like a Dostoyevsky novel, or a Hitchcock film. But growing up can also go horribly wrong.

IR Lots of dreams go unfulfilled. I'm always telling my daughter to learn what they teach her at school, that you can make it if you really want to. But I also tell her she should go through life as if she were on a surfboard, because life has a stronger influence on you than you do on life. There are more important things. Don't cling to your hopes too much, life is like a wave, and you either ride it as a good surfer or fall off and drown—in bitterness.

SM Do you think that there's a difference in the way Europeans and Americans approach life? The Americans have more of a "We'll make it" attitude, but often it isn't very realistic. If your fate dictates that you're a postman, you can try as hard as you like, you'll never be president of the USA.

IR In Italy they teach you to accept things, to conform. They point at someone and say: "The fact that the sun is shining is enough to make that person happy." But at the same time, this behavior is a very philosophical attitude towards life. I learned that from my father. He had an easygoing side to him, despite all of his creativity.

SM That's a very enviable ability. It's almost spooky how much strength it's possible to call up. I think that that's what character means: if it doesn't kill you, it'll make you stronger. But tell me, you're such a busy woman, do you still find enough time to spend with your children?

IR Yes, but a lot of the time we don't do a great deal, in the time between eight and nine in the evenings, for example. We watch television, and if there's nothing interesting on, then we read a bit, talk about what's in the papers. Although nothing is actually going on, these are really precious moments, because I can really get close to my daughter. Well, you know how it is yourself. You've got five children. However did you manage to have five children?

SM How?!

IR No, I know how. (*laughter*) But did you want to have so many?

SM I wanted them. Honestly, I really wanted them. Jeffrey and I were the absolute exceptions. We got married when almost all the men we knew were leaving their wives for younger women. It was a time of affairs and divorces. And suddenly we were swimming against the current and decided to get married. I was already pregnant at the time. But we would have married anyway.

I had a vision of home and family, and then I made the whole thing like a feature film. Jeffrey was terribly busy at the time, his best never seemed to be good enough. (*laughter*)

IR Were you frustrated that the children took up so much of your time?

SM On the contrary. The moment I left the agency, I had the feeling that I could become the artist that I wanted to be; I even thought about becoming a doctor.

IR You would have made a great doctor—one of the crazy, creative kind. If you had operated on me, I would have been afraid that you would tie my insides up into highly artistic, but painful, bows. (*laughter*)

SM If I were a surgeon, I'd sew you up with very intricate little stitches, that's true. And my bandages would look great! I actually did that. I put a bandage on my arm and made sure that it looked good. My children loved it when I asked them to pretend they had broken an arm. Then I put it in a sling so that the kids could show off and flash the fantastic bandage around. I always had that sense of drama in me. Our family life was almost like a scene from a play or a film. I got the children to look like the roles they played in my imagination. If one of the daughters was supposed to be a French schoolgirl, then I dressed her like one. The children let me get away with it for years! (*laughter*)

IR It almost sounds as if you were trying to compensate for something. What were you like as a teenager?

SM I must have been awful. The reason was that I didn't consider myself particularly attractive. And now people often say: "You look really great." That really hits me. Why are people telling me that now? Why did no one say that to me when I was thirteen and really needed to hear it? But as far as appearances are concerned there's always something to worry about, at all stages of life. When I was twenty-three I thought I had reached the end of the road.

IR I was the exact opposite. Giggling the whole time, happy, never grumpy or withdrawn. It was only when I was twenty-one that I started to laugh less. And then I thought, this is what it means to be grown-up, you don't laugh anymore. But two years later, I started to have fun again, and later I realized that I had actually been suffering from depression—my father died at that time. For some reason I didn't make the connection between his death and my sadness. I thought I was at the end when I was twenty-one. My father was a kind of god to me. I remember sitting on a plane and being scared, and he said: "You don't need to be scared." And I relaxed straight away.

SM The power that parents have!

IR It's phenomenal. But power also requires subservience. That's the awkward thing about it. If women admire a patriarch, even if he abuses his power to subjugate them, it's because he guarantees them freedom from fear. He constantly assures them that everything will be okay. Not that my father put pressure on me; I'm not referring to him here. But whenever I find myself taking a lover who gives me a sense of security, and who I find attractive for that very reason, then I remind myself that I have to be prepared to stand up to everything that I come up against. I want to be able to confront my fears on my own.

From VOGUE 02/1995; The conversation was recorded by Rogier van Bakel

ISABELLA ROSSELLINI — SHEILA METZNER

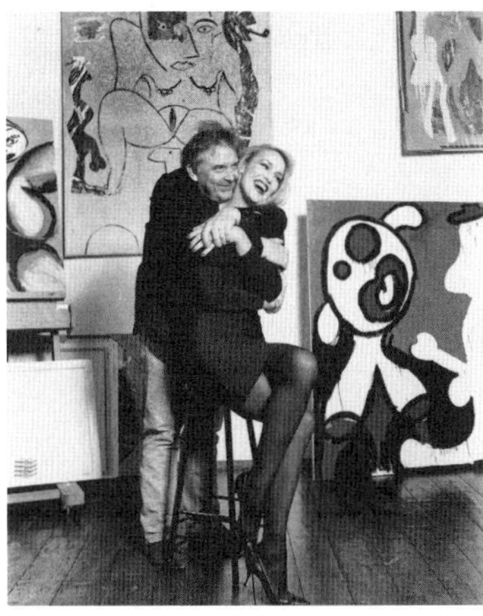

DREAMING OF DRAGONS

Sex is still great for JERRY HALL—and it's best of all with
Mick Jagger. Here, she discusses vices and virtues with her old friend
DAVID BAILEY.

They have been friends now for two decades—but it takes months to get even old friends such as these into the same room together. Finally, Jerry Hall and David Bailey meet one mild spring morning in Bailey's photo studio. As always, he is wearing jeans and cowboy boots. Her hair is freshly highlighted and well groomed—his, quite clearly, is not. Jerry Hall is wearing a tight black skirt and low-cut top from Hervé Léger, high-heeled shoes and an enormous Victorian diamond ring, which Mick Jagger gave her on their engagement. Bailey—photographer, lover, husband to some of the most beautiful women in the world, including Catherine Deneuve, Jean Shrimpton and Penelope Tree—has become rounder and grayer. "I'm like a rhinoceros," he states defiantly. "Ridiculous, but elegant."

JERRY HALL I must have a ciggy before we begin. I need it to get me started. You know what it's like with us addicts.

DAVID BAILEY I'm surprised that someone with a strong character like yours smokes. I can't believe that you're that weak.

JH Last year I quit twice—one time for three months. I'm going to try again as well. I never smoke in front of the children. They still think I've stopped. I'd die if they found out. But you know what happens when I give up? I move on to other bad habits.

DB Like what? Do you start picking your nose?

JH No. I start drinking too much or eating too much, for example.

DB When I stopped smoking—that was when I got fat. Funnily enough, it was Catherine Deneuve who got me to quit. I'll never forget it. One day she said: "You know, the only reason you don't give up smoking isn't that you're weak. You're strong. You know that you can stop, and so you aren't bothered." That was very clever Deneuve psychology. I'll never forget that—and it worked. I always smoked and drank at the same time. And the day I stopped smoking I gave up drinking as well. That was twenty years ago, and I've never started again. It made me fat, though.

JH Heaven forbid! So, Bailey, when are we going to make our film? Did you know there are two films with me coming out? One of them is already in the cinema, *Princess Caraboo*. I made another one last year with Richard Harris, *Savage Hearts*, and then shot a film last November with Eddie Murphy in Los Angeles, called *Vampire in Brooklyn*. I play this really awful, neurotic woman from the Upper East Side. A bitch, an absolute bitch. He kills me and everyone breathes a sigh of relief, you can actually hear the audience sighing with relief: "At last …" We had to work nights on it, every night until six in the morning. The movie business isn't easy.

DB And I often think that it's not all that glamorous, either.

JH It's much less glamorous than modeling. You know, when you work as a model they all take good care of you. When you're making a film you live in a dirty old trailer, no one comes and sees how you are.

DB What kind of films do you like? Have you seen *Reservoir Dogs*?

JH Yes, of course. But I have to say that I find it too intense when there's so much violence. It doesn't bother some people, but too much violence in films gets to me.

DB It doesn't bother me at all. I mean, you have to trust the audience a bit. People are able to differentiate between films and reality. My seven-year-old son can! His favorite film is *Alien*. I mean, he shouldn't really watch it until he's eighteen, because of the violence. But he comes to me and says: "Dad, I know those are just special effects." He's not stupid. But what's your favorite film at the moment?

JH Well, I really liked *Princess Caraboo*. I mean I have a part in it, and I think it's great. Kevin Kline plays the lead role.

DB I recently saw a really bad film: *Prêt-à-porter*. It's not bad, it's worse than that, it's awful, terrible. I mean, I know the fashion business is shallow, but I thought Altman could have done something clever and funny with it. Something amusing! But the film's just chaotic. No ideas! It's absolutely awful. One of the worst films I've ever seen. Really! Don't go and see it. Go and see *Pulp Fiction* instead. One of my favorite films of the last ten years. Have you seen it?

JH No, I haven't because I don't really like John Travolta. Although I worked with him on *Urban Cowboy* and must say he was pretty good. Filming itself is really good fun! You put so much of yourself into it. You need quite a bit of courage and imagination. It's hard to get the thing exactly how you imagine it. I never have problems with the lines. Luckily I've got a good short-term memory. I only have to flip through something and I can remember it. Two weeks later everything's gone. Great for school and filming, but not much else.

DB So you prefer being a film star to a model?

JH As you know, I'm one of the few models who loves her profession. I've been in it a long time now, as well. When I started in Texas I was fourteen. And then I went to Paris—I was almost sixteen, and I met Antonio Lopez, the fashion stylist. He was great. God, how I miss him! He was so talented. He was the one who introduced me to Helmut Newton and got me into my first fashion show, where I met Marie (*Marie Helvin, Bailey's ex-wife.*). A month later I was on cover pages everywhere. And then there was an article about me in *Newsweek*, about this young, sixteen-year-old little thing that had taken Paris by storm. Then, when I was almost eighteen, I got an offer to come to New York.

DB And what happened? You fell in love with Brian Ferry?

JH Brian Ferry hired me for the cover of his new album with Roxy Music. The funny thing is that on the cover of his first album was Carey-Ann Jagger—who is now my sister-in-law. At the time it was really cool, being on an album cover for Roxy Music. One look was enough and I was hopelessly infatuated with Brian.

DB In one of his suits?

JH No, in him. He was so good-looking.

DB And then Mick snatched you away from him?

JH Well—Brian was away a lot, and I had very bad manners.

DB I remember calling Mick at the Ritz, and he said: "Guess who I'm with." And I said: "Jerry Hall?" It was a just a wild guess. Sometimes that's all it takes. Intuition. But you two suit each other. You know he was a real rogue when you met him. It's like with me and my wife: She knows that I couldn't say no if one of those gorgeous models were to come on to me. But Mick was really lucky to find you.

JH And this year we'll have been together eighteen years.

DB Did Brian really go mad?

JH He sure did! It was really hard, because it was in all of the papers. Very unpleasant.

DB What was it like? Did you break a lot of hearts when you were younger? Did anyone ever break your heart?

JH My first boyfriend in Texas dumped me. That was really tough. He was my first lover, and I was absolutely devastated. I was fourteen or fifteen.

DB You started early.

JH Well, you know, in the countryside there's not much else to do.

DB How old were you when you lost your virginity? I was fifteen, and it was in an alleyway in the East End. How old were you?

JH I was fourteen.

DB Can you remember it? You lived in the country; was it in a haystack? In a barn?

JH Shame on you!

DB Did he take his spurs off?

JH He left me for an older woman. She was nineteen.

DB Better than if he'd left you for a twelve-year-old. Don't you get lonely when Mick's on the road so much? What do you miss most?

JH The sex. That he buys the drinks. My ideal weekend is to be in bed with Mick in a hotel. That's my idea of paradise. Not so long ago we spent a great weekend at the Carlyle in New York. It was terrific. From time to time you have to get away and spend time on your own. It was great to be able to act like we did when we first met. Most couples forget what it was that first brought them together. They forget what it's like to be a couple. Every spare minute you spend talking about the children, about bills, things in the house that have broken. It's a real drag. We've had our bad times as well, and I think that that was partly due to the fact that for years we never traveled alone. We do that now, and it really does us the world of good.

DB It must be strange, living with a sex symbol.

JH True. I've got this enormous fan T-shirt, it reaches to my knees, and on the front it says: "I screwed Mick Jagger." I sleep in it. Sometimes you really need something to laugh about.

Life's too serious otherwise. I still swear by dancing the night away from time to time. Getting drunk and having fun. Most of the time, at home, I'm mom, a housewife.

DB And how do you spend your time? You've got a house in the West Indies.

JH That's right. We spend Christmas on Mustique. And then we have a house in France, as well, where we go in the summer. And we have a house on the Upper West Side in New York, but we aren't there very often, only occasionally with work. Mick has an office there. These days New York is too dangerous for the kids. I don't like to take them with me. The children go to school here, in London, to a day school. We didn't want to send them to boarding school. Even if it means that I have to do a lot of homework at the moment. I have to walk around and buy all of these math books. But being a mom is really fun. I get up at seven. One of the children is usually in my bed. Somehow they always manage to end up there. They come in and say they've had a nightmare or something like that. Doesn't that happen to you as well? No? You're probably really strict. Mick is very strict. He doesn't let them get into bed with us, but when he isn't there they come in anyway. I try to be a good mother. But I find that being a parent is a very hard job. You have so much responsibility.

DB When you were a little girl, did you know that you were going to have a career? I always knew that I was going to make it big. The art historian James Harrison once visited the East End and walked through the street where I grew up. He met a woman that I knew as a kid and she told him: "I knew Bailey when he was thirteen or fourteen, and he always said to me, 'Better to meet me now, I'll be too busy later.'" She was right. I always knew that I was going to be successful.

JH Well, I had a lot of imagination. I come from a family of five girls. We were all tall and slim. And my mother always used to say: "You should be proud of being so tall. Stand up straight. You're heavenly amazons." She taught us that we could have whatever we wanted in the world. Nothing is impossible. And you know, once I had an erotic dream involving Mick. After swimming I fell asleep on my bed. I must have been twelve or thirteen. I was probably looking at a poster of Mick before I fell asleep. And in the dream it was a dragon with a tail. It may have symbolized a penis.

DB And what do you fantasize about today?

JH About Mick.

DB Do you have any other fantasies?

JH Well, I certainly wouldn't tell you!

DB I don't just mean erotic dreams. I mean dreams about what you still want to do in your life.

JH Oh yes, I want to play the leading role in a film directed by you. That's my next big goal. I'm waiting for you to give me the starring role, dear, where I can really shine. By the way, Mick has just signed an absolutely fantastic contract.

DB Really? Is he playing a part or doing a film production?

JH A production, with Steve Tisch. So, we have to come up with a project. Then I'll sleep with the producer and get the parts.

DB I'd rather you slept with the director. Do you collect art? Does Mick get angry when you spend a lot of money?

JH No. But I spend a lot of my own money. I often buy him paintings and sculptures for birthdays and Christmas. He likes those kinds of presents best. But you know I'm on the board of trustees at the Tate Gallery. I appear at those charity events and help collect money. They don't really pay much attention to my opinion when making their purchases. But they're building a new museum of modern art and they need a lot of publicity; so they need someone who generates public interest. I'm sure they didn't want me for my knowledge of art or good judgment.

DB Are there any living painters that you like in particular?

JH Well, he's been dead for a long time now, but the last exhibition that I really liked was Poussin at the Royal Academy. I thought that was great, all the naked women and lovely naked men and cupids, wonderful.

DB I find them silly. People are having their guts ripped out and these little cupids sit around and smile sweetly. That has nothing to do with real life. There's no beauty in art any more. If you look at a Baselitz or a Julian Schnabel—they aren't beautiful. Beautiful pictures are so smug. It's easy to lull yourself into a false sense of security. Artists should be provocative. They should make you think. There's no room for beauty in painting.

JH Why is that? People don't paint attractive landscapes. You hardly ever see that any more.

DB I think that part of the reason is that photography and film do that. I don't really like landscapes. But if I were to buy a landscape, then it would probably be one photographed by Ansel Adams.

JH Do you know what I actually collect? Photos! I think that Edward Curtis is great. You know, his Indian photos, they're wonderful. And Brassaï, and all those Hollywood pictures, I think they're great. Cecil Beaton, I've got lots of his. And I've got lots of Warhol pictures. He painted me, you know. And every birthday, every Christmas he gave me one of his little paintings: dollar signs, or a chocolate box, or a few desert flowers. They're worth a lot of money now. Photographs are often not so expensive.

DB And what about David Bailey?

JH Oh, I've got a great picture of Mick as Chairman Mao, that you took. I buy your photos as well, of course I do. I bought two recently. Very expensive.

From VOGUE 05 / 1995; The conversation was recorded by Fiammetta Rocco

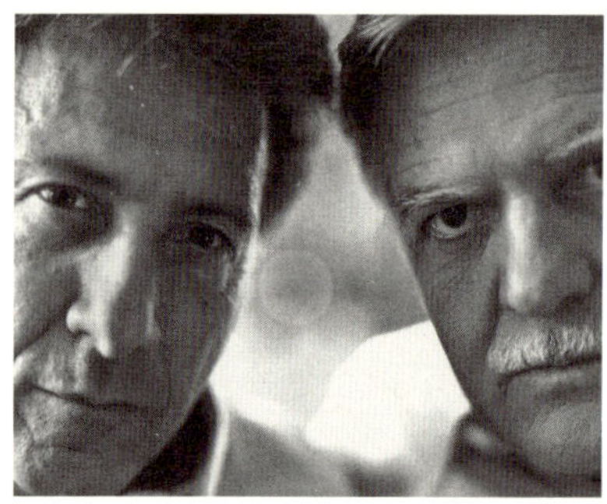

A LOOK INTO THE ABYSS

DUSTIN HOFFMAN and cameraman MICHAEL BALLHAUS
were brought even closer together through a dramatic event,
an event that sets off a conversation about cinema, women,
and the mystery of human existence.

A Bach piano concerto ripples crystal clear through the two living rooms, flooded with California sun. "Christoph Eschenbach and the Hamburg Symphony," says Helga Ballhaus with a friendly smile. "A piece of home in Hollywood." It's not the only reminder of home. On the wall hangs a picture of the flowering bushes of Krumme Lanke near the Ballhaus family's Berlin apartment in Zehlendorf. Michael Ballhaus has been living in the United States for a dozen years, in a New York apartment and in this huge L. A. mansion with its pool and guesthouse, not far from the movie studios. In the course of these twelve years, Ballhaus, who first made a name for himself as "Fassbinder's cameraman," became one of the true Hollywood greats, an award-winning cinematographer in great demand among directors like Mike Nichols and Martin Scorsese.

And Wolfgang Petersen as well, with whom he made the thriller *Outbreak,* starring Dustin Hoffman. Michael Ballhaus had worked with Hoffman once before. Ten years earlier, they collaborated with another German director, Volker Schlöndorff, on *Death of a Salesman.* But the two men, who are almost the same age, became really close friends due to a recent dramatic event, tells Ballhaus: "My wife and boys, Florian and Sebastian, stayed in Berlin when I was called back to Los Angeles to prepare the Robert Redford/Michele Pfeiffer film *Up Close and Personal.* I hadn't been feeling well for several days and then suddenly one morning I collapsed in the bathroom. When I regained consciousness, I was spitting blood, a lot of blood. I could just barely drag myself to the telephone to call the emergency number 911. The hospital notified my wife in Germany, who, in turn, called several of our friends here. Dustin was the first to respond. He came to the hospital and told the doctors that I was under his auspices, and there began to unfold the magic power of a movie-star—everybody at the hospital started jumping. A short while later, three specialists from the university appeared in the emergency room. The situation was terrible, but Dustin's presence gave me incredible strength.

Four weeks after the operation (they removed a stomach ulcer), Dustin Hoffman and Michael Ballhaus meet again for the first time for this VOGUE conversation. As Hoffman gets out of his Range Rover and walks toward the house in rough work boots, Michael Ballhaus comes out to greet him. The men embrace.

DUSTIN HOFFMAN My God, you look marvelous. Fantastic. It's hard to believe. (*turning to Helga Ballhaus*) This man has the strength of a bear.

MICHAEL BALLHAUS I feel good.

DH What are you doing with yourself all day? Don't tell me, you're back at work already.

MB No, I cancelled my next job. But I get a pile of scripts every day, some of them very interesting. I read a lot. And I enjoy my free time. I stay fit, take long walks, and every day I feel a bit better.

DH Have you ever had a closer call in your life?

MB Never. Many people say that you saved my life. From now on, I'll be your slave—forever.

DH Terrific, a slave. But you saved your life yourself. Did you know before this happened that you're this tough? I couldn't believe how stoically you endured all those tortures. Did you ever have that kind of pain before?

MB No. I thought I would faint if they put another one of those tubes, thick as a sausage, down my throat. As you know, unfortunately I didn't conk out. It was down my throat for forty-five minutes.

DH In your place, I would be ruminating day and night about this "eerie encounter" with death.

MB I do incessantly. I reflect on it. Every night I dream about being in the hospital. But I must tell you, despite everything, it was a positive experience. I'm sure it was one of the most decisive experiences of my life.

DH I'm sure you changed as a result of it. Changed as a person, and changed as an artist. Your work will become even more profound, more grounded. The doctors told me: "He needs an operation," as they were pushing you down the hall on a stretcher. It must be tough, I thought, to be in a strange hospital, with strange doctors, and without family, so I went with you. When we came to the hallway leading to the operating room, I was told that I couldn't go any further. The image is still in my mind. Michael, laid out on a gurney, blazing lights, snow-white walls. Without thinking—just to say something—I say goodbye with: "Just look at how bright everything is here." And you are lying there, half in a daze, and you mumble: "That's what I just thought too."

MB It's true. I really was watching the lights …

DH It was as if a thunderbolt hit me, a man on the verge of death, about to go under the knife, takes note of the atmosphere of the surrounding staging area. Really unbelievable. I bet one day we'll see this scene in a movie! (*pounds the table enthusiastically with his fist*) One day you'll recreate this atmosphere in front of your camera, and it'll be a realistic thriller. To me, all this was unbelievably suspenseful. You were aware that you might die.

MB When the doctors thought that the bleeding had stopped, I told them: "No, I'm still bleeding." At first they wouldn't believe me, then—I had already lost two and a half liters of blood—they stuck a tube down my throat once again, and I thought: "That's it, now I'm done for."

DH I was deeply moved when you said: "I had a wonderful life. I'm only sad on account of my wife and children." I didn't want to contradict you. One doesn't contradict a man who is experiencing the greatest pain of his life. But what I wanted to say was: "What are you talking about, man, this is only the first curtain, the end of the first act. Not the end …"

HELGA BALLHAUS How many acts does life have?

DH I hope three. We're now in the second act.

MB This means, then, that you've gotten the first act behind you?

DH I had a close call, too, and was confined to the hospital for a month. Afterwards I became dependent on Demerol. I was in my twenties then, but it changed my life. Everybody believes himself to be God's personal favorite and lives by the motto: Bad things only happen to other people. A sudden confrontation with our vulnerability and mortality is a shock, a mental shock: "My God, any moment could be my last!" And it's stuck with me to this day. I'm especially aware of it in New York. You see old ladies—loaded down with their shopping bags—crossing the street without looking right or left, and New Yorkers drive like lunatics. Don't they see that they're risking their lives? Strictly speaking, it's a miracle we survive so long.

MB That's very interesting: Everybody believes himself to be God's favorite, but in the back of my mind I now have the feeling God wanted to teach his favorite a lesson. I'm not religious in the sense that I go to church on Sundays. But I do strongly believe in a higher spirituality.

DH I do, too.

MB I believe in one God, absolutely. Maybe not the God the church presents to us, but there clearly is …

DH Isaac Bashevis Singer, the writer—I once heard him give a reading at UCLA—answered a similar question: Yes, he believed in God. But he said it in a beautiful way, which a visual person like you will appreciate: "When I go out into the night and look up at the sky, I see all those stars and the special way they are arranged—somebody must have done that. They couldn't possibly be grouped like that by accident—an 'aesthetic force' was at work here."

MB And it can be seen everywhere.

DH We're surrounded by an aesthetic.

MB I think we must adjust our lives according to this aesthetic. We must seek to lead a responsible life, an honest life. Abiding by the rules we feel inside ourselves. But to say: "I'm a good person and therefore I will go to heaven. I'm a bad person … and so on."—these terms don't exist in my way of thinking.

DH My view is exactly the same. We're obligated to lead a life with a moral center. And it's my task to make sure that I'll be a better person today than I was at twenty. And better than I was in my thirties. Now I'm in my late fifties and my goal is to keep working on myself.

MB Of course, you don't merely mean in your profession as an actor …

DH I mean: I'll never be without envy. I'll never be without jealousy. Never in my life will I be without rage and anger. But I'm learning to handle it better. I used to have such blind hatred for people! Now I would be hard pressed to point at someone and say: "I hate him."

MB What kind of people did you hate especially?

DH People who put down my work. I give my best in my work, the product becomes my own child. If someone attacks it, it's as if a teacher spanked my child in school. It drives you crazy; you grab the teacher and yell at him: "Don't you dare touch my child ever again!"

MB I presume you're talking about studio people who believe it's their right to interfere in the creative process.

DH Exactly. I'm talking about producers and studio bosses. People who have more influence. There's a general conception that we're the ones who hold all power: Michael Ballhaus, one of the world's greatest cameramen, and I, one of the movie stars. But the truth is, we do our job and then we've got nothing more to do with the product, what will be cut, and how, and which parts of the film will land in the trashcan for marketing reasons. We do have influence, yes, but only as long we're there. The filming of a movie is only one part of the entire process. Afterwards all the power leaves our hands. And when other people damage my baby, I feel like … feel like …

(*Hoffman imitates almost uncontrollable anger, at least for a moment. Then he reaches for Helga's lovingly presented cookies and continues, munching.*)

God bless all women. I would get into terrible trouble if it weren't for the wisdom of my wife. She looks at me quietly and says: "Fight for things that are worth fighting for. Don't waste your energy on things you can't win anyway." She also tells me I should make sure to get more control, for instance, by making "smaller" movies, movies that are manageable.

MB I can second that wholeheartedly. I've reached the same point in my life. I want to return to movies that are not as expensive to make as the Hollywood movies nowadays. Because the high costs exert tremendous pressure on everyone involved.

DH Every film has to become a blockbuster.

MB That's right.

DH I'd like to get back to what you called "responsibility in our life." Because I feel like one of those pictures in children's coloring books. The images are drawn in outline and the kids have to fill them in with colors. This is how I see us. Our own image is a given, but only in outline. Someone then gives us a name; someone puts clothes on us and gives us our appearance; someone gives us our lifestyle, our world of experiences, our very personal history. The older we get, the more we become responsible for doing the "coloring" ourselves. At some point, we should be prepared enough so that we, and only we, are responsible for our own colors. That's difficult, because others want to mix the colors as well. But we have to fight for our own. We owe it to ourselves. Life is always a battle. But the real battle, the one worth fighting, is the one to maintain control over our own colors.

MB That's exactly the battle. Professionally, it's so difficult because we're exposed to constant conflicts. On the one side are the movies that cost fifty, eighty, or a hundred million dollars to make and will be seen by hundreds of millions of people. Such productions force everybody involved into particular, exactly outlined directions and nobody is free to do what he or she really wants to do. And then there are other movies that cost perhaps five or eight million dollars and will be seen by only a few hundred thousand people. But those films give us freedom of action. They permit us to realize our own ideas, to incur risks, to experiment, and to grow as artists.

DH I know exactly what you're talking about, namely, what we both want to do during our second act: direct movies ourselves.

MB That's it. For instance, I have an offer to do a project with Demi Moore, who gets for her role, believe it or not, twelve million dollars.

DH No woman has ever made that much …

MB With that kind of money alone, we could make two fabulous movies. For example, there's a project titled *Distance*. It's about Berthe Morisot, who became Edouard Manet's lover, but was, at the same time, a self-reliant woman, a painter in her own right, who shocked the whole world with her free spirit.

DH That would be a role for Juliette Binoche. She was a painter before she was discovered for the movies. And who plays Manet? Hey, let's talk business!

MB This would be something for you. Their story as a couple begins when Manet is forty-two years old. We can swing that, Dustin.

DH Maybe. On my way over here, I got a call from Gene Hackman. He told me I looked fabulous in *Outbreak*. I told him: "Film with Ballhaus, then even you'll look good." Who directs? You?

MB No. A talented young German woman, Katja von Garnier. Her film *Abgeschminkt* (*Without Makeup*), actually a student project when she was at the Film Academy in Munich, became a great success. I worked with her on another project: *Lenya*, the story of Lotte Lenya and Kurt Weill. That's the kind of movie I would like to direct myself.

DH I'll take on a role if it helps your breakthrough as a director …

MB And I'll do camerawork for you. Do you have any concrete directing plans?

DH You know how it is. Nobody sends me scripts with an offer to direct. People simply don't think of me as a director. Nevertheless, it's a proven rule of thumb that anybody can be a director. Absolutely anybody. My child can be a director. That's not the problem. But not everybody can be a *good* director, or a very good one. For that you need more than just connections.

MB I'm sure you would be a great director because you're an involved actor who contributes his own ideas. You don't just read your lines, you put yourself into them. When we were filming *Salesman*, I sometimes felt sorry for Volker Schlöndorff because you had ideas that were visually and dramatically fully realizable. Fortunately for Wolfgang Petersen, he had enough self-confidence to listen to you and not feel threatened.

DH Actually VOGUE readers will be the first to know: I do have a project for myself as a director. I have the book right here—a great novel by Balzac. I can't reveal more. I was inspired by a French movie, it was too long, but had impressive scenes—a painter, played by Michel Piccoli, and his model. What was the name of that film?

HB I'll look it up.

MB She'll find anything. I couldn't live with without her. I also discuss everything, absolutely everything with her. I never accept a film project without getting Helga's approval. I feel very lucky that I receive so much. Let's say it: so much love.

DH Fabulous. How long have you two been together?

MB My parents had a repertory theater in Bavaria and Helga's mother was a close friend of my father's …

DH Uh, oh!

MB (*Laughs*) No we're not brother and sister! She joined our group when she was seventeen. At that time I was very keen on older actresses. I found them exciting. But Helga became a part of my life, she became my best friend. We got married, the best decision of my life.

DH Fascinating. So you remained close to your roots in the choice of your mate. I returned to my roots after my first marriage. I had known Lisa since she was ten. My mother and her mother were best friends. Her father said to me one day: "Give her a job." So I gave her a job—to tape some videos or something like that. And, suddenly, I had this strong feeling of being at home, to be able to be myself. I didn't have to pretend. I was a boy from L. A. who'd turned out a bit short, who'd had enough problems in life and didn't need to burden himself in addition with problems in his relationships. I have to tell you, Michael, we have an awful lot in common.

MB I think so, too: We were both born in August. We both have achieved a lot in life …

DH Even if we're not completely convinced of it ourselves …

MB And we would be nothing without our women.

HB The movie is called *Divertimento* by Jaques Rivette and with Michel Piccoli and Emmanuelle Béart.

DH There's one scene I particularly remember: He's a totally blocked painter. Midlife crisis. People want him to paint. He can't. He sits on his chair and, suddenly, he looks at a girl: "That's the one I want to paint." She had never been a model. She comes to his studio. She gets undressed, which isn't easy for her. His interest is aroused, and he begins to draw. It reaches the point where she's sitting on her chair completely nude and he's next to her, fully dressed. He doesn't touch her. But the scene is almost painfully intimate. He confesses to her his deepest feelings, how worthless he feels and how difficult it is for him to be the man he actually should be in his opinion. And he tells all that to a young, naked woman. Extraordinary.

MB That scene took my breath away, too. Because it touches on a truth I don't understand myself. Because for men, a nude woman is something incomprehensible: our angel, our mother, our best friend, our mother confessor.

DH That's exactly the reason why I want to film this Balzac story: to show the problems men have with intimacy. I believe that men have problems with it because we all descended from women. We men begin our lives by sucking on our mother's breasts—that's the most intimate scene imaginable. The image of mother Mary breast-feeding her male child runs through the entire Christian mythology. And when we detach ourselves from our mother, puberty begins, meaning: away from the mother. The American slang word "motherfucker" wasn't invented by a woman, but by a man. He wants to put down another man who can't detach himself from his mother. In order to become a man, one must detach oneself from the breasts of a woman. Then he has to confirm this detachment before himself and the whole world by lusting after hundreds of other breasts from then on. This separation from the mother, which women don't experience—for they develop their own breasts and become mothers—drives men a bit crazy. For the rest of our lives we feel the loss and try, by any means, to return to what we had to leave behind as a child. That's why we're always looking for a mother substitute in the women of our lives. And when we find it—as you and I obviously have—then we've really returned to our roots. And we again permit ourselves to be protected, guided, and helped along.

From VOGUE 09 / 1995; The conversation was recorded by Elmar Biebl

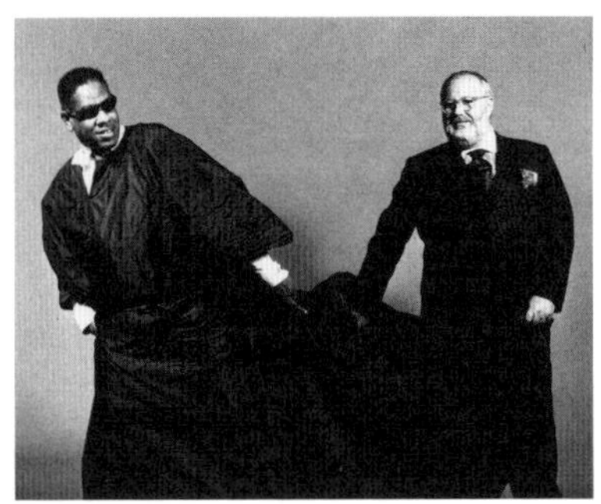

MAKING FASHION—
IT'S LIKE SEX

GIANFRANCO FERRÉ and ANDRÉ LEON TALLEY:
two giants of style meet at Karl Lagerfeld's. He takes photos.
They talk about obsessions, their roots and the subject of wealth.

Karl Lagerfeld is to take photographs. Gianfranco Ferré and André Leon Talley will talk. Scene of this summit: Lagerfeld's Paris residence. Situated on the left bank of the Seine, both decor and dimensions indicate that this is the home of an emperor. The crowd of people bustling around the *palais* also calls to mind the court of a ruler: friends, domestic staff, assistants, two male models styled for another photo shoot. Standing out amongst them all, the bulky form of André Leon Talley, fashion journalist—no, larger-than-life fashion guru. He is wearing a beige-colored Gucci jacket in foal skin, trousers from Savile Row and a pair of green crocodile leather sandals, a birthday present from his friend Manolo Blahnik.

Gianfranco Ferré is coming from Brussels, his flight is delayed. Talley waits without any apparent signs of impatience. Finally—more than two hours later—his counterpart enters the *palais*. Ferré is wearing a three-piece pin-striped suit and apologizes profusely for the delay. The two men decide to retire to Lagerfeld's book-filled salon to talk, seating themselves upon a fur-covered burgundy sofa. "We'd make good husbands, don't you think?" jokes Ferré. The butler serves a double portion of McDonald's chicken burgers and chocolate cake. Talley ordered both, after rejecting the offering of the host—cold poached bass and green sauce—as being "too subtle." Ferré helps himself to a burger. The dialogue can begin.

GIANFRANCO FERRÉ When we met for the first time in New York's Studio 54, I noticed your sharp tongue—and your heart of gold. We've been friends ever since—although we sometimes have no contact for months on end. Then I think to myself: "Why doesn't the son-of-a-bitch call me …" But I know that you have your sad times, times when you want to be on your own.

ANDRÉ LEON TALLEY Every intelligent person knows that—you can't be on top of the world everyday. I like being alone—time to read, think and dream—I enjoy being able to escape the whole whirl of the fashion world. My first memory of you: a collection with red dresses and black sashes, which you designed in 1972. I've always loved the dramatic elegance of your dresses and your sense of detail. By the way, I wanted to tell you that you were splendid in the hectic months following your split with Dior.

GF I'm proud of what we achieved at Dior, and how we achieved it. It was an extraordinary experience, eight years long, and I don't regret a thing. Now I plan to start something in Paris; it's still a big secret at the moment. It won't be a fashion house; I think it would be too fool-hardy of me to start from square one again, but I can't say more than that. Let's start at the beginning: I know that you spent your childhood in the Southern states of the USA.

ALT I was raised in North Carolina by my grandmother and great grandmother. My mother never lived with us. At the time, my father was working during the day as a printer in the US patent office in Washington D.C. and working nights as a taxi driver, so that he could provide for his only son. The South is very different to the rest of the USA. There's something romantic about it, eerily romantic.

GF Eerily romantic?

ALT When you're in New Orleans, there are these shops selling chickens' feet, snakes' heads and snake skins—there's something a bit eerie about that. I remember that I went to a show of Lena Horne, when she was on Broadway. After the show I went backstage and she had rigged up a washing line in her dressing room with snake skins hanging on it. "It's how I keep away the evil spirits!" she said. That's the South, as it lives and breathes. Personally, I find that very homey. As a small boy I was baptized in the small pond of a country church. Dressed in white robes, we had to accompany the pastor through the graveyard and into the forest, where there were snakes, before we came to the baptismal pool, which had been created for that purpose. As I was immersed in the water, my only thought was: "Where are the rattlesnakes?"

GF Was it a big shock for you when you left the South for New York?

ALT Absolutely not. I had read VOGUE, *Time*, *Newsweek* and other magazines; so I already had a cosmopolitan idea of life. I wanted to become a French teacher so that I could see the world, and that's why I had to leave the place where I grew up. I went to Brown University, to be trained as a French teacher, but I was already enthralled by the New York fashion world. I had a letter of recommendation to Diana Vreeland, and in 1974 I began to work for her— not at VOGUE; it was during her time as curator at the costume institute at the Metropolitan Museum. She introduced me to Andy Warhol, and I began to write for his magazine, *Interview*. My first big interview was with Karl Lagerfeld when he came to New York in 1975 in order to promote Chloé. Sparks flew between us like fireworks on the Fourth of July, and we've been friends ever since. But let's talk about you now.

GF You know that I spent six years in India after my architecture exam? I worked for the Indian government and had to complete an inventory of all Indian products—textiles and such that could appeal to European tastes. That was a great experience because I'm more of a reasoning kind of person and India is a country of fantasy and confusion. I had time to read, to study and to think. When I came back to Milan, I founded Ferré. Later, I got more experience in France, working at Dior. They suddenly asked me to come to them; I thought it was a joke at first.

ALT What are the differences in fashion habits between an Italian woman and a French woman? I can't see a difference.

GF I think there's a difference in mentality. An Italian woman is more concerned with the minute details and the quality, whereas the French woman is more interested in the overall impression made. I think that has something to do with the fact that Italians are used to small dimensions, tiny little streets, whereas the French are all focused on their metropolises, on cities. That's reflected in their style.

ALT Italian women place a lot of emphasis on appropriate appearance. In Rome they wear lovely fur coats from Fendi—even when it's twenty-seven degrees. The American style, on the other hand, is based on light sportswear—even where it's luxurious. Even C. Z. Guest (*a wealthy American society woman*), who I think is one of the most elegant women around, wears her clothes in a casual manner. A brocade and sable outfit looks like a Kashmir twinset. At the same time, young people today, the young people on the street, have completely turned American fashion around. Rich Americans no longer dress in a way that shows their wealth. Today, the superrich turn up at the office in polo shirts and khaki trousers. I live in Paris at the Ritz, and I see John F. Kennedy Jr. coming out of the hotel in a tracksuit and going to the flea market. They don't make a big thing of fashion like Europeans do. By the way, how did you manage to remain a gentleman in this cutthroat business—are you religious?

GF I think that I have an instinct for morals, a strong feeling of right and wrong, but I'm not a practicing Catholic.

ALT I was raised as a devout Baptist. Nowadays, I believe that religion is something that everyone should work out for themselves—the biggest hypocrites are found in the church. If you act in a decent manner and follow a moral code based on justice, kindheartedness and helpfulness, then you're a good, religious person in my book. If you look at it like that, the fashion business can be hell. Only a gladiator can survive in it.

GF People in the fashion business have lost the feeling for poverty; they're only interested in a spectacle. I continue to design because I believe in what I'm doing, and because it's the way for me to express my creativity. It's like when you're sleeping with someone: sometimes you do it four times a day.

ALT Have you ever slept with someone four times in one day?

GF Five times!

ALT I must say, that's quite a lot. You would get along very well with Mick Jagger. I don't think that I've ever slept with anyone five times in one day. I've never been in love …

GF What, you mean to say you've never been in love?

ALT I think it has something to do with the way I grew up. It wasn't consciously stated that sex was something disgusting, but it wasn't exactly discussed in sensible terms—so that you could have learned what a loving relationship was like, for example. Of course, I've had great romantic love affairs in my life, but more of the infatuated kind you see in novels. Let's talk about something else. I want to know what you wear when you go to the beach. I never go to the beach because I don't want to present myself half-naked in public. But if I were to do it, then I would wear some kind of floor-length, double-breasted garment in white piqué, with trousers, that I had designed in Paris. You're very elegant, but we're both big men. How do you manage to feel good about your body?

GF (*Protesting*) I don't feel fat or awkward. I've learned to live with my face and my stomach, and that's that—even when I'm sometimes surrounded by beautiful people. When I go to the beach, I wear black shorts and sometimes a wrapped loincloth, and if it's a private beach or I'm on my boat, then I go naked. I love to feel the sun on my naked skin.

ALT But we both have a weight problem. Two years ago I discovered this great fruit juice diet. After three weeks I could get back into suits I'd had made in 1977. I don't have a housekeeper, so I got up in the mornings and put apples, pears, beetroot, carrots, celery and kohlrabi all in the blender.

GF How awful …

ALT I read that Jacques Cousteau, the famous diver who is now in his eighties, said that from a certain age—maybe fifty onwards—we should only drink liquid foods. He does it himself, and look at him—I saw a photo of him, slim as can be. "Aha, so that's the solution," I thought.

GF What was your favorite food when you were a child?

ALT Cake and soft rolls. We weren't rich, but there was always food on the table. Every Sunday, my grandmother made a tray of twelve soft rolls, just for me, and I ate the lot. On Sundays, the menu consisted of a giant breakfast with freshly-baked bread, eggs, ham, sausages and cup after cup of coffee. Then, after church, we ate fried chicken or ham with all sorts of vegetables, followed by at least two desserts—cakes or tarts—everything homemade by my grandmother. She loved to watch people eat.

GF I recall, as a child, the best thing was to smell the aroma of typical Italian food coming from the kitchen. Saffron, for example, while our cook carefully steamed a risotto, or the aroma of vanilla and walnuts as he prepared dessert … Are you still in contact with your family?

ALT My grandmother, who I was very close to, died in 1989, which was a catastrophe for me. Then Mrs. Vreeland died in the same year, the other important person in my life. That's why I decided to move to Paris. But those two women are still very close to me, I think about them every day.

GF The people that we lose are always with us, especially when we're alone. I've lost almost everyone now, only my brother is still alive—he's an engineer, very clever. And my sister-in-law, who works with me, and my cousin, who I grew up with and is like a sister to me. We're very close.

ALT I remember as a young boy being dressed in a smart blue suit and white shirt on Sundays. In the respectable world of the southwestern blacks, every boy and every man grew up with half a dozen white cotton shirts. Even today, they're still a guarantee of elegance in my wardrobe.

GF I come from a wealthy industrialist family; my brother and I were dressed very conservatively as children—papa made sure of that. Twice a year we had to go to a special children's tailor. It was really strange for us; none of our friends had to dress so formally. We wore checked trousers and even had light summer coats and navy-blue jackets with red piping. In the winter, we wore double-breasted camel hair coats, and the following year they were navy blue—we were always dressed identically.

ALT Washing day was a real ritual in my grandmother's house. If the weather was good, she washed the laundry outdoors and made fires to heat the water. When my grandmother finally got a washing machine and a dryer, she never used them. She preferred to wash everything by hand, right up until the end. I watched her slaughter chickens without batting an eyelid, as well as skinning squirrels and opossums. I think that American women are tougher and have more energy than even the men have. I've seen American women from all classes and regions do the most extraordinary things.

GF I always think of *The Color Purple* when I think of that country. American women, to me, are a mixture of strong will and inexperience—naivety, even. They can also be very chic: One of the pictures that had the most effect on me was of Jackie Onassis leaving a New York hotel in a red kimono coat.

ALT I love very well-groomed, extremely slim women. I just have to be surrounded by beautiful women. What gives you the most pleasure, apart from designing clothes?

GF I love beautiful things, and I love to buy books of all sorts. No one in the whole world has as many books as Karl Lagerfeld and I. In my house on Lago Maggiore I've got an enormous library. It's a big, nineteenth-century building in a park.

ALT I have a house in North Carolina, but I'm only there for Christmas; otherwise, I've lived at the Ritz in Paris since 1989. It's best for me. Someone always says *bonjour* or *bonsoir* to you, and when I go to my room, someone has always made the bed already.... That reminds me of that guest performance—the pictures that we did for *Vanity Fair* in the style of *Gone with the Wind*, with Karl as the photographer. It was Lagerfeld's idea to have the blacks playing the whites and the whites as blacks, and you were Scarlett O'Hara's beloved black nanny. You were a great success.

GF I remember you calling: "Naomi Campbell is Scarlett, and you have to play her servant." Straight away I said: "But of course!" and I even made the clothes for the role myself....

ALT Is there anything that you regret in your life?

GF No, thank God! I've been very lucky, because I could always do what I wanted. Of course, it wasn't always easy—like when I came to Paris and had to prove myself as an outsider, as an Italian. I still recall how a politician at a dinner at the Elysée Palace said to me: "Lucky you have a French surname ..." He thought he was paying me a compliment.

ALT The only thing that I regret is that I was too busy with work to be at my grandmother's side when she died. Now, I know that you have to drop everything when one of your loved ones is dying. I was making a video for VOGUE when she died; I'll never forgive myself for that. The video could have waited.

GF I saw my mother die. She had a heart attack; the doctors at the hospital said that everything was blocked and that she would die in the next few hours. She was really calm and tried to persuade us to go home because she didn't realize that she was dying. When she was dead, I was overcome by an enormous feeling of peacefulness. Maybe you don't know this feeling, because you weren't there when your grandmother died.

ALT You're probably right. On the other hand, I believe that everything in life happens for a reason, that everything is for the best—I try to remain optimistic. Actually there's one other thing that I regret: I live at the Ritz but I'm very poor—like a revue girl, wearing a mink coat but without a penny in her pocket.

GF There are more important things in life ...

ALT Oh spare me!

GF I remember that my grandfather had a large painting by Fernand Léger behind the desk in his office. He had other paintings by famous artists, like Modigliani, but he never told us that they were worth a lot of money. Instead, he told us why Léger and Modigliani were significant painters, and I think that that was a very sensible, pedagogical thing to do ...

ALT But listen, money is important, so that you can buy the things that make life agreeable. For example, you need the right Porthault bed sheets—ones that you can fold back two meters. Then there's my collection designed by Versace. Underwear—men like lace as well, you know.

I would need at least 500,000 dollars a year to be able to live well and be completely happy.
I would buy all the books I wanted, travel to St. Petersburg. People think that I'm extravagant,
but, in fact, my needs are modest.

GF Of course, it's nice to be able to afford a few nice things, but I don't really consider it to be
all that important.

ALT Spoken by the man with two navy-blue Bentleys. How can you claim not to find money
so important?

GF (*Laughs*) Oh stop it! I only have one Bentley and two Mercedes in Milan. In my opinion
there's no difference between a Bentley and a Fiat. Who cares? Of course, it's nice to have
money, to be able to buy people things. For example, if I knew that you wanted a python leather
jacket, it would give me great pleasure to buy one for you.

ALT What I want is a Rolls-Royce or a Daimler from 1967.

GF What for? You can't even drive. When I want to feel really free then I leave my car and
driver and go on foot. Then I really realize what it means to be a rich man …

From VOGUE 02/1997; The conversation was recorded by Louise Baring

GIANFRANCO FERRÉ — ANDRÉ LEON TALLEY

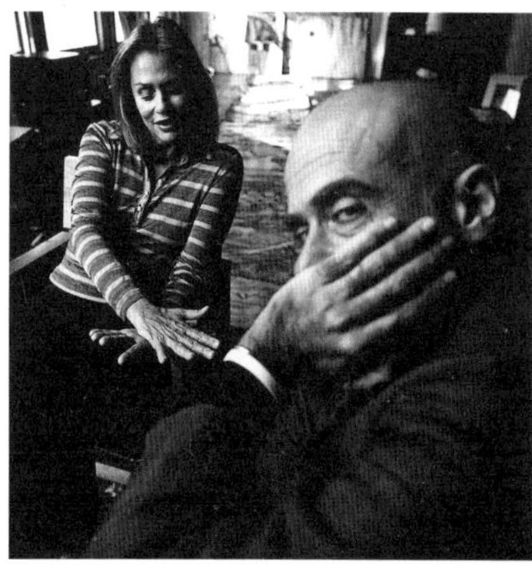

NEW YORK—A MONASTERY

LAUREN HUTTON and FRANCESCO CLEMENTE on penknives and rattlesnakes, the madness of everyday life, and the need to get away from it all regularly.

U sually they meet spontaneously. In fact, they just call out each other's name. If Lauren Hutton wants to know if Francesco Clemente or anyone of his family is at home, all she needs to do is lean out of the window and ask. The supermodel from the American South and the Italian painter, who first met in the early eighties in SoHo, New York's artists' colony, are now neighbors in NoHo (North of Houston Street). But this time, for VOGUE, they met instead at Clemente's studio on Broadway—a large room flooded with light and full of pictures, books and mementos of the two years that the painter spent in India. This time it wasn't their usual spontaneous meeting; it was an appointment by written invitation.

FRANCESCO CLEMENTE You have visited Africa many times. What is it that attracts you so much?
LAUREN HUTTON When I was a little girl I saw a Tarzan film on television—with Johnny Weissmuller—Waahaaahahaa! (*She beats her chest and imitates Tarzan's jungle cry.*) It was the first time I had seen an adult living in an intelligent sort of way. The adults I knew were all very busy working and never had any time for me. My father was in the war, and my mother was always working. But Tarzan lived in the trees, disguised himself, wore feathers and painted his face. He swung from one vine to another, rode on elephants and played with animals. After that, I always dreamt of Africa. In 1966 that dream came true. When I landed in Nairobi and felt the heat of Africa, I knew instinctively that I had come home. One day I will take you with me. You would like it there.
FC Oh no, I would be too scared to go on a dangerous adventure like that. I've got to look after my old bones.

LH My bones are fine, and I've been there twenty-four times.

FC You really are very brave. I've seen a photo of you wrestling with an alligator. Did you learn that when you were growing up in Florida? There must be a lot of wild animals there too, aren't there?

LH I was born in Charleston in South Carolina which was the old metropolis of the South before the Civil War, like New York is now. But my mother left when I was three. She married a wild man who had lived on the Amazon and who had a house in the marshes of Florida. In our garden there were alligators and lots of poisonous snakes: coral adders, water moccasins, rattlesnakes …

FC I've always been fascinated by the American wilderness. As soon as you leave the cities you find yourself in wide-open spaces—unspoiled nature. In Europe, everything has been cultivated for centuries. In any case, there were no rattlesnakes in Italy. We didn't even have a garden.

LH But you grew up surrounded by Neapolitans instead. That's far more dangerous than rattlesnakes. In Naples you've got the Mafia around every corner.

FC No, no. If anything, Naples is a big theater. It is impossible for the people there to behave in a neutral way. Even the most mundane daily incidents turn into full-blown dramas. For example, if you go into a café and order something, there will always be someone who says something amusing or provocative. And then everyone expects you to respond in the appropriate way.

LH Here in the USA, people are afraid to say what they think. It could cost them their job or trigger a libel suit. Americans used to hit each other when they had a difference of opinion, but today everyone holds their tongue.

FC But you don't hesitate launching into controversial discussions—you must be one of America's last patriots.

LH What do you mean?

FC America also has traditions which should be preserved. Today, people do nothing but complain that America assumes the role of a superpower and ruins the cultures of other countries. But American culture has also been destroyed. Thank God there are still a few people who remember the old traditions. And you are one of them.

LH Yes, I have very strong roots here. My family came to this continent in the seventeenth century and has been living in the South for generations. I was the first to go to the North—to New York. I thought that New York was the gateway to the world, and for me it turned out to be true. I have found my fortune here.

FC It was very much the same for me. I never once thought that I would land on this side of the world. When I was living in Italy, my trips abroad were always to India. But when I came to New York for the first time in 1980, I was fascinated. It was a significant period when all trends converged in New York. There were artists from Europe, rap music had just been invented, and everything was still under the influence of the wild seventies. A fantastic mix! As a newcomer, I was surprised that I could take part in everything. In Rome, where I had spent the previous ten years, I always felt as if I was on some sort of threshold but that I had lost the key.

LH I remember those times well. We met through Julian Schnabel, who was working as a cook at the *in* restaurant Max Kansas City at the time. You looked like a monk. I asked myself: what on earth is a monk doing here in New York? It must be far too loud for him here—monks love silence and isolation. (*laughs*)

FC Basically, New York is nothing but a big monastery: everyone lives according to their own vows. (*both laugh*) Manhattan is very small—only twelve miles long and one mile wide. New York has a unique skyline, just like the Italian cities of the fourteenth century with their characteristic church towers and castles. And it is an island—even if we sometimes forget it. An island shaped like a large boat.

LH I think it looks more like a large cigar—a cigar which explodes in Downtown.

FC I like the extremes. Rich and poor live next to each other in a very confined space. And usually they are extremely interesting people. Do you remember when we were going down the Bowery? There was a homeless man on the other side of the road. When he saw you he raised his bottle and shouted "Lauren, you're the greatest model of all time!" His face was beaming as he said it. This sort of thing only happens in New York.

LH (*Laughs*) I'd forgotten all about that. That was when I had a loft in the Bowery—at the corner of Third Avenue—a completely run-down area full of homeless people and junkies. We called the street "crack alley."

FC I painted a portrait of you then. I painted everyone who visited me in my studio.

LH Do you know, that portrait changed my life!

FC Really? What do you mean?

LH When I first met you I always carried a penknife and tear gas in my pocket. I used to carry the knife as a young girl—because of the snakes. When I saw your portrait of me I was shocked. The woman looking at me was terrifying. If I had met myself on the street, I would have crossed to the other side of the road—I looked so dangerous, even without my weapons. After that, I left my knife at home. You freed me from my weapons.

FC Oh, I didn't realize that at all. When I paint a portrait of someone, I don't look at them too closely. I paint instinctively. Everyone has a dark side to their nature, and it shows through if you look long enough. Painting a portrait is different from taking a photograph, because a photograph only captures one particular moment. Drawing a portrait takes at least two or three hours. The facial expression changes with the course of time. I see at least fifteen different faces which overlap.

LH At any rate, you captured me well. And you changed my life. I was going through a difficult phase. I was full of anger. At the age of forty-two I was still suppressing a lot of my childhood problems and had never really worked them out. I decide to do some therapy and started a Jungian analysis. By the way, where is the portrait now? I would like to buy it.

FC I still own it. Perhaps it will soon be shown in an exhibition. I am just preparing an exhibition of portraits at the Andy Warhol Museum in Pittsburgh. I'm going to include a few older pictures too.

LH That's great.

FC I'm looking forward to it. I've always been an admirer of Andy Warhol. Otherwise I'm not really concerned about what other artists do. But I was always a bit envious of Andy's celebrity portraits.

LH Has the art scene changed much in the last few years?

FC I think it's become a lot more conservative. In America, there are always certain phases which reoccur. Sometimes there is a very extroverted and more cosmopolitan phase, followed by a more provincial and introverted phase. But that has never been important to me. I originally started to paint as a protest against society. I didn't want to take part in conventional games.

LH Your father was a lawyer. He must have wanted you to be a lawyer, too. But when you were young you wrote poetry, didn't you?

FC Yes, I was an overprotected child. My mother published my first poems when I was ten. That was something of a shock. Try and imagine what that meant in Naples in the fifties. Poets were almost criminals. Naples is like a Mason's lodge without any ideals, a club without any guiding principles. You have got to fit in. And as far as poetry and painting are concerned, the Neapolitans say, "Hey! We've had all that already! Why should we hang any more pictures in the museums? Enough. It's all over and done with." Painting is not "elegant," doing nothing is "elegant." I suppose that's why I'm here. New York is so vulgar, and it's a very inspiring place for innovative poets and painters.

LH I think that's a typical European problem. So many ideas and great thinkers have been born there that it's difficult for young people to develop their own creative ideas.

FC But in Europe, many cities still have a liberal tradition. As far as art is concerned, Amsterdam, Basle, Cologne and Berlin have always been very productive. In particular, Germany still demonstrates an intensive dedication to the arts.

LH I did some filming in Germany recently. I was surprised to see how many good museums and galleries there were in Cologne and Düsseldorf. And it seems that everyone knows their opera. You go to a gas station and the man sings Wagner while he fills up the tank.

FC Which film did you shoot there?

LH *The Story of Monty Spinnerratz*, a children's film which is just about to show in Germany. It was a collaboration between the Augsburger Puppenkiste and Warner Brothers. I played an art dealer. The story is about a fat, clever rat. The rats are moved around by fantastic puppeteers—they are real artists. The puppets come alive in their hands and they can convey real feelings. When I felt nervous, I went to them, talked to them and took one onto my lap. I think children will love the film.

FC My children were very impressed when they heard that you danced with the American president last week. Do you like the Clintons?

LH Yes, very much. They are clever people from the country—old fashioned somehow. They're far-sighted and stand by the old American principle that everyone should have an equal chance. Hillary is just as smart as Bill. But Washington doesn't like clever women. The First Lady is allowed to express her opinions behind closed doors, but not in public as Hillary does. They are both continually under attack, for example, from the tobacco industry. Bill Clinton has declared war on the tobacco barons. (*Lauren coughs and extinguishes her cigarette; they are both smoking Camel Lights.*) That's why they hate him and spend thousands on publicity campaigns against him.

FC When were you first invited to the White House?

LH The first time I was there it had to do with breast cancer. Clinton's mother died of breast cancer in 1994. As a member of the NBCC, the National Breast Cancer Coalition, I campaigned for new legislation and more research funds. This time they invited me because of my late night show. Clinton used to see it regularly. I think he just wanted to say: "Hey, I love your show." And what do you think of them both?

FC Oh, I'm a foreigner. I don't have to bother about American politics, do I?

LH Come, come. You're more interested in politics than you want to admit. I still remember very clearly how we watched the Iran-gate reports on television that afternoon at Kenny Scharf's. You were practically glued to the screen.

FC Yes, I remember. Kenny had a crazy TV with plastic figures and small palms stuck all over it.

LH I hear that you've thrown out your television!

FC Nobody believed I would really do it, till I actually did.

LH That's totally anti-American. I'll have to call the police and put you in handcuffs!

FC It wasn't because of the programs themselves. I simply couldn't stand the short attention span any longer. Nothing on television lasted longer than five minutes. That's dangerous. It's OK if you concentrate on something, even if it's rubbish, for a longer time. It's the constant interruptions I hate. Our minds need time to follow through our thoughts, feelings and movements. Television trains us to do the opposite.

LH I know what you mean. The idea behind my talk show was to let people talk for half an hour, not for five minutes. But the program was interrupted four times by advertising slots.

FC You're doing exactly the right thing. Everyone should be on the television instead of sitting in front of it.

LH How did your children react to you throwing out the TV?

FC Before, they were addicted to it. After I threw it out, they simply forgot it. Now they're bored sometimes. But I am very much in favor of boredom. Without boredom there are no feelings, no intelligence. You have to be bored before having a new thought or desire.

LH You are doing the right thing with your children. They are familiar with very different worlds: Italy, India and America. They're inquisitive and cheerful. I've known the twins since they were babies—and even before they were born. Can you remember Alba when she was pregnant? She had an enormous stomach that looked like a Volkswagen!

FC People nowadays have very low standards when it comes to upbringing. As long as my children don't resort to cocaine, they're good children. Parents don't expect so much any more. Children are independent personalities. All this talk about you being responsible for how they turn out—it's all rubbish. Each child chooses its own path.

LH Unfortunately I missed out on that experience as a young woman. But thank God I've got lots of friends with children. You, for example. You're stuck with me for life! And then there are the four sisters I brought up. That's probably the reason why I never had a family of my own—I know what a hard job it is.

FC You have family, but you're not caught up in family life. You can come and go as you please. As for me, I never actually decided to start a family. It just happened. And it only works because my wife, Alba, and I take things as they come and don't have any set notions about how things ought to be.

LH I can see that you've done a lot of new paintings. (*Points at the floor where some watercolors are drying.*) It's always difficult to find the right words to describe your paintings. For example, this picture looks like a woman with a beautiful bottom, leaning over. In the middle is a perfect triangle, the center of her being, her vulva. She's got two eyes on her behind and hands are growing out of her thighs which are caressing the heads of two men. The ferns on either side look like angel's wings. For me, a woman's bottom is almost divine, don't you think?

FC I don't know. But bodies are certainly the central element in my work. People here see their bodies in a very definite and technical way which has nothing to do with the reality. The reality is much more disturbing—experiencing our body is the only wilderness left to us. If you look at your body, everything is always changing. Nothing is certain and nothing remains forever. When we realize this, our conceptual and categorical way of thinking breaks down.

LH I like the way bodies entwine themselves with others in your paintings.

FC I see the human body as a dividing line between our physical and spiritual selves. In the West, we put emphasis on the outer world. But other cultures give the inner self just as much attention; dreams, imagination …

LH Is that why you find India so fascinating?

FC India is a country where life and death are still very closely related. In my opinion, this is a very intelligent way to live, instead of separating them as we do in the West.

LH Yes, death is hidden away here. We never see any dead bodies, and we never talk about it. But if you're not aware of death, how can you live life to the fullest?

FC In the West, we only look towards the end of things. But death is not the end of life. We are in continuous circulation, experiencing constant renewal and change.

From VOGUE 04/1997; The conversation was recorded by Ute Thon

LAUREN HUTTON — FRANCESCO CLEMENTE

187

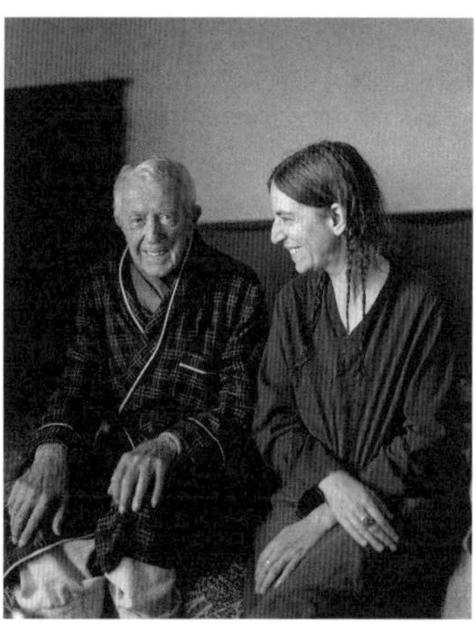

LIKE TWO PLANETS

The rock poet PATTI SMITH reaches the end of her pilgrimage:
she has traveled to Tangier to visit PAUL BOWLES. They discuss life,
love and dreaming.

The port of Tangier is still famous for its reputation as a lawless international zone up to 1956, when it served as a place of rendezvous for gangsters, artists, pimps and adventurers from all parts of the world. Today, it is not shrouded in quite as much mystery as it used to be. Most of the young women have discarded their veils; the muezzin no longer has to exert his vocal chords when he calls the faithful to prayer from the top of the minaret because a recorded tape does the work for him. Of all the literary figures of the Beat Generation—William Burroughs, Tennessee Williams, Truman Capote and Gore Vidal, who were all overcome by Tangier's charms—only one remains: Paul Bowles, the "Titan of Tangier." Today, he is Tangier's most famous resident. Those who read his books continue to make pilgrimages to Tangier, but most of them are refused audience. One of Bowles' prominent admirers, Patti Smith, arrived on a day of pouring rain.

Paul Bowles You've brought the wrong sort of weather with you!

Patti Smith Can I take my shoes off? Otherwise there'll be a squeaking noise on the tape. Actually, I can always tell when it's going to rain. I even knew when I was a child; my bones used to vibrate and a pain spread through my whole body—like "Uncle Wiggly." Do you remember that song?

PB Of course. (*He starts to sing this American children's verse and Patti Smith joins in.*) "How the hell / Can real folks tell / It ain't gonna rain no more."

PS I think it has something to do with the fact that I was born an old person. But first I have to tell you how happy I am to meet you at last. Tell me, all the books say that your birthday is on December 30th. Is it really true?

PB Yes, that's right. Why do you ask?

PS Because it's my birthday too. And Rudyard Kipling's—I was very proud of that as a child. When I was seven, I left New Jersey and went to New York for the first time, and one day as I wandered through the streets I came across a sort of *Who's Who*, a book of biographies of writers, and I chanced upon a picture of you which I liked. Of course, at that age I had never read anything you'd written. But I said to myself: "Hey! Look! There's someone with the same birthday!" (*laughs*). I mean, wasn't that a wonderful stroke of fate! I hope you're well?

PB No, I'm not.

PS You look well in spite of it.

PB Well, I don't really know. All I know is that I have to go to America soon for an operation. I'm not very enthusiastic about going, especially for an operation. The arteries in my legs have to be connected up by some tube—femoral bypass is the official term. All the doctors say the same: "At your age it is too dangerous to have a full anesthetic. But I hate local anesthetics. I had the last one a few years ago in Meknès due to a hernia. In the middle of the operation, the Moroccan medical assistant asked me: "*Voulez-vous voir la comédie?*" I could have watched the whole operation through a mirror, but I didn't want to, and I told him to draw the curtain. I didn't want to see the "comedy," as he put it.

PS Lots of women like watching operations. In America there are special TV programs which show operations which go on for hours and hours. My mother often used to make me faint when she related detailed descriptions of operations she had had, or rather, which she had enjoyed. I hate to see myself bleeding, but it seems that I'm an exception.

PB You're quite right. Blood belongs in the body and nowhere else.

PS I suppose if nature or God took it from me, it would be OK. But not someone who works in a laboratory, unless he had wings, of course.

PB If you ever do meet anyone of that description, do give them my fax number.

PS Oh yes, before I forget. Bruce Weber sends his best wishes.

PB Oh yes, the photographer ...

PS Yes, I've known him for ages, but he's only just taken photos of me for the first time, for the French edition of VOGUE. I don't usually wear extravagant clothes, but for him I put on a ball gown. It was a very amusing photo shoot. I felt like a child dressed up for a fancy dress party, and Bruce kept on jumping up and down and could hardly contain himself because I'd mentioned I was going to visit you. And before that I visited William Burroughs in Kansas. He sends all his love.

PB Has he still got all those cats?

PS Yes, and goldfish, whole ponds of them.

PB Don't they freeze in winter? It gets so dreadfully cold up there.

PS (*Laughs*) No, I don't think Bill would allow that—he loves his fish too much. They all have names and he knows each one. When we were there, one fish had just died and was being greatly mourned.

PB I really must write Bill a letter, but it's difficult because I spend most of the time in bed.

PS Is it because of your hands? Let me have a look. (*She takes Bowles' right hand and feels it cautiously.*) They still look quite strong to me. That's probably from playing the piano, isn't it?

PB Well, I'm a composer as well, of course.

PS Well, I don't think you have much of an excuse not to write to Bill. He might not admit it, but he'd be very pleased to hear from you.

PB Yes, Bill isn't one for showing his emotions.

PS He does to me though.

PB Really? In what way?

PS Well, first I have to admit that I was very taken by Burroughs in my youth and followed him about everywhere, like a groupie. It was very obvious (*laughs*), but he ignored me. As I grew older, I didn't stop, but I showed him my admiration in a different way—by treating him as a gentleman.

PB Yes, he certainly has a remarkable gentleman-like quality.

PS …real gentlemen are few and far between. He responds in his own way: every time I visit him, he dresses up. He puts on a double-breasted suit and waistcoat. This time he was wearing a tie out of silk which he had painted himself. Usually he receives visitors in bed, but he got up just for us.

PB But he's four years younger than me, so he hasn't got as much right to stay in bed. (*looks round*) This is not the ideal place to welcome a visitor.

PS (*Gets up to look at various things in the room*) You know, this looks just like our home in New York: small piles of books all over the place; even the patterns and materials are similar.

PB And the chair—is it comfortable?

PS Well, as I've got a rather bony behind, it doesn't really matter what I sit on because it always starts to hurt anyway.

PB Do you like New York?

PS I still think it's one of the most friendly places I have ever been.

PB What about all the muggings we hear about?

PS It's never happened to me, even when I spent the night in the underground or in graveyards. Perhaps it's because I grew up in the country and wasn't afraid of empty fields in the dark. Quite the opposite—the fact that the city is so full of people gives me a feeling of security. I was not very communicative, but when I was writing I always liked having people around.

PB I wouldn't be able to stand that. I need absolute silence if I'm working—the sort of private sphere which most people haven't the slightest idea about.

PS When I was small, I was never unhappy if I got a children's illness like the measles or the mumps because I always preferred to be by myself with my books, and the illnesses shielded me.

PB Me too, although I wasn't allowed to have any books. But at least it meant I could be by myself— a blessing if you felt that your parents pestered you, as mine did. They came into my bedroom without knocking and told me how I should lie properly so that I wouldn't get a twisted spine.

PS Wasn't there anyone—a relative or somebody—to comfort you?

PB There was my mother—but she was restricted because she was under the tyranny of my father. The wonderful thing about being ill was that I didn't have to go to school.

PS I liked going to school because it meant that I got away from my mother. Originally, I had the strange idea that school was a place of inspiration, but I was quickly cured of that. But it did nothing to dampen my enthusiasm for books, and I continued to go to school because of the library. Did you ever have problems keeping yourself entertained as a boy?

PB Oh no, I was never bored as long as I was allowed to be by myself. Of course, I know what boredom is, as a concept so to speak, but it's a feeling I never actually got myself.

PS Did you ever feel restless?

PB Yes, I often felt restless, but that's a physical state. I didn't like staying in one place for a long time, not even when I was at my desk. After ten minutes I would get up and wander around the room before sitting down again to write. I couldn't get rid of this feeling of restlessness until I discovered pot, but I got restless again later on.

PS You felt a great urge to travel when you were still very young …

PB Yes, and my motives were negative rather than positive; I wanted to get as far away from home as possible.

PS Do you still read a lot?

PB My eyes have got weaker, but it might have something to do with bad light. The lamp is not so bright.

PS Do you still write?

PB In early 1996, I wrote music for a film, but I haven't written any more literature. Perhaps it's because I don't have much inspiration. But I also lack the energy it takes to throw myself into my work. It's very unpleasant to suddenly find that my energy level, which was once so high, has now slackened off.

PS And what about your spiritual energy?

PB That's much better, as I don't need to put any muscles into motion for that. Of course, spiritual energy is the prerequisite for physical energy.

PS If we assume that the spirit is still very strong, is it possible to put one's trust in another person and speak through them, like you have done for other people?

PB You mean Mohammed Mrabet and the others? (*Illiterate Moroccans who told their stories to Bowles, and who then transformed them into books.*)

PS Let me tell you about my own personal experience. One day during a concert I fell off the stage and broke my neck. I couldn't move at all for five or six months, but I had a book deadline to meet. I love the writing process of putting words on paper. I love filling blank white pages. Luckily I was able to find someone who—after a few initial difficulties—was able to act as a medium for my writing …

PB Like a sort of secretary …

PS More than a secretary—as if they were actually the page itself. Can you imagine something like that happening? Would that be an option for you?

PB No. Life here is too complicated. To trust someone as much as you describe, they would have to speak the same language. Fluency in a language is not enough. It's a completely different cup of tea.

PS Your last novel was published in 1966.

PB Yes, I gave up writing when Jane fell ill (*Bowles' wife, the renowned writer Jane Auer, who died in 1975*), and when I had to be at her bedside at a moment's notice. We had a sort of telephone system which connected the two floors. Each time she rang and said "Can you come down?" I said "Yes" and went down. But by the time I was back up again, I had lost the thread and had to start all over again. You just can't write a novel that way. A short story, perhaps.

PS Do you regret the fact that you don't write any more?

PB I don't regret anything, except that I have to die soon. No, that's not true either. Everything will continue as it is, even without me. I won't mind being dead. What I don't like is worrying about whether I will die in pain, for dying is usually accompanied by suffering.

PS Somehow, I think you are not going to have to suffer.

PB How do you know?

PS I don't know. It's just a feeling. I feel that fate has something else in store for you. Perhaps you will just drift away in a dream …

PB That sounds good …

PS Where do you go on your daily walk?

PB My chauffeur drives me up to an area near to the Country Club golf course where there are hardly any cars and where breezes rustle through the trees. I love the sounds of nature, that's why I bought an island off the southern coast of Sri Lanka in the late forties. On one side, you could hear the waves lapping the shore, and the other you could hear them breaking against the cliffs. The powerful music of the sea.

PS What happened to the island?

PB I had to sell it. Jane hated it because all you could do there was read and write, and she couldn't do either after her stroke. So she drank half a pint of gin instead, which only made things worse. After selling the island I was stuck in Colombo for six weeks; the authorities didn't want to pay dollars or rupees. In the end I thought I had sorted it all out and left the country. But then that horrible Bandaranaike lady came to power. She was in contact with Mao Tse-tung, and that was fatal because he persuaded her that Americans were wicked. And so it was publicly declared that I had a transmitter on the island, that I was a CIA agent and all sorts of other rubbish. And as for the money, I never saw another penny.

PS Have you ever felt threatened by your surroundings?

PB Well, earthquakes in Central America are unpleasant; they happen too often and are too violent. There was one that took only a few minutes to kill 20,000 people. I've been in earthquakes in Mexico, Guatemala and Costa Rica. There was one in Antigua just as we were about to have lunch. The others all jumped up and began to scream. The women grabbed their children and ran out. At first, Jane and I just looked at each other because we didn't understand what was happening. We were the last ones to feel the earthquake. And Jane immediately began to laugh. She always laughed when something dangerous happened. One day, the gardener came in with a rattlesnake, which he was holding tight between two sticks. As he entered the dining room, he dropped it by mistake and it got ready to strike. Jane had a kitten which was very curious. When Jane saw the kitten run up to the snake she rushed up and grabbed it, although the snake couldn't have been more than half a meter away. She was not afraid.

PS She was worried about the kitten.

PB I was, too, but I wouldn't have dared to go that near.

PS It must be the maternal instinct.

PB Is that the way mothers are? In any case, I always admired Jane because she was so fearless. I remember when we lived on 10th Avenue in New York. We were up on the roof and I was making corrections to the musical score of a composition. Suddenly, a strong wind blew the sheets of paper to the edge. There were no railings, and the roof slanted at a steep angle. I was rooted to the spot, but Jane didn't think twice. She picked up all the pieces of paper and pressed them into my hands. I was very impressed.

PS I don't want to sound indiscreet, but there's something I'm very curious about. You have never used the word "love" in any of your discussions or interviews. The characters in your books are very egocentric in the sense that their feelings or spiritual development are the main pivot. Exchanges between two different people are very rare. Am I exaggerating?

PB Certainly not. You're probably quite right.

PS If people could meet on an emotional level rather than an intellectual one—which never actually seems to happen in your books—couldn't we call that "love"?

PB It's difficult for me to imagine that two people can feel the same emotions, simply because everyone is different …

 PS It's certainly a challenge …

PB … like two planets in orbit which perhaps touch each other fleetingly for a single moment when their paths cross. And then they go their own way. That isn't a very human perspective, but rings true to me. People don't have the same feelings—that is, not at the same time. It's possible but not probable.

PS But it's worth working towards.

PB Why?

PS (*Hesitates*) I can only say what it means to me. As an inhabitant of this planet, I think that self-expression is worthwhile, whether it happens through writing or in the course of my work. And in addition, all forms of enlightenment are worthwhile in so far as they have something to do with what we generally call "God." And involving others is worthwhile, too, because it widens our horizons rather than restricting them. Did you and Jane communicate on this sort of plane?

PB Oh yes, all the time. I suppose that that's what is usually called "love"—complete understanding for another human being. And I don't know why life with her was so easy, and why it was so difficult with everyone else. I didn't need to make any great effort at all when I was with Jane. How sad she had to go.

PS Do you think of her often?

PB Not during the day, no. But I often dream about her. There's not much point in thinking about her, but dreaming is quite different: dreams are not under our control, and we have to take what comes. It's a bit like television somehow, but I must say, I prefer dreaming!

PS When Jane died—and she evidently didn't look after herself and was moving along the path of self-destruction—didn't you feel responsible all the same?

PB Initially, yes. I did everything I possibly could, but you always ask yourself if there was anything else you could have done.

PS My situation was very similar. I hope that my feelings of guilt will soon pass. In the eighties, I had a phase when I lived very much in retreat—which was something completely new for me. I battled with myself and developed a strict work routine, and I wrote up to twenty pages a day.

PB That's an awful lot …

PS I was married with two children—and suddenly my husband fell ill. I was witness to the constant process of his demise, although he was still young, and one day I just stopped writing. That was about two years ago, and it's still the same today.

PB Just like me …

PS Writing has always been an integral part of my life! At first I said to myself: "Just be patient, it will come back." But so far, it hasn't. How would you define "writer's block?"

PB You mean, as an occupational disease? I would say that it's the inability to express thoughts in words. We should regard writing in the same way as any other activity—like cleaning the house or washing clothes—something to which we can dedicate our available time and energy.

PS (*Laughs*) I sort of imagined that after visiting you, I would be transformed in some wonderful, magical way and be able to write again.

PB Perhaps you will.

PS My nine-year-old daughter didn't understand everything I told her about why I was traveling to Morocco. But when I told her that we had the same birthday—she understood immediately that I had to go.

PATTI SMITH — PAUL BOWLES

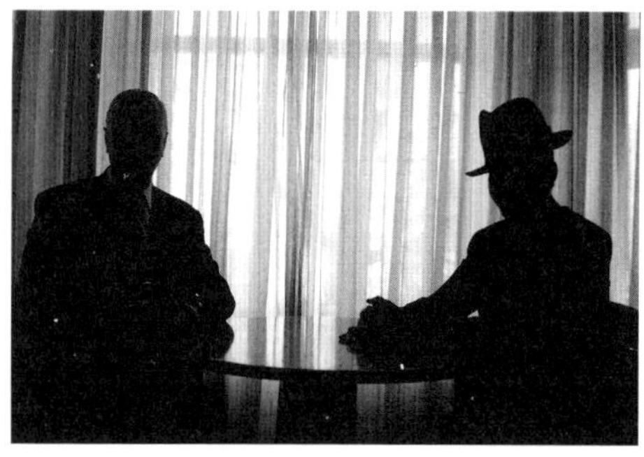

TWO MEN, ONE DREAM

MANOLO BLAHNIK, shoe couturier and gentleman meets
JOHN GALLIANO the fashion rebel. Opposites? It only looks that way;
they both burn with the same fire.

Rock stars and film moguls love the Halcyon on Holland Park. John Galliano recommended it as the meeting place; Dior's new chief designer always stays here when he is in London. His interlocutor, Manolo Blahnik—who his fans have dubbed the "Balenciaga of women's shoes"—is waiting already. He is rewarded for his patience: Galliano makes a theatrical entrance. Wearing an enormous black hat, and followed by two assistants, he storms into the hotel's restaurant. Anyone who does not know both men and observes how they greet each other and sit down would hardly come up with the idea that they both work in the same branch: the eccentric versus the gentleman, the volcano and the tranquil alpine lake. Galliano: wiry, dark, with a razor-sharp goatee and moustache and two-tiered earrings—falling, in a flash, from one enthusiasm to the next. Manolo Blahnik, silver-haired and well-groomed, appears to be reserved and discretely elegant, he makes polite requests and brings fine nuances into the conversation.

JOHN GALLIANO What does your ideal woman look like?
MANOLO BLAHNIK I love women from the Romanic countries, because the way they move exudes so much grace and sensuality. They really enjoy getting dressed up for any occasion.
JG That's right, they really do. I can remember how it was when I was a young child in Gibraltar. My Spanish mother used to put on a special dress just to go with us to the café across the street. When I was six, we moved to London. My father was a plumber and therefore didn't earn much money, but my mother was obsessed with fashion. My sister, too. When she was seventeen, she wanted to enter a beauty contest, so I got out the sewing machine and made her a clinging evening dress of apricot-colored silk. I really have no ideal impression of a woman—a girl is beautiful and sexy when she finds herself that way. When I think back to the dress which I made then, it makes me wince—it was the color of a bathroom. But my sister felt good in it and that's what's important.

MB I don't like it when women go under the knife for their beauty. I know a famous American television actress whose breasts get bigger year by year. I met her recently on Rodeo Drive in Beverly Hills and asked her: "My dear, can you see your feet when you're standing up?"

JG I can only accept plastic surgery if it takes place after an automobile accident or something like that. In this respect, I find American culture somewhat uncanny.

MB I've known you since 1984—I became aware of you at the fashion show of the St. Martin's School's graduates in 1984. You were already making clothes, cut on the diagonal, and it was immediately apparent to me that somebody quite exceptional had entered the fashion world. Dior is a wonderful platform for your talents—their tradition and quality! The very best people work there. But it was courageous of them to hire you—a real iconoclast.

JG Yes, I was extremely lucky—a few years ago, I was still sleeping on the floor in a friend's apartment in Paris.... For me, bringing haute couture into the twenty-first century means making clothes which are both seductive and wearable—they must exhibit a powerful modernity and still respect the past. That's why I try to imagine which of today's influences Monsieur Dior would have assimilated. I also love Madeleine Vionnet's work (1876–1975), particularly her diagonal cuts. The ingenious designs from the past are still a source of inspiration for us today, and fashion has a very exciting future; I've never before felt such a seething atmosphere. In the past two months, Dior has received several dozen orders for corsets and evening dresses. If a woman can afford it—why not?

MB How do you feel about the rebuff Yves Saint Laurent gave your work and which was so blown up in the media? (*YSL, referring to Galliano and Alexander McQueen, his own successor at Givenchy, talked about "a ridiculous spectacle, better suited for the concert stage."*)

JG I take things like that fairly calmly. Monsieur Saint Laurent gave so much to fashion. He's a genius and I can understand how he feels. But things must go on. I see it as my responsibility to thoroughly clear out haute couture, to give it a new freshness and ease. I got my job completely unexpectedly. Last summer, I was at a small evening party which Bernard Arnault had arranged. (*Arnault is the head of the LVMH Group—Louis Vuitton, Moët Hennessy— which owns the Dior, Givenchy, and Kenzo fashion houses, along with Louis Vuitton.*) It was Gianfranco Ferré's last season with Dior. When they started to talk about it, I became more and more enthusiastic and then finally, as a joke, said how much I would like to be his successor. To my astonishment, Monsieur Arnault took me seriously and telephoned me a few days later. He explained: "You know, what you said the other evening was really not such a bad idea ..." It was that simple.

MB You design six collections a year—that's quite a lot of pressure.

JG Of course, but I love it. Designing sets energy free, it's a way of letting off steam creatively, a great passion. The sensuality of a cut, the fabric, the color: an absolute delight.

MB I love my work, too, but I find the commercial aspects—promoting—very strenuous. Traveling is so inelegant. I just spent a month in America, three days here, three days there, visiting department stores, appointments with the press and clients. Sometimes I feel discouraged and intimidated. But I always try to be as friendly as possible. In Los Angeles, I have a young client, Todd, who comes to my department-store promotions every year. He always shows me photographs of himself and his girlfriend—they always wear the same clothes, even the same Manolo Blahnik high heels with artificial flowers—crazy!

JG In my case, it was the fabulous American twins. They were about sixty and wanted identical Galliano outfits. Another woman wanted me to tell her what she should wear to her son's bar mitzvah. These women wanted detailed instructions. That can be quite tiring—especially seeing that I get dozens of these enquiries every day.

MB Rich American women are often very special and super-organized. Some of them have wardrobes as big as rooms—one for the day dresses, one for their cocktail dresses and so on. My sister Evangeline, who manages my flagship store in London, knows a woman who keeps her countless Blahnik shoes in a commode lined with green velvet. Just imagine: a light goes on as soon as she opens it.

JG Yes, they take good care of their clothes; they have lavender sachets everywhere. These women also know how to take care of the interior decoration of their houses.

MB That is definitely a way of life we have to accept. They put a lot of effort into that, just as much as other women invest in their work as a lawyer or banker. They invite me to tea and show me around their homes, which are usually decorated all the way up to the ridge of the roof and stuffed with vases of flowers and heavenly potpourris. People who don't know them think that these women lead lives of unimaginable idleness, but that's not really doing them justice. Many of them—the New York society lady Nan Kempner, for example—are tireless in their engagement for charity and use their benefit banquets to collect hundreds of thousands of dollars. There are many baser interests.

JG And what are you interested in—apart from fashion and your glorious shoes?

MB Unfortunately, I don't have much free time. But I go to the cinema as often as I can. When I was a child, I knew all the Spanish and American film stars, directors, set and costume designers. I enjoyed Jane Campion's filming of Henry James' *Portrait of a Lady* a great deal. The film shows how repressive life was for women in the nineteenth century, even for a girl who was as brave as the heroine, who made such a tragic mistake in choosing her husband. I found the film divine, even though I know that most critics tore it to shreds.

JG I liked that modern *Romeo and Juliet* version, with a set like Miami Beach or L.A. That was fantastically well made. Apart from that, I love music; it makes no difference if it's classical or independent. I usually listen to music when I'm working, also when I'm designing my collections.

MB I can't stand any of this pop music; for me, it's acoustical garbage, destructive to the soul. I like Arabian music best—probably because I spent my childhood on the Canary Islands, where we heard broadcasts from North Africa. At the moment, I'm particularly fond of rai music from Algeria.

JG Did you know what you wanted to be when you were a child?

MB My career was a complete coincidence. My father owned banana plantations. He sent me to a Swiss boarding school and then I studied international law at the University of Geneva. I learned how to make shoes from my Spanish mother. She never had enough patience to wait for shoes from the cobbler and so she taught herself the craft, and I watched her. She made wooden plateau soles with colorful bands or red-chiffon ribbons which she tied around her legs. I made my first shoes for our dog—he lay on his back while I tied the laces. My mother is now eighty-three years old, but she still corrects all my sketches. Whatever I am today comes from her. My sister, on the other hand, is more sporty and business-minded, like my father.

JG I don't know where my talent comes from—both my parents were not at all creative. But when I was young, my mother said: "Good gracious, you really paint well!" And she encouraged me by giving me flowers and all kinds of other objects to copy. My love of design definitely comes from this early enthusiasm. In school, I was a daydreamer and outsider—for example, I seriously imagined that my bicycle was actually a horse. It was only at art school that I came into contact with an entirely new world of sensitive, artistic people, whose existence had been completely unknown to me up until then. Even today, I use stories as a source of inspiration. I think about a Russian princess, fleeing from the revolution: she has sewn her jewelry into her bodice and travels throughout Europe until she finally ends up in Scotland. It's enormously inspiring to try to discover precisely who this woman is, how she lives, her lovers and affairs.

MB Different from you, it took me a long time before I could start my career. I didn't finish my studies; I went to Paris, where I worked in an elegant boutique and studied stage design. In my late twenties, my good friend Paloma Picasso introduced me to Diana Vreeland in New York. At that time, Ms. Vreeland was the publisher of the American VOGUE and I showed her a few of my stage designs. I think that she found them somewhat mannered, but she seemed to like some of the costume details—particularly a pair of pumps with snakes winding their way up the leg. She advised me to try shoes.

JG A great story! With all the work you do, do you have a special way to stay healthy? I think that it's really difficult to keep a stabile energy level. When I think about the collection weeks— I get hardly any sleep for three days. It's like dancing in a crazy dream! Then I really have to be careful. I'm always tempted to eat unhealthy stuff and, of course, that makes things even worse. I used to hang around in clubs until the early hours of the morning, but now I have a personal trainer and a nutrition consultant and live quite sensibly. I have only the freshest foods on my menu—and the Hay diet. To compensate, I still smoke a bit. When I'm in the atelier, I light a cigarette and then put it down to do something else. Sometimes I don't pay attention and have four or five cigarettes burning at the same time. Impossible!

MB I'm very careful about what I eat, usually only soup for lunch. However, I'm mad about chocolate—my only vice. Last night, I ate a whole box of Godiva chocolates while I was in bed, between fresh white sheets, reading a biography. What luxury … what on earth have you done to your eyes? They're unbelievably blue.

JG They're naturally dark brown, but I wear colored contact lenses, depending on my mood. That's why I also change my earrings. Yesterday, I found the most beautiful one—with a pink stone—at an antiques market in King's Road in Chelsea.

MB I'm terribly neurotic about my appearance; I could comb myself to death—everything must be firmly stuck in place. I become crazy if a strand falls into my face. Then I take the scissors and cut it off.

JG I have to admit that I always like to look somewhat like a British eccentric.

MB Yes, but you combine that with a kind of Romanic extravagance, which is great. If you always had to wear the same thing, what would you choose?

JG For everyday work, I wear magnificent black suits handmade by the Dior atelier. But if I had to select one single piece, I would choose a long white shirt, to be worn with or without trousers. I also like manicured, polished nails—colorless polish for the city and dark red when I'm tanned on the beach.

MB Nail polish for men—to be quite honest, I find that a bit drastic.

JG Your fashion basics?

MB A white or black, fine cashmere, polo-neck sweater and beautiful cashmere socks. Tina Chow (*legendary model, 1950–1992*) was a friend of mine and she was, in her day, unquestionably the most elegant woman in the world. She always wore a simple white T-shirt under a knitted cashmere jacket from N. Peal in London, black slacks from Azzedine Alaïa, and an unusual piece of jewelry.

JG What makes you happiest?

MB I don't take drugs and I don't drink alcohol, and I've never had any great scandals or love affairs. Andy Warhol once said that I must be asexual. I'm not that. I just don't allow myself to be categorized. The most important thing in my life, and its happiness, is my work—if I ever stop talking, if I ever stop working, I would drop dead on the spot. When I prepare a major collection it's as though I was giving the world a wonderful gift. A woman quite simply has to walk differently when she's wearing my shoes—she floats. It's wonderful when a man says to me: "Thank you for making my wife so beautiful."

JG You're absolutely right. I love finding aesthetic solutions to technical challenges. Making women happy—that's also the greatest thing for me.

From VOGUE 07 / 1997; The conversation was recorded by Louise Baring

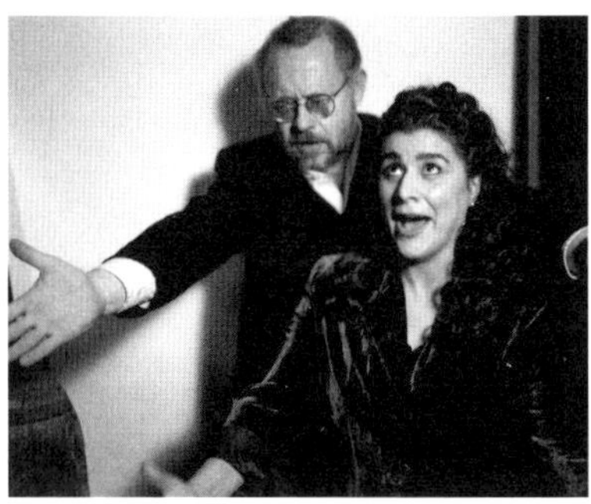

SECRET LOVE

When CECILIA BARTOLI sang the aria "Caro mio ben,"
JÜRGEN FLIMM would have liked to have been able to hide himself
under his seat. The singer and the director: a subtle duet.

A small, well-wrapped woman quickly pushes her way into the elevator. It is, as is usual in New York, cramped and dirty. Contrary to all local customs, we look into each other's eyes and recognize each other even before the elevator stops at the photo studio's floor. After greeting, Cecilia Bartoli goes immediately to the makeup table. Soon, Jürgen Flimm appears; his cunning eyes behind the round spectacles do not seem to miss a thing. The VOGUE photographer Mark Abrahams is uncomplicated and speedy. Punctually, we are in the stretch-limousine which is to bring us to the San Domenico restaurant on Central Park South. The driver wants to collect us in an hour. I decline. First of all, we are expecting the entire Bartoli family and they are not used to eating in fast-food tempo. Second, I know that things will only become interesting after the second glass of Soave. Third, we all live just around the corner. We can find our way home without any help.

JÜRGEN FLIMM It's truffle season, Cecilia …
CECILIA BARTOLI We only have pasta with truffles on Sunday. How about risotto?
JF I'd rather have pasta.
CB With pomodoro and basilico!
JF You sing in so many cities—do you look for places like this, where you feel at home? Or for something new?
CB I love the things I know, but I also need new experiences. I want to see everything, hear everything and learn. But if I'm by myself in a strange city, even the best Italian restaurant can't help against loneliness. Sometimes, I manage to drag a few colleagues along with me—or my whole family, like tonight. They came over from Italy because I've now finished my rehearsals at the Met.
JF The thing I like so much about you is your interest in words. At rehearsals you behave exactly as you did now with the waiter, where you told him precisely what you wanted, in Italian. You want to understand the meaning behind the words. That's why we'll have to wait a while until

you sing German *lieder*. You want to be in complete control of our language before you do that. (*The VOGUE conversation was held alternating between English and Italian.*)

CB Words transport thoughts. It's only when I completely know and instinctively comprehend their meaning that a complete fusion can take place: a blending of meaning and expression. That's immediately apparent with Mozart and his librettist da Ponte: amazing how the meaning and sound become one. The music already exists in the words. It's a miracle that an Austrian had such a command of our Italian language. He not only understood the meaning of the words, but also their sound; in Italian, in particular, the sound changes the meaning of what is said or sung.

JF Opera singers didn't always pay such attention to those aspects. Now, we have a new generation of singers who are prepared to take physical risks for the benefit of expression. Can you remember when we did Joseph Haydn's *L'anima del filosofo* in Vienna? I had the idea of you singing your death scene lying down; even worse, you should roll around the stage and sing! That's when you said: "Jürgen, I can do whatever you want. I belong to the new generation."

CB … to those people who try to give everything they have. By the way, it was my first death scene on the stage. You taught me how to die convincingly. Today, the audience also wants to understand the meaning of what is being sung. And that demands more than impeccable vocalization.

JF You give the audience everything, but what do they give you in return?

CB Energy. I need a place where I can share energy with others. Every good singer, every good actor, in every theater, knows immediately how the audience will react.

JF And the audience is only as good as we are on the stage. That's theater. What happens between you and others cannot be repeated, it remains unique. But I'm still afraid that I've not recognized the true spirit of a piece or interpreted it correctly in spite of the many rehearsals. We'd probably need about 200 years of rehearsal to perform Mozart's *Figaro* "correctly." In my opinion, that opera is the greatest piece of theater in the world. If you rehearse, normally you always say: "We're getting closer to the ideal, but we're not quite there yet." And that's the thing which always makes me sad. It makes me sad that, after these rehearsals, I have to leave these wonderful people. I don't only mean the actors and singers, but also the characters in the piece. The rehearsal period is the best time, the period of research and discovery. You come closer and closer to the goal. And it becomes clearer and clearer that you'll never reach the longed-for, elusive ideal. Mozart and da Ponte are too great. You'll never be able to express everything they said.

CB We can only try to come close to that. We need partners for that. I'm not an artist if my director is not an artist as well.

JF If I understood you correctly, it was a genuine passion which led you, as a fifteen-year-old girl, to music, even though, up until then, you had wanted to be a flamenco dancer. Your parents were both opera singers and your mother started teaching you.

CB I find that it's a great privilege to be able to do something that brings me so much happiness. I don't see my profession as a job, even though I earn my living from it. I don't show my real life on the stage. But what happens up there is a part of me. Sometimes I'm on the verge of a lie, but still display the truth.

JF When you're on the stage, you're always lying. That's the basis of the trade: fiction! The stage is always at least one millimeter above the rest of the world. Everything which takes place on a level above normal life, even if it's only this one millimeter, is what we call the stage. It's a sacred region. You enter into it and start lying. When you go on stage and say: "I'm not Cecilia, I'm Cenerentola," you're lying and the audience plays along.

CB But when I get into the character, it begins to allow me to determine how I can breathe life into it. There are thousands of ways.

JF Yes, every evening is different. A good production changes every day, develops further.

CB *The Marriage of Figaro* should really be called *The Marriage of Susanna*, it's really her story.

JF I feel the same. As director, I once had to say to an American singer: "I'm sorry, but you are not the main character in this opera, Figaro is not the leading role." He wanted to know why the opera was named after him. I replied that the real stress in the title was on "marriage."

CB In Italian, it's actually "the marriages," *le nozze*, plural! We don't have a singular word for marriage. There are always at least two who marry. Is it true that you're really afraid of going to your own premieres? That you sit in the canteen?

JF First of all, I'm afraid that the audience could reject the piece. And second, I'm sad because, after the premiere, the piece no longer belongs to me.

CB Don't you ever go to your own productions?

JF Usually only to the last performance. I like to see how the piece has changed over time.

CB It's probably more important to try to do things better every time than to try to immediately reach the pinnacle.

JF That's why you like to cook so much. There, you have the possibility of getting better every day …

CB And I like to eat everything up! I can't keep things for later.

JF In spite of that, you've gotten thinner.

CB The fact that everything in life and art is subject to permanent change is one of our main problems. Everyone needs a center for their life and a support. For me, it's my family. They're all sitting there at the next table waiting for us to finish this conversation: my mother, my grandmother and my sister Federica. When we've finished here they'll all come over and we'll go on eating together. This trip was my grandmother's very first flight: first class to New York! Can you see how her eyes are gleaming? My *nonna* is one of my idols, so alert and vital. She gives me something that's more important than success: it's love. Since I lost my grandfather a few months ago, I'm even closer to my family, and I have even more fear of loss …

JF Cecilia, do you think that love requires a belief in an afterlife?

CB That's a topic which goes beyond my capabilities. Like so many other musicians, I have a credo. It's an absolutely personal belief, not the Pope's. I believe in the existence of a *forza*, a power, which leads beyond our understanding, which lies outside of our field of vision, outside of our mental capabilities.

JF Is it possible to find God?

CB He finds you. Sometimes.

JF Theater is one possibility for seeking the good, for finding the good. For me, there's no other reason for having anything to do with theater. It's difficult to describe and hard to convey: it's a view beyond the horizon. Sometimes, it happens with Mozart—I can't describe it. But, I know that, then, I'm content, even if it's only for a moment.

CB This contentment exists outside of art … possibly in my garden in Rome. No matter how much I love other cities,—Zürich's sense of balance, Berlin's feeling of progress, the magic of Venice in winter—Rome is always in my heart.

JF I've often asked myself how you manage. You're sensationally successful, loved wherever you go, you see the world from a new perspective every day, and you've still remained the same: the same young woman from Rome, who lives with her family, who hasn't changed, hasn't turned into a prima donna, even though a thousand people want to do that to you every evening. How have you managed to stay the way you are, to stay so human?

CB You cannot develop into a prima donna, you have to be born with a prima donna mentality. I have no time for intrigues and tra la la. There are people for whom life itself is an art form. It's different with me. I want to live my life. It's just like this: you reap what you sow. You can cheat a bit, but not very much.

JF You must have really sown a lot.

CB Success makes it possible for me to see things with more calmness, but it also results in a great deal of loneliness. I've been here in New York for two months rehearsing Rossini's *Cenerentola* and have missed my family and friends terribly. I'm also a little homesick for my lovely garden apartment near the Villa Pamphili—that's the biggest park in Rome—where I go walking with my dog (called Figaro, of course) while my sister protects the wounded sparrows, which she keeps bringing home, from the cats. I wouldn't find traveling so bad if I didn't have to be alone.

JF You hate flying?

CB From the bottom of my heart.

JF And how do you plan on getting back to Europe?

CB I am going to fly, but full of hate! I would never fly in Europe.

JF And if you had to get from Rome to London?

CB With the train or by car—and then the ferry from Calais. That can be managed.

JF There are trains in America.

CB I tried that: by sleeper from New York to Los Angeles. Mamma mia, what a big trip! Three days, bu-bupp, bu-bupp, bu-bupp. Unpleasant and not at all comfortable. I can't believe that Americans travel by train. I love the German ICE and the French TGV: There, nobody goes through your luggage.

JF Just what is so terrible about flying?

CB You are continually told what you have to do and what not. When you have to eat, fasten your seatbelts, sit down, stand up. And then there's this claustrophobia …

JF You appear to have everything in life. Do you have any wishes?

CB Everything. I want really everything. I'm a bit like Don Giovanni: I don't have enough time! Donna Giovanna … there are so many things which I have missed and which I lack. For example, oxygen in New York. I've been breathing the same bad air for the past two and a half months I've been at the Met. I didn't visit the homes of any people who live here. I know just how different Italian people who live only one kilometer apart are from each other. How different must they be here in America? But what about you: do you have any unfulfilled wishes, a secret love life?

JF Just one secret love: Cecilia. A short time ago, she gave a concert in Hamburg with bel-canto arias. I was sitting in one of the front rows with my wife. After endless applause, she turned to me and sang *"Caro mio ben"*, an old aria which I love so much, as her last encore. She said: "This is for a friend." Everybody craned their necks. My eyes welled up, I would have liked to have hidden myself under the seat. Susie, my wife, and I bawled our eyes out. It's such a wonderful song, sung so wonderfully. It's simply irresistible …

CECILIA BARTOLI — JÜRGEN FLIMM

  From VOGUE 02 / 1998; The conversation was recorded by Gideon Bachmann

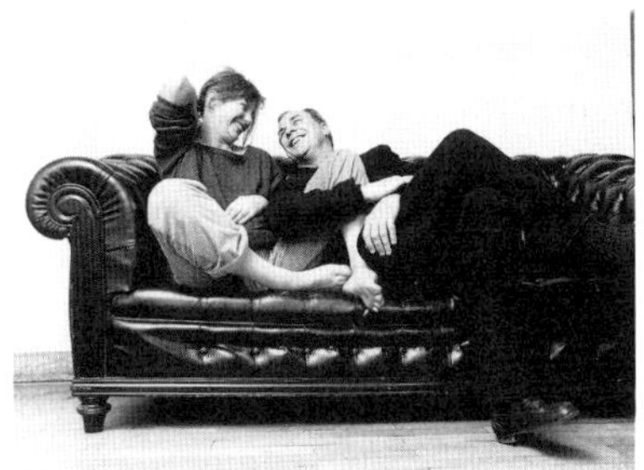

CHILDREN OF PARADISE

He's the Eros of the theater. She's the quintessence of "Je t'aime."
ROBERT WILSON, JANE BIRKIN, and an intoxicating night.

Jane Birkin glides coolly into the auditorium of the Berliner Ensemble, sporting a men's cashmere sweater, corduroys, and sneakers. The English actress, who soared to sudden fame in the 1960s with the song *Je t'aime, moi non plus*, has kept her ecstatic beauty and girlish voice. Beaming, she approaches the stage, then looks on in fascination at Robert Wilson working. The cult director is rehearsing *The Lindbergh Flight,* a young Bertolt Brecht's knavish play about Lindbergh's first crossing of the Atlantic. The American paces back and forth confidently and gracefully, giving his performers a few last comments in a soft voice. There are no props or equipment on stage. Wilson's materials are the human body and light. The actor playing the pilot even mimes the airplane he's sitting in—a vivid image of the fusion of man and machine. By the time Jane and Robert arrive at the "Borchardt" for a VOGUE conversation, it's already one o'clock in the morning. At this hour, only cheese and salad are available on the menu. But who cares when there's plenty to drink? Wilson orders vodka, Birkin wine. This isn't going to be a night for just light drinking.

Jane Birkin I noticed how gentle you are with the actors. I always imagined you as somewhat austere …

Robert Wilson *The Lindbergh Flight* has had a difficult birth. I've worked in many theaters in Germany, but I've never been as moved as I am by the Berliner Ensemble. It still has a touch of the old East Berlin to it. This production is a big challenge for the actors and the technicians. They've been going like wildfire.

JB Even 93-year-old Bernhard Minetti is working like an inspired novice under your direction!

RW The language of the body has always fascinated me. That's what we're working with in *The Lindbergh Flight.* When I was 27, I adopted a 13-year-old African-American street kid. His name is Raymond Andrews. I found him just as a cop was about to bash him on the head. The authorities said he was uneducable, and they wanted to lock him up in a prison for adolescents. I noticed that he made noises the way a deaf person does. I went to court and became his legal guardian. That was unusual at the time. We're talking about 1968. I was a gay man attempting to adopt a black child. As it turned out, the boy was very intelligent, except that his thoughts took the form of visual symbols and signals.

JB What ever became of him?

RW He lives in New Jersey. Now he speaks in sign language and works in a lab. I wrote my first play, *Deafman Glance*, with him. It had no words. The premiere was in 1971 in Paris. The theater was a hole in the wall, and we had to work hard to get the thing off the ground. We worked only with amateurs. For the second staging, I even got some people from an old folk's home.

JB Twice a week I trot off to a retirement home on the outskirts of Paris. One of the old ladies there is my friend. I've been visiting her for fifteen years. What was it like working with old people in your play?

RW It went very well. I've always been fascinated with the idea of memory loss, as if you had a hole in your head with all the information slowly seeping out. Maybe that's why I like those old ceramic Indian heads so much, the ones with a hole in the middle …

JB Name some women you admire.

RW Lady Diana. I've seen her twice. I like the dignified way she holds her head. She also has the lovely quality—when she's at a social event where she's the center of attraction—of looking people in the eye for a few moments and being able to make a real connection with them. That's an exceptional gift. Jessye Norman has this quality too—whether she's talking to a stage hand or a wardrobe person. I'm also an admirer of Marlene Dietrich. When I was a young man, I went to see her perform in Paris 17 times.

JB I remember she called us up once in Paris. She asked for Serge [Gainsbourg] and said, "I'm so lonely," with this magical, throaty voice. At first I thought someone was imitating Marlene Dietrich. But it was really her. And when she called I knew Serge happened to be sitting right at the Bar in the Hotel Raphael. He had just been released from hospital, where he'd had half his liver taken out. I gave her the number there, and she called him. After that she rang rather often, because she felt so lonely. One day she sounded so depressed, that I told her, "I'll come see you." I went out and bought her some candy because I knew she hated flowers, but at the last moment she was afraid and didn't receive me.

RW When we had dinner together, Marlene always had a lot to drink. She was always very carefully dressed and had beautifully manicured hands. But most of all she was a magnificent actress. About a year and half before she died, I visited her in her apartment. If you had an appointment, you weren't allowed to be late, something I'm always prone to be. Marlene was a true Prussian in such matters. Anyway, I asked her, "Who are your favorite performers?" She said some disparaging things about several of the most famous actresses and singers of our time. Then, finally, she said: "There's really only one I truly admire: Tina Turner. She has the legs, she has the voice, she simply has it all!" Tina was pretty surprised when I told her that!

JB It's odd that there wasn't much of a commotion made around Marlene's death in Germany.

RW I found that pretty shocking. She was the most famous international star Germany ever had!

JB She left Germany in the 1930s and went to Hollywood, and then only came back for visits. That's really all she could do, when you think about what happened. Maybe it was her instinct that forced her into exile. Sometimes I think with only the slightest inspiration we do the right thing at the right time …

RW Are you English through and through?

JB I think so. My family comes from Nottingham. Papa always used to ask me, "Which room shall I heat up for you at Christmas?" whenever I came to visit from Paris. So beautifully English! My mother, Judy Campbell, was a disturbingly beautiful stage actress. Noel Coward wrote plays for her.

RW That's where you inherited the talent …

JB The encouragement … She helped me learn my lines for my first audition. The script suddenly escaped my mind. But Graham Greene, the author, said he was looking for the embodiment of innocence and gave me the role in spite of it. I married the composer John Barry at age sixteen and had Kate, my first daughter. Thank God John left me, otherwise I'd still be running his bath water and frying his eggs. Back then I really wanted to lead a normal, bourgeois life.

RW Did your husband just disappear?

JB He explained that we'd both be better off going separate ways. I was overcome with despair and left the house with the baby. I spent the night in a telephone booth trying to reach my parents.

RW Isn't it interesting how we both were taken in by the French?

JB That's true! When I wanted to give a big memorial concert for Serge in London, I first had to convince the English how beloved Serge was in France. Mitterrand, Jack Lang, Yves Saint Laurent, Brigitte Bardot—they all had to write letters so that the concert could happen. The French are used to emigrants. That's why they take in artistic outsiders with such warmth.

RW Like Picasso, Stravinsky …

JB … or Romy Schneider and Claudia Cardinale. When Isabelle Huppert came to London to play Mary, Queen of Scots, a newspaper criticized her for her French accent. But Maria Stuart was raised in France! Speaking with an accent was the most natural thing in the world for her … Potty! When was the first time you went to France?

RW I was born in Waco, Texas, and visited France for the first time when I was seventeen and hitchhiking through Europe. I spent one fourth of all the money I had just to see Maria Callas in *Norma*. Her voice wasn't so good any more, but what a performer! Now I'm doing two or three productions a year in Paris.

JB Is it important to you what people in Waco think of you today? Do you care if they've followed your career or not?

RW Of course I do! But they don't know very much about me down there in Texas. America has very little awareness of the rest of the world. We're a very puritanical people— just look at what's happened to Clinton. I remember reading somewhere that Isadora Duncan once danced in Boston, all clad in red. At the end of the performance she proclaimed, "My entire life is red," or something like that. Whereupon the dumb Americans wrote that she was a communist!

JB You take things very literally over there.

RW I grew up in a community where a woman sinned if she wore pants. Communal dances were a sin. It was even sinful that the president of the USA, Abraham Lincoln, died in a theater. I couldn't wait to get out of there, even if I wanted to hold on to my American roots.

JB At least your parents had a sense of humor, didn't they?

RW No. My father was a lawyer, and my mother, who was born in an orphanage, was very withdrawn. She had only a few dresses—maybe seven or eight—all of them extremely rigid and tailored. As a small boy I had to dine four times a week in formal attire, with my parents and my sister, which I hated. One evening, I pulled out a dinner jacket that was way too big—it was

my father's—and one of my mother's stockings. I pulled the stocking over my head, got a flash-
light and stuck it up the front of the jacket. I climbed out the window, went around behind the
house, then came in through the living room right into the dining room. My father and my sister
were scared out of their wits and screamed. But my mother, who was sitting with her back to
me, said, "It's only Bobby …"

JB How do you approach a production? Do you have many thoughts about it before you begin?

RW Not at all. It was a shock for me in the beginning when I first came to Germany. Here the
actors sit at the table for hours on end, talking about the theater. I'm someone who likes to
respond to a situation. If I feel something, I simply let loose. You too?

JB Are you talking about intuition? Let me tell you something. About six years ago, I was
working under the direction of Bertrand Tavernier in the film *Daddy Nostalgia*. It was about
a relationship between a woman and her father, who later dies. I was terribly afraid of shooting
this film, but at the same time, I also felt obligated to—I felt as if it was somehow expected of
me. And then my father and Serge died four days apart from one another. They were the two
men who had loved me … Blindly …

RW But it didn't break you. Your career went on …

JB I think I have a series of coincidences to thank for my success. I was always stumbling upon
people who somehow understood how to use me as an actress, which always surprised me.

RW Where do you feel at home? In a pinch, I do in a hotel. I know I need to move on when
I've stayed in one place too long. When I first started in the theater in New York in 1968, I put
together my own experimental theater company on the top floor of the building where I lived
in Soho. Every Thursday evening I played the host. Whoever wanted to come was welcome,
and it lasted the whole night. There were three stages, one for dancing, one for eating, and one
for discussion.

JB I live in Paris on the left bank, alone for the first time. I remember, not too long ago, wandering
around the Place du Palais Royal with a pack of cigarettes, thinking, "How free you are!" I didn't
really feel sad, I just knew I didn't have anyone any more. There was no one I had to adapt
myself to, or for whom I would be whatever he saw in me. I've always seen myself through the
eyes of my partners and my children. Maybe I'm feeling grown up for the first time, but I don't
really know what to do with myself.

RW In that respect, I've always had the good fortune of children entering into my life. Like
Christopher. He's autistic and lived in a home for brain-damaged children. I wasn't interested in
changing him through therapy—I just cared for him. Once I took him to a Jessye Norman concert.
Christopher brought a tape recorder along. He started recording Jessye, then played back the
tape while she was still singing, which, of course, totally irritated the rest of the audience.

JB Have you ever captured your work on film? How else will you be remembered?

RW You have a point. But an artist creates one single piece. In my opinion, all of his pieces are
just one piece. Proust said that he always wrote the same novel. Cézanne said he always painted
the same image. I have created only one piece. And it will live on exclusively as memory …
*(Was that the final word? At least for now. But Robert Wilson didn't want to be alone that night.
Jane Birkin accompanied him to the hotel where they both were staying, and, many vodkas later,
when dawn was just breaking, she guided him, as he staggered to his room.)*

 From VOGUE 04/1998; The conversation was recorded by Louise Baring

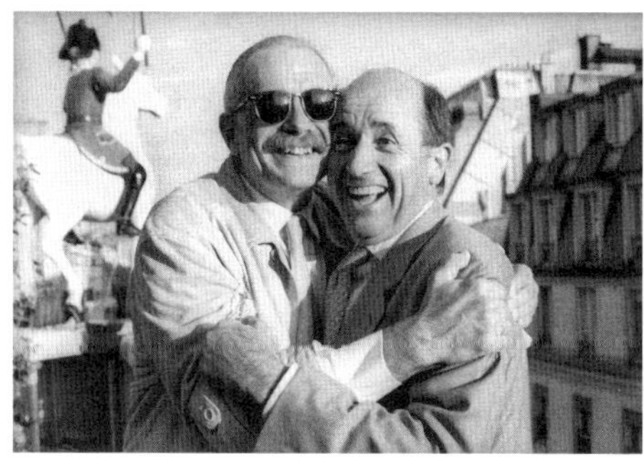

A LIFE OF LUXURY

It is often the little things that are of true importance:
Screen poet NIKITA MIKHALKOV and
JEAN-LOUIS DUMAS-HERMÈS, creator of beautiful objects.

Despite belonging to two very different worlds and having to rely on interpreters to converse, they still feel like soul mates. They both believe firmly in God, love, and human potential, and share the indestructible conviction that life is a positive experience. Both are capable of ruthless business enterprise, and both have tears in their eyes when they talk about their children and grandchildren. They are business magnate Jean-Louis Dumas-Hermès and filmmaker Nikita Mikhalkov, and they conducted their VOGUE discussion in the traditional family seat of the Hermès enterprise in Rue Faubourg St-Honoré, Paris. Both the Russian and the Frenchmen tend to talk in the slow, flowing manner reminiscent of Oblomov—probably one of the most original characters of Russian literature created by Ivan Goncharov. In the first 500 pages of Goncharov's novel, Oblomov does absolutely nothing except gradually persuade himself to get up. However, while our two protagonists may have adopted something of Oblomov's style, the content of their conversation is very much more arresting.

Nikita Mikhalkov I feel very much at home here. Everything in your house is beautiful in a peaceful, unobtrusive sort of way—as if it would allow us all the time in the world.

Jean-Louis Dumas-Hermès Perhaps that's something which will one day be—or which has already become—our greatest luxury: being able to escape the excruciating pace of daily life and living according to our own personal rhythms.

NM The luxury of slowness has, of course, always existed in Russia, and it's embodied by the character of Oblomov. As far as luxury goods are concerned, my fellow Russians will want to have all your products up to the point where they realize that they'll have to make sacrifices for them. Then they'll decide to dream about them, rather than buy them, and rummage about in their closets for their old handbags.

J-LD-H I'm sure that those old bags will also have something quite special about them.

NM I was very impressed as we went through your house just now. You might think I was taken by your heirlooms—the attractive old sled and baby carriage—but what I mean is the special aroma of the treasures rather than the things themselves …

J-LD-H You're certainly a connoisseur. The aroma of an object—whether it be furniture or wine—always betrays its quality.

NM There was something else I loved. Tolstoy once said: "Do what you have to do, and then one day you can turn around and see what you have done." What I mean is your ledgers, which have recorded all orders from the last century and which have not changed to this day. It's a fantastic thought: people today, living in a world of advanced technology, do exactly as people who had never set eyes on a typewriter; to order a saddle, they write on exactly the same lines with their ink pens and carefully fill out the same forms.

J-LD-H But it's not exactly the same. Of course, we could deal with all orders by computer. It's just the blink of an eye in the history of mankind. It's like a beat of a dragonfly's wings—however efficient it may be.

NM *Njet, non*! I don't really see it like that. I did not mean to make a compliment, Jean-Louis. What I wanted to say was that every person is an enigma, an individual cosmos. And their greatness is usually to be found in small things. People might be able to fly to the moon, but that doesn't necessarily mean that they understand the universe. I would rather look at stars in the reflection of a puddle than chase them through the sky in a rocket.

J-LD-H Nikita, I really think we must be some sort of soul mates. I'm just the same. If I wanted to find heaven, I would be more likely to look in a drop of water than at the domed roof of a planetarium. It's our family tradition to create, perhaps not eternal, but long-lasting quality through attention to tiny details.

NM And that's just what I mean when I say that everyone has their own cosmos and is the embodiment of a unique structure, and this is why it is so difficult to shed one's own skin. People have often envied me—my family upbringing—because the house was always full of artists and writers. But how did I feel about it? I didn't think it was anything particularly special. I was introduced to them, I shook their hands, and took it all for granted …

J-LD-H What luxury!

NM When visitors came it meant that I had to be on my best behavior and got dark rings under my eyes from staying up late. I don't know how often I wished that all those prominent guests would just go home, especially when I had school the next morning, so that I could finally go to bed. The world we are born into initially seems like normality—we have never known anything else. And as for your particular world, I have seen—and smelt—the conviction that this is normality in every corner of your house. It's a wonderful feeling.

J-LD-H That brings us to the question: is it still possible in this age to be different, to be in harmony with oneself? Nowadays we are subjected to aggressive global influences; the international media is trying to make us believe the same, think the same and to wash our clothes in the same way (*he suddenly bursts into laughter*)—especially our dirty laundry …

NM The way the Americans have dealt with the Lewinsky affair has given the expression "doing your dirty laundry in public" a whole new meaning.

J-LD-H Yes, but we should really just let them get on with it. What I wanted to ask is: can we produce something—in your case films and in my case quality products—which helps people to escape the grasp of these global forces? What I say to them is: buy my products so that you can be yourself, because of their quality and the time we have invested in them.

NM That's very clever. You place them under an obligation to buy a particular piece of clothing or accessory so that they believe they have at last found a sense of their own unique quality.

J-LD-H Each purchase helps them to feel more like who they really are!

NM You took over the business when it was already an empire—in my eyes this is in some ways easier and in other ways more difficult than founding a new company. It's easier because you already have a basic foundation to build upon. But it's more difficult because your vision of yourself also has to reflect a centuries-old heritage. What do you think is more challenging: setting up an empire or retaining one?

J-LD-H I don't know. But let's get back to the question of how my products can enhance your sense of self. When we were in the saddle department you mounted the wooden horse for a fitting, and I watched you very carefully. I simply tried to put myself in your place as much as I could, and I saw that you needed a saddle which provides a bit more strength and support around the knees. The moment this thought entered my head, the assistant came in with some extra leather and measured you up for this very purpose. Just as you want people to watch your films with open eyes, I want people to buy our products with all their senses engaged. I don't want to just sell a brand name.

NM That's your film, your theater!

J-LD-H (*Slowly, thoughtfully*) It's my survival strategy.

NM Good. I can accept that, and for you it is a valid statement.

J-LD-H What are your long-standing values, or why not call them "eternal" values?

NM Ah, let me tell you: my criterion is inner freedom. Irrespective of what people say about me, I never comment. Once I was at a press conference and someone asked me why I don't defend myself against journalists who don't write the truth about me. I answered: truth is something which I only discuss with God when I'm lying on my pillow. And then I told the journalists: If you write so much about me, it shows that you think I'm interesting. In some ways, I'm earning a living for you. But am I under any obligation to talk to people who make a living out of me? I prefer to choose who to talk to.

J-LD-H But you talk to everyone—you talk through your films. You tell stories.

NM That's absolutely right. My films say what I want to say. That is the message I want to convey to everyone who is willing to listen.

J-LD-H And this message is more than just an intellectual or political message, when I think of your film *Burnt by the Sun.* If I remember correctly, you tried to get the filming done extremely quickly so that you would have more time for your daughter. And didn't you tell me that you were adamant that your little girl should be able to understand the film?

NM That's true. And my daughter could not even read at the time.

J-LD-H I find this very interesting—it's a small, delicate poetic aspect. Even though my business has little to do with yours, I also try to capture this attribute. I happen to have a miniature paint box here in my bag, in a red leather box. And can you see this tiny leather pocket? There's a tiny water bottle inside. It's this little piece of poetry which, in my opinion, flavors the character of the whole.

NM It makes me want to touch it. I will tell you a story which illustrates that all handmade objects have soaked up traces of the energy of their maker. Pictures still breathe the brushes of paint applied by the artist. A while ago I was in Madrid and had enough time to visit the Prado. On that particular day I seemed to be possessed; I wanted to say hello to Hieronymus Bosch. But it wasn't enough to just stand in front of his paintings. I looked for the large haywagon triptych, and I waited for four hours until all the tourists had gone. The guard must have thought that I was a particularly devoted Bosch admirer. Then, when everyone had gone and when the guard's back was turned, the moment had arrived. I quickly put my hand on the picture. And I felt the old master immediately—I could feel him under my skin.

J-LD-H My wife is Greek Orthodox, and so I know what it means to touch an icon. Paul Valéry was right when he said that the skin is the most sensitive organ we have. Recently, I was watching one of our craftsmen placing a lid on top of a box containing a new handbag. I asked him why he was so lost in thought. He said it was strange to think that the woman who bought the bag would take it out of the tissue paper and think that she was the first to touch it, when actually it has been through so many hands already.

NM That's exactly why I refuse to cut film electronically—quite apart from the fact that we don't have the money. Touching a roll of film, knowing that it's an embodiment of experience and history—for a director it's a fantastic feeling. Writers must feel that same when they run their fingers over the pages of a newly-published book.

J-LD-H Thank you, you have brought the subject around to my favorite text which I've brought with me and which serves as a sort of compass in my life. It's a letter which Tolstoy wrote to his grandmother in 1857. These lines are about happiness, the despicable fear which stems from self-love, the uneasy peace which rests on idleness, about life's battle, which demands again and again that we give up everything and start again from the beginning, encounter failure, lose our way, and start all over again.

NM I've read that letter. Tolstoy was twenty-five when he wrote it, and even at that age he knew so much about life. As we went through your house just now and when you showed me your grandfather's travel diary or the rocking horse you used to sit on, I asked myself what really lasts for ever. Perhaps it's the soul which lives on?

J-LD-H Isn't the soul the root of all life?

NM Yes! How can a root simply stand in water without any concept of time? A few days ago I visited friends in the south of France who showed me an old olive tree. It was more than 2,000 years old. It was a very moving experience. Of course, I've also seen artifacts which are thousands of years old and which all have their history, but running your hand over the bark of a very old tree and feeling the young shoots emerging from the old wood—that is little short of a miracle.

J-LD-H Now you have taken away the last chance we had to disagree about something; the only thing I ever wrote was a booklet about olive trees which were 2,000 years old.

NM Tell me more!

J-LD-H I have the privilege of owning a house on a hill on a Greek island. The view stretches across a whole plain of olive trees which are *pre Christu,* as the Greeks would say, dating from the period just before Christ. I hope you'll visit me there one day, Nikita, and look at these olive groves. But more important than looking is feeling. You have to walk barefoot over those old gnarled roots—it's as if you are walking on waves made of stone. This experience can release an unbelievable flow of positive energy. It is as if you are walking on the stones of an ancient road— and thereby open the door of a time capsule. You feel as if you are back in the times of Christ.

NM It sounds wonderful. Trees and people have a lot in common. But there's one difference: people have roots but can still move on.

J-LD-H Yes, and one of our most important tasks is to build roads. That is exactly why I'm so enthusiastic about your films, because I've seen what a difference roads in Russia make. They are the arteries of the whole country. I find that very interesting. Roads are—if you like—my concept of the world. Because that is my craftsmanship: enabling people to travel in beauty and style.

NM Which film were you thinking of?

J-LD-H I'll never forget the scenes in the film *Black Eyes*. The road suddenly becomes the symbol for the man's intense longing for his beloved. The man has been dreaming about his love, the woman far away, for a long time. And then he starts off on the journey to her, feeling the road under his feet. The French say *prendre la route*, taking the road. I think that the leitmotif in your films is traveling along one's own path, and this is also my life's theme on a different level, on the level of craftsmanship. Traveling the road in its most concrete sense is really the traditional motif of this family, however solid and settled it may seem.

NM I live in Moscow opposite the Alexander Cathedral. Recently there were festivities to celebrate the name day of Alexander, and many people went to take communion. It is tradition in the Russian-Orthodox church that even babies take communion, because we celebrate baptism, confirmation and communion all at the same time. The small children were carried to the altar first, and then came the very old; some of them were so frail that they had to be carried too. Between these two poles, the small babies up to three months old and the old people of nearly ninety, there was a moment of union as they ate the bread and drank the wine and celebrated the Eucharist together.

J-LD-H A magic moment, when "the beginning ends" and "the end begins."

NM Yes. In the Alexander Cathedral I was an eyewitness to what we call "the path of life." As young and old met before the altar, I experienced an intense moment of the essence of life.

J-LD-H The symbols of communion—the bread and wine—are very elemental and lead us again and again to the beginning and to the end of life. It is a symbolic encounter between the material and spiritual. On the one hand, there is a spiritual union, and on the other hand, there is union with basic elements.

NM It's a symbolic celebration of the purpose of life.

J-LD-H Of course, we can say it more simply if we again resort to the words of the great Tolstoy, who once said: "The reason for life is living."

NM No one has ever provided a better answer to this question. Who could possibly surpass this weighty conclusion?

From VOGUE 12 / 1998; The conversation was recorded by Isabel Grüntges

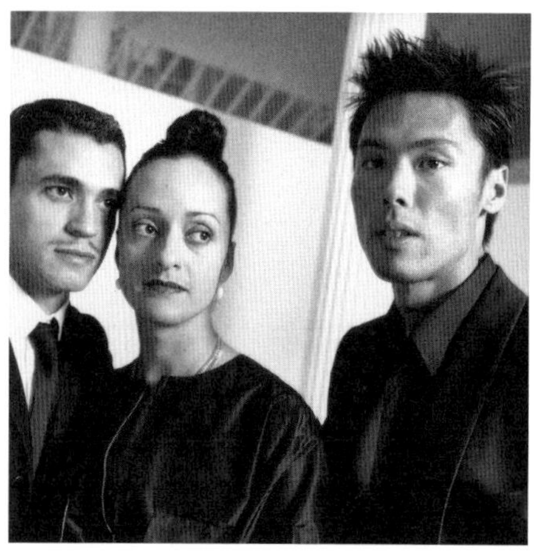

NEW YORK VISIONARIES

ISABEL and RUBEN TOLEDO meet STEPHEN GAN: the trio enthuse about fashion, art, tropical paradises and metropolitan living.

There is a dreadful storm outside. The wind is whipping rain down SoHo's small cobbled streets. There are puddles up to your ankles. But the atmosphere in the *Visionaire* office is bright and sunny. Stephen Gan plumps up the Louis Vuitton cushions on the armchairs, Ruben Toledo is joking with the photographer, and Isabel Toledo sits regally on the makeup chair with her hair in a bold knot, the very image of a Latin goddess. They have converged here for a discussion for VOGUE. This is a first for *Visionaire*, New York's avant-garde magazine for art and fashion, which has just moved into brilliantly white new offices in Mercer Street. It also marks the official opening of the *Visionaire* Gallery, presenting *The New York Kaleidoscope*, an exhibition of drawings by Ruben Toledo. This new showroom at the front of the *Visionaire* office is Stephen Gan's attempt at a three-dimensional "creative showdown" in addition to his two-dimensional glossy magazine.

Isabel Toledo Congratulations, Stephen! Your new rooms look fantastic. Now *Visionaire* is not just an avant-garde art magazine but an art gallery too.

Stephen Gan Thank you. It didn't look all that fantastic until recently. It looked more like the ballroom of the Titanic after being underwater for a hundred years. Everything had gone to rack and ruin. Even the beautiful glass roof was smeared with tar. The gallery we've installed now is more like a lounge going through to the offices at the back.

Ruben Toledo A salon for creative lounging—sounds great! Every nucleus of new ideas needs its own space where people on the same wavelength can get together. Andy Warhol had the Factory. You are part of the same tradition. I remember when you were still publishing *Visionaire* in your one-room apartment. Sometimes you had thirty visitors at once. It was the clubhouse of the avant-garde.

IT You allow people to penetrate your world. Ruben and I, on the other hand, need to preserve our sphere of privacy. In our penthouse in Herald Square, we are in another world. We work mostly in isolation and only exhibit our products from time to time.

SG You are real artists, whereas I'm just a commercial artist.

RT Art and commerce, what's the difference? It's a question of personality more than anything else.

SG You're right. Our generation doesn't really distinguish between art and commerce any more. Nike running shoes or Chanel handbags are just as attractive to me as a fine painting.

IT Do you know how to tell that something new is on the horizon? It's when old structures disintegrate, like the separation of fashion from art.

RT The fine arts are completely infatuated with fashion at the moment. We recently saw the new acquisitions of the International Center of Photography: Lillian Bassman, Richard Avedon, Irving Penn—all fashion photographers from the fifties and sixties. The museum has evidently just discovered them as artists.

SG For me, that's pure art. I only look at photos and illustrations from the fashion perspective.

IT Nothing is elite any more. Nowadays we're subject to so many different influences. We can visit museums or order clothes via the internet. In the final analysis, the real question is: which object makes a lasting impression on us? And it could be designer clothes, a bag of crisps or a painting.

RT Yes, there are no "highs" and "lows" anymore, just endless opportunities. For some it's a striptease bar and for others it's the opera. Both are valid. I even think that avant-garde has had its day; we don't need it any more. It's almost as if we've suddenly noticed that we've turned into adults and that we don't need our parents any more.

IT Talking of "highs" and "lows," I've been following the scandal at the White House with great interest. What do you think about it all, Stephen?

SG Oh, I don't want to talk about it. (*lights a cigarette*)

RT Hey, when are you going to give up smoking?

SG Shh, smoking is absolutely forbidden here! I really don't smoke much at all.

RT I tried it once, too, but it made me cough. But it looks cool. Really, everything depends on outward appearances in the end. Be honest, Leonardo da Vinci painted *Mona Lisa* because she was a mysterious woman with the right look.

IT By the way, do you know where we're going to be for New Year 1999? Kenny Scharf (*a New York artist*) has invited us to his house in Brazil. It's supposed to be very isolated and very beautiful there …

RT … and dangerous. Some people picked up parasites from walking around barefoot. The worms had to be pulled out of the soles of their feet with a pair of tweezers.

IT Perhaps we should think again.

SG What about all this euphoria about the new millennium?

RT We're already ten years into the new millennium. We were already in it while others were still waiting for it. I think this is always the case when significant dates come along. At the end of the last century there were already quite a lot of very modern people. The rest of mankind needs fifty years to catch up. I love the future, new developments, the latest craze!

IT We attach great importance to the New Year. We think that the way we bring in the New Year sets the tone for the whole year. That's why we have certain rituals. At midnight we throw water out of our windows—a Caribbean custom. You should always have a bowl of water in your house to catch the bad spirits. At New Year you throw them out and make a fresh start.

SG You'll have to watch out then, won't you, living in a penthouse?

RT Where will you spend the New Year?

SG I would like to be in southeast Asia—my favorite destination. You must come with me sometime!

IT What's so special about it: is it the culture or nature?

SG I feel completely at ease and surrounded by luxury when I'm on the beach in Phuket or Bali. And I don't mean in some expensive resort. What attracts me is the beauty of nature, the atmosphere of calm and a feeling that everything is in harmony.

RT I understand. We all come from tropical climes—places where even the fruit seems to grow more than anywhere else. You were born on the Philippines, and we come from Cuba. But you're of Chinese ancestry. Did that make you feel different?

SG My grandparents emigrated from China to the Philippines. As a second generation immigrant I didn't have any real problems. I learned Chinese, English and Tagalog—the native language of the Philippines—at school, and I speak all three. But I was always aware of belonging to a minority. People always used to ask me where I come from—even more than in New York.

RT Is there racism in the Philippines?

SG Racism is too strong a word. But the Chinese have the same sort of reputation as the Jews here. People say that they are profiteers.

IT Cubans are often called "the Jews of the Caribbean" because it seems they're only out to make money.

SG There are other parallels too. The Philippines used to be a Spanish colony. The Latin influence is still very strong—like the influence of the Catholic church. I was raised a Catholic.

IT Not a Buddhist? I would never have thought it. I was also raised a Catholic. But our religion is strongly influenced by Santeria, a nature-worshipping African religion.

RT We're also similar because the paranormal is quite familiar to us. Cubans and Filipinos regard magic and superstition as part of everyday existence. Americans always look for logical, scientific explanations. Our cultures allow more fantasy.

SG The Americans have Walt Disney. They make a business out of fantasy.

RT Every time we're on vacation lying under palm trees somewhere, Isabel says: "Wouldn't this be a nice place to live?" But I always feel attracted to the busiest parts of the world, for example the corner of 42nd Street and Times Square. We used to live there once.

IT Yes, right above a peep show.

SG Did New York help you to become the people you are?

RT Definitely. In New York, you can change into a completely new person. I came here when I was seven. At that time, I had no idea about rules of behavior in America, and so was free to develop as I wanted. If I had stayed in Cuba, I might have turned into a typical Cuban. Here, I was allowed to determine my own fate. I even invented new memories. That's why I'm happy to be an immigrant. If we have any children, we'll take them to another country so that they can have the same sort of experience. How was it for you?

SG I came here from Manila when I was eighteen and felt at home immediately. It doesn't actually matter where you come from if you work in the fashion industry.

IT Do you think people in New York are lonelier than anywhere else?

SG No. I think they're the best communicators in the world. People say that all New Yorkers are lonely and unfriendly, but I've met so many nice, warmhearted people. Perhaps it's because they all live so close together. Everyone knows their neighbors.

IT But they all live on top of each other, so it would be only natural to avoid close contact. Isn't hiding in the masses one of the things that New Yorkers do best?

SG Lots of them try. But for me it's like going to a fashion show with sunglasses on and thinking that no one will recognize me. Everyone thinks that they have to travel incognito—out of the limousine and in through the back door of the restaurant. That's a part of the glamour that everyone associates with New York.

IT To be honest, I feel better away from New York. I never felt part of the city.

RT Isabel's a real country girl. She grew up in a village where hens run around on the road. You should see her when she visits her sisters in Puerto Rico. She runs through the garden in her underwear and waters the flowers. She looks really glamorous, but she thinks she's just a simple country girl.

IT I'm glad I grew up like I did. I don't want to feel the hard edge of the city all the time.

RT Isabel would probably never lock the door and would trust any stranger who turned up if I didn't keep reminding her that large cities can be dangerous places. On the other hand, my hometown, Havana, is just as tough as New York.

SG The good thing about city life is that you can have both—peace and action. Once I was at a tea ceremony in Tokyo in a beautiful little Japanese house surrounded by a garden of bamboo. I nearly forgot that we were actually on top of a fifty-story skyscraper. What a fantastic paradox! The owners run around in kimonos like Zen monks. And then they take the lift, pick up their car in the underground garage and go to the movies.

RT New York has changed a lot in the last ten years. It's much more business orientated now. Before, you used to meet really amazing people in the streets. Now, you have to have an appointment. And our interns are already talking about their "career" at the age of twenty! They're under enormous pressure. We can still afford to try out new things.

IT New York has lost its innocence. Nowadays it's a theme park with Walt Disney in the middle.

RT Have you seen the new *Condé-Nast* building at Times Square? We can see it from our window. It's got enormous advertisements right at the top, like in *Blade Runner*, that science fiction film. Worldwide, New York is still the city with the most sex appeal.

IT I don't agree with you there. It's got a sexy facade, but down here (*she pats her stomach*) it's as cold as ice.

RT That reminds me of a good anecdote. In 1979 I was working for Fiorucci. Once, on my way home, I saw a man and a women in an office having sex—at half past four in the afternoon in a doorway in Midtown. I liked them for their naivety and simple desire. You don't see things like that any more in New York.

SG Wasn't that the time you applied for a job as a dildo designer?

RT Yes. I answered an advertisement which read: "Firm requires artist for design of rubber objects." I thought they were talking about toy dolls. But when I visited the small back street factory they were producing dildos.

SG Did you get the job?

RT No. The only people working there were old Italian men and women, and I think they were too embarrassed to talk to a young man about penises. A shame really.

SG Why would you have liked to work there?

RT Well, I'm actually very familiar with the shape! And I think that artists should be employed in all walks of life—designing dildos, trash cans, teacups, or whatever. It improves the quality of life.

SG Isabel, does your Latin background influence your work?

IT I don't know. I'm always very precise in my work, very clear. Is that a Latin attribute?

RT And there's something inquisitorial about you. I don't know if that's just your Spanish blood. Perhaps it has more to do with your character. When we were working with the choreographer Twyla Tharp, I was struck by the similarity between Twyla and Isabel—the American grande dame of dance, next to Isabel with her strict Spanish look. It reminded me of the time I first saw Kabuki dancers and geishas in Japan. I immediately thought of flamenco dancers. Kindred spirits find suitable forms of expression, even if they're in different parts of the world.

IT Some tribes are related to each other in that they demonstrate the same body language, rather than belonging to the same nationality. As a fashion designer, this is very important for me. That's why I immediately noticed your sandals, Stephen. They're a sign of your closeness to the earth.

SG I wear them as a sign of protest; I don't care what sort of storm is going on outside, I'll still be wearing my light summer shoes. I love this sort of paradoxical philosophy. If war breaks out, let's open a bottle of champagne!

IT I watch people for hours—the way they walk and stand, and seeing why they move in a certain way. Sometimes the question "why" is almost more important than the visible result.

SG When you stand in front of your wardrobe, does it take long for you to decide what to wear?

IT No, that happens intuitively. Often I'm in a certain phase which can go on for weeks, or even months, and I dress accordingly. It's like slipping into a role.

SG A friend once told me that he had never seen his mother without false eyelashes. Even if the house burnt down, she would probably stick them on before running out.

RT Vanity can be a source of strength, or even a virtue. I think it can even protect us from stupidity.

SG How do you dress?

RT I choose my clothes according to how they feel, not how they look—except on special occasions, of course. Sometimes I wear the same jacket all year round.

IT Women are really different in that respect. Sometimes I change three times a day because I love change!

RT Perhaps women are more confident than men. They know who they are and can shed their outer skins more easily.

SG Women are always more concerned about their appearance. And they have more opportunities to express themselves. They can put flowers in their hair, they love tight belts and the pain of wearing high heels.

RT But wearing nothing at all is the most comfortable—being completely naked in warm weather.

IT That's the great difference between us: I love clothes, and Ruben would rather take his off. When I get home I change clothes, and Ruben does a striptease.

RT Clothes annoy me, just like jewelry. I don't even wear a wedding ring. I would feel

  strangled.

IT I like feeling something tight. Sometimes I wear a belt underneath a dress because I like the feel of it round my waist.

SG Clothes are something of a paradox. On the one hand, they can be practical: we develop smart new material which keeps the rain off and lets the skin breath at the same time. But on the other hand, we still have shoes with high heels—which are probably the most impractical piece of clothing you can think of. How do you explain the high-heel phenomenon?

IT It's all to do with sex. When women wear high heels they move in a sexy way, their hips swing and their breasts are pushed forward. You can see the effect best on men who wear high heels. They move differently, in a more feminine way.

SG Well, not always. I once wore high heels for two hours. I felt incredibly clumsy. I wish I were graceful enough to walk in them.

RT I don't know if I like the idea of men in high heels. Is that your concept of beauty?

SG Let me ask a different question. What is beauty anyway?

RT Beauty is, for example, when something has been extremely well thought through and constructed, like these Charles Eames chairs we're sitting on.

SG The dividing line between really brilliant objects and pure ugliness is paper thin. The great art director Alexey Brodovitch always used to say: "Try and surprise me." That should be our guiding motto today.

From VOGUE 04/1999; The conversation was recorded by Ute Thon

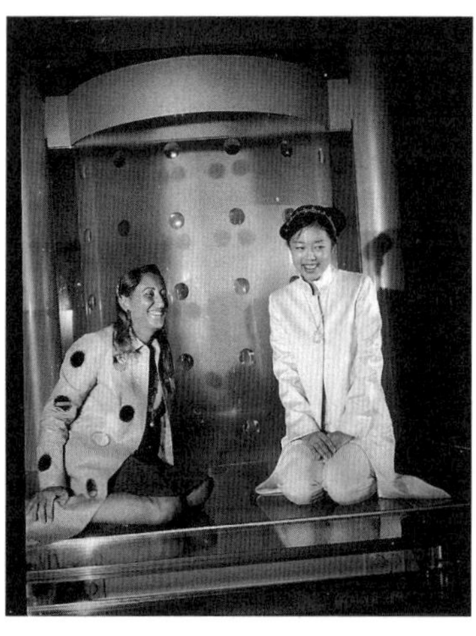

TEMPLE TALK

Tryst in a high-tech pagoda: Milan's fashion sphinx MIUCCIA PRADA and Japanese artist MARIKO MORI unfold their visions for the future and voice secret desires.

They meet in the temple of dreams. Using a combination of high-tech plastic and Murano glass, Mariko Mori has erected what resembles a small pagoda or an enchanted Japanese pavilion in Milan's Fondazione Prada. In the dusky light of the room which surrounds it, the *Dream Temple* seems to float effortlessly in the air. But actually, it is the visitors who float into a dreamland. One by one they enter a cabin at the heart of the temple, and then Mariko Mori's hallucinatory computer-animated video projection sends them on a journey through oceans, galaxies and abstract spaces—through a material and spiritual cosmos.

The artist arrives first, wearing a high-collared Miu-Miu coat and a small, glittering, fragile diadem in her hair. She is the very image of a Japanese princess, removed for a few hours from her peaceful, secluded life within the walls of a royal palace. Miuccia Prada arrives shortly afterwards. She is wearing a coat spangled with round mirrors—an item from her new collection. Whenever she moves, the mirrors reflect the lamps set up for the VOGUE photo shoot, and bursts of light dance across the walls of the hall where Mariko Mori's temple stands.

Mariko Mori Look at all that light! It looks as if you want to send out messages or signals.
Miuccia Prada Perhaps I do, because I'm in your *Dream Temple*, which has given me so many signals and messages. And I certainly wanted to wear something glittery because this place shines and shimmers. And what could shine more than all these mirrors? By the way, what is that shimmering sand underneath the temple?

MM Oh, it's not actually sand at all. It's tiny fragments of the same sort of transparent plastic as the temple steps, and they change color according to how the light falls. For me, this smooth transition from one color to the next is a wonderful reflection of our own state of consciousness, which is also constantly changing from second to second.

MP Isn't it strange how we've been working on your exhibition here for so long, but haven't had a chance to sit down and talk? Our medium of communication up to now has always been your work. It has introduced me to whole new worlds—like the work of a number of other young artists I know. The art I used to be involved with was much more intellectual and restrained. Nowadays, artists—and you in particular—work on a much more spiritual level.

MM Perhaps it's because we address old longings. The dream of creating a utopia or some sort of ideal environment is part of the history of civilization. It goes back 4,000 years.

MP Your new works are very architectural. In the large photos you made earlier, you were always taking on new roles. Sometimes you look like a woman from the future, and sometimes you look like a figure from the distant past.

MM Those photos and performances are an attempt to clarify my position as a woman in Japanese culture caught between ancient tradition and extreme experimentation. I believe very strongly in individuality and self-discovery.

MP That doesn't sound very Japanese.

MM That's true. And I know I can't sever my identity from my social environment, but that doesn't mean I'm tied to it—or to any other political or religious ideas or institutions. But we were just talking about the way I change roles—isn't that just what you do with your new fashions? Offer women the chance to slip into new roles?

MP No, that's not really my aim. I don't think a dress can change someone's personality. And I don't think much of the idea that fashion is art. It confuses issues. Of course, you have to have a certain feel for where society is going with regard to fashion and art—the sort of social conscience which influences our work. But that's where the similarity ends. But what do you think? You've lived in both worlds. I heard you used to be a model and a fashion designer.

MM No, no, not really. In the mid-eighties I studied fashion for two years, and then I did a bit of modeling. But I never had a career as a model, and I certainly didn't have one in the fashion business. It has nothing to do with my present work. Your career wasn't very straightforward either, was it? Didn't you study politics, and drama at Giorgio Strehler's theater?

MP (*Waves off the remark*)

MM What were your goals then?

MP Did we have goals at that age? Dreams perhaps—but not goals. Well, I was a member of the Italian Communist Party, and I was very involved in the feminist movement during the seventies.

MM What did Comrade Prada wear when she went to the party meetings?

MP (*Laughs*) I expect it was rather repulsive for some. I was used to wearing finer clothes, as I had always been dressed in classic children's clothes. And I didn't see why a member of the Communist Party shouldn't wear Yves Saint Laurent or Kenzo.

MM Wasn't it very difficult to adjust when you took over the family business? How did you cope?

MP It took a long time. To be completely honest with you, it's only during the last few years that I really feel at ease.

MM Do you think your fashions can influence politics?

MP Oh no! As I said, you have to know a bit about what's going on to create fashion. But if I wanted to go into politics, I would do something completely different. Fashion is just about as political or apolitical as art.

MM What does your family think about what you do?

MP Oh, my mother still nags at me when I wear Prada because she thinks it makes me look too fat. But often, a little while later, I'll see her wearing the same thing. She's over eighty and looks great in it! But in situations like that, I still feel like a little girl. You're probably better off. I heard you made one of your sculptures with your father.

MM Not quite. My father died eight years ago. He was a scientist, and his inventions still exist today. I use his discoveries in my *Enlightenment Capsule*—a way of transmitting natural light over long distances. In my model of a transparent meditation bubble, this technique enables light to travel along certain plastic elements. But in the future, it will be used to transmit light underneath the earth, for example, to underwater bases or cities, because this is a system which transports light energy and filters out the heat.

MP That sounds wonderful, but also very utopian. You must be fascinated with modern technology—you do so much work with high technology, computer photos and three-dimensional videos—but you use them to show aspects of ancient mythology.

MM I use modern techniques like virtual reality because they allow me to pick up on themes from the past and move into something which I call the "eternal present." What I mean is that there are formal and symbolic elements which have their origin in the distant past or extinct cultures, but which reach into the present and predict the future. Both art and technology look ahead toward the imminent future in search of what is "new." They operate under similar conditions and aim to solve the essential problems of humankind. But from a practical point of view, working with the newest possible technology means that I need help from lots of different people—specialists—and I have to get them to visualize my ideas. You have to explain your ideas too, don't you, so that people can carry them out? Do you have to quell opposition, as well?

MP Not really. In my experience, good ideas are always well received. Of course, they have to be worked at, and sometimes it's a battle. But if the idea is really good, it will be realized and turn out to be a success. If it's not successful, the idea wasn't good enough.

MM I envy you—you've got concrete criteria which can measure your success. People either buy your clothes or they don't. In the art world, you have to learn very quickly how to deal with opposition, criticism and disapproval. Some people have such a different experience of life and think in such a different way that my work means absolutely nothing to them. I have to be aware of these differences and accept them. But I mustn't let myself be influenced by them. Have you never experienced failure in a project you loved, or made a mistake that you loved?

MP A mistake I loved? No, I haven't made any of those. A mistake is a mistake. The best thing I can say about my mistakes is that they were always my own mistakes and I never made them to please other people.

MM While we're on the subject, does it please you to see all sorts of women wearing your clothes, or do you sometimes think to yourself, "Oh God! She really ought to have bought something else!"

MP I don't presume to judge. Everyone makes their own decisions and is responsible for themselves. On the other hand, I love seeing an interesting or beautiful woman wearing Prada. I always like beauty and find it fascinating. Beauty is certainly better than ugliness.

MM Strange that you should say that, seeing as you've just made fashion history by launching your "Ugly Prints" and "Bad Taste" collections.

MP What do you mean, "ugly"? I always liked those patterns! (*laughs*) Those prints remind me of the seventies; the really wild girls wore them while I was still running around like a good well-behaved girl.

MM Do you miss that element of wildness or freedom? Wouldn't you just like to travel around the world?

MP No, no. I love being here with my family. When I was younger I traveled all the time, so now I'm very careful when it comes to deciding whether it's really worth going to some exhibition, trade fair, play or some other event.

MM I'm quite different. I absolutely love traveling. I can think best when I'm in the air, and I get my best ideas on airplanes. If I had the choice, I would live on a plane and spend all my time flying—looking at the sky, the clouds, the sea and the land beneath me and the stars above—without ever having to land. But of course, the most important place is our own inner sanctum. It's not so important where we live or what our outward circumstances may be. We can only find peace and love within ourselves.

MP In spite of that, I really do want to have a nice place to sleep, eat and enjoy some peace. But of course, you're right. Everything depends on your priorities. Everyone has to define what they want and to feel in harmony with themselves. I think your *Dream Temple* is a place where people can feel this way.

MM Right from the very beginning, cultures of every description—East and West—dreamed about an ideal place, beautiful and pure—about a happy, non-place. The Yumedono, Japan's oldest temple, is an attempt to create such a place. *Dream Temple* follows in the same tradition.

MP That's in keeping with the principles of the Fondazione Prada, which is only intended for exhibitions which are preposterous and wonderful at the same time. But tell me, what was the inspiration for those wonderful, flowing, but also disturbing, abstract video pictures in the temple's cabin?

MM At the beginning, my attention focused on the experience of the human fetus. I thought about its perceptions, its level of consciousness inside the womb. That was the starting point for the projection. I decided to create a space where everyone could take a look at themselves. Because enlightenment is something which necessarily involves the body and the conscious mind. I have tried to develop the contact between microscopic and macroscopic worlds and move on into a new dimension where everything belongs to a universal whole and where "now" lasts for eternity.

(*For the photos, both women sit on the platform of the temple. Miuccia Prada sits at ease, like a European, while Mariko Mori kneels in a position which is almost ceremonial. When they have finished, Mariko momentarily has problems getting up. Her legs have gone to sleep.*)

MP Strange that that should happen you!

MM As you can see, Japanese women don't spend much time on their knees anymore.

From VOGUE 08/1999; The conversation was recorded by Bernd Skupin

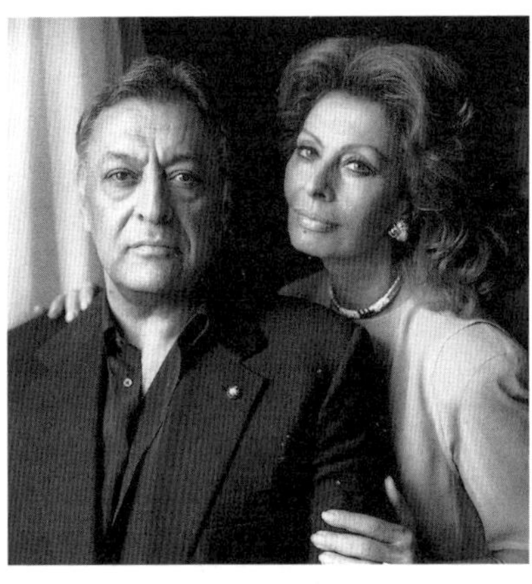

FAME FROM THE INSIDE

Nobody's perfect, not even film stars and idols:
SOPHIA LOREN admits that she is shy, and ZUBIN MEHTA
smuggles roast chicken onto airplanes.

The audience is looking at the stage in great anticipation. It is waiting for the appearance of Zubin Mehta, who is about to conduct Wagner's monumental opera *Tristan and Isolde*. But suddenly the attention of the Florentine public turns away from the conductor's podium to one of the boxes, where Sophia Loren has just taken a seat. Suddenly, as if reacting to some directive, all the Wagner lovers and Mehta enthusiasts jump up and wave their programs for the diva to autograph. It is at this very moment that the maestro appears and smiles in a generous and understanding manner. For of course, Mehta—the musical genius from India—and Sophia Loren—the film icon of Italy—are actually very good friends and even neighbors. For some time now, they have both been living in Los Angeles for at least part of the year. However, what binds them even more is their mutual love of music. Sophia's youngest son, Carlo Ponti junior, has decided not to follow in his mother's footsteps. He aspires to Mehta instead. On Mehta's advice, he studied music at Vienna's Academy of Music. Also, he received private instruction from Mehta's ninety-year-old father, who was the former conductor of the Los Angeles American Youth Symphony Orchestra. This discussion for VOGUE took place in Hotel Excelsior in Florence. As a sort of overture, Sophia Loren and Zubin Mehta talk about culinary delights—about ingenious Italian pasta, delicious Indian chicken and scandalous airplane menus.

Zubin Mehta Sophia, smell the aroma of this insalata caprese—those fresh tomatoes and wonderful basil—I warmly recommend it! But then, you have to eat something more substantial. In Florence you should eat meat …

Sophia Loren Yes. I get enough fish in Naples.

ZM I will order pasta first, although it can't possibly be as good as that fantastic lasagna you cooked for me at your house in Los Angeles.

SL When was that?

ZM Sometime during the last four years. The first time we met was four years ago, wasn't it?

SL Yes, I remember. You were having a party. I wanted to meet you so much that I asked a mutual friend, the costume designer Norman Miller, to get me an invitation. But I felt as if we had known each other for years—as if we had always been friends!

ZM You know how much I love food. That unforgettable lasagna, followed by that sensational tiramisu—that was the beginning of a wonderful friendship. And I thought that a world famous star like you would never set foot in the kitchen! I really thought you would hang around decoratively and pretend to be a good cook.

SL Really, what did you think of me! Do you remember when you unpacked your mother's cooked chicken in the airplane? And how we got all those disgusted looks when we ate it?

ZM They weren't disgusted; they were just jealous because food on airplanes is dreadful. My mother knows that, and even now, although she is over ninety, she would never forget to pack a picnic lunch for me if I'm about to go on a journey. Especially when I fly to Israel—where I go a lot because I conduct the Israel Philharmonic Orchestra. The food on El Al is kosher, but apart from that, it's the worst food you can get on an airplane. As the Rabbis also sit in first class, I always have to hide my mother's fried chicken when I unwrap it. Otherwise I would get into trouble.

SL Your mother seems to be worse than the Italian mamas. I have never spoiled my sons like that. But I ring them up every day, and recently I've been spending more time at my house in Geneva to be closer to them. Carlo is studying in Vienna, as you know, and Edoardo, who is gaining his first experience as assistant director, is in Italy getting ready to start filming with Michelangelo Antonioni.

ZM Do you think I don't call my parents? If I don't call for three days, mama has a fit. My father is a bit more patient, but on the other hand, he's very critical of my work. He's always got some comment to make, especially about the pace of the music. He often complains that it's too quick. On his ninetieth birthday he came to Munich to hear Tristan. And afterwards, the only thing he said was: "Why did you keep the orchestra so quiet? I don't just want to hear the soprano—I want to hear the lines of musical development, too!" He never fails to comment on something he's not happy with, my dear papa. That's why you should be very pleased when he says Carlo is good! H's always saying it. And I can only add that your son loves music with a rare passion—that's the best prerequisite for becoming a good conductor.

SL Well, let's hope so. He always loved music and playing the piano, even when he was very young. But it's not easy to become a conductor.

ZM Why don't you fly to St. Petersburg next week to support him at the small concert he's conducting?

SL No, I don't want to cling to him. Perhaps it's because everyone used to cling to me—first my mother and then my husband, Carlo, who has always given me my marching orders.

ZM Even now that he's over eighty?

SL No, now I'm in command—at least I think so. But I rule more through diplomacy. Mostly, I do things which I know Carlo likes—even before he asks me to. And who is the boss in your relationship, maestro, you or your wife, Nancy?

ZM As a conductor I have to conduct, and that means giving orders—otherwise nothing works. On a private level, I find it very difficult to act differently, and music takes up such a big part of my life. For the first time in years, I've taken seven weeks off. It's only very recently—since I started with the Munich opera—that I've come to understand what free time is. My colleagues are all wonderful people and excellent musicians. And on Sunday mornings I do sports. I'm a member of the Munich cricket team! Foreigners—including lots of Indians and Pakistanis—are in the majority. And we're a mixture of professors, cooks, waiters and doctors. We just won a match against Frankfurt!

SL Have you got any other conductor friends?

ZM That's rather a strange thing. In the old generation—the Karajan generation—all the conductors hated each other without exception. Who knows why. But we—the so-called young generation of conductors—we like each other, value each other and like to be in contact. I'm good friends with Riccardo (*Muti*), Claudio (*Abbado*), Daniel (*Barenboim*) and Lorin (*Maazel*). We all regret not being able to attend each other's performances, but we simply don't have the time. We're not jealous of each other because we all have so many commitments—not a day goes by without having to refuse a new contract. And jealousy is very destructive anyway. But you know that better than me—the film world is in quite a different league from the world of music.

SL Yes, unfortunately, but I'm not actually affected. I'm not jealous of anyone, and I think that I'm generally liked by my colleagues. Of course, there is always someone or other that I'd rather not meet again. But there's no way I would say who that is. And then there are those I carry in my heart, especially Marcello Mastroianni, followed by Vittorio de Sica, who I worked with for many years and who I owe much of my career. Cary Grant, Walter Matthau … But I love many of the younger actors, too: Richard Gere, Julia Roberts, and the wonderful Italian Raoul Bova and, of course, the other Italian, Robert de Niro—though unfortunately he can't say much in Italian except *ciao*, *buon giorno* and *bello*!

ZM Don't you have any other friends among your colleagues?

SL I'd say I've got lots of acquaintances. And anyway, I'm rather shy.

ZM What? I can't believe it!

SL Lots of people can't. But I can assure you that it's something I've been carrying around with me since early childhood—and I just can't get rid of it. I think it's the way I was brought up. That's why I have always put myself under the protection of my husband, Carlo—even at the age of sixteen. He was thirty-six at the time.

ZM Sophia Loren, the shy goddess!

SL There are lots of things about film stars that the public doesn't know. People watch films and see actors playing certain roles, but they can't see inside the person who is acting. They don't know anything. They don't know that I'm shy; they don't know that I crammed and practiced like a madwoman to lose my accent. Otherwise, I would have been the laughing stock of Hollywood because they look down on Italian accents. Marcello Mastroianni, who used to get into a huff quite easily, felt that very keenly …

ZM What happened?

SL He felt so unsure of himself when it came to speaking English that he became very distrustful. Once, on a set, someone said to him: "How do you do?" And Marcello, who couldn't speak much English, turned grimly to me and asked: "What did he say?" Afterwards, we both laughed, but initially he almost took offense.

ZM In the music world it's basically the same. The public only sees and hears what it wants to see and hear. People have no idea about the difficult rehearsals, the diplomacy I have to use on a daily basis so that the singers and the orchestra work together to achieve a harmonious result. And they have no idea about the miracles we always have to perform before managing to launch a premiere. And they have no idea of the good luck we need for it all to happen.

SL Good luck is also a key element in the world of film and theater. At least once in your career, you need good luck. Best if you have it right at the beginning!

ZM Yes, landing a role for the first time is often a piece of pure luck. And you don't get much further unless you throw yourself into it with a passion. By the way, my mother wanted me to become a doctor—not a musician like my father, who spent his whole life playing the violin and conducting. Like the dutiful son I was, I obediently took a few medical examinations. But then I bolted and fled to the world of music. Because that was the life I'd always dreamed of!

SL As for me, I never ever imagined I could become a film star. I didn't even think of becoming an actress. I lived in Pozzuoli near Naples, and my mother was a piano teacher. The greatest achievement I could imagine was to be like her—or perhaps to move to Rome and marry a handsome young man. But then Hollywood came: and then the Oscars, the traveling, the houses, and friends all over the world. I just let myself be carried away by events—and I really don't know if I have deserved all that.

ZM Do you have any regrets?

SL No, none whatsoever.

ZM I do—in my private and public life. Like never meeting Stravinsky, for example. I loved his music and often conducted his work. But I never actually went ahead and looked him up, although he lived in Los Angeles, too. I never rang him up or asked to meet him. Why? My own stupidity, superficiality, perhaps youthful pride—I don't know. When I realized, it was too late. He was already dead. I can never recover the loss. As far as my family goes, my reactions were quicker. I noticed my mistakes in time and it was possible to make changes. For example, I saw to it that I wasn't solely consumed by my work. What about you, Sophia, have you ever had to fight for your family? Or did everything go smoothly right from the beginning?

SL I'm sure you know, maestro, that women always fight for their families. In this sense I am very traditionalist—typically Italian.

ZM Are you homesick at all?

SL No—for several months in the year I live in Geneva, and Italy isn't really far. I can always go and visit my sister Maria or my nieces in Rome. Life in Switzerland is very pleasant; peaceful, tranquil and ordered—that's the way I like it. The house and garden are nice, and I have my two cats, who are graceful and quiet, and my sons visit me whenever they can. And the Swiss are very charming: friendly, helpful …

ZM You can say that because you're a beautiful woman. Beautiful women don't know anything about the world because everyone is on their best behavior. It's just the same with my wife. She enthuses about everyone she meets. Nancy's always saying: "They were so nice to me!" When she travels, she never has to pay for excess baggage, but I always have to. I bet the airlines don't ask you to pay either.

SL You're right! And I travel so often!

ZM But you also do mad things. Like flying to Peking for a day to hear Puccini's *Turandot*.

SL Because you were conducting the opera!

ZM Thank you, madam. But after your heart problems last year, I hope you won't embark on any more escapades like that.

SL Yes, I really have quieted down a bit. We've talked about this before, Zubin. I was very frightened when it happened—I thought I would die. When the heart is affected, people always think about dying. I have prayed a lot, to the Virgin Mary and to Mother Teresa of Calcutta, but it didn't help me to get over my fear of death. After that experience, I often think about death.

ZM I think a lot about death, too. But I'm not worried about it because I'm sure I still have many years of life before me. I still have so much to do; so much wonderful music to study and perform. The God of the Parsees—I belong to the Parsee religion—cannot let me die just yet. I'm so convinced of this that I'm happy for all the other passengers when I'm on an airplane, because there's absolutely no chance of it crashing!

SL You're lucky! What are you working on at the moment?

ZM We're just casting actors for the film of *La Traviata*—the director is Giuseppe Patroni Griffi, who directed *Tosca* in 1992. We have already decided on Ruggero Raimondi and José Cura—two wonderful personalities and, above all, they have excellent voices.

SL Oh, I would love to be Violetta in your film! I'm very good at sync too, as they call it in Hollywood. When I appeared in *Aida* a long time ago, everyone thought I could sing. But actually it was the voice of a great soprano singer, Renata Tebaldi. What a shame, I'm probably too old for Violetta now. There just aren't enough good parts for mature actresses. Let's hope that Michelangelo Antonioni will soon start work on his film *Destinazione Verna*. My son Edoardo is assistant director, and I'm playing a role I like very much.

(*Every five minutes during the conversation, a waiter approaches Sophia Loren with autograph requests from the other guests, but this time he hands a note to Mehta. The maestro nods and whispers. A moment later, the waiter brings back a box. Mehta opens it—and takes out some large, golden-colored mangoes.*)

ZM May I offer you a mango from my home country? A childhood friend of mine who lives in Bombay sends me some every month. Even if we don't see each other for five or six years, he never forgets. They're a gift from the gods—and so, for you, they're the perfect thing!

From VOGUE 11/1999; The conversation was recorded by Isabella Bossi Fedrigotti

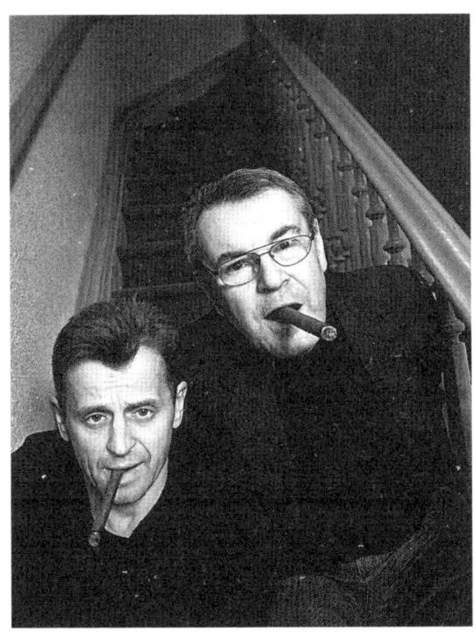

THE ZOO OR THE JUNGLE

Hollywood director MILOS FORMAN and the dance-god
MIKHAIL BARYSHNIKOV are in agreement and sing the praise
of life, its dangers, and real emotions.

Meeting place, Broadway, New York City, in the private room above the Russian Samovar restaurant. Milos Forman is the first to arrive. Fifteen minutes later, Mikhail Baryshnikov appears. They have been friends since the beginning of the seventies, but this is their first meeting in the new millennium. "Milos!" "Mischa!" Mischa hands Milos a cigar. He thanks him for it: "Wonderful! You know I can't stand the taste of these things—but I am addicted to them." The masculine ceremony of cutting the cigar takes place, then both smoke in solemn reverence. After the major portion of the tobacco has turned into white ash, Baryshnikov cries out: "I'm dying of hunger!" Change of scene: the main dining room of the Russian Samovar. He orders vodka, caviar and smoked fish *à la russe*. The VOGUE conversation can begin.

MIKHAIL BARYSHNIKOV How is the young father doing?
MILOS FORMAN I'm not sure if I'm a better father today at sixty-eight than I was thirty-five years ago. That was when my sons, Matej and Petr, were born—identical twins, exactly the same as Andrew and James who are already two years old. At least, I take more care of the two little ones than I did of their half-brothers in the sixties. In those days, I was still very young and wrapped up in my work. Now, my priorities have changed. I devote a great deal of time to the boys and realize just what a wonder children are. You're also a father. The role suits you! I've got photos of you all.
MB Along with golf, photography is my favorite hobby.
MF Mine too, and I find that children are the most wonderful models. I spend a fortune on film. (*They have emptied their first glass of vodka.*) Ah! I recognize that taste. I think I could easily get used to it again.

MB I have learned more from photos than from all the history books. Once, I discovered photographs by Richard Avedon and Irving Penn and, through them, the ballets of Balanchine and Stravinsky …

MF On my first journey to the West, I searched everywhere for photo books. To be able to show somebody in Prague a picture of New York meant so much in those days. My English was really miserable then.

MB And mine, nonexistent.

MF We both have a similar biography; we were looking for freedom.

MB But not for an abstract form of freedom. You had concrete longings, didn't you?

MF At that time, freedom for me meant being left in peace and being able to do what I wanted—without permanently controlling myself and holding myself back, no matter what others thought or said. That is the core of freedom.

MB Yes, the freedom to be able to accept your own failings, without blaming anyone else for them! That's still the same today in the former communist countries: So many people make others responsible for their own misery and talk, full of self-pity, about all the wonderful things they could have done if they had been allowed to.

MF They don't know what to do with their new liberties.

MB Just look at the presidential elections in Russia. The people want a leader. I really had to laugh when President Putin, a former KGB man, was asked about his wishes for the new millennium. He replied: "Love." What was he trying to say by that?

MF There are so many different kinds of love. It can be very destructive—like love of money or false ideals. Love is also something crazy; in the end, Romeo and Julia killed themselves. I ask myself whether love should be championed no matter what the circumstances. (*they laugh*)

MB The highest form of love is generosity. When people say "I love you" it usually only means that they are trying to possess the other one.

MF I recently read that we Slavs are more nostalgic and romantic, by nature, than people from other regions. That's also a cliché.

MB But it's true that in the former Eastern bloc, human relationships are more closely bound and go much deeper. The political system forbade feelings. A personal relationship was seen as a secret, precious treasure. The relationships with the opposite sex are also much more intense in a dictatorship: you cling to the other person like a lifebuoy.

MF The problem with the famous Russian soul is that the Russians don't know precisely what they want. You overcame that. That's what I like so much about you.

MB Until I was sixteen, I lived in the Soviet Union, in my homeland Latvia, but I never felt really at home. My father was an officer in the Red Army. That's why I had to do everything secretly. After that, I studied in the Russian provinces for ten years—and I didn't feel at home there, either. We Latvians were much more open; for example, we wore Western clothes.

MF After your success in Leningrad you progressed, in America, to become the best dancer in the world. In your home country, you remained a god living the dreams of the people there. Don't you owe it to them to return?

MB I visited Riga once, because my mother is buried there. At that time, I visited my old school friends—and realized that an abyss had opened up between me and those I had known before. They thought I was a show-off. It took me a long time to find myself. Today, I know that I belong in America. Here, I don't have to play any games or disguise myself—here, my life is authentic.

MF I was in Paris in 1968 when the Russian tanks crushed freedom in Prague. I had three possibilities: to go back and submit to the regime; to go back and do what I wanted to do—but then they would have thrown me into prison, as they did with my friend Vaclav Havel. The third possibility was to beat it! I didn't have the courage to go back. I landed in the USA—and had a hard time getting used to life here. At the beginning, I fell into a dark hole, but all in all life here is really very comfortable.

MB I also didn't have the strength to go back. I'm not one of those everyday heroes who stand in line all day to make sure their children don't lack anything, and still remains a cheerful human being.

MF The situation in the former Eastern bloc was like being in a zoo; life there was comfortable. You weren't attacked, you didn't have to work very hard and still didn't starve, because they always threw something your way. And the best thing: in his cage, everybody could dream about the beauty of the jungle without experiencing its danger. Suddenly, the bars are opened and you realize that the freedom of the jungle is dangerous, unjust and full of traps. A lot of people long for their former, easy life in a cage. Who needs freedom?

MB After all these years here, I couldn't live anywhere else. I hate bureaucracy, and you can't get rid of that in European countries. When I first came to New York, I went out every night— theater, cinema, parties—an intense, chic life, a real overdose. About ten years ago, I said to myself that I had to get away from the Moloch of the city. I couldn't even sleep. I find peace on my farm with my family.

MF Strange. It was the same in my case. Here, in this city, you can live the same life as in your homeland. When I arrived here, I had a small apartment in a Czech neighborhood. Some of my former neighbors had lived there for sixty years and still spoke only Czech.

MB It's the same in the Russian districts or in Chinatown; you hardly hear any English there.

MF That's why this country is forced to be peaceful. Look at the Albanians and Serbs; they're killing each other. On the other hand, America is a mixture of so many races, ideologies and cultures which simply have to respect each other.

(*A not entirely sober woman in a transparent black blouse enters the room and rushes over to Baryshnikov. She is a Russian dancer … Mikhail remains patient and polite until she finally leaves.*)

MF Maybe one of Putin's female spies. Do you know something? I really have to laugh about all that talk about men ruling the world. Women have the power, beginning with simple things in the family. The world relies on them. Women change us men. They are stronger than we are, and the female form is one of the most beautiful things that was ever created. That's something we two have in common: we like everything about women.

MB My best friends were always women—and I have to thank female choreographers for my best performances. Women exude a wonderful tranquility. I don't believe in the battle of the sexes—particularly not in the twenty-first century. It is true, however, that different sensibilities play a role in the female universe and masculine world. In the past two years, my ballet company "White Oak Dance" was made up of five women—and me. A fantastic combination! A magic, sensual, generous energy hovered around us. But I can just as easily go to the other extreme and play golf with my male friends for two weeks.

MF I always flirt with the actresses in my films. The fascinating thing about the opposite sex is their mystery—and they should keep it as long as possible.

MB I think we would make a great couple, Milos!

MF No question about that. Can you remember? I once brought a happy couple together. Actually, *I* had that date with Jessica Lange. We had been to a preview of a film—and after the showing she dashed off with you!

MB But I'm sure you were happy for me—or not?

MF OK, you're right about that. What one doesn't do for a true friend!

MB I have to thank you for ten wonderful, happy years and my daughter Alexandra. By the way, she'll be going to University soon.

MF Jessica has simply everything: she's an exceptional actress, intelligent, talented, beautiful.

MB She and I—we both didn't believe that you can work on a relationship. When there are no longer strong feelings it's time to call it a day. The emotional intensity between lovers does not last forever—that's how it was with us.

MF You always had luck with women.

MB I was never a charmer or seducer. I simply lived my life—it is too short to waste time seducing somebody. I love women. People were really surprised that a ballet dancer liked women. But I'm not the first—and this prejudice doesn't exist in Russia. I have three other children—Peter, Anna, Sofia Luisa—and this produces a completely different form of dynamism. My wife, Lisa, is a very independent person—like all the women I've ever been attracted to. With my lifestyle, I need security. She works as a choreographer and ballet dancer. I'm not exactly a model father, but Lisa is a dream of a mother. She keeps our family together.

MF My profession takes so much out of me that I need a woman who takes care of me. Feminists would say: "He needs a slave." If beauty is attached to it, then I am completely happy. However, if I had to choose between beauty and talent, I would take talent. Happily, the choice is so great that I have never had to make the decision. In addition, female beauty becomes more intense with time. It becomes more mature, softens and develops into personality. Courtney Love once complained to me about a small crease on her lip. I said to her: "Sooner or later, the first wrinkles appear. Don't complain about it. Learn to love your wrinkles and develop with them. It makes your inner beauty even greater." Did Mischa, the dancer, never fall for the body cult.

MB Because of the way I'm built, I always had complexes. Until I was sixteen I was only 1.5 meters (*four foot, nine inches*) tall. My limbs were hardly created for classical ballet—particularly not in Russia, where ballet dancers are traditionally tall. I liberated myself from that because I knew that, one day, I would go in a different direction, in any case. That's the good thing about modern ballet: everybody is well built, but beauty isn't a prerequisite. My shortcomings opened my eyes—made me realize that I had to go in another direction.

MF After your legendary performances I often found you completely depressed—almost as if you had given too much of yourself. I was there when the Metropolitan Opera was out of control with enthusiasm. But you kept your distance; success never took hold over you.

MB Each and every artist who goes on stage wants to be loved. Sooner or later, you reach the point where you no longer care about what people think about you. Today, I don't have to prove myself.

MF I adore great stars and hate vanity.

MB And how about your Oscars for direction? Did they leave you cold?

MF Winning two Oscars gives you a great feeling which lasts for about twelve hours. (*laughs*)

MB It lasted a bit longer. I can remember that after *One Flew over the Cuckoo's Nest*, you sat opposite me in the hotel and filled out a check for one million dollars. You said "Those are my taxes for a year." You were really proud of that.

MF The Oscar doesn't only produce a kind of high, but also money—and money produces freedom. In the USA, money doesn't result in as much envy as in other countries, and that's why people are not so ashamed of their wealth.

MB That's right! Here, money is a public affair. For example, everybody knows how much a film director earns. OK, maybe they're off by one or two million. (*they laugh*)

MF I wouldn't want to say that the USA is free of envy, but here, people have it better under control. When I should have been deported from the USA, my colleagues convinced the immigration people that it would be a loss and disgrace to expel me. On the other hand, when I was filming *Amadeus* in Czechoslovakia, some of my local colleagues and party members tried to prevent filming. The only reason they weren't successful was because the government was in urgent need of dollars. Now I remember: Didn't you once say that you wanted to stop being a dancer when you turned fifty?

MB I even said forty! I have actually stopped with classical ballet—and started with modern dance. Ten years ago, I couldn't have danced the way I do today. The thing that I find so exciting about ballet is the immense eroticism. Life is short—and that's why everybody should be obsessed with the things which arouse genuine feelings in him.

MF Real life takes place in only a few moments. The tragic romance of Romeo and Juliet probably lasted for about two years. If you had to experience that in real time, it would bore you to death. Shakespeare reduced that to two heavenly hours.

MB Shakespeare brings me to one of the few aspects of American life which does not make me happy: my children don't have enough contact with culture. They play a lot of sports, see their friends, sit in front of the computer, watch television—and, from time to time, they glance at a book. I'm also to blame for that. It's so easy to send the children to school and settle back into the routine of a middle-class existence. The American way of life means that all problems are removed from you. I have a problem with the fact that seventy-five percent of life here consists of sport.

MF I think that will change, it only takes time. The USA is a young country. I often long for my old Prague. That's where I developed my feeling for beauty. That was where I first kissed a girl. It was winter and her lips were frozen … Memories! What would we be without them.

MB Milos the romanticist. Everything which gives life elegance is beautiful: education, manners, the ethics in certain situations—and poetry.

MF What is elegance? Maybe it's a harmony of the appearance, spirit and lifestyle. Or maybe it's just personality. (*Two more vodkas follow.*)

From VOGUE 07/2000; The conversation was recorded by Cristina Carrillo de Albornoz

MILOS FORMAN — MIKHAIL BARYSHNIKOV

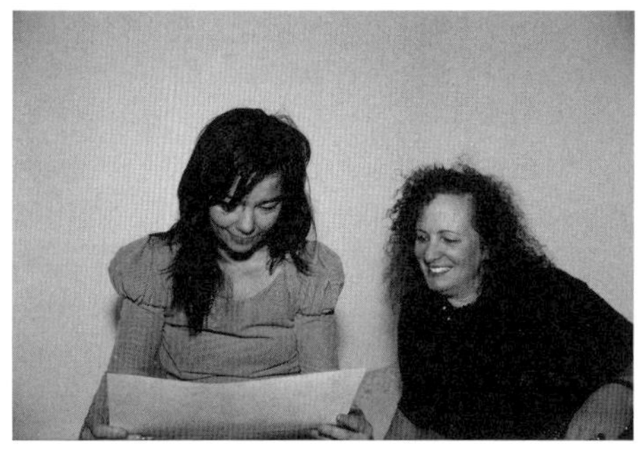

MIRACLES?
WE CREATE THEM OURSELVES

Instead of dreaming, NAN GOLDIN captures the fascination
of reality in her photographs. And BJÖRK trusts in the ability of
genuine feelings to assert themselves—in life, in music, in cinema.

The protagonists: a shimmering icon of pop music and a living legend of the art of photography. Contrary to the traditional idea that goddesses can rarely stand each other, Nan Goldin and Björk became friends for life after their first meeting in a club in London two years ago. Meeting place: a huge loft in the heart of New York. Björk had rented it from an artist for a few months and turned the living room into a recording studio full of all kinds of technical equipment. Nan Goldin rings the doorbell at the appointed time—dressed in a skirt with hundreds of glittering sequins. Björk looks at her silver shoes and cries: "We're both made of silver!" Arm in arm, they go up to the roof terrace of the apartment to shoot a few photographs in the last glow of sunset over Manhattan. The only makeup is a lipstick which Nan produces from her handbag. After this spontaneous shooting, they go downstairs and sit in the bedroom—the room with the least of Björk's equipment. The conversation takes place in the stimulating contrast between Goldin's New England accent and Björk's Nordic one. A particular characteristic: the woman from Iceland rolls her "R" excessively—which sounds wonderful but, at the same time, frightening. With her enigmatic smile, she serves water and Coca-Cola.

NAN GOLDIN I can still remember what we drank in Blake's Club in London when we met in 1998. The drink was called "Purple Haze" or something like that. Somebody had said that he would introduce me to Björk. The evening was fun, but there was no chance of having an intelligent conversation! I was surprised at how friendly you were to me.
BJÖRK You simply feel immediately close to some people. Why, is always a puzzle. I felt a bond to you from the very first moment—and that's strange, because it's not easy for me to become close to other people.

NG Friendship is an intuitive thing and has nothing to do with sitting down and exchanging the same ideas about art and music. I found it great that we talked about children, food and drink.

B I think that our entire life is a matter of intuition. In northern countries, particularly in Denmark where we filmed *Dancer in the Dark,* people always have to analyze everything. I have another philosophy: I dive into each new day and let myself be led by my feelings. A life without secrets and surprises would be death for me. That's the reason that I'm so protective of my private sphere and tell people: "Keep your secrets to yourself!" (*they laugh*) I'll probably never need a psychotherapist.

NG Seeing that you were just talking about secrets, I feel that intimacy works just like friendship.

B Yes, both happen when you least expect it and, over time, develop more and more quality. In my entire life, I've only worked with five people—and not 5,000 as many think. I'm fed up with having to deal with people I don't know at all.

NG I can also only be creative around people I feel for and who are close to me spiritually. For example, this week I couldn't photograph Julia Roberts because there was no communication between us.

B It's often the same with me. (*Among other things, Björk turned down a project with Madonna.*)

NG I see my colleagues as my friends. That's precisely the reason that I have problems with art dealers. I could never have a relationship with anyone which was based only on business.

B My manager has worked for me since I was sixteen. In those days, we were friends. I hired him because I liked him—and because he wasn't a manager. (*they laugh*)

NG I was lucky enough to grow up in the seventies. I "educated" myself by going to movies and museums. I always believed that art consisted of creating art, and was not a commercial product. Without that, I would never have come so far. The profession of an artist is the toughest one around. In the traditional sense, you get nothing for what you produce—a salary or anything like that. You get no external help; you alone have to believe in yourself. That's really difficult for good artists because they often have doubts about themselves in their attempts at reaching perfection. But most people take their art lightly according to the motto: All you have to do is release the shutter!

B And as soon as you have success you're tied up in the next project. You have no time to catch your breath. The audience is always looking for something new.

NG Today, artists are treated like fashion designers: You're only as good as your last collection. A genius like Picasso did not worry about criticism—he simply painted what he wanted to paint. No matter what one thinks about him, he had something to say.

B I just read a critique about me. Terrible. But that's nothing compared to what I go through when I'm composing.

NG How do you come to grips with fame?

B I never dreamt that I would ever become the famous singer "Björk." I could be sitting at the organ in any old village and my attitude wouldn't be any different. I want to make music until I'm eighty-five. Fame has never meant anything to me. In Iceland, I made a record when I was eleven years old—suddenly, people turned around when they saw me in the street and schoolchildren talked about me. I quite liked that because everyone wanted to be friends with me, but I still had no idea about how to deal with so much attention. Overnight, I had become a child star and couldn't handle it. After the first platinum disc, I was supposed to record the next. I refused and, instead, played in a punk band with kids of my age. I died my hair bright orange, and everybody hated it—but that was precisely what I wanted.

NG Were you a wunderkind?

B I went to the music school from five to fifteen and was taught classical music. My teacher, a German, thought I was a genius. We had a strange relationship. Sometimes, in the middle of instruction, he would call me into his office and beg me to make use of my talent.

NG What did you play when you were a child?

B Flute, but I always wanted to compose. When my teacher kept hounding me, I left the school to play something typically Icelandic in a punk band. Even fifty years ago, there was no individual music in Iceland, so my friends and I let ourselves be inspired by our feelings and created something unheard-of: mystical music, close to nature. Only later did I realize that I couldn't merely draw on the pure Icelandic—because I wanted to communicate with the whole world.

NG You've been doing that for many years, and you're still seen as an exotic creature. Artists are always seen as being over the top. I find that funny, because I have never disguised myself. I always want to be what I am. Do you feel attracted by the *outré.*

B When I was a young girl, I liked being different from the others. I have to say that, in the meantime, I have problems with people who are too weird, or surreal, as they're called today. It's absolutely in to say: "How surreal!" The wonderful sex photographs you make are also called "surreal." (*they laugh*)

NG The film writer and director Hanif Kureishi said: "Sex is the peak of mysticism!" I haven't had an orgasm for such a long time that I can't remember if it is really such a tremendous spiritual experience. But I've always been interested in why orgasm is experienced so differently by men and women—although, in the meantime, there are a few men who …

B … who hold back longer. Is that what you mean? (*they laugh*) Sex plays a central role in your work. Why is that?

NG When I was young, my brothers were always doing things I was forbidden to do because I was a girl. That really annoyed me—and so I became a comrade-in-arms in the battle of the sexes. In those days, sex was still a taboo in the USA and I wanted to know why it had so much power over people. I grew up in the hippie era and made my own personal contribution to sexual liberation. (*they laugh*) At the moment, there's a renaissance of the gay revolution but lesbians and gays are, unfortunately, still bashed on the streets. I was always bisexual, I lived with drag queens when I was seventeen.

B I admire people who have no taboos.

NG It's not completely that way. For example, I don't like to see myself naked.

B You can change that. Put on an elegant swimsuit … (*they laugh*) I don't know what to do with taboos. As long as you're happy …

NG Happiness has something to do with sharing. When I lived in a commune, I learned what solidarity means. I share the money I earn today with others.

B I agree with you completely. If you make music or art, you must be prepared to give your all—to be a generous person. Greed would destroy my talent.

NG It might sound silly, but I'm happy when I'm sitting in a comfortable seat in a cinema waiting for the movie to begin. When I was fourteen, fifteen, sixteen I watched all the Greta Garbo, Joan Crawford and Marlene Dietrich movies. I'm still fascinated by the glamour of Hollywood in the thirties and forties.

B I don't have a clear impression of what glamour really is. I'm not a fashion expert. I don't have any fancy clothes. I have dressed myself since I was four—and my friendship with the designers Alexander McQueen and Jean Paul Gaultier has nothing to do with their fashion creations.

NG I'm a real designer queen. When I was young, I found the clothes of Balenciaga and Jacques Fath—as well as the fashion photography of Guy Bourdin—absolutely fabulous. During my punk period, in the seventies, I was crazy about Chantal Thomass' underwear and Vivienne Westwood's shop in London, which was called SEX. For me, the greatest fashion designer was, and remains, Jil Sander with her amazing cuts and attention to detail. At the moment, I wear Prada, Helmut Lang and Martin Margiela and—on my feet—Manolo Blahnik, of course.

B I have a better understanding of acoustic glamour. This happens when I listen to Edith Piaf or the Brazilian singer Elis Regina—when she sings, she runs the gamut of emotions: up one minute, down the next. I admire people who have the courage to do that. It's the same with Angelina Jolie. She's my favorite actress.

NG You find people like that everywhere, from Billie Holiday over Uma Thurman to Catherine Deneuve.

B Catherine Deneuve is a mind-boggling beauty!

NG My idea of beauty has a wide scope and is completely the opposite of what Americans usually understand. I find beauty mainly in women and in faces. Bodies aren't so interesting for me, and recently I've also become enthusiastic about light and nature.

B I've always been surprised at how important people perceive eyes. In my case, everything is hearing. I can remember sounds, voices …

NG And what the voices say?

B No, there's something logical about words. I remember things I feel.

NG You're looking for emotional beauty.

B Beauty is a characteristic of how one experiences feelings and how one deals with other people. I wanted to express that in *Dancer in the Dark*. In the role of Selma, I showed a part of myself, for the first time—my concept of beauty and even of my religiosity. I always thought of myself as an atheist but, during the filming, I discovered that I'm really very devout. If you have the choice between light and dark, you have to take the light.

NG Are you devout in a spiritual or religious sense?

B I think, I'm somewhere in between.

NG Strange, I also find myself at a stage in my life when I'm concerned with light, spirituality and introspection—things that take place outside of this, at parties and on the other stages of self-representation don't interest me any more. I consider myself a religious person— without belonging to any denomination which wants to reorganize my life and have control over me.

B I can't stand control. I experienced that during the three years I spent working on the film. What a blessing that music is my real calling!

NG You could say that you became a religious person out of thankfulness for your talent.

B It's not really all that bad. (*laughs*)

NG I only wanted to say that you orientate yourself towards the light. When I saw *Dancer in the Dark* I burst into tears and almost flipped out. You were so good. All the other women at the movies cried, too.

B Filming was really tough work. If I hadn't had my friends and family, I wouldn't have survived that time.

NG When we talk about love, I automatically think about my friends. Romantic love is something wonderful—but, for the past four years I've only come across the wrong men. I have lousy taste. Unfortunately, I can't live without eroticism.

B You need love like air to breathe. I have the steadiest relationships with people in Iceland who I've known since I was a child. My best girl friend, who lives four streets away from me, delivered her child, at home, under the Christmas tree and I helped with the birth. I think that I'm a product of my friends—and that's why I can't separate myself from them.

NG My friends formed my personality—beginning with my name to my strongly developed sense of humor. But, romantic love …

B Yes, romantic love is the dot on the "i" …

NG I've had a lot to do with lovers in my work. In the beginning, I was interested in estrangement in a relationship. That had a lot to do with my lifestyle at the time where drugs and sex played a major role. Later, I experienced that two women could be mothers, sisters, sexual partners for each other—simply everything. Now, I'm more interested in tenderness than in the dependence on a partner—maybe because I lived together with a man for three years and thought that he was my soul mate. When I was young it was unfortunately the case that the father played the role of the suppressor and the mother, the suppressed. Children tend to copy their parents—that's why I almost always fall into the hands of possessive men.

B The quality of a relationship isn't necessarily that it functions well, but that both partners sincerely try to make it work. In life, one should try to make miracles happen.

NG I believe that you're very courageous and live very intensively.

B I grew up in a hippie environment, happy anarchy. I could do whatever I wanted. It made no difference to my mother if I said I wanted to eat ninety-seven bananas or take a bath in honey—she thought that everything was ok. That's why I grew up with the firm belief that feelings and a sense of humor were the most important things.

NG My parents were not so spontaneous and loving—but at least they were liberal. I was only fourteen when I joined a hippie commune. I never had a formal education, in the classical sense, but my brothers studied at Harvard. However, I taught there last year. (*laughs*)

B That's an irony of fate. How was it at Harvard?

NG The students there think that life is all straight uphill. They're not prepared for the fact that it can be a roller coaster. A lot of them sacrifice their youth for their studies; have no fun, do without sex. Maybe they're smarter than the others, but they have no hunger for life, no daring to dream …

B When I was a child, one of my dreams was to buy an island someday. From time to time, I still go through the advertisements, but today I dream more of leading a normal, everyday life; cooking, ironing, that's exotic for me! I'm not interested in a holiday on a beach under coconut palms. Each day is different and full of surprises. You get up in the morning and have no idea how you will feel at five o'clock in the afternoon. Or you leave the house and meet a friend who was always depressed and has just fallen in love.

NG My dream hasn't changed since I was a child. I want to spend the rest of my days in freedom. The older I get, the more radical I become. That goes from my computer allergy all the way to my political position, which was formed by flower-power ideals. I would rather watch any old video film than do a job which doesn't satisfy me.

B Being free only means being able to stay—or become—what one really is.

NG That's why I like to photograph people I like, to document the fact that they have remained true to themselves. (*Nan gives Björk some photographs which she took when they last met each other at an exhibition in Iceland.*)

B The photos are really beautiful, Nan.

NG Glamour! (*they laugh*) We must take some more. You should take some of me.

B Tomorrow, at noon?

NG Agreed. Bring your camera!

From VOGUE 12/2000; The conversation was recorded by Cristina Carrillo de Albornoz

NAN GOLDIN — BJÖRK

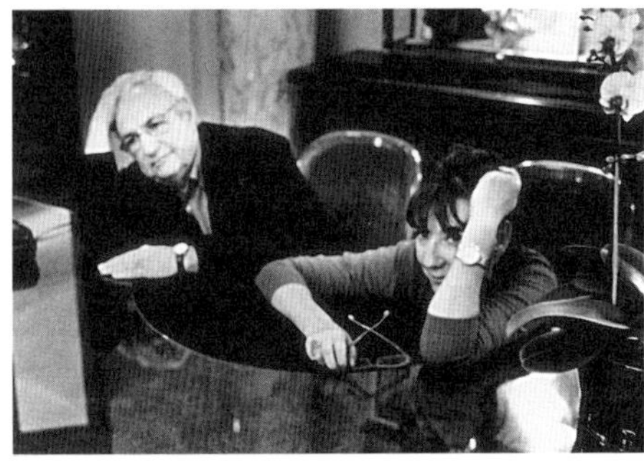

THE INNOCENT AND HER ANGEL

To this day, SOPHIE CALLE and FRANK O. GEHRY still squabble about how and when they met each other. What is beyond dispute is that the architect-genius has taken the provocative photo-voyeur under his wing for a good fifteen years.

On his journeys throughout the world, Frank O. Gehry often comes across good acquaintances in many of the places he visits—the Temporary Contemporary Museum in Los Angeles, the Guggenheim Museum in Bilbao, the American Center in Paris, or the DG Bank at Pariser Platz 3 in Berlin. Critics are often lost for words when they attempt to evaluate his work: "controlled shattering, vibrating dynamism, a wonder of telemetric communication." It is much easier to describe the man himself. Gehry is the eternal provocateur among the global players in contemporary architecture—a playful choreographer, who makes whole urban landscapes dance with his buildings.

Whenever the American visits Paris, he has a date with Sophie Calle—a woman who also cannot be forced into a conventional job description. The Frenchwoman, who has made the investigation of human relationships her passion, lies in wait of strangers, like a detective, with her camera, and transfers their everyday expressions into fascinating photographic passages, which are exhibited in the world's major art houses. They meet in the Hotel Lutetia to talk about those things in life which move them, over pink champagne. Calle and Gehry have been friends for a good fifteen years—and for just as long, they have been fighting about where they first met. This time was no exception, and their subtle, affectionate ritual took place once again …

Sophie Calle You don't remember, but it was during the Olympic Games in Los Angeles in 1984. The city had invited me to organize an exhibition there. And I had the idea of asking people just what had become of Los Angeles' "angels." A friend gave me your address and thought that you might be able to answer that question.

Frank O. Gehry And I did that, didn't I?

SC Yes. Then you said to me: "Los Angeles' angels? They're my family!"

FOG I didn't have to think about it very long. I'm very happy with my family—they are really something quite special. Just like you. You opened my eyes to so many things I wasn't previously aware of. That's an artist's job, don't you agree? But let me repeat myself; I really don't think that we met at that time.

SC It is a fact, though, that you ordered me, over the telephone, to come to your studio—with the somewhat sobering addition that you didn't have much time because you had a dinner date. When you were ready to go, you couldn't remember where you had parked your car— you had to make it beep so that you could find it. And then, to my great surprise, you asked me where *we* should go for dinner!

FOG Not a bad trick, that! (*laughs*)

SC Yes, and it worked. And afterwards, you took me back to your house to show me pictures of your wife and children.

FOG Yes, I can still remember that—even though my initials are FOG. Sometimes they call me that because of the gray wisps of fog which waft through my head (*laughs*)—and, that's also the name of my hockey team.

SC How did you ever come up with the crazy idea of founding a hockey team?

FOG Berta, my wife, is quite a bit younger than I am. When our sons wanted to play sports with me, I was already sixty. In spite of that, I began playing hockey with them. After a while, more and more people joined in and, in the meantime, we've become a pretty good team. I am really proud of it, even though I'm no longer an active player myself.

SC I was also very proud when you called the next day and asked me if I would like to have you as my impresario—do you remember that?

FOG To be honest, no. Remembering dates is a real problem for me. I also don't know why I get everything confused.

SC And I don't know how you managed to get the best gallery in Los Angeles interested in me. Shortly after that, they organized my first retrospective. You were my guardian angel at that time. The exhibition was a great success. That was the beginning of my international career.

FOG I remember that a bit differently. Let's face it, at that time you were no longer an "unknown." I believed in you and couldn't understand why you weren't already world-famous. Your work exuded beauty and drama—it was like a revelation for me. Isn't that when you also met Dennis Hopper?

SC Yes, and he also became a fan of mine. How can I ever thank you for all that?

FOG I'll think of something. For example, why don't you accept my version that we met in the south of France?

SC No, we already knew each other before that! You were invited to take part in the competition to build the museum in Nîmes, along with Norman Foster and Jean Nouvel. That's when you came to the south of France …

FOG … and we danced in the square; I want you to accept that. There's something else I have to clarify with you: Do you really like what I do?

SC I would never dare comment on your work. My vocabulary is just good enough to tell a few anecdotes. That's why I like to go to the theater or movies alone; I don't want to have to discuss the play or movie with anyone afterwards.

FOG Can't you really express your thoughts and feelings in words?

SC It's just that I'm afraid of being asked for my opinion. If I don't like something, I can more-or-less express myself—but if I do like something, I have to remain silent. This is why I refuse to take part in talk shows, where you have to have an opinion on everything: art, politics …

FOG So, you would have told me if you didn't like my work.

SC I would have found a way. But I can tell you this: I admire you as an artist and I also think your cowboy boots are great. (*both laugh*) The only thing I can say when I like something is "I like it." It's easier to explain why one doesn't feel anything—because one sees it from a distance.

FOG I think what connects the two of us is our positive attitude towards life. We believe in humanity and try to change the world, just a little. That's how we take on social responsibility. We're convinced that we're more likely to help people with our work than harm them.

SC A lot of people think that I really do harm others—that I'm even cruel. For example, take what happened with the address book I found on the street. The owner was deeply hurt that I traced him and dialed his private telephone numbers. He reacted really strongly because I had interfered in his life. In spite of that, I would do it again any time, because the suspense is greater than my feelings of guilt …

FOG That all sounds very innocent.

SC His friends told me many candid things about him, probably because they thought that they were doing him a favor. I was convinced that he would throw his arms around me, and that's why I was so disappointed at his reaction.

FOG Even though you're such a smart woman, you've managed to keep your innocence. Most adults lose it, but, just like a child, you're always asking yourself "What would happen if …?" or "Why is it like that?" That's the strength of your work. And, talking about the owner of that address book, I don't think that he really found it so bad.

SC Really? He suffered so much that he took revenge. He got hold of a nude photo of me and had it published in a newspaper, so that I would feel just as compromised as he did. I found it all very exciting—suddenly, everything that had so far been fiction became reality for me.

FOG You're too hard on yourself. All artists work for their own interest. When I design a building, I do it because I want to use my talents. Artistic freedom should be limited by only one rule: don't do anything to others that you wouldn't want them to do to you.

SC The problem with the "address-book affair" is that some unpleasant truths about that man were uncovered. Nobody likes to be exposed.

FOG That depends. It was very important for my development that somebody told me quite frankly, "That's the way you are."

SC I have to admit, I'd rather not know what people think about me. How do you feel about that?

FOG I spent two years in group therapy with fifteen other people. Whenever they said something against me, I thought: "What rubbish! What do they know about me?" The strange thing is that, in the end, they all came to the same conclusion.

SC Now I'm interested.

FOG I can't remember what it was …

  SC Come on, Frank.

FOG All right then. The therapy group criticized that I was always moaning about being bankrupt—even though it wasn't true. This openness helped me. Maybe you did the man with the address book a favor? You should try to get in touch with him.

SC I did try—but, even today, sixteen years later, he despises me as much as he did then. And he's not the only one. I've received stacks of insulting letters. I know what it means to have enemies.

FOG The same thing happened to me when I was building my house in Santa Monica. In that neighborhood, broken-down cars were repaired on the street and there were boats on trailers parked behind iron fences. Aesthetics and fantasy weren't words in their vocabulary. From the very start of construction, the people were shocked. My neighbors went to the mayor; they wanted him to stop construction and have the house torn down. One day, one of them cornered me on the street and said: "I think your house is terrible," and I replied: "Just have a look at your own, with the boat and the wire fence. I find *that* really depressing, but I can live with it." His answer to this was: "The problem is, your house is different." That's the real problem: the way an artist sees the world is different, and that upsets a lot of people.

SC I often think about why unpleasant things inspire me. Once I made a film about me and my husband. The subject was that we no longer loved each other. The film would have been rather boring without the unhappiness and sadism which existed between us. It's really crazy to make a film about a love story that was a flop, or to ask a blind person what he or she considers beautiful, or to tell a stranger's story without his permission. There are always unpleasant emotions attached to my work.

FOG Whenever I build something that the neighbors don't like, they consider that unpleasant …

SC And we are both really nice, kind-hearted people.

FOG Of course, (*laughs*) but, above all, we're different. We give people something, even if they don't like us, and we believe that, in the end, something good will come out of it. What interests me about your work is its merciless veracity. You watch people, and then always show exactly what's happening. Other people wouldn't dare do that. And, almost everyone is a bit of a voyeur.

SC The only difference is that I usually put this desire into action.

FOG Just what did the blind people tell you about beauty?

SC For a year, I stopped all the blind people I met on the street and asked them how they imagined it. I got some wonderful, tragic and sometimes humorous answers. One spoke about the vastness of the ocean, another about Alain Delon, and some had no idea at all. I can easily understand that. I have never really asked myself what beauty is—and am not even specifically interested in it.

FOG I am. For me, striving after beauty of expression is a very personal, innocent attitude to life, borne by a profound longing for love and peace. The most beautiful building I have ever seen is Le Corbusier's church in Ronchamp. Whenever I stand in front of it, I simply have to cry.

SC Would you like to know how a Jewess, with a Polish background, became French?

FOG I've known you for such a long time and only now do I find out that we have the same roots!

SC When my grandfather left Warsaw to emigrate to America, he made a stopover in Paris. He went to a restaurant. He couldn't speak French so he pointed to a dish on the menu—and got an artichoke. He had never seen such a thing and had no idea about how to eat it. The waiter noticed that and showed him how. My grandfather was so touched by this gesture that he said: "I would like to live in a city where a waiter helps a Jew with his meal."

FOG My grandfather delivered goods with a horse and cart. He had a Polish helper, who was causing him trouble and had even become violent. My grandfather went to the police, but because nobody listened to him or helped him, he sold everything and emigrated.

SC Isn't Gehry your real name?

FOG I changed it because of my first wife. When I'm in love I agree to everything. Anita thought that Gehry sounded good—and, because of our sons, she probably was afraid of anti-Semitic reactions.

SC I'm going to China soon, to meet a man. I also can't control my emotions—that's why I try to stick to some rules in my work, at least.

FOG The most sorrow in a love affair comes from false expectations. I have never expected anything from the people I love—I like them the way they are, and that's why they never disappoint me.

SC I also have no specific expectations from a relationship. Of course, intelligence and beauty never do any harm. I find it particularly erotic if somebody can make me laugh. What I expect from people I'm in love with depends on how I feel at the moment, whether I'm sad or happy. On Monday, I could say that I would find it best if somebody could cheer me up. But, on Tuesday, I might want somebody just to be nice to me. On Wednesday, I want tenderness when I'm weary. And, on Thursday, when I'm in top form, I just want to be surprised.

FOG That's the right attitude. I also want to live everyday as it comes—always in the present.

SC What does that mean for you?

FOG That I'm always investigating new technologies and can follow the developments in the world. For example, I'm a great fan of teleconferences because they allow me to avoid a lot of traveling. And, of course, my cell phone is always ringing. Last week, somebody in London said to me: "Mr. Gehry, you receive a great deal of criticism because of your preoccupation with technology."

SC Which criticism has hurt you the most?

FOG I'm really my own toughest critic, because I'm always coming up against barriers in my work. What really annoys me are silly comparisons. For example, when Luis Fernandez-Galiano, *El Pais'* famous critic, compared the Guggenheim Museum in Bilbao with a garbage heap.

SC I felt worst at an exhibition in New York when my work was mentioned in the same breath as Vito Aconci's. I visited him in his studio and told him about my work—that I followed people around and wrote about them. Aconci replied that he had completely different intentions: he followed people to study their movements. My observations, on the other hand, were aimed more at finding out which kind of relationship they stemmed from. Vito Aconci gave me his blessing. That was a great relief.

FOG I find the idea that everything has already been done, somehow and somewhere, rather comforting. I've seen my architectural ideas and curves in Borromini's work. It feels good to know that somebody else has already attempted the same as you—then you don't feel so alone and lose the responsibility of having to invent something. When did you actually start following strangers?

SC In 1979, after I had traveled around the world for seven years. In those days, I felt completely lost in Paris and didn't know what to do with my life. I had no work, no desires, no friends—there was no sensible reason for me to get up in the morning and go out of the house. Then I hit on the idea of following passersby on the street, to give my day a meaning. The first person to cross my path should show me the direction.

FOG So, you left everything to chance?

SC Yes, because I had no idea myself. That I would become an artist was not planned, it just came from the situation …

FOG Creativity has a lot to do with chance—some scientists call that "chaos theory." When I was a young man, I worked as a trucker and studied in the evening at the University of Southern California. You see, I could have ended up as a truck driver …

SC I can remember that, in a restaurant, you once looked over at the dessert on the next table and called out loudly: "A swimming island! They've copied one of my buildings!"

FOG I always proceed very seriously with my work—but, at the same time, I don't take it seriously.

SC It's the same with me, I make a game out of everything—but, first of all, I have to clarify the ritual. When I was five, I held a solemn funeral for my goldfish. I dressed him finely and, in the background, played sad music.

FOG It's too bad no one filmed that!

SC I would never go straight to a neighboring table and photograph a woman sitting there, just because I found her beautiful. I can only be indiscrete, even abominable, when the rules have been set up. But, at the moment, I feel absolutely fantastic.

FOG Because you're soon going to meet a man in China?

SC The main reason I feel so good is because our meeting was so extraordinary. (*takes out a photo book*) Before we part, I would like to give you my book *Double-Jeu Violette*, which I dedicated to you.

FOG (*opens the book and looks, in astonishment, at the first picture*)

SC Whenever I have an exhibition, you send me enormous bouquets of flowers, which have to be wheeled into the room. What do you think I do with all those flowers? My house is overflowing with dried bouquets. On this photo, you can see all the flowers you ever sent me.

From VOGUE 02/2001; The conversation was recorded by Cristina Carrillo de Albornoz

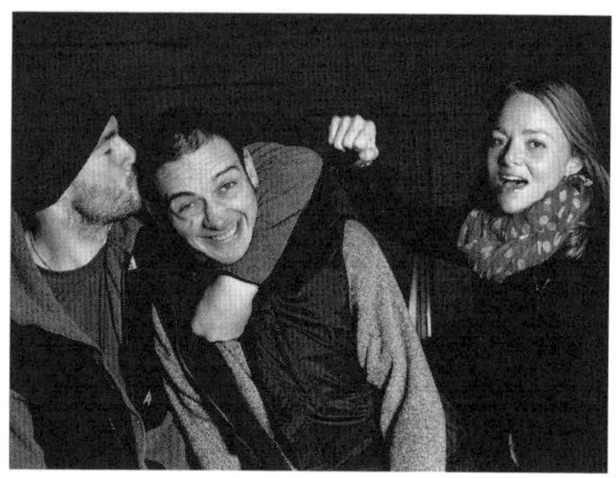

TRIUMPH AND DISASTER

There are many aspects of success: STELLA McCARTNEY, the power girl of the fashion world, between JAKE and DINOS CHAPMAN, the bad boys of the contemporary British art scene—a VOGUE trialogue.

Before the two evil brothers went at Stella McCartney with their axes, they almost let the twenty-eight-year-old freeze to death; Jake and Dinos Chapman's studio in southeast London, where England's most dazzling success-children met for this VOGUE conversation, is not heated. Stella, who had just returned from a trip to the Caribbean, was completely unaccustomed to the local temperature and had to jump up and down to keep herself, more or less, warm in the polar atmosphere of the atelier.

The contrasts between the top designer and the Chapmans could hardly be greater. Stella has put her talents to the service of beauty. Since the daughter of ex-Beatle Paul McCartney and his wife Linda, who died from breast cancer three years earlier, started working for the French fashion house Chloé, she has enriched the world of fashion with young, erotic, imaginative collections. In 2000, the video channel VH1 awarded her the coveted title of "Designer of the Year." On the other hand, the central subject of the Chapmans—who the *Independent* dubbed the "Brothers Grim"—is shock. With their highly controversial installations dealing with the themes of death, war and mutilation, the megastars of the current YBA (Young British Artists) boom cultivate an anti-aesthetic which is both disturbing and fascinating, and is exhibited in the world's major art houses.

Stella McCartney and Dinos and Jake Chapman had recently met each other at a gala dinner in London and their small talk made them interested in getting to know each other better. The reunion, organized by VOGUE, was arranged to clarify the questions: "How do you deal with success? What do you have in common?"

  STELLA McCARTNEY Do you actually consider yourselves successful?

DINOS CHAPMAN Yes—because we now have the freedom of being able to accept, or turn down, things as we want. There are also artists who are successful and still don't make any money. We're financially very well off—we don't have to accept any commissions which don't suit us.

JAKE CHAPMAN On the other hand, there are some unpleasant aspects of success because it gives rise to fear. When you're in demand as an artist, people expect more and more from you. That's why we're continuously thinking about how we can maintain our verve, our punch, our creative energy.

SMC When I see myself on a front page, I think: "Just look, I really am successful." But I feel like you two. I'm always under the pressure of having to surpass myself in my next collection. My strong feeling of self-confidence helps me in that …

DC … a result of success?

SMC No, I draw my strength from the feeling of being in harmony with the world and of being myself. A positive person, a sexy woman—that's my ideal for this life. Professionally, I feel most successful when I come across a young woman on the street, or at a party, who is wearing one of my pantsuits or chiffon dresses—and even more so, when she tells me just how much she likes my creations. That means much more to me than famous colleagues telling me that they think I'm wonderful. That many people see me as competition is what I consider the drawback of success. Is it the same in the art scene?

JC A crazy kind of egocentricity is rampant in the upper echelons of our business. There, you find a group of artists who consider revealing their innermost feelings and receiving public acclaim for their work, as their natural due. And, of course, they're all completely well informed about exhibitions, commissions and prices—and the social prestige which goes hand in hand with these things. The two of us don't have much contact with our colleagues. And, personally, I don't think artists are very interesting as a social group.

SMC There are only a few who really get to the top in art, in fashion or in music. At the most, there are sixty or seventy major stars in each area. I know a lot of them and it always struck me that their relationship to each other is often characterized by rivalry. I find that absolutely bizarre.

DC That's hardly a surprise. In business, no matter in which branch, it makes no sense if too many are successful. The market is always making a selection—even the superstars have to be on their guard.

JC As an artist, I have real problems with the fact that our works are so expensive. The people who can afford to pay so much for our works aren't necessarily those who one would like to have as clients. You're better off in that regard. We'll never be in the pleasant situation of meeting people in everyday life, on the street, who like our things.

SMC The things I design are also quite expensive.

JC Who buys your clothes?

SMC There are sixty-year-old women who buy my double-slit pantsuits and look great in them. And, sometimes, I have twelve-year-old clients. That unnerves me a bit: girls who are so young buying designer pieces. When I was their age, my parents taught me not to throw my money around. They give me very little pocket money and I bought cheap copies of the clothes I liked. In those days, the most fabulous feeling was to be able to go to the disco after-noons organized by the school. I can still remember that, when I was eleven, I went dancing in a pink and gray spotted plissé skirt, a little top and pink rolled-down stockings. I grew up in the country, in very simple surroundings, but well protected. Today, I'm grateful for my normal childhood.

JC I can hardly imagine that there is anything in your boutique in Paris which costs less than 5,000 francs.

SMC I'm not convinced of the sense of the second-lines which many labels and designers push. I think that it's an affront to the clients. You should be able to buy everything in a single shop. When a young woman comes into my Chloé shop, she can clothe herself in my look by taking one of my T-shirts, a pair of jeans or sunglasses with a crystal heart on the lenses. If she can't afford this and buys fakes then, in my opinion, that's fine, too. I would personally find it strange to come across somebody walking around dressed, from head to toe, in original Chloé. My main goal as a designer is to help women to feel stylish and unique.

DC Is that the philosophy of your fashion?

SMC Yes, precisely. You should have enough self-assurance to be able to combine something hot, bought at the flea market, with an haute-couture jacket which costs 1,800 francs. That's what I call class.

DC Whoever starts talking about "class" shows that he, or she, wants to belong to the elite.

SMC No, I think that's nonsense. But I'm not very interested in getting into an argument about it. I'm much more interested in finding out how your collaboration came about.

JC We decided to work as a team because of the ideas we had in common—not because of any genetic connection. When we were children, we didn't have much to do with each other. We're five years apart and we went to different schools. There's no telepathy between us— that's why each of us has a mobile phone.

DC Our joint activity began in 1992 with the work on *Disasters of War*—deformed children's figures, which we spread out on the floor of Jake's rented apartment. It makes no difference to us who comes up with an idea. The production of the objects is a purely mechanical process. I often get things moving at the beginning and Jake gives the product the final polish—which I hate with a passion! We are often at odds over ridiculous details or philosophical principles— but we're brothers and can't turn against each other.

SMC What do you think about the contemporary art scene?

DC We went to the opening party of the new Tate Gallery in London. It was a nightmare— it was like coming to a giant airport just after the plane had left. First of all, a glass of champagne was thrust into your hand, and then you just stood around with all of those great artists and important people, who have nothing to say—and, if they did have some- thing to say, you wouldn't have been able to understand it because the music was so loud that it hurt your ears. But, I have the impression that you like going to openings and art exhibitions, don't you?

SMC Art and I are secret lovers. When I was at college I hung around with the boys who were studying sculpting—probably because most of them were heterosexual and sweet. I get invited to almost every artistic event—but, on most weekends, I take the "Eurostar" from Paris to Sussex, to my parents' house. The first thing I do is saddle my horse and ride off.

JC So you don't often go to parties?

SMC I prefer staying at home and drinking a glass of wine with a friend. Most of my friends are simple people—but the only photographs which appear in the newspapers are those of me with this or that celebrity. I'm really defenseless about the fuss made about me.

DC Jake is much more active in society than I am …

JC That's how you can gauge how miserable I feel! I hang about in the scene because I don't
have any children like you do—and because I find television a bore. For a period, distraction
was really quite important for me. In recent years, we were sent packing mercilessly. In the
middle of the nineties, we had some major successes—but then some problems came up in
connection with an exhibition in New York which we had organized with Larry Gagosian;
the critiques were bad. I believe that the reason was because American art is so concerned
with itself and isn't capable of dealing with other points of view—particularly European ones.

DC We made the best of that defeat; we threw ourselves into our work.

JC I have nothing against a bit of animosity. But the American disaster was a real blow to us.
Relying on our previous success, we had bought houses in London and were counting on the
income. That's why we put all our energies into our work and occupied ourselves, intensively, for
an entire year, with *Hell*, our installation for the *Apocalypse* exhibition at the Royal Academy
of Arts. This was a giant volcanic landscape, arranged like a mirror-inverted swastika, where a
series of brutal scenes, inspired by the Holocaust, were shown. We used the most common ideas
of an inferno which occurred to us, the darkest moments of the twentieth century. However,
hell is a spiritual place—our *Hell* is simply one impression of this imagination.

SMC The work made an enormous impression on me when I saw it, just recently, at the Royal
Academy. It shows a human abyss which we would prefer not to see.

JC But these abysses rule our subconscious. The thing which interests my brother and me is
beauty without aesthetics. We want to eradicate the difference between the beautiful and the
ugly. Of course, some people were repulsed by *Hell*. Complete strangers who were disgusted
by the work attacked us verbally as well as physically. It's clear that something like that has
repercussions for our personal lives.

DC Let's talk about beauty with aesthetics: What was the first piece you ever designed, Stella?
I bet that at that time you didn't come under fire from all sides.

SMC You're right, there—but, like you, I've also been subject to some rather harsh criticism.
I try not to be intimidated by it and to be just as strong as my mother. The positive attitude, which
I try to have, is her legacy. Her credo was: "Don't let yourself be put down by self-important
people." I have to laugh whenever I think about it. To answer your question: I believe that
I was thirteen when I designed my first jacket. It was dark blue, made of imitation velvet,
with a pink lining—typical eighties, with masses of buckles and a big, puffy collar.

DC Just how did you discover your style?

SMC I can't say exactly. A style is the result of so many different experiences and emotions.
Of course, my mother had the greatest impact on me. She was often attacked for the way
she chose her outfits. She always wore flashy socks, and ancient clothes—precisely, typical
seventies. She looked really cool! No offence meant, Courtney Love! When I started at Chloé,
my ambition was to bring the brand's coquette, crazy style back to life—the style of a period
thirty years past, when my mother was my fashion ideal. In a way, I grew up in her wardrobe.

JC Do Frenchwomen actually have a different attitude towards fashion?

SMC London's street culture is much cooler than Paris'—and that's reflected in the way women
dress there. Frenchwomen are very chic but, at the same time, terribly conservative—there isn't
much humor or surprise in their clothes. The thing which makes me so happy with Paris as my
location is the fantastic craftsmanship and skill which goes into the work of my atelier. I couldn't
find anything like that in London. My seamstresses put so much pride into their work; the
tradition which is part of their trade has developed over many generations.

DC Are your proud of your profession?

SMC When I was younger, I was usually embarrassed when people asked me about my work; I was afraid they would think that I was superficial and not very serious if I admitted to being a fashion designer. But today, I think that fashion has a profound, positive influence on people, particularly on women. They're gaining more and more social power and, through this, their relationship towards men is changing—and, as a result, men themselves. We women no longer want to be pushed around, but we want our success to be founded on femininity. Fashion should be sexy without being aggressive.

JC But don't you think that the British find it difficult to spend a lot of money on clothes? It's the same with contemporary art. We Britons have only recently learned that being successful, and being able to afford beautiful things, can make one happy.

SMC I just bought some works of art which I liked and am terribly happy that I possess them. Of course, success can also be measured by the amount one earns. I'm happy that things are going well for me—but having money in the bank doesn't mean very much to me. All the riches in the world can't make you a better or more interesting person. Just imagine if everything belonged to you—what then? You can't buy good friends—and, even less, a happy life.

JC Could we possibly work with you sometime? We have a few fabulous ideas.

SMC That would be wonderful. What I desperately need are a few good film sequences for my next show!

From VOGUE 03/2001; The conversation was recorded by Louise Baring

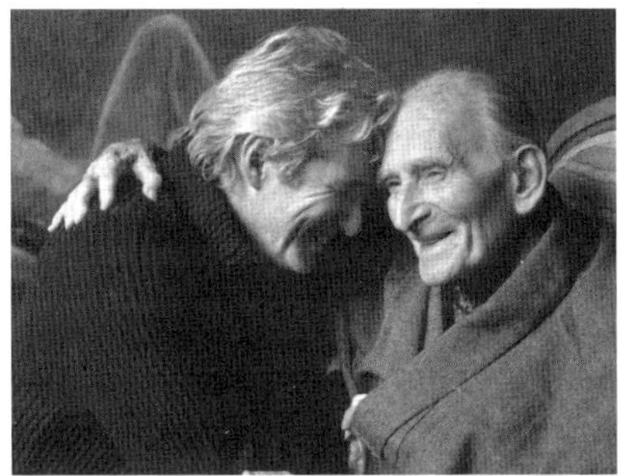

THE FAREWELL

The friendship between Richard Gere and Balthus will undoubtedly surprise many people, but it also reveals the best and most subtle nature of both men. Twenty years back, young Richard Gere was filming in Italy. Younger than his real thirty years, Gere was passionately interested in all forms of artistic creativity and held Balthus to be one of his favorite painters. Verde Visconti, niece of the brilliant director, introduced the two men and later Sydney Picasso, a good friend of the actor, gifted him a drawing by Balthus. From that time on, the actor and the artist have met many times. On this occasion, Gere has come from Rome, where he was presenting "Autumn In New York" and will be staying for two days in the Grand Chalet, an 18th-century wooden mansion in the Swiss Mountains and home to Balthus since 1976. Richard Gere is greeted by Balthus' extraordinary Japanese wife and they wait in the living room for Balthus to come down. The door opens and the artist appears, with Doctor Lui, his constant companion. The actor and the artist embrace. "My friend, my friend!" Gere says softly. Balthus looks at him and, as he always does with his closest friends, strokes his face and grasps his hand. There is a feeling of great happiness in the room. The men sit down and a long conversation begins, full of the twists, turns and happy accidents that are the fruit of the human mind.

RICHARD GERE It's over a year since we last met! The last time was in Zurich at your wonderful exhibition at Sotheby's and then onto the discotheque where you danced the night away. (*Gere is joking; Balthus now walks with great difficulty.*)
BALTHUS I no longer dance, but in my time I was a great tango dancer. (*He then sings a tango. Balthus can hum almost anything from a Russian folk song to a Mozart opera.*)
RG (*Looking at the painting "King Of Cats," a self-portrait of a super-thin 25-year-old Balthus*) I expect that with those long legs you must have been. I adore Astor Piazzola. I had a great time learning to tango for my film *The Cotton Club*. Not very well, mind you, but I had fun.
B I learnt in my national service in Morocco; it was one of the best times of my life. I was

spoilt and I brought out such tender feelings in people that they would even argue about who would dress me. I had a horse called "The Arab" which I rode every day. When I returned to Paris, it stopped eating and pined to death. A true love story.

RG I've had a truly wonderful Appaloosa gelding for 10 years. There'll be much sadness when he is gone. (*There are days when the 92-year-old Balthus, still an imposing figure, has an aura around him. I comment to Gere how handsome Balthus looks.*)

RG You do look great. And you seem much stronger.

B (*Grasping his hands*) Richard, Richard! I'm so happy to see you!

(*Setsuko, who had left the room, returns with a drawing by Balthus, "Sabine," and gives it to Gere both as a present for his 50th birthday and to celebrate the birth of his son, who is now ten months old. The baby spends his time crawling around and makes all of Richard's nights a special time.*)

RG (*Moved*) Thank you so much! I'll hang it in his room.

B What is your son like?

RG He's a healthy, happy little guy. Look. (*He gives him a wonderful photograph taken by his friend Herb Ritts. It shows Gere's arm embracing the baby, a beautiful boy with lively eyes and a smile matching that of his happy father.*)

B It's wonderful having a child that smiles all the time. You know? My mother painted me and my brother. I'll show it to you later. It's a work that I like a lot. What's your son's name?

RG Homer, the same as my father. He's very secure and easy … laughs a lot. Already very conscious, very aware, I think. His Tibetan name is Jigme, which means "fearless." One of my teachers, Ribur Rinpoche, has been staying with us and Homer sits on his lap for long periods most contentedly.

B I used to sit on Nijinsky's legs and I still remember that they were hard as iron. One of my most frequent dreams is that I'm in the Trojan War, talking with Archimedes and Homer.

RG In fact, I was unsure whether or not to call him Homer, but my wife insisted on it and also, she became pregnant when a terrific new translation of the *Iliad* appeared. It's not an easy name. But most certainly he is Homer. I can't imagine any other name now. Fearless one … make voyages … make voyages.

(*Dusk is about to fall and Richard picks up his camera and begins to take photographs of Balthus, one after the other.*)

RG You're a very patient model, where did you learn patience?

B I have studied patience all my life. As you know I paint slowly and I have observed the patience of my models.

RG It has cost me a lot of time and effort to achieve some patience. Anger comes so easily.

B Me, too, I was also very impertinent. It was a defense mechanism against those who didn't love me. Over the years I have learned to control myself, because there are many types of behavior that provoke and annoy me.

RG (*Laughs*) When we first met years ago in Rome I thought you were so patronizing. The first thing you said to me was "How many languages do you speak." You were so sophisticated, giving the impression that you knew everything. I was very young, and green. I answered: "Only two … English and Japanese." And I proceeded to fake some Japanese gibberish with great confidence. But as you didn't know much Japanese either, it didn't really matter.

B Oh yes. How peculiar! What I remember is my surprise that someone from a milieu so far removed from painting wanted to meet me. What's more, with your Irish roots, I thought that you might perhaps be an angel. (*Balthus has an obsession with a certain aspect of Celtic culture.*)

RG (*Gere smiles gently*) Your universe has always interested me. It isn't immediately obvious why your paintings act on our hearts and minds so powerfully. It's so very subtle, this interaction. The surrealists, the abstract expressionists, the conceptual artists engage certain parts of our brain and it's fairly obvious how their effect works on us. You, on the other hand, use recognizable images in naturalistic settings, fragmenting time and space, creating an effect outside of both. But the sleight of hand is invisible. The illusion of normalcy slips us past thoughts and opinions. The painterliness of your work misleads us completely.

B Outside of time, yes. What I'm most interested in are recognizable images, what Braque called the pictorial effect.

RG So the content is of no interest to you.

B No. For example, when I began, I painted *The Guitar Lesson* to cause a scandal. (*It was a double entendre and one of its meanings was an act of masturbation.*) It was the only way of getting attention, but what pleases me is that now it's regarded as painting. The theme is a mere pretext.

RG Exactly. When we see your painting there is the illusion of a story. It has all the comfort and narrative cues of storytelling. We all love to sit around the fire and be told a story. It fulfills the needs of the heart and the mind, but this narrative is exhausted immediately; then comes your magic, that is, to open and enter the space between thoughts. It's like a hole in the wall. From far away you see very little through it but if you go up close the view is infinite.

B It's passionate what you say. Your words are full of sensations and imagery and your conversation has all the qualities of a film.

RG It's true that I usually see things and ideas in terms of images.

B Fellini also and me, when I see someone, I'm sketching with my eyes.

RG It's because we're children and children communicate very quickly in images.

B I've never stopped looking at the world through the eyes of a child and with a sense of wonder. The world of a child is infinite and as you grow up, it starts shrinking.

RG Right. A child's field of awareness is limitless because it has 360-degree vision. There's no defining center. A great sadness of getting older is that we tend to lose this all-around vision. As soon as the umbilical cord is cut you start to feel insecure and hungry. Your field of vision reduces around needs for food, love, affection, survival … and you begin to manipulate your world in order to achieve them. You learn strategies for self-preservation and this unfindable "self" takes on the appearance of solidity. The world narrows.

B I enjoyed an idyllic childhood and my youth was a brusque change, something completely different. I discovered life's difficulties and suffered a lot. (*They go off to rest and return at teatime, resuming the subject of suffering and Antonin Artaud, the French writer and great friend of Balthus.*)

RG Artaud was influencing everything in American theater in the 1970s which was my most formative decade. Even photos of him had enormous impact on me. He had the eyes of a saint.

B Artaud and I were so alike that people confused us. He said that his theater of cruelty was cruelty against oneself.

RG I took it to be cruelty against the notion of a solid self … cruelty against irrational self-cherishing.

B Everyone forgets about the terrible accident that Artaud suffered as a child. He fell flat on his face.

RG Also it seems he suffered from terrible headaches all of his life … and visions.

B He had to take all kinds of drugs to get rid of his headaches and he did suffer from hallucinations.

RG This is all very Romantic, but I think this "cruelty" was much misunderstood. We need to be "cruel" to ignorance and find a way to open our hearts and genuinely care about each other. If we have the courage to tame our unruly minds, not be fooled by conceptual reality, there is a beatific, a transcendent possibility awaiting all of us.

B Yes. It's a sort of game of inversion, which could lead you fatally in the opposite direction. We should read Artaud again carefully.

RG It's like the image of Saint Sebastian: cruelty to the "self" … or the idea of the "self" which is unfindable, unknowable, a hallucination. You have to be brutal to this self-cherishing. But it is extremely difficult work. Still, it's the only way to achieve freedom.

B Everyone is cruel to others. It's very easy; it's our law. In German there's a word "to suffer with." When I was young, I suffered greatly. I had no money and with the exception of a few people (*Picasso and Giacomerti*), no one helped me. I was alone against the world in Paris. I did everything, from painting chairs to translating. This suffering, which to begin with was like a game of ping-pong, took me to a state of religious ecstasy. As Baudelaire says in one of his verses: "Blessed Oh Lord are you who send suffering as the supreme cure for our impurities." Finally Artaud saved my life.

RG How?

B Artaud had gone off to Africa and suddenly he had the feeling that he had to come to Paris and visit me. He arrived literally at the moment when I had attempted to kill myself for the love of Antoinette, who would later become my first wife.

RG Literally at the moment. Amazing! How did you try to commit suicide?

B With an overdose of medication for treating the malaria I had caught in Africa. In a way, I was a very romantic person, like those of the 19th century.

RG It was a very expressive century, full of grand gestures, full of fantastic voyages.

B Romanticism still exists now, but in a different guise.

RG The moon has footprints and is littered with trash. The 60s and all its revolutions finished off the Romantic gestures, but we clearly deal with the same eternal issues of anger, hatred, jealousy, compassion, creativity, love and meaning. We live in the age of irony; the pure Romantic gesture now finds expression through humor, although I suspect that women even in these political times still approve of gallant gestures.

B A certain finesse has been lost. A woman immediately reveals herself in all senses of the world.

RG That can be quite wonderful and exciting, but I think that men do miss a certain sense of modesty.

B I understand this nostalgia for a certain type of woman. I also feel the same nostalgia for the figure of the gentleman.

RG What is interesting about the woman of today is that she tends to be totally straightforward … no artifice. The man doesn't have to push, and she doesn't have to withhold. It's more flowing. Setsuko is an incredible combination of Japanese modesty and western directness.

B She is a very special type of Japanese woman. When I met her in Tokyo she was twenty and was a "modern garu." She did a lot of things in the Western way. Now she's more traditional; I asked her to wear a kimono. Our encounter began with an argument because I was against compulsory education and defended a highly instructed type of illiteracy.

RG Kyoto is one of my favorite cities. When I began studying Buddhism, my first teachers were Japanese Zen masters. I loved being in Kyoto, loved everything about it. The spiritual and worldly esthetic is in perfect balance … heartbreakingly beautiful.

B You know, prudishness for me is only a social issue. Malraux said that the 20th Century would be religious or it would definitely not be. Prudishness is something religious.

RG Religion is a difficult word. Misunderstandings about this word have led to so much unhappiness. The Dalai Lama is very careful when he talks of religion. He always says "my religion is kindness." Kindness is something everybody responds to no matter what "religion" one does or doesn't follow.

B When I met the Dalai Lama I was surprised by his aura, an almost tangible force which very few people have. Strangely, he was scandalized by how, as a painter, I sold my works.

RG Twenty years later. I can say with absolute certainty that my meeting the Dalai Lama has been the greatest fortune of my life. I met him at a time when I was quite lost and unhappy. He's a true and completely trustworthy spiritual friend … forever in my heart.

B Like the Irish, I'm very Catholic; I believe profoundly in prayer.

RG Who are you praying to?

B To God, naturally.

RG What is your vision of God? Who is God?

B Everything.

RG So your prayers are directed to everything, everywhere.

B Praying is a way of getting out of yourself.

RG Well, if everything is God, are you not also God? So then is God trying to get out of himself?

B I'm not God, but I'm probably part of Him and when I pray I try to reach the light, a higher level. When I paint, it's like a prayer.

RG Who is the one who paints his prayers … and tries to reach the light?

B God. Man can't create, he can only invent. He who paints creates.

RG I like this image. The one who paints is praying to the one who creates but both are the same. Perhaps the one who prays paints the creator. Perhaps the creator paints the one who prays. In the end it's all problematic, for who creates the creator? It's an infinite regression.

B The one who paints tries to get out of himself and in that way approaches his Creator. If you paint, you try to leave your ego behind and at that moment I feel the light which is God and my mind and my hand are merely machines which listen. You listen to what you've got to do.

RG Who listens?

B The listener.

RG Who paints?

B The painter.

RG If you find the "Listener/ Painter" please let me know. (*laughs*)

B What I think is that we are living in the age of personality, which is absurd. Today, painting is dead. If you have personality, the best thing you can do is get rid of it. I'm not interested in expressing myself. Expressing oneself is the end of everything.

RG You're probably right, there probably are no painters in the painterly sense today and part of the problem is we live in the age of such irony. Everything emerging now is commenting on itself. Nothing is just what it is, everything is analyzed and commented on to death. The purity of the image no longer exists.

(*After a pause for tea*)

RG I do think though, with the greatest of respect, if one were to look at your paintings, one would say that there is a personality who made these paintings; there is the filter of your personality. There is Courbet, there is Balthus. I don't think that's a negative thing. You're the only one who could have painted your paintings.

B It's not my fault if I'm recognized.

RG The act of emptying the self creates openness, or rather *is* openness. What creates art from that openness will have a personality. I am an actor and I am different all the time, but everything I do is filtered through my emotions. And they're expressed instinctively. That's my gift. It's impossible not to have a personality. And surely personality is not a negative thing in itself. It depends on the level of wisdom that empowers it. A lower conscience can only express lower thoughts. Self-cherishing betrays us all.

B Perhaps the ego and personality are not the same thing but I prefer anonymity. I could never paint a naked woman. Adolescent beauty is more interesting. Adolescence represents the future, the being before it becomes perfect beauty. Woman has already found her place in the world, the adolescent girl, no. The body of a woman is defined.

(*Dinner time has come. The women have dressed and Richard Gere arrives in jeans.*)

RG What a nice surprise, all these beautiful women! This is such a European thing, this dressing for dinner. Well, these are my elegant jeans. I've changed from my casual ones. (*He jokes*) It's a pretty boring uniform. But you all are so lovely. I'm fortunate to be here.

B A book on elegance in men was published recently and its cover was a picture of me taken in the 40s by Man Ray. I was wearing a suit—the only one I had at the time! The example of elegance! Richard, do you want some Scotch? A Drambuie?

RG No, that's only for people with personality. (*they laugh*) I'd love a glass of wine.

B Naturally I've been a vegetarian for a long time now.

RG I stopped eating red meat when I was twenty-seven. My mother and father would find it impossible to give it up.

B My family always helped me though, not materially, but if it hadn't been for them I wouldn't have been a painter. Their social milieu was the intellectual elite of their time. They gave me the culture that I needed to become a painter. How did you get to be an actor?

RG It started quite early. Second grade. I played Santa Claus. My mother made the costume. I'm sure I was brilliant. (*laughs*) An actor is like a puppet; they're the same word in Hindi. It's a license to be, to feel. I was very shy and at school I gravitated to the theater, music and performing. Emotions are my oil paints. Emotions are that which moves the mind. The mind is the ground of all experience. If we want to release ourselves from confusion and, hopefully, help others, we have to understand what moves the mind. Who better knows emotions than an actor! Our entire craft is generating and playing with emotions.

B Didn't you ever feel you were in the wrong place?

RG No. Acting has given me a home and a context. It's been a good friend. A loyal friend. But sometimes a very needy friend. (*laughs*) It doesn't exactly lead you to emotional responsibility. It's probably a little harder on women. Movies are a very masculine world, ninety-nine percent of filmmakers are men. Balthus, you've met many actresses.

B I've met so many actresses and it's difficult to label so many different women. Sharon Stone was here recently, just before she adopted her child. She drove me crazy at first because she was so beautiful, but also because she has something inexplicably attractive.

RG I worked with her some time ago and saw her again during the last Venice Film Festival at a fundraiser for AMFAR. She's done extraordinary things raising money for AIDS research and treatment. A very committed woman.

B An actress I admired was Audrey Hepburn.

RG Very beautiful and very fragile.

B Yes, extremely fragile yet at the same time with an extraordinary strength. We admired her more as a person than as an actress. She was a real lady who had an extraordinary ability of not showing her emotions in her private life. We met her the day we threw a party in her honor in Villa Medicis in Rome. Her son Sean Ferrer had just suffered an accident with a lion in a zoo and no one was sure if he was going to lose his sight or not. We told her that we would understand if she couldn't come, but she did. She was fantastic and she left for Los Angeles at midnight.

RG I'm surprised you say she was not a good actress. I thought she was amazing, magical, her emotions were so transparent, the movement of her thoughts so vivid. That was her true beauty. It's something really difficult to do without appearing ridiculous. Being that open … that willing to share your emotions.

B What's the most difficult aspect of being a celebrity?

RG The fact that nobody is prepared for it. One's first response is an animal response … to run away. As quickly and as far as possible. But I have always kept my life extremely private and simple. You learn the lessons and adjust your life accordingly. In the end, it doesn't really matter what anyone thinks. It's all nothing more than a rather splashy spectacle. The surface of things is unreliable. The internal stuff will always be mine. That's all I really care about, anyway.

B I know less and less about myself. I'm always surprised by things and myself. It's as if I'm always seeing things for the first time.

RG (*After some silence*) Balthus, do you ever think about death?

B All that I know is that I'm not afraid of it, but I ignore how I'll react when it arrives. What I do not like is the brave position before it. I have exposed myself for the sake of doing it, usually to stupid situations such as jumping into a minefield. My bold side had always assaulted me.

RG So everything will work out fine. I think the key to death is the same as to life: to overcome all hope and fear. Fear comes and goes. Hope comes and goes. Nothing remains but our karmic legacy. Belief in karma leads to wisdom and responsibility and *that* is the ultimate protection and a most reliable path to destroy death. (*Setsuko says she's not afraid but admits she's completely materialistic and will feel sad to leave it all behind.*)

RG In the end nothing need be rejected. Every emotion, every sensory input can be an opportunity to break through, to transcend. Each sensory experience can be unique and alive. When a liberated person tastes something, it's like tasting the universe; when he hears the most mundane sound, it's like listening to angels chanting the most celestial songs. Pristine and ecstatic.

B Absolutely. I'm definitely bound by all sorts of things. My family, my daughter, Mitsou (*the cat*), warmth, my wife. I take or leave things according to my needs.

RG Grasping or rejecting things is the same jail. Giving power to things is a dead end. (*silence*)

RG I remember taking photographs when I was eight thinking "how do I balance this image to make it feel alright." The balance came by itself. The composition was innate.

B I have to show you photos I did.

(Setsuko goes to fetch some pictures taken by Balthus of Italian models when he was living in Rome. Setsuko shows Balthus' photograph to the astonishment of Richard Gere, who finds them incredibly beautiful and a complete mastery of light. He compares the extraordinary similitude of them with Balthus' paintings. Balthus, as usual when he wants to leave the room, addresses Setsuko in Japanese and retired to rest. The next day at 8:30 Balthus, wearing a kimono, is having breakfast. Richard appears at 10:30, full of energy and with an especially attractive positive light.)

RG I spent the night thinking, "Who is the one who paints?" (*They laugh*)

As I was meditating this morning, the light was coming through the windows and illuminating the mountainside. It reminded me of many of your paintings.

B That's what I see. I often wonder why people these days no longer paint from nature.

(Gere gets up and feels the Balthus kimono.)

RG I really like your kimono. The material looks European. Was it made in Japan?

B Yes.

RG How long have you been wearing kimonos?

B For over forty years. They gave me the first on a trip to Japan. It's very comfortable and also beautiful because it's a tradition.

(Mitsou II, Balthus' cat, walks across the breakfast table.)

B My cats come and go across the table, to the great consternation of my dinner guests.

RG I don't mind. I remember having lunch at Zefferelli's villa, outside Rome. He let his enormous dogs roam the dining room as he threw them chunks of meat. They would be crazy throughout the whole meal, jumping on the table. I ate like this (*He puts his arms around his plate.*) It was awful. (*laughs*) I spent time years ago in a primitive village in Borneo, and curiously, their first commandment was literally: "don't laugh at animals."

(From Zeffirelli, they pass to all memories, from Fellini to Rossellini, great friends of Balthus and greatly admired by Gere. They also discuss the future of cinema and painting.)

(In Balthus' studio, Richard studies the painter's latest paintings, which he has been working on for the last ten years. He takes more photographs and then goes for a stroll in the mountains, whose features remind Gere of the mountains in Bhutan.)

RG Bhutan is such a beautiful place, but unfortunately many of the houses there are no longer being built in the traditional way with mud. They use cement, which isn't as beautiful and doesn't retain heat.

B Do people have a sense of efficiency in Bhutan?

RG No, they do it to be "modern."

B I hate modern. It seems that ugliness has conquered the whole planet.

RG It is unfortunate that wherever you go, it looks the same. Fifty years ago it wasn't like that. Music, art, architecture was different and uniquely indigenous everywhere.

B We live in a general flatness, but what I don't understand is why the ugliness, too?

RG Bad Bauhaus influence nearly destroyed our cities. But, I think today, architecture and design are becoming more human, more sensual. Simple but soulful. I hope so, anyway.

B I find all architecture unbearable, like the cities themselves, and for me, design is the end. Fashion moves everything. The world today is more intolerant. Everything has to meet a standard. It's ridiculous.

RG Now fashion is 'ethnic' so they mix Hindu and Chinese or Indian Moorish and Japanese or African elements, but if you really want to preserve traditions and their innate strength, they must be pure.

B Obviously. The world is like a strange tasting salad … or more like a broth. The invention of stupidity is the loss of tradition.

RG I think we all prefer things with a sense of history. To me, they feel alive, with their own soul, like antique cloth. Many of the things I do are made to appear older than they really are, like my photographic style. I have no interest in being current. I'm building a house which looks and feels to be a hundred years old. It was built with an appreciation of imagined memory, a kind of yearning. But I suppose ultimately it's theatrical. Not real. History can't be faked but it can be suggested. Soul is a factor of time.

B So modernity is like a feeling of expropriation.

(*They go on discussing the sense of modernity like expropriation. Modernity as synonym for "alive." Gere tells the story of Italo Calvino and Don Quichote.*)

RG I still feel good and alive around Shaker architecture and design. It's purity and directness I find very moving.

B There's a town called Wallenberg, in Switzerland, which is very similar to the Shaker style. It's all very traditional. We must go there.

(*Setsuko jokes that modernity is to change your wife.*)

RG Balthus, you're modern.

B Perhaps in the end we're both modern. (*pause*) Just like we were talking about ugliness, poor Francis Bacon, a friend, and intelligent man, was irresistibly attracted by ugliness. I think that he would be what is today called a good painter.

RG What is today called a good painter? (*laughs*) Very skillful. Along with you, he's one of my favorite painters. He explored extremes of emotional experience. He tried to communicate distortion and madness and I would suppose his personality requires that he expresses it that way. To say "Bacon ugly," "Balthus beautiful" is irrelevant. He transcends what is traditionally considered ugly and you transcend what is traditionally called beautiful. Both incredibly beautiful to me because I feel the delicate soul that is the painter. Anyway, beauty is completely subjective and therefore most likely false and ultimately meaningless.

B I don't agree. I believe that beauty is an objective thing with universal canons; everything was done in a common atmosphere where only beauty in the largest sense of the term could come out. That's why I was talking about cathedrals. Beauty comes from within. Bacon's interior was unfortunately above all ugly. Do you remember the film *Primal Fear*, in which the innocent boy is the murderer?

RG The surface of things is unreliable.

B I'm sure of it. But we're playing on words that don't get to the interior.

RG What I'm interested in is what lies behind the idea of beautiful and ugly. In the film, the boy is innocent and monstrous at the same time.

B Exactly. In the end we discover that deep down he's irredeemably ugly and that's what counts.

RG It depends on how deep you look. At the deepest level we're all the same. At the deepest level we're clear light. Oceans merging into a drop of water. Anyway, I'm more optimistic than you.

B You find the optimist by getting to know the pessimist. That's what I'm like. I hope you come to my exhibition at the Palazzo Grassi in Venice in September. It will be the largest yet. Before you go, you can come to Montecavallo with all the family. (*This is a property with a fantastic castle that Balthus owns 50 km from Rome.*)

RG I'd love to, but I hope it isn't during the cinema festival. That's terrible time for actors. I can't walk: every step people ask for autographs and photos. The farthest I get is from the Cipriani to Harry's Bar. (*laughs*)

B But that's what being an actor is, wanting everyone to love you.

RG Everyone needs to be loved, probably actors more than most. I don't take it badly but sometimes it's just too much.

(*Sadly, the time to day good-byes has arrived. Gere approached Balthus, puts his forehead against the painter's and says a few words in Tibetan, a Buddhist goodbye.*)

RG Regain your strength, Balthus. Are we modern?

B It's my seductive side, perhaps inherited from my relation Lord Byron, but don't say so. Don't tell anyone.

From VOGUE 07/2001; Text: Richard Gere/Cristina Carrillo de Albornoz

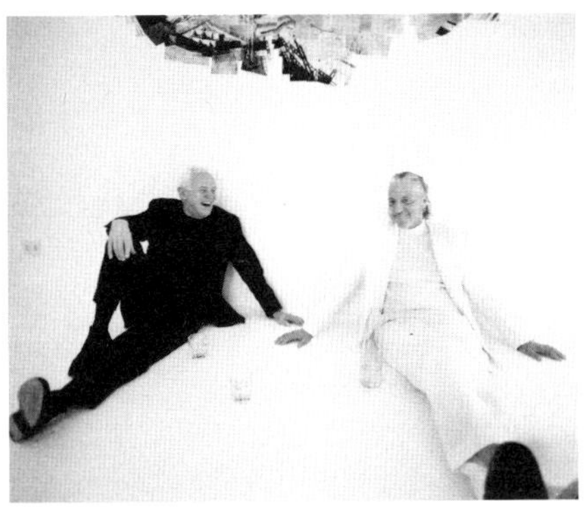

DREAM MEN

Both men can imagine doing something completely
different: Fashion entrepreneur WERNER BALDESSARINI
and Munich barkeeper CHARLES SCHUMANN
on women and men, looks and lifestyles.

The two make a good team. There is nothing they hate more than sitting around idle. In order to dive into the ebb and flow of the never-ending current of their thoughts, the conversation begins in the makeup room where they are being prepared for the photo shoot. In the mirrored ping-pong of glances, they exchange thoughts on lies and the truth, self assurance, fashion and the relationship between the sexes. The *séparée* atmosphere makes both of them relaxed. The current favorite topic of the "grand old men" of German lifestyle: planning the future. Werner Baldessarini is retiring as CEO of the Hugo Boss AG. Charles Schumann has just opened a new location and dreams of a hotel with a bar on the French Atlantic coast.

CHARLES SCHUMANN I think we saw each other for the first time at the beginning of the nineties, when I was modeling for Yamamoto and Comme des Garçons.

WERNER BALDESSARINI No, we met long before that. I met you in the seventies when you were still in Harry's New York Bar. When we engaged the world's top models for the first Baldessarini catalogue, it was too boring for me. I wanted people who had something to say and where you could see that they had some experience in life. I asked you, and you were a hit. Today, the catalogue is a cult object. Even though you're a little bit past puberty, young men today want to be as cool as you. In addition, you appeal to women and they make the most decisions about men's fashions. That's why our models have to appeal to them, first of all. Women find you exciting; they see a lot in you. I hope you can fulfil their expectations.

CS I'm really a pretty great guy.

WB Others find you a bit of an odd fish. But nobody finds you boring.

CS I have a new woman every day.

WB And I dream about a new one every day. How did you actually get started with Yamamoto?

CS In Japan, they saw a photo of me in a magazine and contacted me. In those days, Yamamoto didn't hire models but lots of actors—Dennis Hopper, for example. Then, I stopped working in fashion for a while. When Marvin was born, I got married and lived my life exactly as before. Of course, that didn't go so well. Since then, I'm a sworn bachelor.

WB I was a sworn bachelor, too, for a long time. I had a highly developed timidity about getting into a permanent relationship. And the divorce statistics show that I'm right. The most important thing for me was not an exciting sex life. I thought that if I got married, the woman and I would have to have a great deal in common and still give each other plenty of leeway. I finally found one like that!

CS I'm married to Schumann's Bar. Sometimes I wonder if that's right. What you're doing now, Werner, dropping out completely, is something I couldn't do. If I could manage to leave the bars to themselves, I would love to spend two years just looking. Maybe an event or a woman could make opting out easier. I always wanted to live in another country, to open a hotel and a bar. And I also have a weakness for women from southern Europe.

WB Dropping out is something you should really consider. Things are closing in around you …

CS As long as my name is on the door, I can't say "I'm a member of the board" and come in the evening and count the cash. The team would lose their respect for me. The motivation is completely different when I take on a full part. That's why I thought so long about opening a "day bar." Everybody advised against it. Luckily, I did it anyway. It gave me many new ideas. And today I find myself thinking once again: That can't be all there is!

WB Some people can't understand my getting out of business. But for me, a certain life plan is crucially important. I know a lot of people, top managers, who simply can't let go. Life is too short to waste your time talking. I would say that I'm fairly truthful. Of course, if you're honest, you make yourself vulnerable. It's a great feeling never having to disguise yourself.

CS You never disguise yourself? You're always telling me you like something and, in reality, you don't.

WB I'm a bit careful with you. I might be somewhat sensitive, but you're the greater prima donna.

CS When it comes to the truth, I'm your complete opposite—I lie all the time.

WB I believe that I'm an authoritarian team player. It's important to give others some leeway, but not too much.

CS I always say: "I'm in favor of democracy, as long as we do things my way."

WB With an attitude like that, you might still be standing in your bar when you're ninety.

CS You manage things better than I do. You don't have any choice. Your business is so much bigger and, therefore, you have to delegate.

WB That's right. If not, you become so inflated that, sooner or later, you'll explode over something insignificant. And if you're always putting on a show, you hinder communication and waste your strength on nothing. But the audience always needs new stimuli. In our advertising campaigns, we no longer use normal model photos. We're always asking ourselves how we can get better. Charles, you're a perfect example. We can let your own personality come to life in a photo; we don't have to hide you in our rags. You help the outfit, you as a person. If we recognize your type and present it in the right way, the suit immediately seems much better.

CS I'd like to comment on that, since we have been working together, I've changed. For example, I've discovered colors. I always used to gripe: a bordeaux corduroy suit!—who could make such a thing? For me, male fashion was black and white, perhaps dark gray. I think it's great that I now wear all colors, it's much more fun. When I put on a red or purple pullover, everybody wants to know where I bought it!

WB Gastronomy needs something like you and your bar—the same way as fashion needs the courage of the owners of small boutiques. In the big ones, you only see managers, rationalization, statistics. When all is said and done, they don't take any risks. The passion for fashion is missing.

CS Passion—that brings me back to partnerships. Normally, you can't cultivate a relationship when you're as involved in your work as I am. I'm busy from dawn to late at night. When I come home, I'm exhausted. It's just not possible to get into the car and drive to you in Kitzbühel. My father died some time ago. Marvin and I wanted to visit him over the Easter holidays. We couldn't make it during the first week. In the second week, my father passed away. Then I thought I couldn't continue in this way.

WB It was a great loss for me when my mother died—she committed suicide.

CS How old were you then?

WB It was about fifteen years ago.

CS Oh, then you weren't so young. You could handle it better.

WB It was very difficult for me. She had a serious illness and didn't want to become an invalid.

CS You can accept that. It's really amazing that she had the courage and strength to make such a decision.

WB It was only later that I realized how strong my mother was. She brought up her children, ran our textile shop and saw my father as Tarzan. In those days, there were no equal rights. My mother did everything on the side. For me, she was the embodiment of femininity, intelligence, warmth.

CS Women don't get any benefits from emancipation. They lose their femininity. I don't need that—then I would look for a man as a friend.

WB But that makes cuddling so difficult.

CS In the meantime, the trend has moved a little in the direction of femininity. Women want to be like women and not like men. Thank God!

WB Charles, what are you wearing today? You look like nothing on earth!

CS What do you mean? I'm wearing a great shirt, from you, by the way …

WB Your trousers are much too wide; your jacket is too short. If I were to wear that, I'd look like a bum. But you are sexy, it suits you.

CS The trousers are tailor made!

WB Your tailor needs glasses.

CS The tailor followed my instructions, precisely!

WB Then he needs a hearing aid. Most men wear jackets that are too short—it really ruins the figure.

CS Why do we have jackets anyway?

WB Women have an ideal conception of the male body: upright stance, broad shoulders and an ass like a plum. When you go to the sauna and see reality—it's a drama! So, we put shoulder pads into the jacket. And the trousers, no matter how wide, must cling to the ass, here (*he points to the base of the spine*).

CS Arabs wear baggy trousers …

WB … and their women wear veils.

CS I wouldn't want to be a woman. But I was always jealous of children. Children have such beautiful things to wear, simple things, too. Now kids also want to wear "labels." That doesn't really bother me. Nothing bothers me any more.

WB I don't believe that.

CS Okay, the problems kids have today bother me, now that Marvin is here. The environment, the brutality of human relationships—that worries me …

WB Since September 11, it's clear to me just how unimportant fashion is. On that day, I was on the way to a showing in New York and then the captain said that the airspace over the USA was closed and we would have to land immediately. It wasn't a landing, it was a nosedive. I never used to be afraid of flying—now I am.

CS Fear of flying is a problem for me, now that I have Marvin. What if something were to happen to me?

WB You can come to grips with fear. Through meditation.

CS Do you do that?

WB I meditate for twenty minutes every morning and evening. I'm so restless, it's an immense help.

CS Do you think I should try it?

WB Yes, it wouldn't be a bad thing for you. But to get you to do it! I can remember the week we spent on a boat in Turkey. At the beginning, you bitched a lot, but then you liked it. That was an exception. Usually, you say "maybe" and then you don't come.

CS It's difficult for me to spend a week anywhere in isolation. It's a problem for me to sit in the water with Marvin and wait for the next wave. But every evening I make music for an hour. No matter how tired I am, I do it. I usually play the piano.

WB Your neighbors are going to shoot you!

CS No, I have the whole house to myself. How will it be for you when you have no responsibilities? You were a guiding light. Nobody can take your place.

WB Of course somebody can. That's the good thing about a corporation. "Guiding light" makes me feel good, however, nobody is irreplaceable.

CS The King is dead! Long live the King!

(While Werner Baldessarini tells the makeup artist about the benefits of shoulder pads for the female silhouette, Charles Schumann has jumped up to greet people in the studio, to telephone his team and to get changed, in a flash, for the shooting.)

From VOGUE 06/2002; The conversation was recorded by Ingeborg Harms

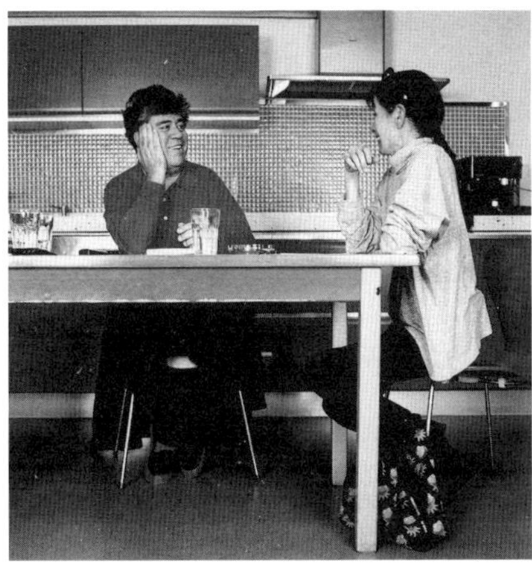

THE ANGEL AND THE VAMPIRE

GERALDINE CHAPLIN is a star without any affectations.
Actors think of PEDRO ALMODÓVAR as a "vampire" because
he demands everything from them—the ideal coupling for
controversial topics: bodies and dreams, love and lust, spirit and liberty.
Plus, the desire for luxurious fashion!

L ike a character from one of his films, Pedro Almodóvar enters the gaudy kitchen of his production office El Deseo (desire). He gives Geraldine Chaplin the seat at the head of the table and squeezes himself into a place in front of the oven. The studio—a multistory building with a glass facade—is located in a narrow street in the old center of Madrid. The glistening green facade, the interior decoration of steel and glass, and the cheerful colors of the furnishings are a symbol of the longing for modernity which drove Almodóvar from his native village in La Mancha to the metropolis, more than thirty years ago. While he pours his guest a glass of water, he gushes that he loves everything about Geraldine—her natural friendliness, her sharp sense of humor and her complete lack of prejudice. Both are in high spirits—they have been chased upstairs and downstairs by photographers for more than an hour looking for the perfect angle—the staircase has become their stage. And the director found himself in a slightly different situation —in front of the camera.

Pedro Almodóvar Yes, you are the born diva. I don't like being photographed, although … they should be able to find the attractive side of my face.
Geraldine Chaplin As Charlie Chaplin's daughter, I was photographed from the day I was born. I grew up with cameras, studios and fame.
PA I just don't like being the center of attention. On the contrary, at that moment my desire for liberty and independence becomes greater.

GC How do you feel when you look in the mirror?

PA It's not really all that bad! A short time ago, I started making a lot of self-portraits. But I don't like being photographed by others. And I particularly hate those pictures which show me how time is flying.

GC Time! (*covers her face with her hands*) Good old time! I also find it terrible that it passes so quickly. The mirror has always been one of my enemies. For years I hoped that I would wake up in the morning, transformed overnight into a sensual, curvaceous woman. In vain!

PA I've been thinking about "time" since I was a little boy. When I was ten years old, I was fascinated by artists who showed their talents at an early age, such as Mozart and Rimbaud. When I was eighteen and still hadn't produced anything earth-shattering, I started to look around for other role models and, to my relief, discovered that many famous writers only began when they were forty. I always feel a certain time pressure. It doesn't have anything to do with getting old—more with the fact that I would like to leave behind something permanent.

GC My father had the same wish. Recognition was important to him, right up until his death. I can still remember how, shortly before he died, he was supposed to get an Oscar and was invited to America for the presentation. He really never wanted to return there after he had been treated so badly in the McCarthy era. He even took the American passports away from us children, and we were given British ones instead. But then he went, in spite of everything, and I realized how much the Oscar meant to him.

PA There are so many things I want to ask you about your father, but tell me first of all: Are you leaving tomorrow, for Switzerland?

GC No, Miami. To visit my son.

PA I don't think that there is a better reason to travel than to visit family who are scattered all over the globe. Unfortunately, I don't have that.... What do you like about Miami?

GC For me, Miami is like a vision of the future. Everybody is young, beautiful, muscular. After a certain age, nobody notices you any more, which can be an advantage because you can then sit back and watch the amazing fauna.

PA There's always something wonderful, unexpected about beauty. I'm mainly fascinated by expressive characters, slight blemishes, and faces you don't see every day. What does your son do in Miami?

GC He's studying psychology, and wants to set up a practice there.

PA He was here once and I can remember that he looked very Spanish.

GC That's right. There's lot of Spanish in him.

PA He should come over here and cure us of our obsession with time—that's really an enormous problem. On the other hand …, he's much too young to know what that is. And your daughter? What does she want to be?

GC Oh, at the moment her hormones are determining what she does. But she's turned into a fabulous woman.

PA When you see her, you would never guess that you are her mother.

GC My daughter is how I always wanted to be: tall and sensual, with an enormous bosom. I would have liked to have looked like Marilyn Monroe or Laetitia Casta.

PA You should be happy that, at least physically, she fulfils your expectations.

GC Oh yes, I am. But she looks like she's twenty-three. My intention was to be a liberal mother who lets her young daughter do what she wants. And now, I have become quite authoritarian.

264

PA (*Laughs*) Internal contradictions are completely natural! Our entire life consists of contradictions.... How old were you when you left home?

GC Seventeen.

PA Me too! In those days, we left home some time between fifteen and twenty. It's different today where kids live with their parents forever.

GC It was a disgrace to still be living at home when we were eighteen.

PA In our village there was only one chance of finding work—a bank. When I refused to start working there, they looked at me as if I was from Mars. I think that, even if you know nothing, you should at least know what you don't want. It was clear to me that I wanted to be as free as possible in organizing my life.

GC Where did you go?

PA I came here, to Madrid. For me, Madrid was a synonym for "everything is possible" and "all modern things."

GC Did you know anybody here?

PA No, and I found that exciting. I had the feeling that the city was wide open for me—ok, not completely, I only wanted to go to the film school …

GC … which the good old dictator Franco had just had closed.

PA That's how I became an autodidact. A seventeen-year-old has to experience things for himself. He has to discover for himself those things which suit him or not. In spite of the dictatorship, compared with my village, Madrid was the best: a place where there was a film premiere every day, where I could rent films and where I really developed. I discovered other eras, other countries—it was a dream. I decided what I wanted to read. At that time Latin America was in: García Márquez, Cortázar, Borges … one after another.

GC A bit later, in the seventies, the "*movida*" began. Madrid became famous for its wild nightlife. I was already living here at that time, but always went to bed early and never experienced any of it. It was only later that I realized what I had missed!

PA In those days, I led a double life. I had a job from eight in the morning until three in the afternoon and then my second life began. I had decided to take matters into my own hands. I abandoned myself to my pleasures.

GC What kind of work did you do?

PA I wandered around with the hippies, made chains of glass pearls or sold books. I kept my job at the national telephone company only to please my family. I wanted to prove that I could do something serious. I was a clerk in a department with several thousand people—like in Billy Wilder's *The Apartment*. The only difference is that there, everything was much more stylish. My colleagues all came from the middle class and I, a lower-class kid, had never had anything to do with all that before. Their tastes were completely different from mine—their interests, too. The awful consumer orientation and their conservative attitudes were utterly foreign to me—and made them interesting objects to study.

GC I like living life to the full, but have a well-structured daily schedule—probably because I'm afraid that, with my inborn tendency to chaos, I would sooner or later go under.

PA Chaos and excess are important themes in my films; yet in reality, they don't play the same role they used to. As a director, I find people who are at peace with themselves unexciting … and, at the same time, I hope that I will one day experience precisely their feeling of inner peace.

GC I believe that it's the artist's duty to break taboos and to break rules. I don't have any respect for prohibition.

PA If something is forbidden for moral reasons, I ignore it. Today, there's no longer any "official" censorship in Spain, but there is an economic and moral form of it. And all over the world, censorship comes from political correctness. I'm politically incorrect—by nature! But I didn't let you finish. What did you do when you left home at seventeen?

GC I went to work as an au-pair in London. I really wanted to become a dancer in the Royal Ballet.

PA Where did you spend your childhood?

GC The first eight years in the USA and the rest of the time in Switzerland. When I went to England, my father found a proper family for me. I ended up with an impoverished Polish prince. On the first weekend his daughter said: "We're going to Chartwell, to Winston Churchill, for the weekend." So, I spent the weekend playing cricket with Lady Churchill and then spent a bit of time cleaning the Polish prince's house. I led the life of an au-pair deluxe.

PA Did they take you into the Royal Ballet?

GC No, and that's why I went to Paris, to work with the Marqués de Cuevas Ballet in summer. I danced Cinderella. When the ballet disbanded, I went on to the circus.

PA And your sister? She has a circus, hasn't she?

GC No, she was too young at the time. I took part in a charity performance. After that, the same circus offered me a job and I became an elephant keeper and trainer.

PA The first time I saw you was in a photograph with Jean-Paul Belmondo.

GC That was later. When I was nineteen I decided to try films. It was easy for me. The Chaplin name opened a lot of doors. People admired my father. I felt loved and cared for and never had to be afraid that I would have to show my comical side.

PA And then you developed a taste for acting.

GC That only started when I was twenty, with *Doctor Zhivago*.

PA David Lean, the man who made *Doctor Zhivago*, is one of my favorite directors. He was the only one who was able to make those mega-productions without having them look like they were made for a major studio. They also have something absolutely individual—author's cinema, quite simply. Bertolucci tried something similar with *The Last Emperor*, but he doesn't come close to Lean's productions like *Lawrence of Arabia*; they all seem to be absolutely personal. Lean was an exceptionally gifted director, but he must have used just as much talent to defend his own point of view.

GC He remained completely independent. I can remember that sometimes he sat around for days just pondering instead of filming. The bosses of the production companies came around from time to time, but nobody dared put him under any pressure.

PA Did you have to do any auditions?

GC Yes, twelve altogether. The others thought I was too young, but he stood up for me: "I can see exactly how we can make her age." I noticed that he wanted me for the role and, suddenly, I became afraid. He felt that and went with me to my dressing room and confessed, "I'm also scared to death because I'm used to speaking to my crew in English." "Don't worry," I said. "I'll translate for you." And that's what I did for the following fourteen months.

PA Of course, *Doctor Zhivago* was filmed in Spain. And after that, you stayed put here. Later, you worked a lot with Carlos Saura.

GC I usually tell the story like this: "I never unpacked my bags." I kept falling in love, and always with Spaniards. I guess I'm just a romantic type. But you can probably tell more about romanticism and desire.

PA For me, desire is something completely human. I've also noticed that it's rare that two partners desire each other to the same degree. That's one of the great tragedies of mankind. I have to be told, everyday, that I'm loved.

GC When my parents married, my mother was seventeen and my father fifty-four. My grandfather, Eugene O'Neill, didn't attend the wedding out of protest; he never spoke another word with my father. The age difference didn't matter to my parents. They had a happy marriage and flirted with each other like young lovers.

PA Love is a kind of madness, it's like a drug; all-in-all it can't be explained. It can disappear from one day to the next, and you never know if the other person really understands your feelings.

GC Everything depends on sex. That's the animal nature which we try to tame in order to transform it into love. Time changes everything. At twenty, it's pure sex; the hormones are in revolt screaming to be united. Later, it's different. There we are dealing with love. However, sometimes I still feel like a twenty-year-old.

PA I was educated by priests, who even managed to make me find sex disgusting. My education consisted of punishment, fear and feelings of guilt. The worst was the threat of divine punishment, burning in hell—a terrible pressure. In spite of everything, you always find a way to survive. My method was quite theatrical: I sang everything that could be sung, all day long, even Latin masses. I liked the ceremonial, the ritual aspects of the church services.

GC And the incense.... My parents were atheists but not opposed to religion. My father sent me to the strictest school he could find—a convent school. His attitude was: "I would like to believe but I can't." When I arrived there, I had never heard about God and was absolutely convinced that this person, who they were always talking about, must have been the owner of the school. When I found out who He really was, it took me a long time to fully understand it.

PA Your parents had a completely different family background.

GC My father grew up in the street, in comical musical theater, vaudeville. My mother was Catholic and had a fine education. As I said, her father was Eugene O'Neill, the playwright. I had a strict, Irish-American, Catholic grandfather.

PA I find his play *A Long Day's Journey into Night* fascinating. We should film that together. When did he write it?

GC I really don't know. But I can remember that he didn't want it to be performed before his death. It's basically the story of my family.

PA Eugene O'Neill dealt with the problems of women at a time when nobody else did that. He was a hundred years ahead of his time. I find it wonderful that he made a mother the heroine, addicted to ... what was it? Opium?

GC Morphine. That was my grandfather's mother. Her husband, my great-grandfather, was a great Shakespearian actor but later he played only the Count of Monte Cristo—into ripe, old age. He hated himself for giving up everything else just for money. He was always on tour throughout America. He took my grandmother along. She was given morphine during the births of her children so that she could bear the pain. After that, she was addicted. The young brother, who is referred to in the play, is my grandfather.

PA I saw it recently on the stage in London—with Jessica Lange. It was wonderful.

GC I saw it once with Laurence Olivier—uncut. Four hours. Very impressive! The history of my family is full of theatricality and madness. I'm not sure that something like normality even exists.

PA Everyone who talks about himself and his world talks about normality. Even the wolf-man thought he was normal when he saw himself in the mirror. Normality is what we experience twenty-four hours a day.

GC There is a madwoman hidden inside of me with her own, terrible life. At night, she comes out. She's afraid because she has looked death in the eye.

PA Death is something I don't understand, which I can't accept. In 1986, when I made *Matador*, I wanted to find out how I stood to this irrevocable fact. I didn't get very far, and I don't have the problem under control. However, it became clear to me that I can only understand death when I see it as a part of life. That's why I have made a connection between death and sexual excitement. What do you do when this "madwoman" shows herself?

GC I go for a long walk everyday. Not so much for the exercise, but to get my thoughts straight. Finally, reason takes over.

PA In real life I'm much more rational than in my films. I think that I'm absolutely normal although there are many aspects which completely contradict each other.

GC I'm more impulsive than my father, but I'm often just as sober as he was. When I came to Spain, the thing I missed most was discipline—except with you.

PA As far as I'm concerned, nothing is possible without discipline.

GC But you still place the characters in your films in quite extreme situations. They move along the edge of an abyss.

PA One can think up all kinds of stories and present them convincingly. The most important thing is that the actor should not appear artificial. You can tell stories which have been repeated time and time again as long as you do it naturally. Somehow, there is always the possibility of creating a connection with reality. I find it fascinating to see the incredible power which passion can set free in people. We have everything, really everything, inside us.

GC Are you attracted to the evil in man?

PA Sometimes I try to create a character who is absolutely evil. But I'm never successful. I cannot believe that man is man's worst enemy. Actually, I like to appeal to positive feelings, but that isn't always easy. I hate manipulating feelings, like Hollywood does: There, films are often made to make people "feel good." I wanted to ask you something else about your father: How was your relationship with him?

GC My father was very Victorian. He himself was married four times, but with us he was very strict. He hardly ever let us go out, and he was not at all happy with the idea that we could have a boyfriend. I never introduced him to a boyfriend until I was twenty-three. His children were everything to him. He was very witty and often performed for us. My father always saw the funny side of life, and that was a great blessing. I have seven brothers and sisters and there was a lot of laughter in our house.

PA And your mother?

GC She wasn't as strict, but she did what my father said. My mother also had a great sense of humor. I think the most wonderful thing one can give children is a sense of humor and the ability to laugh at oneself in tragic situations.

PA My mother, also, was not as strict as my father, but she had a strong character. I learned a lot from her, for example, that you have to liven up reality with fantasy in order to make life easier and more pleasant. She was a creative person and enormously energetic.

 GC I admire women. And you understand the strength they possess.

PA Yes, thankfully. I don't know why, but women interest me more than men. I find you fascinating and it's great fun to just watch you and listen to you. I grew up in La Mancha— the home of the greatest machos in Spain. Men rule their families like gods. I can even remember that my mother washed my father's feet. However, in our home it was always the women who solved all the problems—discretely. I can also remember that my grandmother, my mother and my sister often avoided a tragedy through their theatrical skills. You women are much stronger, always good for a surprise, and are much more mature emotionally. You tackle problems directly, that's why it's more exciting to talk to you. Men are much more closed.

GC Women were always my idols. I'm absolutely convinced that we are the stronger sex, that we control the world. We were born to govern! In my eyes, there is nothing more attractive than a heterosexual woman who knows how to manipulate and control men. Hillary Clinton is a fabulous sex symbol—and Catherine Deneuve the most luscious woman in the world. Just think of the aura a female body has in a silent movie! In your recent movie *Hable con ella* you gave women a great deal of power.

PA A shapely body and beautiful breasts appeal to everyone; even though, in the fashion industry, the half-starved variety seems to be preferred. When I'm filming, I'm obsessed by each individual figure. That's why I have such a close relationship with my actors. I'm sure you've heard the rumor—that I'm a vampire—and suck the lifeblood out of others.

GC I love intense relationships! The closer they are, the happier I am.

PA In any case, I work like a man possessed, and maybe that's the worst thing because it devours me completely. On the set, the director is symbol of power, a god who creates a parallel world founded on his dreams. It seems as though I transform my dashed hopes into something different.

GC I love my profession as an actress, but you have to be oversensitive in this job. Sometimes it's even humiliating. You can't take it personally. By the way, what do you do to relax?

PA I devour books and I love tennis.

GC Sport? I would never have expected that of you.

PA Physically, sportsmen are perfectly suited for film; they have the bodies of people who demand something of themselves, who have fought. For me, it's a symbol of a desire to which I've found no entrance. And as I want to find an entrance to all forms of desire, it's frustrating and fascinating at the same time. Women's tennis is the only sport which interests me. I don't know why.

(*A few photographs are taken. Pedro Almodóvar's glance falls on the photographer's trousers: black, of exquisite quality. He makes a note because he wants to buy exactly that model.*)

PA I love trousers without pleats or any other extras. I'm a real fashion freak and buy VOGUE as soon as it's published. The glamorous layout appeals to me. I think it's a form of art. Fashion also plays an important role in my work, because a film tells a story with the help of light, color—and fashion. My work is very colorful—I believe that's because my mother always ran around in black. For me, the most wonderful example of elegance is Grace Kelly in Hitchcock's *Rear Window*. I like to stuff my figures into a kind of uniform from Armani or Gaultier. That gives them something mystical and transforms them into abstract, universal creatures.

GC I have a weakness for formal dresses and have an impressive collection of them. But I really don't like to style myself. I love going to the sauna and having massages, but I hate sport. Do you know what? I had to be careful all my life to stay this slim, or I wouldn't have been offered any more movie roles.

PA I don't believe you. My eternal youth is due to the fact that I'm a bit chubby—and that I did a few really crazy things at the right time.

(*They laugh and kiss each other goodbye.*)

GC Take care of yourself.

PA You too.

From VOGUE 07/2002; The conversation was recorded by Cristina Carrillo de Albornoz

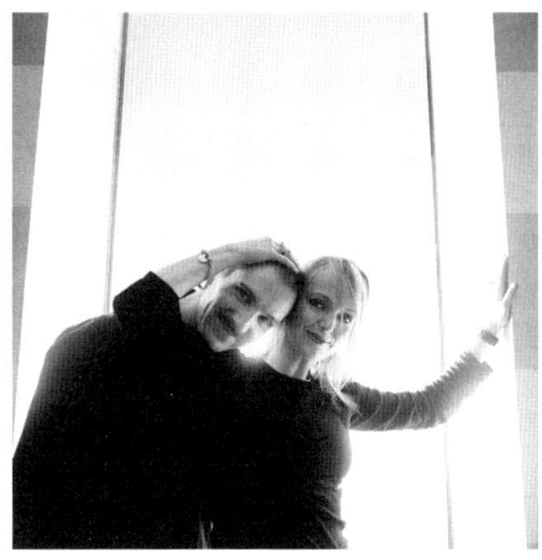

TO FIND AND LOSE ONESELF

MIRANDA RICHARDSON meditates with RALPH FIENNES about falcons and people, stars and fans, problems of physique and the only real sex appeal.

It is late afternoon in an apartment in "The Hempel" Hotel in London. Miranda Richardson goes into a corner of the room, bends down and rummages through a case of personal belongings for a pair of pirate trousers. The look of an angel. The makeup artist touches up her face. At the same time, she chats with the shooting team. Finally, thirty minutes later, Ralph Fiennes appears, completely in black with his hair cut short and with the moustache he has to wear on the stage in his role as the psychoanalyst C. G. Jung. With a mysterious expression he goes up to his colleague and gently places a hand on her shoulder. Miranda presses it firmly. The two sit down close to each other and order. While they are waiting for the Japanese food to arrive, the conversation begins.

MIRANDA RICHARDSON I was at the opening of this hotel. It's very stylish I think.
RALPH FIENNES The ceilings are a bit low, but I feel comfortable in the simple Japanese atmosphere. You know, my taste is very purist.
MR Only the best of everything. (*They laugh. Drinks are served.*)
RF Do you only drink water?
MR Last month I took a purification treatment; I had drunk a bit too much alcohol. Now, even my coffee is decaffeinated. I would start climbing walls if I drank normal coffee.
RF A good wine, some Parma ham and cheese—to me that's heaven. I love simple food. Good pasta is like poetry.
MR Did you know, hypnosis helped me to stop smoking?

271

RF In the fifties, that was a popular method; it seems like it's back in fashion. I only smoke if it's necessary for a role or if I'm alone, to help me concentrate. (*Japanese soup is served, immediately followed by a tray with four dishes for each.*)

MR That looks delicious, but it's enough to feed an army.

RF I'm dying of hunger. Let's eat. I was out with a friend yesterday. He saw you on the stage as the guest star in the comedy *The Play What I Wrote* (*directed by Kenneth Branagh*) and said that he thought you were wonderful.

MR I really only understood the role at the last performance. I'm really convinced that if somebody is good in a comedy, they are good in everything.

RF You have to differentiate a bit. Some actors, Jim Carrey for instance, are always funny; on the other hand, there are performers who only appear funny at the right moment. I don't think that I'm naturally funny, but I do have a sense of humor.

MR I've seen you laugh a couple of times. That's what I like most about you—your child-like smile.

RF And you have a tremendous sense of humor—the quality I like most about you!

MR I chose this profession in order to make people laugh.

RF Can you remember the filming of *Spider*? Even though terrible things happened, we were completely relaxed—a wonderfully laid-back working atmosphere.

MR So uncomplicated. I have difficulty dealing with sad things and suffering. When I'm in a down phase I always try to get a part in a comedy; then I can't do anything which reminds me of my own situation. It has to be the opposite of me. Why did you really become an actor?

RF I think because it's only in this profession that I can be myself.

MR It was completely different with me. I had the feeling that I had to escape from myself. I wanted to slip into other roles, probably because I never really liked myself, never really accepted myself. But the most important motive was: I wanted to make people laugh. At home, they always thought that I was eccentric. Our family was fairly conventional—my mother was a housewife, my father a marketing director. We lived in the country, near a golf course with flocks of millionaires.

RF I grew up on a farm, but we lived like bohemians. My mother, a painter and writer, gave me the initial impulse. When I was eight, she was always playing speech records: Laurence Olivier in Shakespearean soliloquies. And, later, when she took me to experience him in *Henry V* everything became clear.

MR I recently saw a documentary about your mother (*the writer, Jennifer Lash, who died in 1993*). Did she have a large influence on you?

RF She was a very understanding person with unbelievable intuition. She encouraged her children and helped us to develop and find ourselves. It was never her main intention that we be successful: she wanted us to become independent, open-minded, critical people, always 200 percent involved.

MR With a mother like that, the expectations concerning women are naturally extremely high. For me, the most important thing is that one respects the other as he is. Never try to change him, give him his leeway! Is there anything you would never say to a woman?

RF Even when I'm critical, I try to be constructive. You should support the other person, strengthen her self-assurance. By the way, I find that clichés are often rather accurate. A woman does want to hear that she looks super and has a wonderful figure. But, in spite of that, they always ask the counter-question: "Do you really mean it?"

MR Figure and weight—now we're on a touchy subject. I've never felt comfortable in my body. As a young girl, I was always a bit too chubby. Later, I lost a great deal of weight, but I always think a lot about whether I should change my body in some way, whether I get certain roles because of the way I look. Of course, I know that what I have in my brain is much more important. I only start to feel comfortable when I'm on the stage.

RF I was never a good sportsman, and I really don't like sport at all. But I always worked at keeping fit. Movement cleanses the body and clears the head. I go to a fitness studio and do a lot of yoga. You can't separate body and mind. In a way, they're always dancing with each other.

MR I'm not the yoga type. I like to run and I train using the Pilates method. What do you think when you read in the newspapers that you're the most erotic man in the world?

RF Of course, I seem attractive, like other men as well. But, when all is said and done, attractiveness and sex appeal have more to do with inner values. As an actor, I'm aware of my appearance. I spend a great deal of time in dressing-rooms: I get made up and observe my face. That's how I discover myself. It has nothing to do with vanity. I think it's absolutely reasonable to have a feeling for the impression one makes on others.

MR Your fashion style?

RF I like to wear comfortable things, but I pay close attention to what I wear. For me, that has something to do with dignity and self-esteem.

MR I like those flipped-out Belgian designers like Dries Van Noten and Martin Margiela. I've even started designing fashions myself.

RF But you originally wanted to be a vet …

MR … I love animals. My cats are called Ines and Emilie, and the dog's name is Liv.

RF But the most amazing thing is your love of falconry. How did that come about?

MR A wounded falcon fell from the sky above my farm. I let him sit on my shoulder all day long. Having a wild animal so close to me—that was the formative experience. I started to think how I could combine that with my studies. So, I enrolled in veterinary medicine, I read a lot, and, at some time, falconry came into the picture—not hunting with the birds, only studying them. I'm fascinated by the flight of falcons, training them with the intention of later releasing them into nature—and their solitude. We would get no pleasure out of taming them. The relationship between us and falcons is one that you relinquish when the moment comes.

RF Do you like isolation?

MR The best ideas come to me when I'm alone, in the country. However, I often think that I should have got married a long time ago. But, for that, you have to find the right man.

RF I'm usually quite happy alone with myself.

MR What does romanticism mean to you?

RF For me, the epitome of romanticism is to decide, from one moment to the next, to whisk somebody off to a special place, to buy the plane tickets and simply fly away with that person. In my opinion, romanticism is a synonym for genuine spontaneity.

MR But the other person has to trigger that spontaneity in you. When you're ablaze, it's clear that these things happen. Subtle planning also plays a role for me here. So many things were planned in my last relationship—some of them really silly. Once, when we were on holiday on an island, I suddenly got the idea of hanging dozens of little hearts from the ceiling-fan for Valentine's Day.

273

RF Was that a success?

MR No, because he switched on the fan too early and we ended up with heart salad. Really funny! … You played in the comedy *Maid in Manhattan* with Jennifer Lopez …

RF That was great fun, too—a completely new experience. Jennifer is so charming—a really spontaneous actress, who improvised her part in the dialogues. It was liberating to work with her. It's amazing how laid-back she is in her dealings with the press and photographers. We filmed in Central Park in New York and there, it's absolutely impossible to keep the paparazzi away from you. Jennifer let them all photograph her and then asked them to only publish the best pictures. But she was so aware of what she was doing, she looked good on all of them.

MR I saw a photo taken at her birthday party—she was shoving a piece of cake into your mouth …

RF That was awful because they had dreamed up a love affair between us. We're really playthings for the yellow press, which spreads vicious rumors and tasteless stories about us.

MR The reason is to try to destroy the myth of the artist—at all costs. It's like a conspiracy. Do you believe in chance or is everything predestined?

RF I don't think that anything happens in life by coincidence; everything is linked together. There are forces which are beyond our control and which determine whether certain things happen or not.

MR And if you try really hard to get your own way, it also doesn't work?

RF Sometimes a strong will is essential to get things moving, but you often experience that, in spite of all your efforts, nothing develops. A sort of collective energy exists which regulates everything.

MR Maybe that's why I've never come across Mr. Right! The fact that you have everything under control really impresses me. No matter what you do, it's always brilliant and well-considered. I so often feel ill-prepared. I would love to have a method—for my work and life. Do you have something like that?

RF First of all, I always take my time. What did Picasso say when he was asked about his method? "First of all, I 'feel' myself." I let myself be guided by my instincts, my feelings or, as my mother would say, by my emotional intelligence. A concrete method isn't any good.

MR Sounds fine.

RF Think about acting. It's amazingly easy and practical. I need the same amount of technical and practical know-how to be able to play a love scene or a scene in a restaurant …

MR Mmmm, it's not really as easy as that. Sometimes your partner is an idiot. A kiss is not like a real kiss—a kiss in real life—because you have a thousand things in your head and you're surrounded by the director, lights, the technicians. Everything depends on how I feel on that day. But maybe women feel differently about that. You're even completely relaxed in nude scenes.

RF I feel much freer in films. It's all a question of trust, and I'm a trusting person. In films, there aren't so many risks. The true risks exist in real life, that's obvious. In films, suspense is produced artificially. You make your appearance, then you sit around and wait. I like to go to my dressing room and watch videos. That's how I keep my distance.

MR I seem to have read …

RF Yes, yes, I know. I organize orgies with drugs and all that. Absolute rubbish!

274　　**MR** How do you feel when your fans start to squeal when they see you?

RF I also see myself as part of the audience. I've experienced wonderful actors, singers, pop stars and am as fascinated by them as anyone else.

MR I find this star cult horrible. Only dancers and musicians can make me envious because I consider ballet and music the most perfect art forms. I would have liked to have been a dancer.

RF Looking at you, the way you move and behave, it would be easy to imagine you as a ballet dancer.

MR People who do something so complex have to always consider "Can I contribute something new?"

RF No unreasonable demands, please! There's no sense forcing oneself to do something. At the moment, I have at least six books waiting to be read. I just don't get around to it.

MR I like reading biographies. Typical of old people, I'd say. Maybe it's an overreaction to our dismal youth culture.

RF We must do something about that. We must take culture to the old people on this planet. (*They laugh.*)

MR Yes, we must honor and respect them. I wouldn't want to be twenty again.

RF Old people are calmer, more relaxed. They no longer continually ask themselves "How do I look? Will I be able to do that? What does life have in store for me?" I love mature actors who have given their all—seen and done everything.

MR Which prejudices have you done away with over the years?

RF Oh! I think I'm developing more. I don't know that they are genuine prejudices, but they are something like it. I've had certain fears since I was young. I've always asked myself how things will be, was afraid of being exposed to others and of failing. You could say that I was afraid of everything. The older I get, the easier it is to get away from these. At the moment, I'm playing C. G. Jung in a play (*the comedy "The Talking Cure" by Christopher Hampton*) and I've discovered some parallels to myself. I become impatient around reserved people, and in the play, when a patient tells me about his problems, I think: "Be glad you're not me!" Do you understand? One is impatient towards people who are similar.

MR What are you afraid of?

RF My own intolerance and fury. I'm afraid that I suppress them and that's not good. But, there's so much fury inside me that I'm afraid to release it. You seem to be much freer and more independent.

MR That's all a facade. I have the same delusions as other people. Also in connection with marriage: Everybody else gets married, but I'm not quite so far yet. Maybe I'm afraid that everything will become routine.

RF What else did Jung say? "The magical smell of the house disappears," or something like that. It's a very difficult decision, you shouldn't force it.

MR By the way, I'm invited to party in the country on Saturday. Would you like to come?

RF I can't, I'm afraid. But ask me again soon.

MR Will do.

RF I'll wait for you at the theater.

From VOGUE 03/2003; The conversation was recorded by Cristina Carrillo de Albornoz

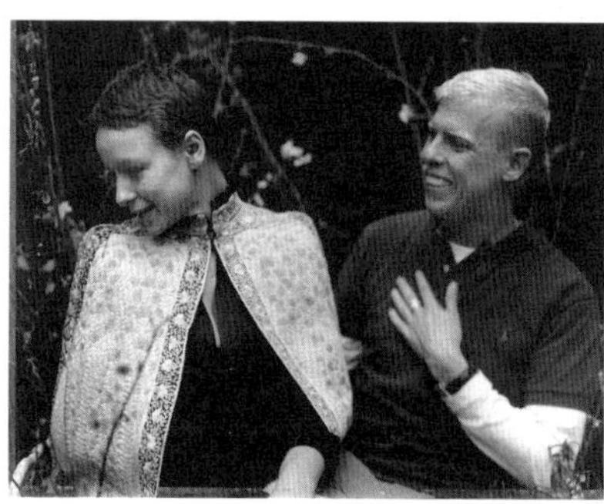

STARS FROM THE DEPTHS

She was thrown out of school at fourteen and conquered the cinema; he fought his way from poverty to the top of world fashion: SAMANTHA MORTON and ALEXANDER McQUEEN.

The gentlemen in London's "Groucho Club" have become used to the fact that women are now permitted. In spite of this, they all look up when Samantha Morton enters the traditional restaurant. The English actress is wearing an Indian hippie skirt, and a washed-out jeans jacket, topped off by a small, green felt, hunting cap. Even Alexander McQueen, famous for his eccentric fashions, cannot hide his astonishment. Then, the British couturier greets her like a caring older brother; Samantha is pale, recovering from a minor operation. It proved very complicated to organize this meeting between her filming and his collection—but that made them all the more curious about each other.

SAMANTHA MORTON Just why did you want to talk to me?

ALEXANDER McQUEEN Because, I assume, we grew up under similar circumstances, fought our way to the top and both hate being forced to do things. I wanted to discuss it with somebody similar, in complete trust, without having to first explain things to the other person. And also, people say so much about you that I wanted to hear your story from you personally.

SM That's exactly the same reason I accepted this invitation. I believe there are people who simply don't fit into predefined structures and have to find their own way. I was thrown out of school when I was fourteen and felt really very relieved. I knew that I wanted to act and thought that that was the only place where I could show my emotions. After a few attempts in the Junior Television Workshop, I was finally accepted by the Royal Court Young People's Theatre. Not long after that, I got my first role.

AMQ I don't think that anybody who has not experienced it himself can really understand what you're saying—to find no support or understanding, in the family, for your dreams. Not even having the right words to be able to describe your dreams, to only know, that's what I want to do, that's how I want to be—and then to have to find out yourself how to get there.

SM Strange, I feel close to you, as if we'd known each other for centuries. I can tell you things absolutely frankly. Today, when I see myself in a film, I'm proud, so proud! Exactly the way

I was when I started. I still can't believe that that's *me*, that *I* managed to do that. Do you know what I mean? I'm not conceited about it, I'm just so full of joy that I'm really worth something, that I've really made it.

AMQ In spite of the bad cards fate dealt you, so to speak? I know that feeling, too. I grew up in a working-class district in East London. My father was a taxi driver, there were six children, and sometimes there wasn't enough money for the rent. I was the youngest and something of a bird of paradise, lost in my dreams. As a child, I used every spare moment for drawing, designed entire collections—and everybody thought I was crazy. I only knew one thing for sure: nobody would help me. That's why comprehensive training, in theory and practice, was so important to me. Parallel to my studies at St. Martin's School, I did an apprenticeship in Savile Row.

SM People always divide things into categories: fashion here, art there, music here, cinema there. For me, everything is connected. That's how I immerse myself in a role. When I listen to music, I act as if I were dancing. Why shouldn't theater have something in common with ballet?

AMQ Maybe that's why people feel that you become one with the part, that it is you—and, at the same time, the other person you are playing.

SM When I see myself on the screen, I always have the impression of seeing a stranger. I believe that when I'm working I'm completely outside of myself, and music helps me achieve that.

AMQ Music is also something essential for me. Some evenings, when everybody has gone home, I sit in the atelier and listen to Johann Pachelbel's (*1653–1706*) wonderful *Adagio*. I sink into it completely. Then I look down at the street, and the people rushing through the city as if they were running for their lives. Sometimes, I start to cry, I just let it flow, don't worry about it. Something happens inside me, my face is flooded with tears. At times like that, I'm at one with myself. And afterwards, I start to draw.

SM Film doesn't come from film and fashion doesn't come from fashion. Everything, what we experience, who we are, is a part of all of our activities. That characterizes creativity. Or how do you see it?

AMQ My main source of inspiration is art. I live surrounded by my collection. I think I need that because artists express something for me that I'm not capable of expressing myself. Maybe they don't have a direct influence on my creations but act more as models, to be courageous, to feel completely independent, to determine my life myself, to work with the greatest possible freedom.

SM Look at what I brought with me: a handbook, a guide through the entire history of art. There might be some ideas for the photo shoot here. I wanted to show you this painting by Caspar David Friedrich, *Woman at Dawn*. Look at the jacket she's wearing—the wide shoulders and this line which makes the narrow waist appear so fragile. I would like to wear something like that later.

AMQ I can imagine something like that for you; I think we have something here.

SM That's a comfort. Even though Esme, my daughter, is already three years old, I have the feeling that, since her birth, I've had to resort to all kinds of tricks to hide my tummy. Look, let me show you. (*lifts up her T-shirt*)

AMQ That doesn't look so bad to me. The modern idea of beauty, that a woman should look as thin as possible, really has nothing to do with the female body. Compared to that, it's wonderful that you have your own child.

SM She really gave my life a focus. I would do anything for Esme. I just bought a real house; I want my daughter to grow up in a stable environment I myself never had. I hardly knew my brothers and sisters because my father had children with several women and we were all brought up by different mothers and permanently-changing nurses. My daughter is going to know, right from the start, where she belongs.

AMQ I can understand that completely. I think it must be wonderful to make a child a part of one's life, to accept responsibility. That must be a radical change, don't you think? Do you dream about having an even larger family?

SM In the meantime, yes. I used to be terrified by the idea. But now, I want at least one more child. I'm separated from the child's father. Now, I want to know for sure if the man I'm living with at the moment is reliable enough and mature enough to handle it. If at all possible, I want to have a real family—father, mother, children. Isn't it difficult, as a gay person, to have a steady relationship?

AMQ I don't know if that isn't difficult in any situation—for gays and heterosexuals. I only find love truly really beautiful if you can imagine it lasting and if faithfulness is taken for granted. Anything else is enervating and takes too much energy away from my work. My friend and I are thinking about possibly adopting a child. He's Catalan and commutes between London and Mallorca. We haven't known each other very long. I'm not quite certain that our relationship could support a family. A lot of people are surprised that I, as a homosexual man, would want to have a family.

SM I can't understand that. Sayings like: "We've always done things like that," or "We've never done things like that," don't get us anywhere. Some of my gay friends have better relationships with their partners than most of the heterosexual married couples I know. I believe that when children grow up with well-balanced, reliable adults who can guarantee them continuity and security and fully support them, that it has more value than the conventional division of roles.

AMQ The Anglican church sees that a bit differently. By the way, is religion important to you?

SM My mother was Polish and my father Irish, so I was brought up in a strict, Catholic environment. Later, I developed another idea about religion. Possibly, it's only important that you behave humanely and responsibly towards others, that you don't turn your back when somebody needs help. Many people seem to need religion as a kind of ID. Then they stand in their church and think to themselves, this is the group I belong to. And how about you, do you believe in God?

AMQ I'm an atheist. When I told my Cambodian housekeeper that a few days ago, she crossed herself. The fact that I'm not baptized shocked her as much as if I were Satan himself. Then I showed her all these medallions and crosses I wear around my neck, see them? That calmed her down a little. I believe in some kind of supreme spiritual force—there must be some way of explaining the unknown. In any case, I'm convinced that we only know and experience a fraction of the world around us. Our knowledge is limited, our ignorance limitless.

SM Don't you feel that a lot of people resort to religion in order to come to grips with their fears? I'm not sure that God exists, but if he does, I imagine that He is in me and not somewhere above me. I think my life plays a part, only I can make things happen. Perhaps it's the same with God, that I have to make room for him within me.

AMQ We have so many possibilities for fighting our fears. I've so often felt that I was balanced on the edge between life and death that I'm no longer afraid of dying. I fully understand our life as an intermezzo between birth and death, an extremely limited affair. You could say that we're just passing through. What's important is to do something during this period which is worth being called life.

SM I think that religion is one possibility to pass on responsibility or to do something in the name of something. The war in Iraq has made me realize once again just how closely religion is associated with aggression.

AMQ But at the same time, we all know that the US government didn't attack Iraq because of Saddam Hussein or for any religious reason. It was all about annexing this country with its oil wells and reconstructing it in a way which would suite the USA. On the internet you could find out that right-wing groups had been planning this for a long time and even consciously used Bush as their marionette. The attack on the World Trade Center finally provided the rationale for justifying this project. Of course, it was important to crush Saddam's dictatorship, but I'm convinced that it wasn't necessary to carry out a conventional war with so many victims.

SM Oh, please stop! One of my brothers is a marine. That's why I wasn't only against this war politically, from the very beginning, but because I had to fear for a member of the family every day when I watched television. Even if I don't know him very well, he's still my brother. Do you think that artists should take a position, that they can maybe even have an influence on politics?

AMQ It seems really difficult to make those in power change their position. But you can inform the people who vote for them. Even fashion can, and must, make a statement. At least, I tried that in my last show. I unraveled a giant American flag as a kind of ironic, exaggerated gesture. Nobody could misinterpret that. And, of course, clothing can say something about your political attitude.

SM Of course. Tell me, we hear a lot about you. For a while, the media reported a new scandal almost every week.

AMQ I can assure you, I wasn't interested in the scandals but only in making a statement. Sometimes I need some fresh air in this artificial world. A few years ago, one of my models lost both legs in a car accident. She modeled for me with artificial wooden limbs. The audience was shocked. But don't you think it would have been a bigger scandal if I had cancelled her contract?

SM Wow! That was brave. Who was the model?

AMQ Aimee Mullins. After that performance, she became so famous that she now has more work than she can handle.

SM Super! The sterile fashion and film world doesn't like it when you scratch away the veneer. But you have to be twice as good as the rest to be able to get away with that.

AMQ I know. Would you be happier appearing in political melodramas?

SM Basically, taking a position is easier in films than in fashion. But I don't believe that we should only make politically-engaged films. Something else is important to me: I try to take on roles which show respect for people. That could be in *Code 46*, which I just finished filming with Michael Winterbottom as director—a fictional story about a cloned woman. That can also be a melodrama like Lynne Ramsay's *Morvern Callar*, which we filmed last year. As is usual, I played a person in a borderline situation, in this case, a girl who publishes a novel, written by her friend who had committed suicide, under her own name. I had to take the responsibility of embodying this injustice.

AMQ I really admire that. I could never be an actor. How do you stand it? How can you accept shaving your head bald for a role?

SM Look, nobody can force me to do anything I don't want to do. Four years ago, I was supposed to wear a miniskirt to a dinner with a producer and a famous director—I refused. I was twenty, and you know that many directors think that young actresses are mainly there to go to bed with them. For the first time in my career, this was a project which would have brought me a million dollars. Everyone was shocked. But as you said before, isn't it precisely the opposite? Wouldn't it have really been a scandal if I had shown up in a miniskirt and laid a married director, just to get the job?

AMQ Yes, it's really strange. I can remember that there was an uproar in the press because you had turned it down.

SM I wear short skirts, but only when I want to. It was the same with the shaved head. I've had my head shaved five times—because the particular roles interested me so much that I decided, for myself, that I wanted to immerse myself into the character all the way.

AMQ I can totally understand that. When I'm working on a collection, I place demands on myself which nobody else could expect from me.

SM That used to be a problem for me. I was so hard on myself that I became hard towards others. Now I've learned to keep things separate.

AMQ What do you mean by hard?

SM For example, 100 percent discipline. In almost every film, I have to deal with a new territory; that can be historical connections, electronic music, psychic behavioral patterns or the problems of drug addiction. The more you understand about the background and surroundings, the better you're able to penetrate the part. That's why, once I've decided to learn something, I immediately become diligent and precise. But you also know a lot about discipline. You've changed you figure completely, haven't you?

AMQ Maybe there's a connection with what we said at the beginning: if you grew up the way we did, you can create the energy you need to invent yourself. Some time or other, I'd had enough of being seen as a "bad boy"—fat and with rotten teeth—who could afford to shock people.

SM Did other people tell you to do that?

AMQ No, but I always knew that just being shocking wasn't enough. If you really want to start a revolution, you have to be absolutely professional and successful. At a certain stage, my image as an *enfant terrible* was so cemented in the newspapers that I felt misunderstood. That meant only steamed fish and vegetables for me and reducing my chocolate obsession to only one day of joy a week—Friday, incidentally. Strangely enough, I got used to it quite quickly. Then I had my teeth fixed and surprised people that I could be a really friendly human being.

SM I think you have to keep on redrawing the line between the image and the real person. My little daughter helps me in that. When I come home and Esme needs me, when I look at her baby face, I know once again who I am. That's so important for me.

AMQ I can understand that. Every day you have to be careful that you don't fall into the gap between your image and your real personality, especially when you enter the world of the rich and the famous, but hail from Nottingham or East London. You're always on a kind of tightrope.

SM I know what you mean. The rich admire you, maybe precisely because of your background, but only as long as you impress them with your best performance. That's the kick for them. If you become a bit sloppy, there's the danger that you'll fall out of favor, in an instant. They would be more tolerant of people from their own circles. High-class society functions the way it always has, only with different codes.

AMQ That's why you have to get into the system in order to be able to change it—you have to be able to probe into the structures and formulas and then change things from within.

SM And that's possibly the most exciting thing about our progress—we see things from within and without, we know the world of the happy few as well as we know the world of the workers.

AMQ Maybe it's an endless journey—who knows where we're going? Samantha, when shall we meet again? I think we simply have to keep in touch. But I think we shouldn't keep the photographer waiting; he also has a schedule.

SM Okay. But you have to help me. I feel terribly insecure when I'm being photographed.

From VOGUE 07/2003; The conversation was recorded by Isabel Grüntges

SAMANTHA MORTON — ALEXANDER McQUEEN

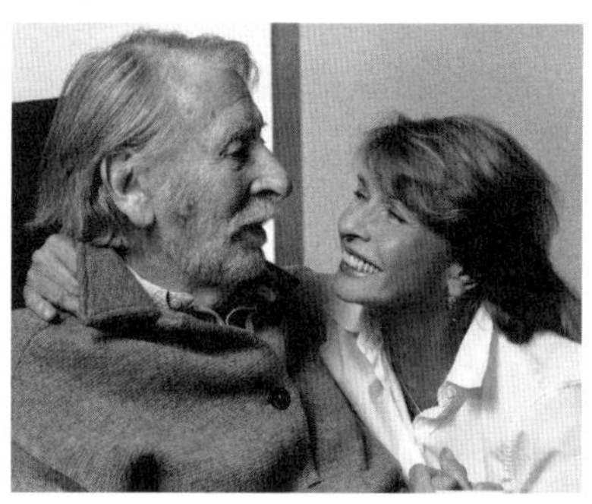

WISE TO THE WORLD

Life's travels have taken SENTA BERGER and GEORGE TABORI
to many places. What these journeys have given them is the ability
to marvel (at the power of days gone by), to be amazed (at Thomas
Mann's humor)—and even to laugh in the face of a catastrophe.

You might almost think the Ganymed restaurant was in the Boulevard St Germain, what with its little red roofs over the windows. The truth is, however, we are in the sober Schiffbauerdamm, right next to the Berliner Ensemble, the theater Brecht made famous. This is one reason why Senta Berger and George Tabori decided to meet here. Another is that Tabori lives next door. The two of them first met in 1958, and have been friends since 1994. Berger's husband, Michael Verhoeven, filmed Tabori's story *Mutters Courage (My Mother's Courage)* and made a documentary about him. They are therefore totally at ease with each other. They embrace and say hello; tea and water are ordered—it's still afternoon. How are the children? Your husband, the dog, the wife? And especially, how's Vienna? Later, when the pictures are taken, there are three people who barely need to communicate to understand each other—Viennese photographer Elfie Semotan, Viennese-born Senta Berger and Vienna fan George Tabori. All three are suddenly homesick at the same time. It's a bond.

George Tabori What shall we do?

Senta Berger Please, George, do what you do best—tell jokes. You've got this special brand of humor.

GT I used to know a lot more jokes. But you know, humor's a very serious matter. There's always a disaster behind a good joke.... I like it when jokes are sad.

SB A lot of jokes really do manage to boil a catastrophe down to a format you can comprehend. They aren't show-off jokes.

GT Do you remember the first time we met? It was making the film of *The Journey* in Vienna, with Yul Brynner and Anouk Aimée. You played a young waitress, and I was the screenwriter. I watched you, but I didn't dare speak to you.

SB Well I was only sixteen!

GT That's just the right age.

SB *The Journey* was the film I got thrown out of the Max Reinhardt College for.

GT How did you get the part?

SB One day, a group of American actors visited the drama school. You could see they were artists—they were wearing duffle coats. I love duffle coats! At that time, they represented the unobtainable. They meant either Englishmen or Americans. So Yul Brynner came to our college in a duffle coat and asked if anyone could read something. I risked it—I've no idea why—and got a small part. But you were not allowed to play parts in films while you were studying, so they kicked me out. I never regretted it. The film did a lot for me. But you lived in Hollywood for a long time, too. Did you feel American or European there?

GT English. During the war, I worked as a foreign correspondent for Britain …

SB You were with the *Geheimdienst* (*secret service*)!

GT That sounds so …

SB OK, let's say secret service, that sounds classier. How old were you? Probably very young …

GT … That was 1942. I had to work it out. I married my first wife, a girl from Palestine; there wasn't any Israel then. Ten years later we separated, and I almost married a fellow thespian of yours, Greta Garbo. We were together for a time and lived together. She'd already stopped making films by then. *Two-Faced Woman* was not a success, which upset her so much that she gave up. She sat at home and had a cook who always made these healthy things. But Garbo didn't like them. She went secretly to a Polish colleague to eat sausages and goose.

SB How did you get to know her?

GT At the dentist's. He looked at my teeth and said they'd all have to come out.

SB A bad moment to meet Garbo.

GT She asked me what was wrong, and I tried to tell her. She then drove me around in her old Chevrolet—the speedometer never dropped below 125 mph. I still remember celebrating my birthday with her that May. It was in Sunset Plaza in Hollywood. Thomas and Katia Mann came. Thomas Mann wasn't too keen on Garbo because she could tell jokes so well and he couldn't. When he got started, no one laughed. And then Garbo came along with two incredible jokes, and everyone fell to pieces. He never forgave her for that. The best of it was when Garbo said on my birthday: "Come and pick me up, I'll take you out for a meal." She normally wore a dark hat and long dress, but that day she wore a marvelous suit, and for the first time I saw her as a film star. We were going to an expensive restaurant, and I noticed too late that her suit was covered with hair from my cocker spaniel. When she got out, it all stuck to her. She just spun round three times, and all the dog hair simply dropped off. She was incredible.

SB Did you speak German or English with her?

GT Both. I was very serious and very left-wing. And I didn't like her films, particularly *Ninotchka*. We went to the cinema in Santa Monica together, and afterwards I was very rude to her. "How can you make a thing like that? The Russians are fabulous!" I said. It was only later I found *Ninotchka* OK, and funny.

SB You couldn't laugh at the film any more than we could later laugh at Billy Wilder's *One, Two, Three*, because it came out at the height of the Cold War. Now I love the film, but at twenty I didn't understand that anyone could have that kind of humor.

GT It was silly of me to be rude about *Ninotchka*.

SB It wasn't silly. You only wanted to be fair to a different system. American self-righteousness always triggers off a reaction. Tell me, did Thomas Mann actually have to tell the jokes in English?

GT Thomas Mann had no sense of humor.

SB In any language?

GT I met Thomas Mann in Hollywood that time and admired him very much, particularly because of *The Magic Mountain*. He gave me a tip, always to begin speeches with a joke if I wanted to be successful in the US. He tried it again and again, but no one ever laughed.

SB When did you start writing?

GT I can't remember any more; the real genius was my brother, who was six years older. He was a great liar.

SB Told lies or wrote lyrics?

GT Lied. He'd already had articles and poems published in newspapers at fourteen. When he was eighteen, my father got him a job at a Budapest newspaper. One day, there was a terrific interview with Thomas Mann in it. A week later, a letter arrived from Thomas Mann's lawyer in Germany saying that Herr Mann had not even been in Hungary at the time of the interview. My brother had made it all up. In 1935, my brother went to London and from that day stopped lying. The books he wrote after that were so boring. The change of cities had a strong effect on him.... When did you first go to Berlin?

SB Oh, I was eighteen, so 1959. Berlin was a dark, mysterious city and remained alien to me. I had no friends and an apartment without a TV or telephone. There was a whole host of things going on politically at that time, but I was never interested in it. I was more interested in whether I was happy or unhappy, in love. But you went to Berlin very young, too, didn't you.

GT My father told me very early on that I absolutely had to find a profession I could do abroad. Then in October 1932 we went by train to Berlin, and I started in catering—first as a waiter, then in reception. But the best was room service. Guests used to leave a lot of food, so we always had something to eat. Once I had to serve Hermann Goering breakfast. He was lying there in purple pyjamas, telephoning. I didn't know who he was, but the situation wasn't so desperate then, although you could already see Hitler giving speeches in Wilhelmstrasse. He always looked so tired and sad. Of course, I was in love with the manager's daughter; she was lovely. She always supervised breakfast. I used to say very deliberately every time, "one bread with ham, one jam, two coffees" and so on. Very slowly, just so I could look at her.

SB You were always a ladies' man!

GT After the war I got a letter from her. She was living in Italy with four children and had seen my name in the paper. She wrote: "If that's you, it's me, Annie, I'm married and very fat."

SB Wasn't it about then you first got involved in the theater here?

GT Yes. My first job was in the US with Elia Kazan, and then I was successful with *Brecht on Brecht*. It was only afterward that I went to Germany. Do you know Germany?

SB Not entirely, even now. But that's OK. What was it like, when you came to Berlin in the 1970s?

GT I came to Berlin from New York. My little son asked me how I could live in Germany. I said I could live here very well, and promised him I'd keep an eye on them. I didn't have the feeling I'd come across Nazis here. But I never think in categories like "the Germans" or "the English" anyway. I think of Mr Smith or Herr Müller. Once I told my father I'd learned in school that all Rumanians were queers. Then he hit me and said: "Rumanians as such don't exist." After that he apologized, but ever since I've known it's wrong to think in national categories. Where were you living at the time?

SB I was in Rome, and saw what Willy Brandt meant abroad. I think he was seriously interested in change. There was a real difference in the air—intellectually and in mood. You could feel a sea change in every country—even America. It wasn't a matter of fashion, or a media sensation, but a development affecting all levels and generations. Everyone had a vision of a better world, and wanted to try out new social structures. The buzz word was *Verwirklichung* (*implementation*). We were the first generation that could ask questions. With hindsight, I seem to myself very untested—particularly when I think of your life or remember how hard we were on our parents. It was right that we were harsh, but were we also unfair? On the other hand, we can't just do what Martin Walser wants—just stop talking about the Nazis. When I went to America, I was twenty-one and didn't know much about it. I found myself constantly getting the once over: "Aha, so you're Austrian. When were you born? And your father? Was he in the war? Was he a Nazi?" And that was in the film business, which is in fact run by Jewish Europeans. The more I knew about the past of Austria and Germany, the better I was able to cope with such situations.

GT These days I dream of the past a lot.

SB So do I—I can't sleep. In the early morning hours, it's a kind of waking dream. Then I go for a walk in my childhood, I'm at my ballet school again, or in my grandparents' apartment, which smells of soup …

GT It's much the same for me. I can't get to sleep before my wife gets back from the theater. She's back around two, because she goes off with the rest of the company for a bite to eat. Do you mind if I smoke?

SB Can you give me one, too? Actually, it's rather nice being awake so early. For a long time, I couldn't help feeling very sorry for myself because of it. Then at some point, I told myself, that's how it is at your age. You should spend more time thinking, remembering and looking forward.

GT (*coughs*)

SB You know, you shouldn't be smoking.

GT Yes, I know. I started smoking when I was sixteen, but I try not to inhale.

SB At any rate, you certainly couldn't live in New York any more. There's only room for non-smokers there.

GT I like thinking about New York. It's a very Jewish place, even the blacks talk like Jews. I lived in a great neighborhood. There was a synagogue, and next door a cathouse.

SB The important things go together.

GT It must have been 86th Street. That's where the German colony began, right by the Jäger restaurant, where Brecht always used to eat. Once I was supposed to play baseball with my son, I'd never heard anything about it before, and only accidentally hit the ball. He was thrilled. And my daughter had to write a piece for school. She handed in a rather sexy piece, where-upon the teachers immediately rang me up because they thought she'd made it up. But I'd done it. A great time.

SB I recently dreamed up a city of my own. It consisted of Wenceslas Square in Prague, Budapest and Vienna. In my dream, I didn't know the way home, and I was too proud to ask for help. At some stage I persuaded myself to ask someone: "Excuse me, what's this place, which way do I have to go?" Then I saw three women, but when I got out of the car, they recognized me at once and started talking about me. I found that so awful that I didn't dare speak to them. I dream a lot about places that have been important in my life. Will you be going to Budapest this year, where you were born?

GT Yes, I thought I should visit all the cities once more that meant anything to me. I want to spend a week in each. Touching, isn't it? I'd go to Vienna, then Hamburg, Sofia, Istanbul, Cairo, London and then back to Berlin. And after that your husband wants to film another story of mine—with you in the leading role, of course!

SB Yes! Do remind me what it's about.

GT The story's called *Premature Death*, and takes place in the future. Everyone over sixty is to be eliminated. A man and a woman meet, fall in love and both act as if they were under sixty …

SB That's a wonderful subject. Particularly now, where generation conflict is such an issue. In the story, people who are too old only come out at night, like rats from cellars. They secretly slip each other the addresses of cosmetic surgeons, and go along with this whole business of worshipping youth.

GT There's a doctor in Vienna who thinks it's good if people die younger. The problem is people living too long. In the last century, they never got beyond forty. But there's another problem there—my favorite playwright is Sophocles, and he was eighty when he did his best work.

SB Tell me, have you always fallen in love with actresses?

GT My first wife was a secretary at the BBC, but otherwise, I like actors. They're what matters in the theater, not the director.

SB There's this great reading by Orson Welles of *Moby Dick*. No film could replace what he did in fifteen minutes. I worked with him for television, his program was called *Magic Hour*. I played a girl magician wearing a number who did a few tricks with him. He was always in a good mood, although there was no reason for it. He had no money, he was never going to be able to finish his projects—but he was so full of life. When I got to know him, he wore these huge flowery ties. They were covered not only with flowers but also ketchup, pastrami, egg yolk and grease spots. It didn't matter to him. Orson Welles is a terrific example of someone who believes in something. That childlike expectation that the next project really will come off—we really need it. And you're a bit of a child yourself—admit it now, isn't it true?

GT Let me think … (*both laugh*)

SB At any rate, you expected more dedication from actors than just to their roles. That was vital, because we had to break away from the craft business, old-fashioned acting. When are you doing something in Vienna again?

GT I do miss Vienna. Although it's always the same. Before people see my things there, they're terribly skeptical. Even Thomas Bernhard was always horribly rude beforehand, and afterwards he was always completely bowled over.

SB I know that Viennese skepticism. They have a saying: "I believe in man's goodness, but depend on the badness." That's Vienna for you.

From VOGUE 12/2003; The conversation was recorded by Anne Philippi.

BIOGRAPHIES

PEDRO ALMODÓVAR caused a sensation in Spain in the 1970s with his underground films dealing with violence, drugs, and homosexuality. The director was born in Calzada de Calatrava in 1951 and, in 1986, became internationally famous with *La ley del deseo.* Additional successes include *Mujeres al bordo de un ataque de nervios* (1988), *Átame!* (1990), *Todo sobre mi madre* (1999; for which he was awarded an Oscar) and *Hable con ella* (2002).

GIORGIO ARMANI, the Italian designer, has been celebrated as the master of purism for around thirty years. Discrete colors, simple elegance and exquisite, personally designed fabrics are the hallmarks of his collections. His "giacca destrutturata"—the jacket without padding and lining—became one of the signature pieces of clothing for the 1980s. The couturier, who was born in Piacenza in 1934, initially studied medicine and came to fashion as an autodidact. He was a window decorator and purchaser for a department store before he started designing men's fashion for Nino Cerruti. In 1975 he established his own business together with his friend and partner Sergio Galeotti, who died just ten years later.

DAVID BAILEY was born in 1938 and has become a classic in the field of fashion photography. The Briton has worked and lived with top models and actresses—he was married to Catherine Deneuve from 1965 to 1972. Michelangelo Antonioni chose him as the model for the photographer Thomas in *Blow Up*, the cult film about "swinging London." In the meantime, Bailey has specialized in unusual portraits, paints, makes films himself, and produces photographic books.

WERNER BALDESSARINI is the creator, licensee, and art director of the luxury menswear label "Baldessarini" for the fashion company Hugo Boss. He was born in Kufstein, Austria, in 1945 as the son of a fabric wholesaler and joined Boss, located in Metzingen, Germany, in 1975. He became a member of the board of directors in 1988 and, today, sits on the supervisory board of the company. He lives in Kitzbühel, Austria, with his wife, Cathrin.

MICHAEL BALLHAUS is the great author among cameramen. His very first assignment with Rainer Werner Fassbinder made cinematic history: in *Martha* (1974) he panned the camera 360 degrees and, after that, used the lens to produce unbridled images, in close cooperation with the director. The genius of the Berlin-born cameraman did not remain a secret from Hollywood for very long; since the beginning of the 1980s Ballhaus has worked with famous directors, including Martin Scorsese (*The Color of Money*, 1986 and *Gangs of New York*, 2002), Francis Ford Coppola (*Bram Stoker's Dracula*, 1992) and Wolfgang Petersen (*Outbreak*, 1995).

BALTHUS belongs to the twentieth century but, at the same time, goes far beyond it. The painter's creative passion was dedicated to the female body in its transition from childhood to womanhood. Other favorites: cats. As a twelve-year-old he processed his sorrow at the death of Mitsou I in a series of moving, ink drawings. The descendent of an aristocratic Polish family was born Balthazar Klossowski de Rola in Paris in 1908 and died in February 2001.

CECILIA BARTOLI is one of the most popular mezzo-sopranos of our time. She was born in Rome in 1966 and both of her parents were singers. For years, Cecilia received vocal training from her mother. She later studied at the famous Accademia Nazionale di Santa Cecilia in Rome. While working on a French television documentary on Maria Callas, she was discovered by both Daniel Barenboim and Herbert von Karajan, who, shortly before his death, rehearsed Bach's *Mass in B minor* with her. Since then, she has recorded many prize-winning albums and appeared in all of the world's leading opera houses.

MIKHAIL BARYSHNIKOV, the son of a Soviet officer, was born in Riga, Latvia, in 1948. He started studying ballet at twelve and entered the famous Leningrad Kirov ensemble at eighteen, where he was immediately engaged as a soloist. In those days he was already a master of all modern and classical dance techniques. While on a tour of Canada in 1974, Baryshnikov defected from the company and has lived in New York since that time. His performances with the American Ballet Theater are legendary. During the 1980s he was the company's artistic director and appeared in several films. To this day, he fascinates us with modern dance theater.

PINA BAUSCH, the world-renowned ballet director and choreographer, developed a completely new art form with her Wuppertal Ensemble: a mixture of free dance, spoken drama and ballet. Existential human problems—love, aging and violence—are the subjects of these danced dramas. The publican's daughter was born in Sollngen in 1940 and made her debut as a dancer, at the age of eighteen, in Essen.

SENTA BERGER was born in Vienna in 1941. She did not complete her studies at the Max Reinhardt College, but became a star in the film *Es muß nicht immer Kaviar sein (Operation Caviar)* in 1961. Shortly there-after, she went to Hollywood, where she filmed with Sam Peckinpah (*Major Dundee*, 1965) and other directors. She achieved international fame through her theater, film, and television roles (*Kir Royal, Die schnelle Gerdi)*. She has been married to the director and doctor Michael Verhoeven since 1966 and, together, they founded the production company Sentana in 1965.

BERNARDO BERTOLUCCI was a poet until he got to know the director Pier Paolo Pasolini. Bertolucci was born in Parma, Italy, in 1940 and gained international renown through his films *The Spider's Stratagem* and *Il Conformista* (both 1970) and, above all, for *Last Tango in Paris* (1972). He strengthened his position as a master director with films such as *1900* (1976)—an epic about the past century, lasting more than four hours—*La Luna* (1979) and *The Last Emperor* (1987) which was awarded nine Oscars. After filming Paul Bowles' Saharan novel *The Sheltering Sky* in 1990, he climbed to the roof of the world to make *Little Buddha* (1993).

JANE BIRKIN saw the light of day in London in 1946. She had her first stage appearance when she was ten and, at seventeen, she made her film debut. Highlights in her career include roles in Michelangelo Antonioni's *Blow Up* (1966), Bertrand Tavernier's *Daddy Nostalgie* (1990) and Jacques Rivette's *La belle noiseuse* (1991). She became internationally famous in 1969 with her erotic hit "Je t'aime, moi non plus" (a duet with Serge Gainsbourg, her partner at the time), which caused an enormous scandal.

BJÖRK regards her acting performance in Lars von Trier's *Dancer in the Dark* (2000), which won the Golden Palm, as a one-time episode in her career. The pop musician, who was born in Reykjavik, Iceland, in 1965, was awarded the prize as best actress in Cannes for her role in that film. She is regarded as Iceland's contribution to world culture and lives with her son, Sindri, and daughter, Isadora, in London.

MANOLO BLAHNIK, the son of a Spanish mother and a Czech father, was born in 1942 and spent his early childhood on the Canary Islands. At his parents' insistence, he studied law and politics in Geneva, changed to literature and architecture after one semester before finally entering the Art Academy in Paris in 1965. In his late twenties, he designed his first shoes, which soon became highly sought after. Today, his name is a synonym for virtuoso shoe couture—models and international stars are his clients.

LUC BONDY was born in Zurich in 1948 and studied acting with the mime Jacques Lecoq in Paris. He was barely twenty years old when he directed his first play: a dramatization of a Gombowicz novella. In 1969, he became an assistant-director at the Thalia Theater in Hamburg. Since then, he has directed at the most famous theaters in Europe. He has established himself as a master of few, but extremely meaningful, gestures and has gained the reputation of giving new life to dusty, classical plays. Since 2002, Bondy has been the Director of the Vienna Festival, where he has sole responsibility for the artistic program.

PAUL BOWLES was born on Long Island in 1910, studied composition under Aaron Copland and became a hard-working composer of film and theater music in New York, writing for Tennessee Williams and Orson Welles. In 1947, he moved to Tangier—his magic city—with the writer Jane Auer, who he had married in 1938. He was repeatedly drawn back to the city and was followed by other authors of the beat generation, including Allen Ginsberg and Jack Kerouac. Bowles' first novel, *The Sheltering Sky* (1949), became a, never-again reached, worldwide success and was filmed, in 1990, by Bernardo Bertolucci. Bowles died in Tangier in 1999.

SOPHIE CALLE has made spying on people, sometimes disguised as a chambermaid, her artistic concept. She was born in Paris in 1953 and became famous through an address book which she found: she called the owner's friends and collected stories about him—which she later published. Ego projects are her trade-mark: she let friends, neighbors and strangers sleep in her bed and documented her observations.

CLAUDIA CARDINALE: CC, along with BB and MM, were the third magic initials in the cinematic firma-ment of the 1960s. The daughter of a Sicilian and a Frenchwoman was born in Tunis in 1938. In 1957, her award as "the most beautiful Italian in Tunis" brought her a free flight to the film festival in Venice. There, she was discovered by the producer Franco Cristaldi, who married her in 1966. Claudia Cardinale, who was named a UNESCO ambassadress in 2000, charmed her audience in films including Luchino Visconti's *Rocco and His Brothers* (1960) and *The Leopard* (1962). Her career even managed to survive tripe like the story about Mussolini's lover *Claretta* (1984), made by her current partner, Pasquale Squitieri.

GERALDINE CHAPLIN, the first of the eight children of the actor and director Charlie Chaplin, was born in California in 1944. She made her debut in 1952 in *Limelight*, one of her father's films. The trained ballet dancer became internationally famous through her leading role in *Doctor Zhivago* (1965). Other important films: Alain Resnais' *La vie est un roman* (1983), Jodie Foster's *Home for the Holidays* (1995) and Pedro Almodóvar's *Hable con ella* (2002).

DINOS and JAKE CHAPMAN, born in 1962 and 1966 respectively, studied at the Royal College of Art and became famous overnight when they presented their works in a joint exhibition in 1993. Their themes: death and war, conveyed with dark humor. The installations *Disasters of War* (2001) and *Hell* (1999–2000) are among the greatest successes of the two brothers. They both live in London.

FRANCESCO CLEMENTE was born in Naples in 1952 and studied architecture before turning to fine arts. After 1977, he undertook many—often long-term—journeys to India. Today, they sill influence his painting. In New York, where he has lived for more than two decades, he soon became one of the stars of neo-expressionism. His mystical, sensual pictures of entwined bodies and flying heads can now be seen in all the major museums.

JEAN-LOUIS DUMAS-HERMÈS was born in Paris in 1938. He has led the company of the same name, which was founded by Thierry Hermès in 1837 as a specialist shop for bridles and tack, since 1978. The original range of goods has been extended from equipment for horses and riders to what is now a comprehensive assortment of luxury articles—luggage and bags, fashion and accessories, porcelain, home collection and perfume. Jean-Louis Dumas-Hermès is married to the interior designer Rena Dumas.

BERND EICHINGER was born in Neuburg an der Donau in Bavaria and in 1974, aged twenty-five, set up his production company Solaris with a starting capital of 20,000 marks. He produced films directed by Wim Wenders, Alexander Kluge, and Edgar Reitz, among others. In 1979, he took over the management of the Munich film rental company Neue Constantin and distributed Wolfgang Petersen's *The Boat* (1981), which was a huge success and received six Oscar nominations. In 1983, the film version of Michael Ende's *Unendliche Geschichte* (Never-ending Story), with its budget of 60 million marks, was widely discussed. This was followed by Jean-Jacques Annaud's *The Name of the Rose* (1986), Michael Herbig's *Der Schuh des Manitu* (2001) and *Nirgendwo in Africa* (2003), which won the director, Caroline Link, the Oscar for the best foreign-language film.

GIANFRANCO FERRÉ was born into a wealthy industrialist's family, in northern Italy in 1944. After studying architecture, he began working as a designer of furniture and jewelry before making himself independent with his own fashion line in 1978. From 1989 to 1996, he was, simultaneously, chief designer of the traditional fashion house Dior. In 2000, Ferré sold ninety percent of his business, while remaining honorary chairman of the label.

RALPH FIENNES, the eldest of six children, was born in 1962 and grew up in England and Ireland. He was a member of the Royal Shakespeare Company and received Oscar nominations for his performances as the camp commander in Steven Spielberg's *Schindler's List* (1993) and as Count Laszlo Almásy in Anthony Minghella's *The English Patient* (1996). The British actor recently appeared with Jennifer Lopez in Wayne Wang's *Maid in Manhattan*. His younger brother, Joseph, is also an actor. Fiennes lives in London.

JÜRGEN FLIMM is one of the very few German men in theater who are equally acknowledged as director and manager. He was born in Gießen in 1941, grew up and studied in Cologne and was head of the Thalia Theater in Hamburg for many years. His productions of *Peer Gynt* and *Hamlet*, which launched his era, were praised as being "theatrical revelations." Since 2002, he has been responsible for the theatrical activities of the Salzburg Festival. He is also famous as a director of operas—usually with Nikolaus Harnoncourt as conductor. His production of the *Ring des Nibelungen* was presented at the Bayreuth Festival from 2000 to 2004.

MILOS FORMAN, American by choice, was born in Cáslav in Czechoslovakia in 1932. His childhood was influenced by the loss of his parents, who perished in the Auschwitz and Buchenwald concentration camps. After his studies at the Film University in Prague, and his first work as a scriptwriter and director, he turned his back on his homeland, which was then occupied by the troops of the Warsaw Pact, and settled in the United States. In Hollywood, he rapidly progressed to becoming a master of large-scale cinema with heroes far removed from normality. Among his major successes are: *One Flew Over the Cuckoo's Nest* (1975, five Oscars) and *Amadeus* (1984, eight Oscars).

JOHN GALLIANO was born in Gibraltar in 1960. In 1966, the family moved to London. In 1983, he completed his education at the St. Martin's School of Art and Design with honors. In the meantime, he has been named British designer of the year on four occasions. In 1995, Galliano became chief designer at Givenchy and, the following fall, succeeded Gianfranco Ferré at Dior. The traditional fashion house's appointment of the eccentric fashion genius was regarded as a sensation.

STEPHEN GAN, a Filipino with Chinese roots, moved to New York at the age of eighteen. After studying design, he worked as a photographer and fashion editor for *Details*. In 1991, he founded *Visionaire*, New York's fashion magazine for the avant-garde. The exclusive publication has become a fetish of the fashion world, for which star photographers like Bruce Weber and Mario Testino work, free of charge! One issue of the magazine might appear in a jewel box, another wrapped in a Hermès scarf—but is always a collector's item.

FRANK O. GEHRY was born in Toronto in 1929. He is now an American citizen and is known as one of the greatest architects of our time. He has designed architectural jewels, full of verve, such as the Guggenheim Museum in Bilbao, the DG Bank in Berlin and the Rock Museum in Seattle. The Vitra Design Museum in Weil-am-Rhein, built in 1989, was his first European project and made him famous on this continent. He lives in Los Angeles.

RICHARD GERE, born in 1949, achieved international stardom in 1980 with his role in *American Gigolo*. Other successes include *An Officer and a Gentleman* (1982) and *Pretty Woman* (1990). An encounter with the Dalai Lama changed the actor's life: he became a Buddhist and actively supports important humanitarian activities. Gere is married to the actress Carey Lowell and they have a son, Homer James Jigme, born in 2000.

NAN GOLDIN was born in Washington D.C. in 1953. She grew up in Boston and discovered photography at the age of sixteen. She is seen as the most important chronicler of the cultural, social, and sexual changes of the past decades. Her home is the New York underground scene and she regards her circle of friends as her family. Nan Goldin travels frequently. Always with her: her technical equipment and the telephone numbers of her soul mates scattered throughout the world.

JERRY HALL was born in Texas in 1956 and was only fourteen when her fashion talent was discovered. In Paris, the beauty advanced to become a star of the fashion scene. She was engaged to Bryan Ferry until she met Mick Jagger, who left his first wife, Bianca, for her. Four children are the result of her relationship with Jagger which ended, after around twenty years, with a divorce in 1999. She has recently appeared in several plays in London but still has a great passion for her work as a model.

PETER HANDKE was born in Carinthia, Austria, in 1942. He started legal studies in Graz because he thought that would give him plenty of time for writing. He stopped studying when the Suhrkamp Publishing Company accepted his novel manuscript *Die Hornissen* (The Hornets) in 1965. In his early texts, Handke struck out against the prevailing language and narrative styles (*Publikumsbeschimpfung* / Audience Abuse, 1966), disturbing the literary establishment by accusing them of "descriptive impotence." Later, he attempted to conjure up the good, true and beautiful and exposed himself in political polemics (*Gerechtigkeit für Serbien* / Justice for Serbia, 1996). He lives with the actress Katja Flint in Chaville near Paris.

GABRIELE HENKEL elevated table-setting to an art form. Philosophers, politicians and industrialists gather around her table pictures, which were praised by the German artist Joseph Beuys. She later extended her table-art into installations, and she has also produced stage settings. She was born in Düsseldorf, Germany, in 1935 and began working for the news magazine *Newsweek*. At twenty, she married the washing powder producer Konrad Henkel (he died in 1999). Today, the benefactress is curator of the Henkel Company's important art collection and teaches communications design at the Wuppertal University.

DUSTIN HOFFMAN became an international star overnight. His first main role, as the seduced young man in *The Graduate* (1967), brought the thirty-year-old an Oscar nomination and fame. This was followed by film classics, including *Midnight Cowboy* (1969), *Marathon Man* (1976) and *Kramer versus Kramer* (1979). Hoffmann is regarded as a specialist for complicated psychological studies (*Rain Man*, 1988) as well as for heartrending comedies (*Tootsie*, 1982). The two-time Oscar winner has remained a loner in Hollywood and resolutely refuses to classify himself as a star.

ISABELLE HUPPERT, the youngest of five children, was born in Paris in 1953. At fourteen, she attended the acting schools in Versailles and St. Cloud, and later attended the Paris Conservatory. Following this, she studied Russian literature. After 1971, she started performing stage, television and film roles and quickly advanced to become a superstar of both the French and international cinema. She has worked with Jean-Luc Godard (*Passion*, 1982), Michael Cimino (*Heaven's Gate*, 1980), Michael Haneke (*Die Kavierspielerin* / The Pianist, 2001) and, often, with Claude Chabrol (*Rien ne va plus*, 1997). She is particularly impressive in her portrayals of women who appear, at the same time, both distant and passionate. Isabelle Huppert lives in Paris.

LAUREN HUTTON was nineteen when she moved from South Carolina to New York, where she was discovered as a model. With her unmistakable look—a gap in her teeth and dazzling blue eyes—she became America's first supermodel. The globetrotter, who was born in 1944, still appears regularly in front of the camera—not only for photographs: in 1980, she played opposite Richard Gere in *American Gigolo*; her other film partners include Robert Redford and Gérard Depardieu. The enthusiastic motorbiker lives in New York and New Mexico.

WOLFGANG JOOP worked as a fashion editor in Hamburg after he had finished his art studies. Joop, who was born in Potsdam in 1944, started working as a freelance designer in the 1970s. In spring 1982, he produced his first fashions for the *Joop!* label, which he later sold in order to get away from business for a while. Instead, the couturier, who is also successful as an essayist, wrote his debut novel *Im Wolfspelz* (In Wolfskin), which was published in 2003. In the same year, Joop made a reappearance in the fashion world and introduced his new line "Wunderkind" with a collection of evening gowns.

DONNA KARAN was born on Long Island in 1948. She started her career as a fashion draftswoman in Anne Klein's atelier in New York. She was soon promoted to her assistant and, after Anne Klein's death in 1974, became the house's chief designer. In 1984, she made herself freelance and, one year later, presented her first Donna Karan collection. The label DKNY soon followed.

CHRISTIAN LACROIX was born in Arles in 1951. After presenting his first collection under his own name in 1987, he rapidly became the darling of the international fashion circuit: a virtuoso who could mix styles as no other; each model was an intelligent etude on themes from the past and future. Since spring 2002, Lacroix is also chief designer of the Italian fashion house Pucci.

KARL LAGERFELD was born in Hamburg in 1938. His career began with the design of a coat which won the International Wool Secretariat's first prize in 1954. After finishing school, Lagerfeld went to Paris, where he worked with Pierre Balmain and, after 1958, as a freelance fashion designer and artistic director for Jean Patou. In 1963, he moved to Chloé, where he held the same position until his departure in 1997. Since 1983, his designs for Chanel have made it a most sought-after label. He also designs the collection for Fendi.

SOPHIA LOREN was born in Rome in 1934 and spent her childhood in Pozzuoli near Naples. In 1950, she returned to Rome, where she appeared as an extra in *Quo Vadis?* In 1954, she made her breakthrough with *The Gold of Naples*, which was her first encounter with Vittorio de Sica, her great champion. She made film history as the congenial partner of Marcello Mastroianni and Cary Grant. Sophia Loren won her first Oscar for *Two Women* in 1962 and received a second, in 1991, for her lifetime achievements. She has been married to the producer Carlo Ponti since 1957.

MARKUS LÜPERTZ is one of Germany's most famous painters. He was born in Bohemia in 1941, and as early as in the 1960s achieved huge success with his individual mixture of expressionist painting and savage, passionate coloration. In the early 1980s he increased his sculpting activities. He has been Rector of the Art Academy in Düsseldorf since 1988.

STELLA McCARTNEY studied at the St. Martin's School of Art and Design in London. Shortly after graduation she became—at the age of twenty-five—chief designer for Chloé, as Karl Lagerfeld's successor. Nowadays, she designs sexy, cool, and femininely playful fashion for her own label, which belongs to the Gucci Group. The daughter of Paul and Linda McCartney is an enthusiastic rider and vegan.

ALEXANDER McQUEEN, the youngest of six children, was born in the East End of London in 1970. At sixteen, he began a tailoring apprenticeship in Savile Row. At twenty, he worked for Koji Tatsuno and Romeo Gigli and studied at the St. Martin's School of Art and Design in London. He became chief designer for Givenchy in 1996. Since 2001, he designs exclusively for his own label as part of the Gucci Group.

ZUBIN MEHTA was born in Bombay, India, in 1936. After studying conducting in Vienna, he began his great career: among other positions, Mehta was chief conductor of the Philharmonic Orchestras of Los Angeles and New York. Since 1998, he has been musical director of the Bavarian State Opera and Bavarian State Orchestra and holds the same position, in this case for life, with the Israel Philharmonic Orchestra in Tel Aviv. He is a regular conductor of both the Vienna and Berlin Philharmonic Orchestras.

SHEILA METZNER confesses: "When I started photographing, I thought that I was the only person who knew what photography really was." In 1968, she gave up her position as art director and shot her first pictures. A mere ten years later, the Museum of Modern Art in New York displayed her works. Today, this mother of five children, who was born in Brooklyn in 1939, is one of the most important photographers in the world. The delicacy, charm and naturalness of her pictures are immune to any change in zeitgeist. Her work is documented in excitingly beautiful photographic books. For some time now, the New Yorker has also made commercials and short films.

NIKITA MIKHALKOV was born in Moscow in 1945. After his studies at the film academy, he worked as an actor, changing to direction at the beginning of the 1970s. *Slave of Love* (1976) was his breakthrough. *A Few Days in the Life of I.I. Oblomov* (1976) and *Dark Eyes* (1987) with Marcello Mastroianni and Marthe Keller, as well as *Urga* (1991) cemented his international reputation. *Burnt by the Sun* (1994) received an award in Cannes which was followed, in 1995, by the Oscar for best foreign film.

CLAUDE MONTANA was born in Paris in 1949. At twenty-two, he moved to London and started his career with self-made jewelry created out of papier-mâché and colored stones. However, he was not granted a working permit and soon had to leave. In 1979, he founded the Claude Montana Company, which proved to be a trend-setter; Montana was the first designer to introduce broad shoulders and set on a "sexy line." From 1990 to 1992, he created the haute-couture collection for Lanvin and achieved world renown.

JEANNE MOREAU was born in Paris in 1928 and, at twenty, became the youngest member ever of the Parisian Comédie Française. In 1952, she turned down a contract with Paramount in order to continue working with Jean Vilar's experimental Théâtre Nationale Populaire and was regarded as the best stage actress of her generation. In the 50s, she appeared in more than twenty films. The muse of the *Nouvelle Vague* achieved international fame in 1958 in Louis Malle's *Ascenseur pour l'échafaud*. Michelangelo Antonioni filmed his masterpiece *La Notte* (1961) with her, François Truffaut engaged her for *Jules et Jim* (1962) and Orson Welles for his interpretation of Kafka's *The Trial* (1962). In 2000, she became the first woman to be elected to the Académie des Beaux Arts in Paris.

MARIKO MORI is one of Japan's most successful artists. The Buddhist, born in 1967, appears, in ever changing identities on giant, computer-animated photo-panoramas and in 3D videos. Mori's work is characterized by a mixture of naïve charm and the attraction of superficiality; they also reflect a longing for more profound truths. In recent years, the most important international museums have exhibited her extravagant, glamorous art. Mori is actually always on the move—she mostly commutes between Tokyo and New York.

SAMANTHA MORTON was born in 1977 and expelled from school at the age of fourteen. In the same year, she appeared in her first television role. Her breakthrough occurred in Woody Allen's *Sweet and Lowdown* (1999), which won her an Oscar nomination as best supporting actress. Her recent films include *Minority Report* and *In America* (both 2002). She lives in London with her daughter, Esme.

ARMIN MUELLER-STAHL was born in Tilsit in 1930. He studied musicology in East Berlin and graduated as a music professor and concert violinist. He later went into acting and belonged to the ensemble of the Berlin Volksbühne from 1954. After signing the petition against Wolf Biermann's denaturalization, his career in the GDR came to an abrupt halt. In 1980, Mueller-Stahl migrated to the west. He became an international movie star in films such as Costa-Gavras' *Music Box* (1989), Barry Levinson's *Avalon* (1990) and Scott Hicks' *Shine*, for which he received the Oscar as best supporting actor in 1996.

RUDOLF NUREYEV was born near Irkutsk in Siberia, on a Trans-Siberian Express train in 1938. The world-famous dancer began as a dance instructor in workers' collectives and with folk-dance performances. He was a master-pupil at the Kirov Ballet School and completed the eight-year training in a mere three years. In 1961, he defected while performing in Paris. He was given an engagement with the Royal Ballet in London where he had triumphant successes in *Giselle, Sleeping Beauty, Les Sylphides* and in many other ballets. Starting in the mid-1960s, Nureyev began choreographing and made several ballet films. From 1983 to 1989, he was ballet director of the Paris Opera. The last public appearance of the AIDS-stricken star was in October 1992 at the premiere of *Le Dieu et la Bayadère*, which he had choreographed from his bed. He died at the age of fifty-four in Paris in January 1993.

RIFAT OZBEK was born in Istanbul in 1953, where he grew up and studied architecture before enrolling at the St. Martin's School of Art and Design in London. In 1984, he produced his own collection, inspired by both orient and occident, and became famous with his "Nouveau Hippie Look." *The New York Times* feted him as "the greatest trendsetter since Yves Saint Laurent." Margaret Thatcher honored him as Designer of the Year in 1988. Since 2003, Ozbek designs for the Italian Pollini fashion house.

ANNA PIAGGI worked as a translator of thrillers, among other things, before being promoted to Italy's most famous fashion journalist. She was a columnist for the weekly magazine *Panorama* and was editor-in-chief of *Vanity*, the magazine she herself had founded, for three years. Karl Lagerfeld erected a monument to her in his book *A Visual Record of Anna Piaggi's Creative Dressing and Self-Editing*. Piaggi's wardrobe is legendary: she collects—and wears—clothing from 200 years of fashion history.

MICHEL PICCOLI exhibits, as hardly any other French actor, a mastery of character studies. The Parisian's breakthrough in 1963, at the age of thirty-eight, came with his leading role in Jean-Luc Godard's *Le mépris*. Following this, he appeared in numerous masterworks: Luis Buñuel's *Belle de jour* (1967) and *Le charme discret de la bourgeoisie* (1972), Alfred Hitchcock's *Topaz* (1969), as well as Marco Ferreri's *La grande bouffe* (1973). Piccoli, who always portrays the typical French bourgeois man with the black depths of his soul, lives in Paris and today almost only appears on the stage.

MIUCCIA PRADA took over the Prada leather goods shop in Milan from her grandfather in 1978. The company, so rich in tradition, produced luggage for a conservative clientele. The then twenty-eight-year-old doctor of political science, who had also studied acting at Milan's Piccolo Teatro, revolutionized the company's image. She tailored a small urban rucksack from black nylon—today, this is the world-famous "Prada bag." In addition, since 1988, she has designed a prêt-à-porter collection, characterized by its simple elegance and often wild patterns and details. The "Miu Miu" line—christened after Miucca Prada's nickname—was added in 1992.

ROSA VON PRAUNHEIM (real name: Holger Mischwitzky) was born in Riga in 1942 and grew up in Berlin and Frankfurt/Main. After early attempts as a painter and writer, he discovered film as his individual medium in 1967. In 1971, Praunheim made his breakthrough, with both critics and public, with his films *Die Bettwurst* (The Bed Sausage) and *Nicht der Homosexuelle ist pervers, sondern die Situation in dem er lebt* (It is not the Homosexual who is Perverse, But the Society in which He Lives). His autobiographical book *50 Jahre pervers* (Perverse for 50 Years) also achieved wide acclaim.

EDGAR REITZ overstepped all previous boundaries with his 16-hour-long family saga *Heimat* (Homeland) and, with its follow-up, *Die zweite Heimat* (1992), which lasts 26 hours, achieved a firm place in the history of film. He was born in the Hunsrück region of Southern Germany in 1932 and made this area the middle-point of his chronicle of the twentieth century. His earlier films *In Gefahr und größter Not bringt der Mittelweg den Tod* (In Danger and the Greatest Need, the Golden Mean leads to Death) (1974; he collaborated with Alexander Kluge on the script) and *Stunde Null* (Zero Hour) (1977) were landmarks in modern German cinema. Edgar Reitz is currently working on *Heimat 3*.

MIRANDA RICHARDSON was born in 1958. The British actress began her career in the theater and on television. She became known to a broader audience in 1985 when she performed with Rupert Everett in *Dance with a Stranger* (directed by Mike Newell). She was nominated for an Oscar for her performance in Louis Malle's *Damage* and for a Golden Globe for Mike Newell's *Enchanted April* (both 1992).

MARIA RIVA (née Sieber), Marlene Dietrich's only child, was born in Berlin in 1924. In the early 1930s, her mother took her with her to Hollywood, where she appeared in Josef von Sternberg's *The Scarlet Empress* (1934), playing the same part Dietrich performed as an adult. Following this, she performed on the stage, in radio, and on television. Her book *Marlene Dietrich* was filmed in 2000 by Joseph Vilsmaier, with Katja Flint in the leading role.

ISABELLA ROSSELLINI, daughter of the actress Ingrid Bergman and the director Roberto Rossellini, was born in Rome in 1952 and is a beauty with many faces. She started as a model, had her own TV show in Italy, performed with a comedy group and still loves appearing in amusing films like *Death Becomes Her* (1992). However, it was her saturnine role as Dorothy in David Lynch's *Blue Velvet* (1986) which finally brought her international fame as an actress.

BARON GUY DE ROTHSCHILD is a scion of a banking dynasty dating back to the eighteenth century. From 1949 to 1978, he was director of the Rothschild Bank in Paris. He was born in 1909 and grew up on the family's Château Ferrières near Paris, which he donated to the University of Paris in 1973. His education was in accordance with the family tradition, which held that wealth implied a social and cultural responsibility as well as a "certain elegance in life, which expressed itself, not so much in luxury, but in style." As a prominent victim of the politics of nationalization, introduced by the Socialists he supported, he moved to New York, with his wife, at the beginning of the 1980s, only to return a few years later. Baron Guy de Rothschild has written several books, including his successful autobiography *The Whims of Fortune*, which was published in English in 1985.

CHARLES SCHUMANN was born in the Upper Palatinate in 1941 and is Germany's most famous barman. He is, in addition to being a master in his dealings with people and mixtures, one of Baldessarini's models. His guests have turned "Schumann's," which he opened at the end of the 1980s and is now located next to the former palace gardens, into one of Munich's most cosmopolitan bars.

HANNA SCHYGULLA was born in Katowice, Poland, in 1943. In 1945, she moved to Munich with her mother. Shortly after her high-school graduation, she became Rainer Werner Fassbinder's muse. The actress, who until then, was little known, appeared in many of his films, including *Die Ehe der Maria Braun* (1979) and *Lili Marleen* (1981), as well as other theater productions. She became an icon of the German art cinema. Schygulla also filmed with Jean-Luc Godard, Margarethe von Trotta and Andrzej Wajda. She often appears on stage, sings chansons with texts by Peter Handke, Heiner Müller, Thomas Bernhard, Arthur Rimbaud—and Rainer Werner Fasssbinder. Schygulla lives in Paris.

PATTI SMITH was born in Chicago in 1946 and, since the beginning of the seventies, has performed her own punk poetry accompanied on the guitar. Her first LP *Horses*, was released in 1975 followed, two years later, by her book *Ha Ha Houdini*. This founded her reputation as the "shaman of rock music." Her cover version of Bruce Springsteen's "Because the Night" landed her a smash hit in 1978. In 1980, she married Fred Smith, an ex-member of the MC5 band, had two children and withdrew from the music scene. At the time of her husband's death, in 1994, they had been working on a new album entitled *Gone Again*. She celebrated a comeback, with this title, in 1996 and, in the meantime, has published several additional albums.

SUSAN SONTAG was born in New York City in 1933 and grew up in Tucson, Arizona. The literature fan was invited to tea with Thomas Mann when she was only fourteen. She attended high school in Los Angeles and graduated, with a bachelor of arts degree, from the University of Chicago. She studied philosophy, literature, and theology at Harvard and Oxford. After returning to New York, she became a figurehead of America's cultural and intellectual life with her provocative and pointed essays (including *Art and Anti-art*, 1961; *Illness as Metaphor*, 1978). She has received numerous awards for her work, including the National Book Award (2000) for her novel *In America*, and the Peace Price of the German Book Trade in 2003.

GEORGE TABORI was born in Budapest in 1914. He moved to Berlin at the age of eighteen and fled to London in 1936. He lost the greater part of his family in the Auschwitz concentration camp. Tabori wrote novels, worked for the BBC and became a British citizen in 1945. He went to the USA in 1947 where he wrote plays and film scripts—for Alfred Hitchcock, among others. In 1968 he returned to Germany and, since then, has directed many of his own pieces, dealing with the relationship between Jews and Germans, at the Kammerspiele in Munich (*Mutters Courage*), the Maxim Gorki Theater in Berlin *(Mein Kampf)* and Vienna's Burgtheater (*Die Ballade vom Wiener Schnitzel*). He was eighty-five when he transferred to the Berliner Ensemble with Claus Peymann.

ANDRÉ LEON TALLEY grew up in simple surroundings at his grandmother's house in a small town in North Carolina. He began training to be a French teacher but his love of fashion guided him to New York, where the two-meter dandy became the assistant of Diana Vreeland, the fashion icon, and, later, one of the most distinguished fashion journalists. The brilliant eccentric (born in 1948) today writes his cult column for the American VOGUE. The devout Baptist lives in Hastings-on-Hudson near New York.

ISABEL and RUBEN TOLEDO met each other at high school in New York. Both had migrated, with their parents, from Cuba when they were young. Since then, the fashion designer and the fashion illustrator have been—privately and professionally—an inseparable couple. Isabel's sophisticated collections often move directly from the catwalk into the museum. Ruben, who was born in 1960 and is one year older than Isabel, also manages the business activities of her fashion firm. To compensate, Isabel is his muse and only model.

WIM WENDERS was born in Düsseldorf, Germany, in 1945 and is regarded as the most successful German filmmaker of his generation. He studied in Munich at the College for Film and Television from 1967 to 1970. His films *Paris, Texas* (1984; honored with the Golden Palm in Cannes) and *Himmel über Berlin* (1987) are impressive through their opulent landscapes and peaceful narrative style—aspects which have become rare in Hollywood films. These films, along with *Buena Vista Social Club* (1999), count as his greatest successes.

ROBERT WILSON, the theater and opera director, was born in Waco, Texas, in 1941. The all-round talent—Wilson also studied architecture and is a successful artist—is regarded as "the greatest genius in contemporary theater" (*Le Figaro*). Measured movements, artistic perspectives and a stylized manner of speech are typical of his method. Among his most important productions are: *The Forest*, a dramatization of the *Gilgamesh* epic, *Death, Destruction and Detroit, Hamletmaschine* (Schaubühne Berlin) and *Black Rider* (Thalia Theater Hamburg). His various opera productions, ranging from Mozart's *Magic Flute* in Paris to Wagner's *Ring des Nibelungen* in Zurich, have also met with great critical acclaim.

INDEX

PHOTO CREDITS

Mark Abrahams 199

Bryan Adams 276

Kim Andreolli 244

Rosanna Armani 156

Olivier Boissière 238

Nick Clark 165

Arthur Elgort 150

Richard Gere, Courtesy Fahey /
Klein Gallery, Los Angeles 249

Anton Goiri 263

Nan Goldin 232

Antoine Le Grand 271

Torkil Gudnason 227

Mikael Jansson 104

Vincent Knapp 93

Karl Lagerfeld 176

Jo Magrean 98, 207, 259

Sheila Metzner 161

Nadir Naldi 144

Nigel Parry 182

Manuela Pavesi 218

Steve Pyke 222

Jim Rakete 82

Tim Richmond 188

Satoshi Saikusa 122

Ferdinando Scianna 134

Elfie Semotan 282

Peggy Sirota 170

Alfred Steffen 115, 128, 203

Stefan Studer 212

André Leon Talley 110

Jürgen Teller 194

Tyen 139

Eddie Wong 87

The Library of Congress Cataloguing-in-Publication data is
available; British Library Cataloguing-in-Publication Data:
a catalogue record for this book is available from the British
Library; Deutsche Bibliothek holds a record of this publication
in the Deutsche Nationalbibliografie; detailed bibliographical
data can be found at: http://dnb.ddb.de

© Prestel Verlag, Munich · Berlin · London· New York, 2004
© Condé Nast Verlag, Munich 2004

Prestel Verlag
Königinstrasse 9, 80539 Munich
Tel. +49 (89) 38 17 09-0; Fax +49 (89) 38 17 09-35

Prestel Publishing Ltd.
4 Bloomsbury Place, London WC1A 2QA
Tel. +44 (020) 7323-5004; Fax +44 (020) 7636-8004

Prestel Publishing
900 Broadway, Suite 603, New York, NY 10003
Tel. +1 (212) 995-2720; Fax +1 (212) 995-2733

www.prestel.com

Condé Nast Verlag
Ainmillerstrasse 8, 80801 Munich
Tel. +49 (89) 38 104-0; Fax +49 (89) 38 104-230
www.condenast.de

Project management: Gabriele Ebbecke (Prestel),
Ingrid Hedley (Condé Nast)
Translation from the German: Robert McInnes,
Julian Wheatley, Rosie Jackson, and Paul Aston
Copyediting: by Charles Heard and Danko Szabó
Art direction and cover design: Thomas Giller (Condé Nast)

Layout and production: WIGEL, Munich
Lithography: Reproline Genceller, Munich
Printing and binding: sellier Druck, Angerstrasse 54,
85354 Freising

Printed in Germany on acid-free paper

ISBN 3-7913-3181-7